Daniel O'Connor

GOSPEL, RAJ AND SWARAJ
The Missionary Years
of C. F. Andrews 1904-14

Foreword by
the Archbishop of Canterbury

Verlag Peter Lang
Frankfurt am Main · Bern · New York · Paris

CIP-Titelaufnahme der Deutschen Bibliothek

O'Connor, Daniel:

Gospel, Raj and Swaraj ; the missionary years of C. F. Andrews
1904-14 / Daniel O'Connor. - Frankfurt am Main ; Bern ;
New York ; Paris : Lang, 1990
  (Studien zur interkulturellen Geschichte des Christentums ;
  Bd. 62)
  Zugl.: St. Andrews Univ., Diss., 1981
  ISBN 3-631-42055-2

NE: GT

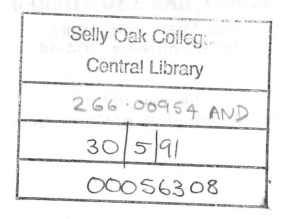
ISSN 0170-9240
ISBN 3-631-42055-2

© Verlag Peter Lang GmbH, Frankfurt am Main 1990
All rights reserved.

Printed in Germany 1   3 4 5 6 7

Gospel, Raj and Swaraj
The Missionary Years of C. F. Andrews 1904-14

STUDIEN ZUR INTERKULTURELLEN GESCHICHTE DES CHRISTENTUMS
ETUDES D'HISTOIRE INTERCULTURELLE DU CHRISTIANISME
STUDIES IN THE INTERCULTURAL HISTORY OF CHRISTIANITY

begründet von / fondé par / founded by
Hans Jochen Margull †, Hamburg

herausgegeben von / édité par / edited by

Richard Friedli
Université de Fribourg

Walter J. Hollenweger
University of Birmingham

Theo Sundermeier
Universität Heidelberg

Jan A. B. Jongeneel
Rijksuniversiteit Utrecht

Band 62

Verlag Peter Lang

Frankfurt am Main · Bern · New York · Paris

For Juliet, Aidan and Tim
who generously admitted 'Charlie'
into our family life.

Foreword by the Archbishop of Canterbury

I must have been about 14 when I met C.F. Andrews. He was introduced at Prayers to speak to the school. It was not an easy assignment, and he was not a great orator. Yet his holiness and integrity penetrated the formality of a school assembly, and held us spellbound. I can't easily remember any other visiting speaker from my school days; but I can still recall that bearded face, the kindly eyes and the quiet gentle voice fascinating us with his love for India and devotion to his Lord.

Since then I have come to revere him as a great Christian figure. He represents all that is most creative in the missionary movement that fanned out from Britain in the last century. Yet his thinking remains strikingly contemporary 50 years after his death in 1940.

No Archbishop of Canterbury can travel the world and not ponder the fact that certain missionary themes recur wherever he goes. A love for the poor, a longing for a faith that is genuinely at home in the culture where it is believed, and a wise and welcoming encounter with people of other faiths. While Churches and Councils of Churches today struggle to express these things in their policies and priorities, C.F. Andrews was a man whose openness to the Spirit and attractiveness of character made him a shining example of how Gospel imperatives can focus together in a single life.

Dan O'Connor traces C.F. Andrews' thinking in his formative years with great sympathy and perception and, as a former Cambridge Secretary to the Mission to Delhi, it gives me great pleasure to commend his study warmly. C.F. Andrews shows us what riches are to be gained, and to be given, when Christians leave the land of their birth and discover the universality of their Lord.

Robert Cantuar

IX

CONTENTS

Foreword   vii

Acknowledgements   xi

Introduction   1

Chapter One   The Background   6

Chapter Two   The Context of Mission 1904–6   24

Chapter Three   Breakthrough to Mission 1906–7   64

Chapter Four   Towards a Theology of National Renaissance   102

Chapter Five   Towards an Indian Church   156

Chapter Six   People of Other Faiths   213

Chapter Seven   Moving On   278

Conclusion   301

Glossary of Indian Words   306

Abbreviations   311

Bibliography   314

Index   340

ACKNOWLEDGEMENTS

I should like to thank those who have assisted in any way with the
preparation and publication of this study.

It all grew out of my work as a teacher and chaplain at St Stephen's
College, Delhi, so that my first thanks must be to that fine institution
and my colleagues there and in the Cambridge Mission to Delhi, who first
set me on the trail of C.F. Andrews, and to my parents who brought me up in
the Church in the Diocese of Durham, where Westcott was still remembered.
My time in India also gave me opportunities to meet and talk with people
like Marjories Sykes and Benarsidas Chaturvedi, Krishna Kripalani, and
members of the Gandhi family both in India and at Phoenix in South Africa.
On returning to Britain, my first job, at the University of St Andrews,
provided me the opportunity for some part-time research and the discipline
of a formal dissertation: I am grateful in particular to Dr John Fleming
who supervised my work at that stage and gave me much helpful guidance. It
has been good to complete the preparation of this study at Selly Oak, where
the encouragement and challenge of Marcella Hoesl and other colleagues to a
sound mission orientation have been very important.

Many people with the care of libraries and archives helped in my search for
information, in particular at the National Archives of India, U.S.P.G., the
India Office Library and Records, the Centre of South Asian Studies at
Cambridge, the University Library at St Andrews, and the National Library
of Scotland. In the same way, many friends and strangers helped me to
trace papers and find answers to my awkward questions, among them Dr Ian
Clark, Mrs Laura Person, Professor Eric Sharpe, Fr James Stuart, and two
former colleagues at St Stephen's, Prabhu Guptara and Harsh Kumar.

A number of friends read over sections of the work at various stages or
discussed aspects of it, among them Drs Judith Brown, Basudev Chatterji and
the late Percival Spear, and Professors Margaret Chatterji, Victor Kiernan,
George Shepperson and Hugh Tinker.

I owe a special debt of thanks to Drs M.M. Thomas and the late Dick Taylor

of the Christian Institute for the Study of Religion and Society, in
Bangalore, and to Fr G. Gispert-Sauch, S.J., of Vidyajyoti, Delhi, for
providing opportunities for me to venture into print with some preliminary
exercises on the present theme.

At the research stage, I had help with the expenses involved from the
Research and Travel Funds of the University of St Andrews, the Edward
Cadbury Charitable Trust, the F.N. Davey Trust, the G.H. Forbes Trust, the
Society in Scotland for Propagating Christian Knowledge, the Spalding Trust
and the Walker Bursaries Patronage Committee.

In the matter of publication, I have to thank Canon Humphrey Taylor,
General Secretary of U.S.P.G., and Mr Nadir Dinshaw, for their
encouragement, Professor Walter Hollenweger for suggesting that the work
appear in the present series, the Drummond Trust, 3 Pitt Terrace, Stirling
for a generous grant, Mrs Margaret Breiner and Mrs Jenny Hodges for the
preparation of the text, and the staff of Verlag Peter Lang.

I am extremely grateful to the Archbishop of Canterbury for writing the
Foreword, with its recollection of his own boyhood encounter with Andrews,
and its reminder of his own former work for the Cambridge Mission to Delhi.

My chief gratitude is indicated in the dedication.

College of the Ascension   Dan O'Connor
Epiphany 1990

1

INTRODUCTION

Gandhi called him 'love incarnate', and even among the imperial guardians,
while he frequently evoked waves of apoplexy, there were those for whom
Charles Freer Andrews was 'the salt of the earth as regards pure goodness'.
More specifically significant, for our present purpose, he was, in Gandhi's
judgement, 'the pattern of the ideal missionary'. (1)

Since his death in Calcutta in 1940, C.F. Andrews' stature within the
history of modern India has been recognised and acknowledged. He is in the
textbooks of school children, and places and institutions are named after
him, while the centenary of his birth was celebrated in 1971 with a
National Seminar and with the issue of a handsome postage stamp bearing his
portrait and the title Deenabandhu, 'Friend of the poor'.

There has also been a good deal written about him in the way of serious
studies. Most of this, however, has dealt with the period from 1914
onwards, as if his leaving a formal missionary appointment in Delhi at that
time to go to live at Tagore's Santiniketan marked his emergence from
conventional obscurity onto the public scene. The present study, which
seeks to correct this misperception, is of his first ten years in India,
from 1904 to 1914, when he was a member of the Cambridge Mission to Delhi
and a teacher at St Stephen's College. This decade has been little studied
hitherto, but was a distinct phase of his life, and has proved to be not
only full of interest for the study both of mission and of modern Indian
history, but also, in the field of inter-religious relations, exemplary and
prophetic.

The decade was also a very important one for Andrews. It was a period in
which, under the stimulus of intense and richly varied new experience, his
thinking on many issues developed dramatically, and when most of his later
concerns were first identified, but while they still had the attractive
freshness of new discoveries. It was also the period when many of his most
significant friendships, with Gandhi and Tagore, for example, began. There
was also a task of demythologizing to be done for this period. The notion

that he was constantly and totally at loggerheads with his bishop and
missionary colleagues required correction; the notion, also, as has been
indicated, that when he went to South Africa to visit Gandhi early in 1914,
he was still an 'unknown' young Englishman. It was also a period for which
there was a wealth of interesting material, much of it not hitherto
examined, including a great deal which enabled me to place him in the
context of contemporary Indian nationalism, particularly as it was
developing in the Punjab. I wanted also to trace the process whereby a
gifted but conventional missionary became, in Marjorie Sykes' very accurate
phrase, 'the rebel devotee' or, in Hugh Tinker's, a 'gentle, humble, but
ferocious seer-activist' in Indian politics. (2) There was also much
evidence in this period to show that he was a serious and creative
theological thinker, and not an activist only, even if a devout one, the
devotion, the action, and the theological reflection all continually
interacting in his development through the decade.

I have approached this piece of work as a mission study. There have been
two fine biographies, an early one by Benarsidas Chaturvedi and Marjorie
Sykes, and, more recently, Hugh Tinker's. A mission study is something
different, an attempt to see and interpret things in a particular
perspective, and if I have had a model in mind, it has been Eric Sharpe's
study of the thought of J.N. Farquhar, published in the series 'Studia
Missionalia Upsaliensia', though I have also tried to take account of John
Kent's appeal, in an essay on 'The History of Christian Missions in the
Modern Era', to take secular history more seriously 'for its own sake' than
was the case with an earlier generation of mission studies, not that any
other sort of study would have made much sense, so active and perspicuous a
participant was he in that history. (3) Hence the title. It might,
nevertheless, be asked whether justice is done in mission studies at the
end of the twentieth century by giving attention to an individual Western
missionary working in the East. I have in mind Bühlmann's appeal for
'Justice in the Writing of History'. (4) That Andrews would have been
himself the first to affirm this particular sense of justice (he was, after
all, an early admirer of K.M. Pannikar for his study of <u>Asia and Western
Dominance</u>) is one clear reason why he is still so worthy of attention, and
why Indian as well as Western scholars continue to find him a subject of

fascination.

I have also suggested that it is helpful to see Andrews in the particular
context of the Cambridge Mission to Delhi and its very distinctive theology
of mission, and, indeed, that this theology found a new authentication in
his work during these years. I have not attempted to review the
nineteenth-century background of 'Protestant missionary thought', because
this has been done very thoroughly in the first part of Sharpe's study.
Sharpe's omission, however, of the Cambridge Mission to Delhi and the other
'missions of the Catholic tradition' ('with one exception, the Oxford
Mission to Calcutta'), because they lie 'to one side of the dominant
Evangelical stream of missionary thought', provides a convenient space in
which to establish the distinctive approach of the Delhi Mission. (5)
Another omission is of any general survey of the history of the Cambridge
Mission to Delhi, partly because a useful one is already available, by F.J.
Western, but partly also because the essential context of Andrews' work was
the completely new situation that developed in India almost immediately
after his arrival there, for which the earlier activities of the Mission
afforded no precedents.

Nor have I attempted, except occasionally and en passant the delicate task
of locating Andrews and his ideas in a framework such as that suggested in
Edward Said's study of 'Orientalism'. (6) Andrews' sensitive and painful
endeavour to work out his Christian path between raj and swaraj would be a
rich quarry for such a project, but it would require great subtlety, not
only because of the scope and complexity of this field, but also in order
to avoid a reductionism no less misleading than that of other, less
critical approaches to mission study.

The sources used are exclusively English-language, for English was almost
exclusively the language in which the matter of Indian nationalism at this
stage, and of Hindu reformation and of much of progressive Indian Islam
occurred. For the unpublished sources, I have relied largely on the
well-known collections, in particular the archives of the Cambridge Mission
and of SPG (as it then was), the papers of two of the viceroys, Minto and
Hardinge, and the correspondence of Tagore, Munshi Ram and Gandhi. The

published sources have been in many ways quite as important as the
unpublished, for Andrews became, from late 1906, something of a compulsive
communicator in the nationalist press, and the evidence for his developing
ideas is to a considerable extent in print here. Many of the published
sources are very hard to come by. There is, for example, in India, only
one known surviving set of the St Stephen's College Magazine for these
years, and the same is true of the journal, Young Men of India, while there
is in Britain, where I wrote this, only one microfilm of the nationalist
newspaper, the Tribune, so important for this study. A full account of
these sources is appended. A considerably more copious version of the
notes can be consulted in an earlier version of this study submitted as a
doctoral dissertation in the University of St Andrews.

There is an illuminating footnote in a recent commemorative volume in which
the author recalls how, around the time of the Tambaram Conference, Andrews
'unceremoniously dumped' his copy of Kraemer's The Christian Message in a
Non-Christian World into his waste-paper basket. (7) As we now, towards
the end of the twentieth century, come out from under the long shadow that
that conference cast over so much of Christian relations with people of
other faiths, it is striking how in fact all the main strands in how we now
think about mission, as dialogue, evangelization, inculturation and
liberation, along with ecumenism, are adumbrated in the thought of C.F.
Andrews as he struggled to come to terms with his Christian identity in the
new context of India at the beginning of the century. Perhaps most
striking of all were his christological formulations, on which it seems to
me that in many ways Christian thought has yet to catch up. All of this,
it has to be reiterated, was forged in the thick of the world of action
with its complexities and ordeals.

My hope is that, as we face the momentous issues of an increasingly
indivisible human and creaturely destiny, this study will enable others to
come closer to the heart and mind of this 'gentle, eager and many-sided
saint', for he still has the power to awaken, enliven and deepen faith. (8)
I hope also that a fuller understanding of him in his own times will
underline his continuing significance as he moves ahead of us along roads
we have not yet had the courage to tread.

NOTES: Introduction

1 From a letter to A. Harrison, 1940, quoted in <u>C.F. Andrews</u>
  <u>Centenary Souvenir</u> (ed. M.R. Bansal) Calcutta 1971; Lord
  Irwin to S. Baldwin, 9 May 1928, quoted in Tinker 1979, p. 230;
  Gandhi 1958 ff., Vol XLVIII, p. 122

2 Title of a centenary pamphlet, Calcutta 1971; Tinker 1974, p. 334

3 Daniélou etc. 1969, pp. 255-70

4 Bühlmann 1986. The phrase is the heading of Bühlmann's chapter
  five.

5 Sharpe 1965, p. 15

6 Said 1978

7 M. Hunter Harrison 'The Study of the Relation Between
  Christianity and Other Religious Faiths: The Contribution of
  Eric J. Sharpe' in Ambalavanar 1985, p. 92

8 T.G.P. Spear <u>Stephanian</u> Jun 1940

CHAPTER ONE
THE BACKGROUND

1. Introductory

For his first ten years in India, his 'missionary decade', from 1904 to
1914, C.F. Andrews was a member of the Cambridge Mission to Delhi. His
arrival in Delhi coincided more or less with a major development in modern
Indian history, the beginning of a new and vigorous phase in the national
movement, though that is in some respects a rather narrow definition for
what he later came to call 'an eruption of a whole continent of humanity
from within seeking to mould itself afresh in new forms'. (1)

For many missionaries, especially in the country districts, the particular
developments from about 1905 cannot have made much difference to their
work, for the movement was as yet largely confined to those who had been
influenced by Western education, the 'educated classes' as they were
called, in the cities and bigger towns. (2) For missionaries among the
educated classes, however, the movement was harder to ignore. No one took
it more seriously than Andrews, for whom, indeed, it became a major
preoccupation, and of critical significance during these years, in itself,
in the new challenges that it presented to the church, and in the new
religious movements and attitudes which accompanied it. He became
convinced that the Christian mission could only be effective as this new
and powerful phenomenon was taken seriously. Rejecting attitudes widely
shared among missionaries from the Church of England, he was led to regard
the movement not only seriously but also sympathetically, welcoming it, and
justifying his welcome with original and interesting theological
reflections.

Andrews' approach had, however, a context, in the mission to which he
belonged. In the 'immense and varied' spectrum of the Christian missionary
enterprise in nineteenth-century India, the Cambridge Mission to Delhi had
its own very distinctive self-understanding. (3) This must be our starting
point.

2. 'An Alexandria on the banks of the Jumna'

The experience and reflection of two men in particular gave shape to the
project of a Cambridge Mission to Delhi, Thomas Valpy French (1825-1891)
and Brook Foss Westcott (1825-1901). When, in 1875, French wrote to a
young man at Cambridge, E.H. Bickersteth, who was interested in the
possibility of missionary work, and suggested to him 'the first idea of a
Cambridge brotherhood' in India, he had himself already spent a quarter of
a century in north-west India. (1) During those 25 years, along with
evangelistic and translation work, he had been instrumental in establishing
two educational institutions for the Church Missionary Society, St John's
College, Agra, teaching arts and sciences, founded in 1850, and, some 20
years later, a Divinity School at Lahore.

We get some indication of French's missiological ideas from his observation
that St John's College, though it might become 'an instrument of extended
usefulness', could never hope to rival 'the ancient Christian schools of
Alexandria, Edessa, Nisibis, in its Platonic reasoning, profound and
original thinking, and masterly methods of grappling with Oriental
subtleties'. (2) The Divinity School, for the training of evangelists,
pastors and teachers, seemed at first to hold greater promise. Believing
that received ideas of missionary work were 'in danger of making the Gospel
too much of an exotic', French envisaged finding 'out of the ranks of
pundits, moollahs, gooroos', those who would 'vie with one another in
coveting the gift of close study of the Jewish and Christian shastras',
thus equipping themselves to develop a new apologetic in the vernacular and
the thought-forms of Indian religious tradition, just as, in second and
third-century Alexandria, 'from converted Aristotelians and neo-Platonists
came the best refuters of Celsus, Porphyry, Libanius and Julian'. (3)

In the earlier years, it is quite clear that French did not see this
missionary method as involving more than a very sophisticated exercise in
translation, 'enlisting for Christianity all the associations connected in
the mind of the Hindus with their venerable and beautiful language,
gathering out what is pure in the language from the mass of corrupt notions

which it has been employed to express'. Later, in planning the Divinity
College, he seems to suggest that he might have come to believe that not
only the language, but also something of the content of the Indian
religious tradition might have its part in the divine economy:

> Is it not hard to suppose that God has suffered that
> vast mass of erudition and result of mental force to
> accumulate for so many ages to be utterly purposeless
> towards setting up the kingdom of his dear Son?

Certainly, the main stress continued to be upon 'Hindu literature' and
'appropriate expression in the niceties, beauties and forces of the
Sanskrit tongue', but it is also the case that a developing appreciation of
some elements in Hinduism and Islam can be traced in his writings during
these years. (4)

French had never regarded the small Divinity School at Lahore as more than
'a mere miniature of a far more extensive plan which time and the growth of
education and of the Church of Christ in India might give birth to', with
the help of 'our seats of learning at home'. (5)   Interest in missionary
work was growing at Cambridge in the 1870's, not least under the influence
of Westcott, and the first plans for a 'Cambridge University Mission in
North India' were being formulated, in which 'the Church's interpretation
and form of doctrine should be presented in such aspects and from such
points of view as would be most intelligible to the Hindoos and most
analogous to the religious ideas which their sages have struck out and
originated during thousands of years of study and meditation from time
immemorial'.   This gave French the opportunity for a further elaboration of
his ideas, the model being, again, the Christian Platonists of the second
and third centuries:

> The Alexandrian Schools of thought and enquiry have
> often been referred to as supplying the exactest and
> most practical model of a Christian Educational
> Institute, which in its class-rooms and lectures
> should be exhaustive of all the great branches of

science and problems of thought on which the human
mind is exercised. It found ready to hand, of
course, in Alexandria, great schemes of education,
encyclopaedic in character, well compacted and
organized in system, expansive and even tolerant in
principle, and it needed only the mind of a
philosopher, and the heart and soul of a Christian to
see how happily all this might be fertilised,
foecundated, refined and even glorified by being
brought into combination with that seed of the Word,
which is God's divinely appointed instrument of
growth into that divine image in which man was
created.

French noted that 'a stir and ferment' and 'an enquiring people' were
necessary conditions for the sort of work in which the Alexandrian Fathers
had engaged. Contemporary India seemed to him to provide similar
conditions, and this, with the interest which he found at Cambridge,
suggested an ideal opportunity for the realisation of his vision. (6)

French's consecration in the December of the following year, 1877, as the
first Bishop of Lahore, seemed a guarantee, as Westcott observed, that his
'great thoughts' would become 'the inspiring thoughts of a diocese', and so
provide the ideal setting for the inauguration of the work of the Cambridge
Mission. (7)

The contribution of Westcott, Regius Professor of Divinity at Cambridge
from 1870, was to bring further definition to the theology of mission which
French had proposed, to demonstrate in the field of doctrine how it might
be applied, and, perhaps above all, to inspire the early members of the
Cambridge Mission in their attempts to put it into practice.

Westcott had first met French in 1868, and was clearly attracted by him and
his ideas - 'a true apostle', he called him - and they became regular and
intimate correspondents. (8) He took a sympathetic and practical interest
in the Lahore Divinity School from its inception, which coincided more or

less with his own appointment at Cambridge. With his 'Platonic theology' taking shape during these years, he found French's ideas about educational missions singularly congenial. (9) The latter wrote delightedly in 1874 that 'in Professor Westcott, the Lahore institution seems to have stirred up a wonderful determination to grapple in Christ's strength with the whole question of Indian, Chinese, and other missions, such as would mark him out, perhaps, in the Romish Church for the head of a new order for the propagation of the faith'. (10) So it was that Westcott, 'the Christian Platonist', with long-standing family connections with India, 'dreamed of an Alexandria on the banks of the Jumna'. (11)

To what extent Westcott's own ideas influenced French, it is hard to say. The latter certainly acknowledged that it was a great advantage to study the broad principles which Westcott, 'more than any other Christian writer and thinker of our universities', had worked out on aims and methods for 'preaching the Gospel to the heathen nations of the world'. He also prayed that Christ's 'Indian crown, among the many He must wear', might have 'some of his brightest and purest jewels gathering for it by the prophetic teaching' of Westcott. (12) More importantly, however, Westcott himself went on from these early contacts with French to a very interesting enunciation of these principles, and so, because of his 'dominance of the Cambridge scene', exercised an important influence in the shaping of the missiological approach of the Cambridge Mission to Delhi. (13)

As early as 1872, in a sermon on 'Universities in Relation to Missionary Work', he had begun to spell out his ideas. 'Missionary teaching' to date had been on the wrong lines. The 'elaborated doctrine' of the churches was 'a priceless treasure', but it represented 'the experience, the thought, the character of the West', and to impose it on Christians in India was to 'impoverish the resources of humanity', and to 'do dishonour to the infinite fulness of the Gospel'. What was needed was 'a gathering together of men' who would be 'as thoroughly Hindu as they .... (were) Christian', and this would require a system of education 'like that of Clement, ... on the lines traced out by Origen'. (14)

What Westcott had in mind becomes clear when we examine his essays on

'Clement of Alexandria' and 'Origen and the Beginnings of Christian
Philosophy', published a little later in the 1870's, more or less as the
Cambridge Mission was in process of formation, and his later very
substantial article, 'Origenes'. Thus, Clement, seeing 'the Incarnation as
the crown and consummation of the whole history of the world', acknowledged
'a providential purpose in the development of Gentile life', and recognised
in Gentile speculation 'many divine elements'. Greek philosophy was 'a
guide to righteousness and a work of divine providence, ... a preparation
for justifying faith, and in a true sense a dispensation, a covenant'.
Origen in particular, 'with a firmer conviction of the universal
sovereignty of truth, a larger grasp of facts, and a deeper sympathy with
the restless questionings of the soul than any other father', was immensely
attractive to Westcott. His firm grasp of the truth of 'the unity of all
creation, as answering to the thought of a Creator infinitely good and
infinitely just', his claiming 'for the domain of Christianity every human
interest and power', his 'grasp of the significance of the Incarnation'
(which 'made an epoch in Christology'), his commentary on St John (which
'marks an epoch in theological literature and in theological thought'), all
find echoes in Westcott's own most characteristic work. What concerns us
in particular, however, is that Origen, 'a learner in the school of
Greeks', discovered through them 'fresh depths in the Bible', and went on
from this to create, in his De Principiis, a 'philosophy of the Christian
faith'.

> This book ... was written ... for those who were
> familiar with the teaching of Gnosticism and
> Platonism; and with a view to questions which then
> first become urgent when men have risen to a wide
> view of nature and life. Non-Christian philosophers
> moved in a region of subtle abstractions, 'ideas':
> Origen felt that Christianity converted these
> abstractions into realities, persons, facts of a
> complete life; and he strove to express what he felt
> in the modes of thought and language of his own age.
> He aimed at presenting the highest knowledge as an
> objective system.

Thus, the De Principiis marked 'an epoch in Christian thought', and
illustrated in a comprehensive way the sort of procedures required of a
missionary Christianity in the context of a great intellectual culture.
Westcott also drew attention to the teaching of Justin about 'the seed of
the Word ... inborn in every race of men', as a result of which there were
'Christians before Christ among the heathen'. He found Justin's ideas
'singularly full of interest'. (15) Here, then, were 'fresh models' (as
French had called them) for a theology of mission for contemporary India.

A course of undergraduate lectures which Westcott gave during these years,
'Introductory to the Study of Christian Doctrine' and published as The
Gospel of Life, gave him the opportunity to demonstrate the sort of
possibilities inherent in this approach. The Alexandrian Fathers, though
they had seen clearly that there was 'a work for and of God going on during
the apparent isolation of the heathen from the region in which the Spirit
revealed Him', had not risen to 'the apprehension of the special office of
the Gentile nations in the divine economy, which a larger view of the
relations of the parts of our vast human life' now enabled Christian
thinkers to gain.

This larger view was now possible because, along with other new knowledge
(and Westcott quoted at length from the latest writings of the physicist,
J. Clerk Maxwell), 'the original writings of Confucianism, Brahmanism,
Buddhism, and Zoroastrianism' were rapidly becoming accessible 'in
intelligible forms'. In his lectures, Westcott then examined the
'characteristic thoughts' which underlay 'the prae-Christian Book
religions', their 'special office' being to enlarge and define the
conception of humanity's religious nature, and (because every human
religious thought has its corresponding thought in the Gospel) to shed new
light on the Christian faith. (16) The exercise, necessarily generalised,
was a bold one, and the accompanying notes which Westcott prepared on 'The
Sacred Books of the Prae-Christian Religions' indicate the seriousness and
thoroughness with which he approached it. (17)

The detail of this exercise, however, is less important for us than the

general approach, and its articulation as a theology of mission for India.
Thus, a serious and sympathetic engagement with the Indian people in their
search for a solution to the problems of life, specifically in the terms in
which these presented themselves to them, was a precondition to a further
'unfolding of the Faith'. Just as Origen's attempt to develop a philosophy
of the Christian faith had marked 'an epoch in Christian thought', so this
'unfolding' would amount to nothing less than a great new 'epoch of
revelation'. (18)

The emergence of the Cambridge Mission to Delhi with its distinctive
theology of mission was not, of course, quite apart from French's own
earlier efforts at Agra and Lahore, wholly unheralded. A handful of
earlier missionaries, such as William Carey and the Baptist missionaries in
Bengal, and W.A. Mill of Bishop's College, Calcutta, civilians like John
Muir and J.R. Ballantyne of Varanasi, and some of the early converts like
Nilakantha Goreh, Krishna Mohan Banerjea and Brahmabandhab Upadhyaya, had
been in varying measure sympathetic to or at least not entirely dismissive
of Indian religious tradition.

In Britain, the beginnings of a scholarly exposition of Eastern religions
had enabled F.D. Maurice, so powerful an influence on Westcott, to open up,
in his Boyle Lectures of 1845 and 1846 on The Religions of the World, the
question of the Christian understanding of other faiths and their adherents
in a bold and generous way. Similarly, Charles Kingsley, in his Alexandria
and Her Schools (1854), which Westcott had read, called for a contemporary
application of 'the philosophy of Clement' in the Christian approach to
people of other faiths. (19)

The work of orientalists also, from about 1875, influenced a number of
Evangelical missionaries towards a more conciliatory approach. Chief among
these were Max Müller, from whom Westcott derived so much of the data for
his reflection on the 'Prae-Christian Book Religions', and M.
Monier-Williams, whom French knew. In Delhi itself, an SPG missionary,
R.R. Winter, who, with his wife, had laboured heroically and effectively
for twenty years before the founding of the Cambridge Mission, responded to
a speech of Müller's in 1874 by calling for a mission directed to Delhi's

new 'literary natives' which would claim 'Eastern thought and culture for the service of Christianity'. (20) There were, then, antecedents of a sort, though none that went so far as to integrate their sympathetic understanding of other faiths into an actual mission strategy.

This was the distinction of the Cambridge Mission to Delhi, that it was established on the basis of what we might call a classical theology of mission, developed in the bold and expansive categories of Westcott's thought.

The Mission was begun in 1877, and St Stephen's College, clearly regarded by French as the main vehicle of its work, in 1881. There were disappointments as well as successes in the early decades. (21) Whatever the balance of these, the stream of reports from the missionaries to Westcott – made public in the series of Occasional Papers published from 1881 onwards – indicate that they held themselves accountable to him ('our beloved Master', as one of them called him) for what they did. (22) Westcott himself continued to make reference to 'Alexandria' as 'the type and promise of Evangelic work in India' and to remind the Mission of 'the power of a great ideal'. (23)

With early members of the Mission still active, among them S.S. Allnutt as Head of the Mission, and G.A. Lefroy ('the clasp that held fast the pearls of the chain from being scattered', French called him) as Bishop of Lahore, this was the heritage into which C.F. Andrews entered in 1904. First, however, we must look at his beginnings.

3. 'Eager enthusiasm'

Andrews was born in Newcastle in northern England in 1871 and lived throughout most of his early years in Birmingham. From 1880 to 1890, he attended King Edward's School, which had also been Westcott's old school, and also that of another founding father of the Cambridge Mission, J.B. Lightfoot. The influences most distinctively discernible later, however, were those of his parents and home, and the Catholic Apostolic Church, of which his father was the Angel, the chief minister, in Birmingham. It was,

by all his accounts, a happy home, and he was equally emphatic throughout
his life that he owed his deepest religious convictions to his parents,
though no doubt his restless and troubled personality also owed something
to these years. The solemn and exalted liturgy of the Catholic Apostolic
Church, at which his father presided, made a deep impression upon him, and
no doubt contributed to his 'theophanic awareness of reality'. (1) What he
seemed to remember chiefly, however, about his father, were his
conservative political opinions and his unquestioning admiration for the
British Empire as 'the one destined instrument in God's hand for setting
right the world'. (2) Such views were very characteristic of the Catholic
Apostolic Church. The Church's strong emphasis on the Second Coming also
found an echo, in a small way, in some of Andrews' own later thinking. (3)

A conversion experience during his last school holiday brought a new depth
to his faith, and he frequently retold the story in later life. (4) His
own account of the experience, '... (Christ's) love had won my heart for
ever', points to the origin of the later description of him as a 'Christian
bhakta'. (5)

Andrews went up to Pembroke College, Cambridge, with a scholarship in 1890
and was there, off-and-on, for the next fourteen years. Throughout those
years, in the Master of Trinity's judgement, a divine blessing rested
'visibly ... on his work and influence'. (6) He read Classics and then
Theology, being placed in the First Class in both, and won various
university prizes. A further result of his early years at Cambridge was
his confirmation in the Church of England in 1895. He spent a short time
as a lay-worker in Durham, where Westcott was now Bishop, and then from
1896 was Missioner at the Pembroke College Mission in south London for
three years, during which time he was ordained by the Bishop of Rochester,
E.S. Talbot. He returned to a Fellowship at Cambridge in 1899, where he
also became the first Vice-Principal of the Clergy Training School (later
known as Westcott House), and then Lecturer and Chaplain of Pembroke.
From there he set out for India 'one bitterly cold morning in February
1904'. (7)

A number of men at Cambridge influenced Andrews during these years, including some to whose ideas we will find him returning in India. Among these was E.G. Browne, who introduced him to Islam and Arab civilisation, and to a sympathetic view of these, Forbes Robinson, whose intense friendships suggested a way through the racial barrier that Andrews was to meet in India, and Lord Acton, whose 'almost startling' teaching on 'Liberty and Nationality' he was to re-interpret in new circumstances.

It was B.F. Westcott, however, whose influence was most important for Andrews. He had already left to become Bishop of Durham when Andrews went up, but, quite apart from the influence which his memory and books continued to exert almost unchallenged in the University throughout these years, Andrews came into unusually close personal contact with him. (8) This was through 'the two greatest friends ... (he) had on earth' at that time. (9) One of these was C.H. Prior, Tutor of Pembroke, who had been taught by Westcott at Harrow and had subsequently married one of Westcott's daughters. Andrews found in Prior's household almost a second home until the latter's death in 1899. The other was Westcott's youngest son, Basil, Andrews' contemporary as an undergraduate. Practically speaking, the latter wrote later, 'never a single day passed' without their meeting, while after Basil left for Delhi in 1896, they corresponded 'every week'. (10) Through these friendships, Andrews spent some of his holidays in the Westcott household at Auckland and on holiday in Yorkshire, times which he remembered as 'golden days', when he drew upon 'the wisdom of the aged bishop'. (11)

There were a number of aspects to Westcott's influence upon Andrews. The most fundamental was in Andrews' whole theological outlook, which he later described as 'liberal orthodox'. (12) The commanding features of Westcott's own strongly incarnational theology, reflecting, as we have seen, his enthusiastic understanding of Origen, and in particular his Christology, we will find Andrews developing in new and very fruitful ways in India.

Westcott's influence was evident in the first instance, however, in directing Andrews' attention to social questions. This was something new to him, for, following his father, he had been 'a Tory of the Tories' and

he had never come under 'liberal political influences' until he came to
Cambridge. (13) Westcott's commanding influence in this field, and
Andrews' discipleship, are illustrated in the fact that the former was the
founder and first President of the influential Christian Social Union, and
the latter the Union's Cambridge Secretary.

Andrews' interest in social issues had a strongly practical side during
these years: in succession to, among others, Prior and two of Westcott's
older sons, George and Foss, he became from about 1894 an exceptionally
energetic member of his College's settlement project in south London. If
he was later to go so far as to say that his experiences there, and more
particularly during his months as a lay-worker at Monkwearmouth, made him
'an out-and-out opponent of the capitalist system', his reports from
Walworth reveal him as a much less radical and much more typical member of
the settlement movement, shocked at the 'open and revolting ... vices ...
of the poor', critical of 'red flags and tub-oratory', and working to
change 'the current ideas in the minds of our people with regard to those
above them in station' by creating within the life of the College Mission
'a practical expression of the brotherhood of rich and poor'. (14)

If these immediate reactions to the College Mission's work reflect so
strikingly his class-background, his more systematic consideration of the
context of the Mission's work, in his prize essay on The Relation of
Christianity to the Conflict between Capital and Labour, indicate the
importance of Westcott's influence. A jejune work in some respects, it
nevertheless clarifies some of the features of Andrews' developing thought
about Christianity and Christian mission. Because 'the world of common
life' has been 'opened up on such a vast scale by modern industry', the
opportunity has arisen to work out 'Christian principles' on a scale
hitherto almost inconceivable, and this represents what Westcott might have
called a new epoch of revelation, for Andrews, with his Catholic Apostolic
background, 'one of the days of the Son of Man'. New modes of thought and
expression, 'ideas of mutual dependence, of society as an organism, of the
solidarity of the race', are now 'being learnt by the workman and the
labourer with a clearness which was lacking even to great thinkers' a
century previously. These are 'ideas which help man to grasp the message

of the Incarnation', because the 'Gospel of the Incarnation' is itself 'the
true basal bond between man and man, drawing each in sympathy towards a
common, mutual life of love and service', or, as 'Dr. Westcott' puts it,
because the Incarnation is 'the inexhaustible spring of brotherhood'. (15)

Westcott, indeed, with F.D. Maurice, is the decisive influence behind this
early, undergraduate effort of Andrews', and they are acknowledged as such
in the Preface. In particular, we must note that Andrews' claim that 'the
message of the Incarnation met half-way the inner workings in the minds of
labouring men', suggests that, in theory at least, he has grasped and
absorbed something of Westcott's theory of mission.

The time and place for Andrews' own distinctive development of this
theology and its practical expression were still to come. The awakening of
his interest in the Cambridge Mission to Delhi, however, took place during
these same years. While he was still in his second year, the visit of the
then Principal of St Stephen's College, J.W.T. Wright, aroused considerable
interest in the Mission. 'One man in particular', it was reported,
'Andrews, of Pembroke', was proving a very keen and active Undergraduate
Secretary and had arranged for meetings and found secretaries in several
other colleges, and appeared to have learnt a great deal about the
Mission. (16) His decision to offer himself as a candidate for work in
Delhi came some years later, reinforced by Basil Westcott's death there in
August 1900, and prompted by an Indian colleague and friend of Basil's,
S.K. Rudra. (17)

In later life, Andrews often explained his attitudes and missionary
approach in India by reference to B.F. Westcott, saying, for example, that
he had 'started with the great advantage of having "sat under" Dr. Westcott
... and absorbed his writings with eager enthusiasm'. Of his talks with
Westcott while staying with him on holiday, there is no contemporary
record, but his lengthy later recollections indicate that these touched
upon Westcott's dream of a new 'Alexandria'. What Greece had been to
Europe, India, as the other great 'thinking' nation, would be to Asia. Her
imminent awakening would make her 'the missionary of Christ to Asia'. (18)
It was these talks more than anything else which shaped Andrews'

understanding of mission. His appreciation and grasp of Westcott's
theology of mission was such, indeed, that when, on Westcott's death in
1901, a need was felt for a record of Westcott's contribution in this
field, the Head of the Mission in Delhi wrote to the Chairman of the
Mission Committee in Cambridge saying that he thought 'Andrews would do it
very well'. (19) The plan seems to have got no further, but Andrews' place
in it is noteworthy.

Of the particular and quite new situation with which Andrews was to find
the Church faced in India, that is, the new context of mission created by
developments in the national movement from about 1905, his years at
Cambridge can have provided few clues. Sensitive missionaries, French and
Lefroy among them, had for many years been acutely aware of the near-
impossibility of effective missionary work in India because, as the former
had put it nearly fifty years earlier,

> The Bible in the one hand has no attractiveness
> when it seems ... accompanied by the sword in the
> other. (20)

Westcott, on the other hand, while aware of the 'temptations' of empire,
could scarcely have had a more elevated view of British rule in India, 'a
monument of lofty policy' to which he knew no parallel. The perspective is
characteristic, that of the 'corporate growth' and 'solidarity' of
humanity. Within this perspective, 'Imperialism' was 'a step towards the
earthly destiny of man, "the federation of the world"', and belonged 'to a
late stage of human history'. (21) Westcott wrote and spoke a great deal
on this topic. It is not altogether surprising, therefore, that when
Andrews went out to India in 1904, while he had rejected his father's
views on 'labour questions', the 'intensely vivid belief in the British
Empire' which he had heard 'from babyhood onwards, ... had never been
challenged.' (22)

To spend 'whole days reading the Sacred Books of the East and Max Müller
and other writers', as he said that he did from about 1899 onwards, might
have seemed a model preparation for his work in the Cambridge Mission to

Delhi. (23) To be learning to expect an illumination of the doctrine of
the Incarnation through looking at what was going on in his own times 'in
the minds of labouring men' in Durham and South London, as they struggled
with life's problems, was, as it turned out, not less so.

NOTES: Chapter One

1. Introductory

1 WIOC p. 214

2 I have used this not very satisfactory term, 'educated classes' throughout for that new élite created in the nineteenth century by the spread of Western education, simply because it is the one most widely used in the literature of the period.

3 Neill 1964, p. 325

2. 'An Alexandria on the banks of the Jumna'

1 Birks 1895, Vol. 1, p. 323

2 Ibid., p. 44

3 Printed annual letter of 1872 (CMS)

4 Birks 1895, Vol. 1, p. 44; 163; passim

5 French 1876

6 Ibid.

7 Birks 1895, Vol. 1, p. 333

8 Ibid., pp. 14, 232

9 Newsome 1974, p. 122

10 Birks 1895, Vol. 1, p. 316

11 Chadwick 1962; S.K. Rudra in SSC Mag Apr 1914. Westcott himself, before Delhi was chosen for the Cambridge Mission's work, had asked 'is it too much to hope that we may yet see on the Indus, or the Ganges, some new Alexandria?' (Westcott 1873)

12 Birks 1895, Vol. 1, pp. 317, 364

13 H. Chadwick 1960

14 Westcott 1873, pp. 25-44

15 'Clement of Alexandria' and 'Origenes' are in Smith and Wace 1877 f., Vols. I and IV, 'Origen and the Beginnings of Christian Philosophy' in Westcott 1891; the remarks about Justin occur in Westcott 1892, pp. 116-7.

16 Westcott 1892, pp. 116-22

17 In a footnote to the Preface of the Gospel of Life, Westcott

regretted that he had not had time to include notes on the sacred books of the prae-Christian religions (p. xvii). He did, however, publish the following year a very comprehensive set of such notes as an appendix in The Cambridge Companion to the Bible 1893, pp. 15–21.

18 Westcott 1892, pp. xxiv, 282

19 It was with Islam particularly that Kingsley envisaged 'a fresh reconciliation' p. 170; Westcott refers to Kingsley's book in his essay on Origen, Westcott 1891.

20 'Report of the Mission in Delhi and the South Punjab ... 1873–4' (SPG)

21 When Westcott heard that the College was to be affiliated to the new Punjab University, which, uniquely in India, recognised the vernaculars on an equal footing with English, he described the news as 'of the most momentous significance and of the highest promise', and made a brief reference to 'Alexandria' (Westcott 1882). Four years later, S.S. Allnutt, first Principal of the College, reported that the policy was not being implemented satisfactorily (Allnutt 1885).

22 Allnutt to Stanton, 14 August 1901 (CMD); several years later, Lefroy still called him 'our great Cambridge teacher' (Ellison and Walpole 1908, p. 67)

23 Westcott 1882

3. 'Eager enthusiasm'

1 J. Pinnington Times Literary Supplement 20 June 1980

2 'My Mother' (handwritten) (Chaturvedi – NAI)

3 For an early example, Andrews 1896, pp. 5, 142

4 e.g. to Munshi Ram and the Gurukula students. Andrews to Munshi Ram, 30 Apr 1913 (Chaturvedi – NAI)

5 WIOC p. 92. Andrews used the term of himself Christ in the Silence (1933) p. 14; others have also used it of him, e.g. Sykes 1973, p. 6 and Gispert-Sauch 1973, p. xxx.

6 H.M. Butler, in his preface to Andrews 1904, p. ix

7 'My Mother' (Chaturvedi – NAI)

8 For Westcott's posthumous influence, see 'Religion in Cambridge'
   Church Quarterly Review Oct 1904

9 Andrews to Herman Prior, 3 Aug 1900 (Pembroke)

10 YMOI Oct 1925

11 Andrews 1933, p. 152

12 Biog p. 66

13 Ibid. p. 51

14 MR Feb-Mar 1915; Mission Report 1897, pp. 4, 5, 8
    (Pembroke)

15 Andrews 1896, pp. 125, 86, 66, 48-9.

16 Stanton to Lefroy, 9 Feb 1893 (CMD)

17 Rudra to Stanton, 27 Nov 1902 (CMD); Gandhi later wrote, 'We
    owe C.F. Andrews to ... Rudra' Young India 9 Jul 1925

18 YMOI Apr 1930; Biog p. 47; NMI Nov 1910

19 Allnut to Stanton, 14 Aug 1901 (CMD)

20 French to Venn, 29 Jan 1857 (CMS); see also, for French, Birks
    1895 Vol. 1, pp. 70, 205-6, 342. cf. Lefroy, 'our position as
    the ruling power puts a dead weight on missionary enterprise,
    which nothing but the direct grace of God can possibly enable us
    to lift' in Montgomery 1920, p. 20, also 30, 173, 175, 179-80

21 Westcott 1900; 'The Empire' in Hocking 1900, pp. 19-20

22 'My Mother' (Chaturvedi - NAI); pamphlet 'How India Can Be
    Free' (1921)

23 Biog p. 66

CHAPTER TWO
THE CONTEXT OF MISSION 1904-6

1. **Introductory**

T.V. French had spoken of 'a stir and ferment' among 'an enquiring people' as a necessary precondition for the sort of Christian mission that had been carried out in ancient Alexandria. Andrews came to just such a situation, to 'the New World of the East' at 'the very epoch of its renaissance'. (1) Of course, this renaissance had had in a more general sense a longer history, of more than a century, by this time. His first year or two in India did, nevertheless, coincide with what a new Indian friend called 'an extraordinary ebullition of feeling'. Although the country as a whole remained 'in a dreamy state of consciousness as to its highest interest', it was 'no longer fast asleep'. The 'middle-classes', who had been, 'according to the Englishman's view, "contaminated" by education', were 'restless'.

This restlessness took a quite specific form: 'politics and politics alone' had, from 1904-5, become 'the predominant interest of this class'. This new Indian friend, looking back in 1910, summed up the new situation by saying that 'a wave of political consciousness' had passed over India in the previous five years, and indeed, 'over the whole of Asia'. (2) For Andrews, the first important question to be asked was:

> How may the new movement in the East be rightly used
> to extend the Kingdom of Christ? (3)

In this chapter, we shall look at the process whereby he came to formulate the question.

2. **Orthodox and ardent**

Andrews arrived in Delhi at the end of March 1904, and he began in many respects as a very conventional missionary, even down to 'a heavy black

European suit', which, as he later remarked, 'no one could possibly call
... in sweltering India, a "garment of praise"'. (1)

The Cambridge Mission likewise presented a conventional if impressive
picture of urban and district mission work. A visitor at the time wrote,
with a touch of the military terminology characteristic of mission-writing
at the time:

> The Cambridge Mission at Delhi - to take one of the
> greatest of our Mission centres - presents all the
> impressive strength of a great organisation. The
> majority of the members of the Mission live together
> and work the city like a huge parish. Every
> department of life is catered for. There is a
> complete ladder of education, from the elementary -
> very elementary - schools in the Bastis, to St
> Stephen's College, which is affiliated to the Lahore
> University. There is a first-rate Purdah hospital
> under the direction of a lady doctor of great
> reputation, and a staff of district nurses, who are
> sent from the hospital to nurse the women in their
> homes. There is a large staff of ladies who
> systematically visit in the zenanas. There are
> centres of Mission work in ten or a dozen different
> districts of the city, under the charge of catechists
> superintended by the Mission clergy. There is an
> orphanage, a boarding house for boys, a hostel for
> students, a staff of bazaar preachers, and in the
> centre of all a fine church with daily services and a
> communicants' roll of 200. Besides all these there
> are several out-stations where individual members of
> the brotherhood live and work on the same lines as
> the main body at Delhi.

> Here then is an organisation which meets the eye; the
> Church in Delhi is putting forth her strength in a

great frontal attack, and the characteristic feature
of the Mission is active work. (2)

Andrews' arrival brought the Brotherhood's numbers up to ten, and the
Mission's numbers up to forty senior members. (3) Although he was to
remain a full member of the Brotherhood for the whole of his ten years in
Delhi, sharing in the community's common life, its prayers and retreats,
and its deliberations, even being considered for the Headship at one point,
he lived at the community house in the centre of the old city only for the
first year or so, moving out then to join other teaching members at a house
which they had secured adjacent to the College hostel, and, for his last
two or three years, to the house of an Indian member of the College staff,
an arrangement which he found the most congenial of all. He had, in fact,
developed reservations about the brotherhood type of mission by 1908,
though he continued throughout the decade a serious member of the
community, by no means isolated entirely in his 'advanced' views, but
a stimulus to his colleagues by his example 'and not seldom his
exhortation'. (4) He made a lasting contribution to its devotional life in
a conventional enough way with the office book which he drew up between
1908 and 1911, and which was used daily in the Brotherhood – and in many
other religious communities – for many years. (5)

About a fortnight after arriving in Delhi, after Easter Day and his
admission to the Brotherhood on 12 April, Andrews went up to Simla, a hill
station and the summer capital of the government of India, where he was to
stay for some six months taking lessons in Urdu. The acting Head of the
Mission was to report at the end of the year that he was making very rapid
progress in the study of the language, but in fact he seems never to have
become very proficient in any Indian language. His teacher was Shams-ud-
Din, a court translator from Lahore and a Muslim nephew of the well-known
Punjabi convert, Dr Imad-ud-Din. He had leanings towards Christianity, and
the conventional missionary reported at the turn of the year that he was
'still trying to keep in touch with him'. (6) At the same time, Shams-ud-
Din inculcated in Andrews something of his own love of Islam, and also gave
him his first glimpse of British rule through Indian eyes, with regard both
to the matter of racialism and also to 'the follies and extravagances of

the "Simla-season"', which filled the devout Muslim with horror. (7)
After the annual Brotherhood retreat, Andrews was back in Delhi for the
beginning of the year at St Stephens's College in October. We shall have
to pay special attention to the importance of the College for the
development of his ideas. He seems rarely during his ten years as a member
of the teaching staff to have spent more than the cooler half of the year
at the College: poor health and increasing preoccupation with outside
concerns were to keep him out of Delhi a great deal. His first two winters
in India, however, saw him settling into teaching and other aspects of the
College's work, combining this with various responsibilities in the local
church - quiet days, bible classes, and preparing a young Muslim student,
Faizal Hasan, for baptism. He visited Rawalpindi at Easter 1905 to assist
the chaplain there, and wrote a lively report, in which he refers to Hindus
as 'heathen'. (8) We catch glimpses of him also making friends with the
Regency President of the princely state of Patiala, and having with him
'long conversations about the Faith', and on a railway journey to Lahore
commending 'the True Way of Life in Jesus Christ' to a Hindu fellow-
passenger. (9)

Just a year after his arrival in India, a new concern was beginning to
intrude upon the emerging routine of Andrews' life as a conventional
missionary. From the inception of the Cambridge Mission, literary work had
been envisaged as a chief part of its programme. Nothing, however, as
Stanton, the Chairman of the Mission Committee at Cambridge, pointed out in
1905, had yet been accomplished in that field, new members of the Mission
being 'dragged at once into the daily routine of immediate duties'. Early
in 1905, Andrews took up the matter with Stanton and Allnutt, stressing his
own desire to make a literary career the main end of his missionary
activity. He identified a serious lack in the Church's work in the Punjab,
perhaps 'the most pressing need in Upper India', namely a more general
literary provision for 'the rapidly rising Native Christian Church and the
rapidly growing educated Native Community'. He saw settling to such a
career as a possible solution to an old difficulty, that of 'having too
many irons in the fire and getting distracted by divided duties', but this
does not take away from the importance of his perception of this new
missionary task. Stanton insisted that this should not be allowed to get

in the way of his regular work in the College and must not be his sole aim, but he agreed to the suggestion, observing that Andrews' 'power of insight into the conditions and requirements of the work' were remarkable. (10)

Andrews' life as a member of the Cambridge Mission was disrupted in 1905 by illness. Ear trouble necessitated a visit to England to consult a specialist, and he was away from Delhi for seven months, returning in November on the condition that he should thereafter always spend the hot months in the hills, where he would - the Cambridge Committee of the Mission announced - 'occupy himself with literary work'. (11) He was to experience poor health for most of the rest of his time at Delhi, with a series of illnesses which laid him low and disrupted his work to such an extent that, looking back, he went so far as to say that throughout those years he 'lived in a kind of morbid state in which it was very difficult to think and act with calmness and clearness of vision'. (12)

He did not allow his visit to England to be taken up entirely with seeing doctors. He continued his language study at Cambridge, and had interesting discussions with Har Dayal, a young graduate from St Stephen's College, who was studying at Oxford, and to whom we shall have occasion to refer later, and also with men who were able to tell him of incipient national movements in Ireland, Turkey, Persia and China. He also seized the occasion to take up a cause, that of Indian students in England who, as he saw it, were frequently 'fleeced and cheated', and drifted into an anti-Christian society of 'theosophists with vegetarian ideas, occultists, spiritualists, etc.'. (13) From this, he went on to float the idea of an Indian students' hostel in London, a move of characteristic foresight. He also wrote three articles for missionary journals which we shall look at in some detail.

Andrews' return to Delhi was a great relief to both Indian and English colleagues in the Mission. One of the former went so far as to say:

> What his presence in our midst is cannot be described
> in words. It is sufficient to say that my heart goes
> up in thankfulness to God for enabling him to
> continue here. (14)

If this suggests a very special contribution to the work of the Cambridge
Mission, Andrews' first two years give only slight indication as to the
form this is to take. Looking at these beginnings, it is easy to see the
justice of his remark that he started his work in India 'perfectly
definitely at this time a missionary in the orthodox sense, and a very
ardent missionary'. (15)

3. 'Things as they were'

> The sunshine touched the Viceregal canopy and flashed
> upon the burnished thrones, before which stood the
> brilliant figures of the Viceroy and the Duke of
> Connaught. The Amphitheatre was a blaze of colour,
> of glittering jewels, of gorgeous dresses. The arena
> was filled with uniforms. Men of all races and hues,
> the greatest and noblest and most famous in India,
> joined in one spontaneous act of homage to the mighty
> potentate who rules over Hindustan, and whose writ
> runs to the farthest corners of the earth, the
> uttermost isles of the sea. (1)

Thus Delhi a year before Andrews' arrival, at what has been called 'the
high noon of empire'. (2) He said later that on arrival he had by no means
got rid of that uncritical admiration for the British empire that he had
learned from his father. (3) It was, nevertheless, the less attractive
aspects of the current arrangements which most impressed him at first.
This would seem to have distinguished him, for all his initial
conventionality, from most of his contemporaries. Certainly, the opinion
of a sympathetic Indian observer in 1904 was that 'modern missionaries'
seemed to be actively committed to upholding things as they found them.

> To non-Christians, their mission appears to be much
> less religious than commercial or political. (4)

The advice regularly given to Andrews by older English residents was that, whatever he might notice, he 'must deal with things as they were'. (5) India was ruled at the time by that least unobtrusive of viceroys, Lord Curzon - 'a rampant Tory imperialist', the leading Indian newspaper in the Punjab called him, who 'outshone the pomp and magnificence of the Great Moghuls of Delhi'. Even his closest associate at the India Office observed, in the year of Andrews' arrival in India, that Curzon 'considered his position to be that of Louis XIV - "L'état, c'est moi"'. (6)

Within a matter of weeks, we catch a glimpse of Andrews close to the centre of Imperial power. His name occurs in a list in an Anglo-Indian newspaper, and he is the only missionary there:

> The Viceroy's Levée. The following were present at
> his excellency the Viceroy's Levée at Viceregal
> Lodge, Simla, on the 27th (May) ... New Presentations
> ... Andrews, Rev. C.F, M.A. (7)

This was, in fact, a levée of the acting Viceroy, Lord Ampthill, while Curzon was on a visit to Britain. During that first summer at Simla, Andrews was tutor to Ampthill's children, and through this developed something of a friendship with him as well as getting to know a number of members of the Indian Civil Service. (8)

Ampthill's brief acting viceroyalty provided the country, in the judgement of an Indian observer, with a 'much needed rest' from the energetic reforming zeal of Curzon. (9) It was, however, Curzon's viceregal style that impressed itself upon Andrews at the time, for news was reaching Simla throughout that summer of the large military expedition into Tibet, which he had organised before going on leave. There is, of course, a great deal more to say about Curzon than this, and Andrews himself came to appreciate some of his policies, particularly his educational reforms, but what he remembered over thirty years later was this venture, and he referred to it to illustrate the 'old blustering policy' that still prevailed in 1904. (10)

Andrews started to learn about India, then, and to reflect upon the meaning of mission there, definitively under the conditions created by the British imperial presence. No part of India presented these conditions with a greater sharpness than the Punjab, his 'very first home in India and ... (his) very first love'. (11) The Punjab was the last of the great provinces to come under British rule, and its strategic position in relation to an imagined Russian threat explains why it had a more evident military presence than any other part of India. The Bishop of Lahore pointed out that his diocese had in it a larger number of British troops (26,000) than any other in the empire, while Andrews observed that five out of every six 'Englishmen' in the Punjab were soldiers. (12) On the frontier - and he was able to say before long that 'the Punjab and every part of it became known to me, right up to the frontier' - military adventurism still flourished. (13)

British rule within the province, away from the frontier, had its own distinctive character. Considerable development had occurred in the last decades of the nineteenth century, with ten million acres recovered for agricultural use through irrigation and colonisation schemes, but the province was notorious for its harsh administration, in what was known as 'the Punjab tradition', a harshness 'verging almost on the tyrannical', as Curzon's successor, Lord Minto, noted, and tempered only by a strongly paternalistic ordering of the lives of the rural peasantry. (14) It is true that a more benign impression is coveyed by some contemporary reminiscences, both Indian and English, but it was the 'English military atmosphere' which struck Andrews as most evident, and as most critical for the Church's mission. (15)

The city of Delhi was something of a special case. Still brooding over the 'mutiny' of fifty years before, and the violent repression which had followed it, it was characterised in the view of the Bishop of Lahore by 'stagnation and dogged resistance to change', and showed 'the greatest reluctance to yield before the tide of change and Western influence which ... (was) rising with such force over most parts of this vast peninsula'. (16) Andrews noticed this in terms of the city's 'mass of poverty and misery', but what struck him initially was the style of the British presence:

I shall not soon forget the strangeness of my first
few days in Delhi - the policemen saluting, the
people salaaming, the Indian soldier standing at
attention, every one making way. I thought at first
it was all directed towards my companion, who was
well known in Delhi. But no! all was exactly the
same when I was alone. It was due to the simple fact
that I was a Sahib. (17)

It was the same in Simla, with regard to the treatment of his Urdu teacher,
Shams-ud-Din:

> He was a very old man and in Simla he used to wear
> boots with patties as he was not used to the cold.
> When he went to teach an officer to whom I
> recommended him as a Munshi, this officer used to
> make him undo his patties and take off his boots.
> The officer was quite young and the Munshi was quite
> old .... Altogether I was quite disgusted with what
> I saw and it made me very unhappy. (18)

If a young administrator could mock such Anglo-Indian attitudes with the
remark that 'an Indian entering with shoes on would be the first sign of
another mutiny', they made a deep impression on Andrews. (19) This was
confirmed by the 'racial poison' that was distilled into his ear night and
day at Simla. He stayed there in the house of the Chaplain, G.E. Nicholls,
a member of his own college, who had with him an English officer and a
Punjab missionary, from whom he was taught a daily lesson as to how to
treat the native:

> Never, under any circumstances, give way to a
> 'native', or let him regard himself as your superior.
> We only rule India in one way - by upholding our
> position. Though you are a missionary you must be an
> Englishman first, and never forget that you are a

Sahib ... do not give away English prestige. (20)

One of Andrews' earliest impressions was of how these attitudes penetrated the life of the Church:

> On the first morning after my arrival in Delhi, I sat
> in church before the service began, and opened the
> Urdu Prayer Book. These were the words I saw –
> 'Edward VI. Ke dusre sal men Parliament ke hukm se'
> (in the second year of King Edward VI by order of
> Parliament).

Andrews says that his heart sank within him. 'Were not only English but also Indian Christians to be bound down by that annus non mirabilis, the second year of King Edward VI? Was that fateful order of Parliament to go on finding fresh fields and pastures new of spiritual usurpation ad infinitum?' (21) This is not to suggest that Andrews immediately formulated a concept of 'spiritual usurpation', though it was a remarkably short time before he was to do so, but only to indicate his perception from the very beginning of the importance within the Church of the imperial factor. It is precisely in these terms that he was later to sum up his first impressions:

> I found in missionary efforts as they were carried on
> in India the conventional touch of a religious
> imperialism which had the same blighting effect on
> the inner self-determination of Indian Christians as
> the ordinary political imperialism had upon Indians
> who were not Christians. (22)

It is equally true of Andrews' attitude to the 'ordinary political imperialism', that, although within half a dozen years he was calling for a Christian critique of the system, we cannot say much more of his earliest impressions than that he was immediately aware of something that would have to be taken into account because he met it in so many striking and memorable forms.

4. 'A dawn of Hope'

Looking back, in his autobiography, to the Indian situation as he first
became aware of it, Andrews, Open Classical Scholar as he had been,
subsumed his varied impressions under the comprehensive simile of the Roman
Empire:

> The scene in India during the early years of the
> present century, when I lived in Delhi, resembled
> that of the Roman Empire nineteen hundred years ago.
> There was the same vast, unbroken imperial peace in
> external affairs, and a settled order outwardly
> maintained. (1)

It was a simile that had been worked hard for the best part of a century,
and it was still in vogue in Andrews' time with writers as different as the
Lt Governor of the Punjab, who even went beyond simile so far as to trace
the current land revenue system back through Akbar and the Sassanian
dynasty of Muslim Persia to 'the just and bold reforms' of Julius Caesar,
and the Punjab nationalist newspaper who enjoyed designating Curzon 'the
prancing pro-consul'. (2) It was a simile that Andrews was to make much
of, both for his general view of British rule, and his reflection on
education in an empire and on the role of the Christian.

We have already seen that there was for him another side to this 'vast,
unbroken imperial peace', namely the 'blighting' effect of the system on
'the inner self-determination' of Indian people. In a lecture by one of
his colleagues, he heard the East referred to as 'a wilderness of dying
nations', and he refers several times to the 'apathy', the 'helplessness
and despair' that still ran through the writings of educated Indians in
1904. (3)

This was, however, a situation that was to be decisively modified within
Andrews' earliest months in India. If the Tibet Expedition during the
summer of 1904 had suggested to him a supreme confidence in the extension
of British influence, it was, in fact, in historical perspective, 'the

swan-song of British Indian imperialism'. (4) The passage in his
autobiography just quoted continues with a more dynamic simile:

> Within this area of apparent calm, a surging, heaving
> ferment had suddenly begun to appear, like volcanic
> lava cracking through the surface of the soil.

It was a ferment so significant that the standard history of India is able
to say that 'the year 1905 heralded a new period in the annals of this
land'. It brought with it changes so comprehensive and so rapid that the
Viceroy in 1911 was 'quite convinced that were Curzon to return to India,
he would hardly recognise' the new situation. The surprising thing is that
Andrews, so new to India, saw this immediately, and in 1905 was drawing
attention to 'this fresh epoch of Eastern history'. (5)

The causes of this were, of course, extremely complex. From the British
side, in particular a series of moves initiated by Curzon - for the
partition of Bengal, the reorganisation of the universities, together with
what appeared to be a public criticism of the character of the Indian
people - all bore down in such a way as to create an inevitable reaction.
That is, in part, how Andrews subsequently interpreted it, as 'an almost
entire reaction ... against European domination'.

From the Indian side, the long evolution through the nineteenth century of
political awareness crystallised at this time in various new ways. There
was the assertion of a more 'extreme' political claim on the part of many
educated people, amounting, he said at the close of the year 1904, to 'one
exulting hope - that the days of servitude to the West were over and the
day of independence had dawned'. Andrews noted, too, the creation of new
instruments of nation-building such as Gokhale's Servants of India
Society,which prepared young men by courses of study and research for
'careers of national usefulness'. (6) There was the spread from 1905 on an
all-India basis of a policy of <u>swadeshi</u>, which meant, broadly, a claim to
develop the Indian economy in Indian interests. (7)

There were also features of the situation that were peculiar to the Punjab.

There had been from 1900 a series of legislative moves by the government, relating chiefly to the canal colonies, designed to favour the rural masses against the educated and commercial classes. For a variety of reasons, these measures led to increasing agrarian unrest. Radical elements among the urban educated and commercial classes, led by Lajpat Rai, aligned themselves with those who were discontented in the countryside, and by late 1906 the situation had so developed that it was possible to say that 'the Punjab countryside was about to burst into flames'. (8) Andrews, not entirely surprisingly, being located in Delhi, missed this aspect of the ferment. His impression in 1905 of the Punjab peasants' 'cheerful acceptance of law and discipline' reflects a view that was certainly not seriously challenged before 1906: the provincial government itself in 1905 rejected the warnings from some of its own district officers of serious growing unrest. (9)

There was one event, however, that seemed in 1904 and 1905 to speak more compellingly than any other to Indian aspirations. This was the Russo-Japanese War, which began in February 1904 and ran on to mid-1905. It was seen through Indian eyes as a struggle between Europe and Asia, and from its earliest stages the Indian press was claiming that 'nowhere in the world can the proceedings be watched with more breathless interest than in Britain's Eastern dependencies'. To one of Andrews' Indian Christian colleagues, the conduct of Russia and her European allies was 'morally unscrupulous', burning 'like hot iron' in the hearts of the Eastern peoples. They had shown the 'the real "White Peril"'. As the news of the Japanese successes was reported, the enthusiasm of the Indian press became more explicit, a leading journal stating that 'for the first time in many centuries, Europe has gone down before Asia', and adding very pointedly for its Indian readers that 'what is first need not necessarily be the last'.

Andrews subsequently came to think that the effect of the Japanese victory had been exaggerated, tending to obscure the fact that the national movement in India had started long before, in the work of people like Ram Mohun Roy and Ishwar Chandra Gupta, 'when Japan was still a closed land'. However, he seems never to have seriously modified his early view that, along with the rise of nationalism, the Japanese success was of primary

importance in changing 'the centre of gravity of the world's history', and
in making the 'dawn of hope' in India in 1904 'shining and radiant'. (10)

This reference to 'the world's history' indicates another feature of
Andrews' interpretation of the events of his first few months in India,
that is, that he was learning to see the ferment in India as part of a
larger phenomenon. Not only was there this evidence from further east in
Asia – the rise of Japan – but also, as he had partly discovered from
encounters at Cambridge in 1905, there were indications of major changes in
China also, and in western Asia, in Turkey, Egypt and Persia, 'literally
... from one end of Asia to the other'. (11) It was out of such a
gathering of evidence that his reflections on his Indian experience and on
the missionary task developed in one of its most distinctive ways, so that,
with all the risks implicit in broad generalisations (and he was fully
alive to these), he began to fit these reflections into the broadest and
boldest of frames. (12)

In the passage from his autobiography in which he summarised his early
impressions under the image of 'a surging, heaving ferment', Andrews went
on:

> Men called it the 'national movement', but its force
> and range were far vaster than that. It was an
> eruption of a whole continent of humanity from within
> seeking to mould itself afresh in new forms.

That such a situation had profound implications for missionary policy, an
observer might have deduced from the form of the Hindustan Review's
exultations over the Japanese victory:

> The irresistible energy of the Japanese has shattered
> the flattering European theory entertained for
> centuries past that there can be no true
> civilisation unless it was of Christian, Greek or
> Roman origin. (13)

Such implications were not lost on Andrews. Indeed, he responded quite
explicitly, pointing out, for example, that among Muslims, 'with whom
temporal power and religious ascendancy are almost inseparable ideas', the
sight of Russia defeated, 'the one Christian Power which has marched up to
the walls of Constantinople itself, the one Empire which all along the
Central Asian border has made the Crescent recede', could herald a revival
of Islam and have 'far-reaching results to missionary work'. (14)

For all this, however, he did not interpret the emerging situation as a
threat so much as a ground for hope, and if we need an indication of the
way in which he was to respond, we might find it in his comment that 'the
close of the year 1904 ... was a time when it was "good to be alive"'. (15)
The 'high noon' of the historian of empire's perspective was rapidly
becoming 'a dawn of hope' in the very different emerging perspective of
the newly-arrived missionary.

5. 'An educated scholarly English gentleman'

When Ramsay MacDonald referred to St Stephen's College, in his book about
India, as 'St. Andrew's College', the London Correspondent of the Tribune
called it 'a very pardonable error.' This view would have been supported
by the Principal, who declared with gratitude in 1914, as Andrews was
leaving, that no single personality had had so great an influence on the
College. The sentiment was reciprocated. In the last year of his life,
Andrews claimed that St Stephen's College had been to him 'one of the most
sacred spots on earth'. This was never merely a matter of sentiment,
however. Also in later years, referring to the decade which he spent
there, he recalled his 'high hopes and ardent educational ideals'. (1)

Quite apart from what he did to transform the College, his connection with
the institution was particularly important for his developing ideas for
three reasons. First, it provided him with a continuing close association
with members of the most progressive element in Indian society at that
time, the educated classes, in this case his own students and his Indian
colleagues. In seeking to define 'the Indian point of view' in his
writings, he constantly drew illustrations from his experience as a teacher

at St Stephen's College. (2) Secondly, it was the foundation of an actual
area of influence, of which he was to make much use, within the life of the
nation as a whole. As early as 1909, Gokhale declared that the students of
India had no better friend. His influence later in this important sector
of society was regarded as unique. (3) Thirdly, it enabled him to develop
an informed critique of educational policy in both church and state. The
Church in India in this period had almost a half share in the higher
educational enterprise - Andrews pointed out that five out of eleven
colleges in the Punjab were under missionary control - so that through his
work at St Stephen's he was well placed to develop such a critique in a
broad, general way. (4)

For all its importance for Andrews' developing thought and missionary
practice, and for all the founder's great vision of a new Alexandria on the
banks of the Jumna, and for all the overall impressiveness of the work of
the Cambridge Mission to Delhi, St Stephen's College when he arrived in
1904 was still a very modest institution. Much solid groundwork had been
done under Allnutt's and Wright's leadership, and there were to be striking
developments during the ten years that Andrews was to be on the staff, in
terms of numbers, performance and standing. (5) In 1904, however, the
College was still very small, and, with only eighty-five students, thirty
of them resident, far below the optimum two hundred resident students that
Hibbert-Ware, the third Principal, was advocating. (6) In terms of results
and standing, Delhi, with St Stephen's and the new Hindu College, was
substantially overshadowed by Lahore with its strong Government College and
Forman Christian College.

Andrews made an eleventh member of staff in 1904. The Principal at this
time was G. Hibbert-Ware. He had joined the staff in 1898, and had rapidly
established himself since his appointment as Principal in 1902, Andrews
himself soon after his arrival coming to regard him as 'a really great
Principal of the College'. (7) The only other European member of staff at
the time of his arrival was one of his own former Cambridge students,
J.G.F. Day. He had arrived two years earlier, and taught on and off until
ill-health finally drove him back to Ireland in 1909. (8) The eight Indian
members of staff included three Christians, among them S.K. Rudra, to whom

we must give particular attention, and S.A.C. Ghose, who had been a student
and teacher at the College for some twenty years, and was something of 'a
stormy petrel of the Delhi Mission'. Andrews called him his earliest
friend in India. (9) Of the three Hindu and two Muslim teachers, the one
with whom he came to have most to do was a young Kayasth, or member of the
writer-caste, the Sanskrit lecturer, Raghubar Dayal. Remembered as a
moderating influence in the College, he was very active in developing many
aspects of its corporate life. He was, nevertheless, also very active in
the national movement. (10)

The eighty-five students came from the city and province, the thirty
residents including some from the country and some richer students from
Delhi itself who preferred to be in residence on the ground of study, or to
learn English and 'English manners'. (11) Although the majority of the
population of the Punjab, and nearly half of the city of Delhi, were
Muslims, there were only eleven Muslim students in the College in 1904,
the student body being made up largely of members of the educationally
more progressive Hindu community, and, in particular, of 'the most
progressive' caste in Delhi, the Kayasths who made up more than half of the
students. (12) There were six Christian students, most such in the
province preferring to go to Forman College at Lahore at this time - though
there was to be a marked increase at St Stephen's from 1905. Altogether,
although there were to be some interesting developments during the decade
in response to the national movement, the College continued in its already
established conventional role of providing recruits for India's emerging
professional classes. Throughout Andrews' time in Delhi, the bulk of the
graduates of the College went in almost equal numbers into law, government
service and education, the three main areas of opportunity for the educated
classes in this period. (13)

Just as the College was in most respects an unexceptional missionary
college, Andrews started off in 1904 very much an unexceptional educational
missionary - though he struck one contemporary as exceptional for his
scholarship at least, being in this respect 'far superior to any other
member of the staff, and probably any other college teacher in North
India'. His part in things, however, was conventional enough:

> ... apart from the first hour of Christian
> instruction, I have been teaching English literature
> daily.

Early references to his part in the Christian instruction – a compulsory
hour daily for all students – show him teaching the Sermon on the Mount to
his Hindu students. (14) With regard to the general teaching, outside of
the more specialised work in oriental languages and science, the missionary
staff had to be adaptable. 'In those days', Hibbert–Ware recalled, 'the
work that had to be done was just divided up among ourselves'. This was
the more understandable in that, at least with the first and second-year
students, the work was, Andrews discovered, 'more or less analogous to
English Public School work', and in fact he found the teaching of English
at the College 'ABC work really'. (15) As the same time, it was also to
the ardent missionary an opportunity.

> Instead of this proving merely 'secular', there is
> scarcely an hour passes without the subject of
> Christianity coming forward.

Interestingly, we get a glimpse in this early period of Andrews at work,
and of how 'the subject of Christianity', and Christianity over against
Hinduism, found its way into his teaching of Tennyson's 'In Memoriam' to a
Kayasth student in his M.A. class:

> ... how quickly he grasped the Christian message of a
> life beyond the grave where personality is not
> destroyed but rather develops into fuller life. (16)

There was, of course, a humdrum aspect to his work as an educational
missionary throughout the decade, with, for example, '850 Intermediate
English papers to look through in a fortnight' one summer. (17) In spite
of the routine demands of the work, however, he was from the beginning
looking at issues of principle and questions of strategy regarding the
College as a missionary institution. Within his very first month there, he
successfully proposed at the Staff meeting that Curzon's Universities Act

should be discussed 'so that the College in its working may be able to
anticipate the Government'. (18)

It would have been surprising if educational missions were not to be
touched by the 'surging, heaving ferment' of the national movement. The
impact of the emerging situation was alluded to by Hibbert-Ware in his
annual report written at the end of 1905, when he mentioned 'a very great
change from what I found when I first entered the College'.

> Then it was difficult to find, in their College life,
> any subject of talk on which they would take fire,
> anything which showed that they possessed hearts.
> Now there is one subject in which they are nearly all
> on fire.

Day filled in the picture somewhat, suggesting that there was not a student
in the College who was not 'to some extent "agin" the Government', and that
there was certainly no student who was not 'Swadeshi'. A new interest in
public meetings in the city was reflected in the College, and before
Andrews was back from sick leave in 1905, Ghose had read a paper to the 'St
Stephen's Club' on the subject of swadeshi. On his return, Andrews
immediately threw himself into things, initiating a series of discussions
on 'such burning subjects as the Unification of India' and how it was to be
attained.

It would be a mistake to over-dramatise either the general climate in the
College at this stage, or Andrews' own response. With regard to the
former, though the awakening sense of nationalism was to become 'a
dominating factor among the majority of the students' by the end of 1906,
Day insisted in late 1905 that there was 'really little to be alarmed at'.
There was no boycott of British goods in Delhi, as there was in Bengal, the
students simply wanting to encourage Indian industry, and they were
'intensely loyal, if not to the existing Government, at any rate to the
crown'. (19) Andrews' position, likewise, was still very cautious: he
later recalled speaking in a College debate 'in the most enthusiastic
manner on England's great benefits conferred on India'. (20) One of his

students, who was himself to become deeply involved in the national
movement over the ensuing year or two, retained an interesting recollection
of him:

> I learned from him - more than from any other
> Englishman teaching at St Stephen's - what an
> educated scholarly English gentleman can be. (21)

That, of course, was only part of the picture, but it may serve as some
sort of indication of where Andrews started from as an educational
missionary.

6. 'The closest friend of all'

A small Bengali élite was an important element in the development of
post-annexation Punjab, and, within this Bengali community, a group of
Christian converts were among the Indian pioneers of Western education
in the province. Andrews was soon able to claim that he had been
'admitted into the Bengali circle' in Delhi, Simla and Lahore, his
admission being by no means limited to the tightly-knit Christian segment
of the community. (1) It was, nevertheless, a Christian Bengali who was to
be the most important single influence in his life during the missionary
decade, and, indeed, a determinative influence for his entire life and work
in India.

Susil Kumar Rudra was born in 1861, the year after his father, Pyari Mohun
Rudra, a member of an old-established land-owning family in Bengal, had
been baptized by Alexander Duff. His mother was received into the church
in the year of Susil Kumar's birth. Like many of Duff's converts, his
father had an impressive subsequent career as a missionary, working for the
C.M.S. in Calcutta and at various other places in Bengal. An important
influence in the younger Rudra's life as he grew up was the Oxford
Brotherhood of the Epiphany at Calcutta - and a visitor to the Brotherhood,
Charles Gore. 'All that I have of faith', he later told Andrews, 'I owe to
those men'. (2) After graduating at the University of Calcutta, he joined
the Bengali Christian 'diaspora' in the Punjab, being appointed in 1886 to

the staff of St Stephen's College. He was soon to become 'the leading
personality' of the College staff, so that his progression to the
Vice-Principalship in Wright's time was a natural one. (3) He was to
remain on the staff until two years before his death in 1925.

When Andrews arrived in Delhi, he entered from the first into an
exceptionally close and warm relationship with Rudra. Rudra was ten years
older than Andrews, but particularly welcomed the affectionate support that
he received from him, for his wife had recently died, leaving him to bring
up their children alone. A student at the time referred to Andrews'
'attending to the education and personal comforts of Susil Rudra's
children'. He added an interesting observation, that Andrews' 'noticed
that the life of ... Rudra ... was melancholy, and he was suffering from an
inferiority complex evidently through the sinister influence of the colour
bar which was rampant .... To redress it,... Andrews began to ... show his
affection for him in all possible ways. We as young students watched them
walking arm-in-arm in moonlight nights ... and in College and outside it,
... (Andrews showed) a respect for ... Rudra which an Indian had never
received from a European'. (4) Andrews' affection was clearly
reciprocated, as one of Rudra's sons recalls:

> Words fail me to describe what he meant to my father!
> ... My father and Mr Andrews were like brothers to
> one another. (5)

This was the first of a series of exceptionally close friendships which
were to characterise Andrews' life in India. A later acquaintance noted
that his life was 'a catalogue of friendship', each stage being marked by a
new friend, 'each one, as he would characteristically say, dearer than a
brother'. (6) Rudra, however, continued 'the closest friend of all' until
his death: this 'deepest love', Andrews once wrote to him, after Munshi
Ram, Rabindranath Tagore and Gandhi had been entered into the catalogue,
'... held its ground as something quite by itself, quite different ...
growing deeper all the whole while'. (7)

These friendships are a most interesting phenomenon, and their character indicates that we are concerned with an unusual personality. (8) From the point of view of Andrews' work as a missionary, one important thing to note is that out of what was clearly a series of spontaneous friendships, he developed a theory about the need of 'sincere and wholehearted personal friendship within the Christian Body ... with at least one fellow-Christian communicant of another race', as 'a practical missionary thought' to be encouraged among younger missionaries. He subsequently extended the idea with reference to people of other faiths. (9) It is also important to note that the unusually exaggerated manner of his friendship seems almost invariably to have been accepted as totally sincere. (10)

Through their friendship, Rudra influenced Andrews from the beginning in several ways. Very important in this respect was the way in which their friendship made India for the latter, 'from the very first not a strange land, but a familiar country'. (11) It was, however, a friendship with its own unexpected disclosures. Rudra's very formal Western clothes, which were a source of lifelong regret to him, concealed a passionate nationalist, of whom Gandhi could say later:

> Of his sympathies with the so-called extremists,
> if he made no parade, he never made any secret
> either. (12)

Andrews was soon learning to see through his friend's eyes, and to see that his own inherited preconceptions about the empire as an unqualified good, required revision. Rudra was a teacher of economics, and it was in these terms that Andrews' assumptions were first challenged.

> I saw India poor the first day I came to India
> through his eyes, and he gave me a true vision. (13)

We get some indication of Rudra's own position at this time from two articles that he wrote for missionary journals, the Cambridge Mission's Delhi Mission News and SPG's The East and the West. (14) In the first of these, written during a visit to England in 1905, there is much admiration for 'this wonderful little island', particularly for its ancient

institutions, the public schools, the universities, and the Church. Rudra
points out how much these owe to generous endowment in the past. Then,
asking whether the English merchant who acquires his wealth from India
could not endow similar institutions in 'poor India', he wonders whether
anything of the sort is to be hoped for, since the English 'rule the
country, but ... have not adopted it'. In the second article, there are
references to 'the present happy rule of England', and to 'the truly
paternal interest of the British government', but these occur alongside
others which are intensely bitter and unmistakably sarcastic, as when he
expresses his admiration for the 'wonderful way' in which the 'British
rulers have ... been able to use the children of the soil to maintain their
supreme position'.

> The masses ... are content if they have scope to
> vegetate, and the British government gives them every
> opportunity to do so ... (but the middle classes have
> had) their political consciousness ... roused by the
> British administrators, by the large advantages given
> to the British as a race, not only in the Services
> under the Crown, but to the British manufacturer in
> England who is able to crush the nascent industries
> in their country.

The ambivalence of Rudra's position is something with which students of
race relations have become familiar in recent years. Andrews noticed it at
the time, writing that 'this inner struggle was continually going on in
Indian Christian lives, dividing their allegiance'. Some of Rudra's
remarks here were unfamiliar thoughts for a missionary journal, and it is
not surprising that Andrews did not immediately accept wholeheartedly
Rudra's interpretation of Indian poverty. We have seen him enthusing in
the College on 'England's great benefit conferred on India'.

> On another occasion when the debate was on the
> subject of the poverty of India, I indignantly
> refuted the proposition that India was getting
> poorer, but Mr Rudra was the truest possible friend

and he would reason with me hour after hour when he
felt I was mistaken. (15)

This was probably during the latter part of 1905, and it was to be some
four or five years before Rudra's reasoning led Andrews to a thorough-going
revision of his assumptions about the empire.

'Far deeper still', Andrews affirmed, than in the matter of nationalism,
was the influence which Rudra exercised in the 'transformation' of his
faith. (16) What Rudra's thinking on religion amounted to was a bold and
original appropriation of the categories of current 'liberal Catholic'
theology, a new and distinctive development of these in the context of the
Indian national awakening. We find this in typical form in the latter of
the two articles just referred to. After dismissing the possibility of
'even the best spiritual pantheistic thought, ... because of its impersonal
character', providing, in the face of new 'materialistic and secular
influences', an adequate 'Vision of the Unseen' for India 'as she awakes
from her age-long sleep', Rudra goes on:

> The only moulding power I know is a personal one; and
> I believe that the Christian Church is able to place
> the figure of Jesus of Nazareth ... in such a way
> before the Indian people that they will ... be
> strengthened in themselves for the huge task of
> setting their own house in order.

Likewise rejecting the possibility that Hindu reforms, which were no more
than 'a reconstruction of an eclectic creed, out of the old sacred books of
the East', would be 'strong enough to dominate the social life of the whole
country', he testified:

> There is no motive power that earth can give which
> can compare with the quickening vital energy that
> will come from the Vision of the Christ, living from
> dead, the personal Saviour of men, the King of the
> East and of the West, the very Image of the Unseen

God.

This motive power would be evident, Rudra believed, in the work of the educational missions, conducted in the new situation 'with far greater wisdom and patience and tact than before', and aiming to direct 'the half-awakened consciousness of India to the source of all power and strength – the Vision of the Unseen God'.

In all this, Rudra is at his most typical, seeming to suggest a process of 'christianising every department of modern life', rather than a programme of conversion in a formal sense. (17) He had not always seen things in this way. His son recalled a change in his father's outlook:

> For many years he continued to be an austere and
> rigid High Churchman. Undoubtedly his upbringing and
> contact with the devout fathers of the Oxford Mission
> Brotherhood at Calcutta, and the members of the
> Cambridge Mission Brotherhood at Delhi, and his own
> temperament, strongly inclined him in that direction.
> But as he grew older, contrary to common experience,
> he grew broader in his views. (18)

Rudra, with a few other Indian Christians, shared deeply in the national awakening of 1905. (19) This seems to have had a good deal to do with the loosening of a rigid theological position distinctively Western in character. In 1906, he wrote:

> A foreign religion with hard dogmas, more or less
> repudiated in the West by some of its ablest
> thinkers, is not suited to remould the life of the
> Indian peoples. The beauty of Christ is one thing, –
> that we can appreciate; the dogmas of the Church are
> another – those we reject.

Andrews expressed his sense of Rudra's early influence on himself in strikingly similar terms:

My mind, which had been obsessed with narrow dogmas,
was gradually widened and broadened in the sunshine
of his love, and my inner nature gained a new
freedom. The inner change was constructive, not
destructive .... I learnt from my friend to
understand what Christ is to the heart of man in new
and living ways. (20)

In another place, he explained that this new understanding of Christ was
related to 'the "Indian"' in Rudra, 'so singularly preserved'. But that
was a later assessment, and it would be a distortion of the perspective of
Andrews' developing thought to go much beyond his remark that 'This
transformation of my Christian faith into a more living reality was the
greatest gift which Susil Rudra's friendship brought into my character and
nature'. (21)

At the same time, it would seen unlikely that the vigorous development of
Andrews' ideas during these years should have had no effect on the thinking
of his closest friend, and there are several at least minor indications of
indebtedness. (22) Perhaps the most important thing, however, that Andrews
did was to encourage Rudra to write at all. There is no direct evidence
for this, but it is interesting that he appears to have published nothing
before 1905 and very little after 1914; in other words, all of note that he
published, some half-a-dozen articles, was written during the decade in
which Andrews was with him at St Stephens's. (23)

In his article, 'Is India Thirsting for Religious Truth', Rudra indicates
that he was thinking at this time about the missionary role of the
Christian colleges. He saw the development of the staff into a deep
religious fellowship, in which, so far as the missionary members were
concerned, their 'natural political, pro-English bias ... (would) have
little or no place', as the only really effective Christian witness at that
time among the educated classes. That this was one of the most significant
effects of the friendship between them, was affirmed in various quarters.
Rudra's own son, recalling 'this great example of mutual respect and
devotion of two men of different races', said that one result was that 'a

unique sense of oneness ... prevailed through the College', and also that
through this 'wider contacts were made and rich experience secured for the
College in the stream of the national life of the country'. A later
missionary member of the College went so far as to call Andrews' creation
of a tradition of close personal association between the different
communities and races 'one of the greatest contributions of St Stephen's to
the national life'. (24)

Like his subsequent friendships, this with Susil Rudra had a rich and
fascinating significance for his developing understanding of his task as a
missionary.

7. 'The vividness of a first impression'

The two friends started writing at about the same time, and for the same
journals, although this was the beginning of something much bigger for
Andrews than for Rudra.

Towards the end of his first cold weather in India, as we have seen,
Andrews had mooted the possibility of making literary work the main thrust
of his work as a missionary, seeing this as a way of serving the Indian
church and also of reaching the non-Christians among the educated classes.
At this point, however, ill-health and the consequent visit to England
intervening upon his plan, he found himself writing his first three
articles for an English readership. For the Delhi Mission News he wrote,
in three instalments, a piece entitled 'Indian Character: An
Appreciation', for The East and the West 'The Effect of the Japanese
Victories upon India', and for the Church Missionary Intelligencer, as 'a
tiny fragment of a big debt of gratitude' to the CMS missionaries in the
Punjab, to whom he claimed, with a rather exaggerated flourish, to owe so
much, a short but vivid piece on 'The Religious Unrest of Northern India'.

Andrews had been just over one year in India when he wrote these, all on
broad themes. He was clearly conscious that the charge of inexperience
could be laid at his door, for he opens the first article with the remark
that he has 'waited more than a year', testing his initially sanguine

impressions of Indian life, before writing, and he mentions later that he
is speaking 'on the basis of only a short acquaintance'. Similarly, in the
article on the Japanese victories, he draws attention to the fact that he
has not attempted to draw conclusions because 'that could only be done by
far older and more experienced hands'. Nevertheless, he adds, for the
Delhi Mission supporters, his article 'may have the vividness of a "first
impression"'.

It is wholly typical of Andrews' work that his first article should be a
defence of people under unfair attack. Indeed, the very act of writing
something entitled 'Indian Character: An Appreciation' was an act of
sympathy in itself, for the indiscriminate denigration of the moral
character of the Indian people, especially of the educated classes, was a
widespread tendency of the British in India, both civilians and
missionaries. (1)

This tendency had recently been reinforced in two significant cases. In
the first, Andrews' own bishop, G.A. Lefroy of Lahore, had reprinted a long
and unrelievedly sombre account of Indian character that he had first
published as an occasional paper sixteen years previously, deploring the
'intensely low moral tone, which ... now broods over the whole country',
Muslim as well as Hindu. (2) Lefroy highlighted in particular 'the want of
trust, whether of trustfulness or trustworthiness'. He conceded that this
was set 'amongst much that is good and worthy of our own imitation in
Indian character', but his paper dealt exclusively with the darker side.

The other case was a much more notorious one, though not, perhaps, more
deservedly so than Lefroy's jeremiad. On 11 February 1905, Lord Curzon had
spoken at the Convocation of Calcutta University, and in the course of a
much more even-handed discussion than Lefroy's, on 'certain ideals ...
peculiarly applicable to ... the Indian character', had suggested that
truthfulness was less highly prized as a virtue in Asia than in Europe. (3)
Curzon's speech caused a furore in the Indian press, which Andrews could
not have missed, although his own article gives the impression of being
much more clearly directed at the sort of points raised by Lefroy.

Whatever, in fact, sparked off his articles, it will be seen that to write an appreciation of Indian character at this time was to fly in the face of received opinion, and this Andrews was deliberately doing, questioning, as he said, 'the ordinary Anglo-Indian's generalizations on Indian failings'. His chief point in vindication of Indian character is that in the 'natural and non-Western' institutions of Indian society, the family and the caste, there is to be observed a 'marked ... mutual trust' and 'fidelity', and that it is precisely in the political and economic relationships created by the imperial situation, 'relations with English rulers and merchants', that these virtues are less evident. While not condoning the latter state of affairs, he suggests that two factors help to explain it. First, that with 'new and foreign methods of business and government, ... the old social conditions ... (are) breaking up, ... (and) moral confusion ... (is) inevitable'. Second, that corruption can be understood as a lesson that the Hindu has learned through centuries of oppression, and is one of 'the weapons of the oppressed'. These are ways of looking at the question that do not seem to occur elsewhere in the missionary or secular literature of the period. He meets other Western criticism of Indian character with a similar exercise of imaginative sympathy.

It is almost equally typical of Andrews' work that another of these first articles should deal with the importance for missionary policy of current events in secular history. In 'The Effect of the Japanese Victories upon India', written a matter of only a few months after the final victory, he looks at this effect, 'with Western prestige weakened, ... Eastern conservatism strengthened, .. the plant of patriotism ... very young and tender, but ... growing rapidly', specifically in terms of its implications for mission. Indeed, one of the features of this article, and one that is to characterize his writing over the next few years, is a plea for what he came to call 'missionary statesmanship':

> Political thinkers in all the chancelleries of Europe
> have already begun to ask, 'What does this mean to
> our political interests?' ... We need ... Christian
> thinkers who will carefully consider, 'What does this
> new factor mean to missionary enterprise? How may

the new movement in the East be rightly used to
extend the Kingdom of Christ? (4)

It seems that even from this early stage he saw himself as providing some
of the required statesmanship, for he has the beginning of an answer to
hand.

Because, he argues, the 'strange' combination of 'the Christian missionary
and imperialism' is a contradiction to the Asian, 'we need to revise our
work', and this calls for a new alignment, no longer with imperialism, but
with 'the new aspirations which are coming to the birth'.

This was a strikingly sympathetic approach. It can perhaps best be
explained as a result of his close and affectionate relationship with men
like Rudra and Ghose, combined with his already developed interest in
social questions. (5) Although he would soon be influencing others towards
a similar approach, it was, nevertheless, one which already separated him
from more conventional church circles, which complacently held 'the task of
the twentieth century' to be the approximation of 'missionary sentiment'
with 'imperial sentiment'. (6) Andrews was, in fact, told by those of
longer experience that he was laying too much stress upon the growth of
nationalism, 'and that any such plant could never take root in India and
the East'. Two years later, he felt able to claim that events had proved
that he had laid, not too much but too little stress upon it. (7)

From the beginning, Andrews saw that the Indian national movement could
never be regarded as a solely political phenomenon. In explaining 'the
awakening of the East', of which the Japanese victories were a symbol, he
suggested that a most significant feature of the new national pride was
that it was, for most people 'not of territory or dominion, but of the
intellectual and spiritual supremacy of their past', and that accompanying
it was the watchword, 'Back to the Vedas'. In this respect, he makes an
important distinction between the nationalist ideas of what he calls 'Hindu
conservatism', and a 'higher patriotism, ... a love of country rising above
the narrower love of caste and sect, ... one of the noblest characteristics
of the more highly educated'. (8) He was, nevertheless, convinced that

Hindu conservatism had to be taken seriously, both because it had a wide
appeal, and also because it would serve to 'awaken the masses from their
sleep of centuries'.

In his third article, on 'The Religious Unrest of Northern India', he looks
at the Arya Samaj as one of the principal expressions of this conservative
religious factor. He does so by describing an encounter on a railway
journey with a member of the Samaj, and he bases much of his analysis on a
pamphlet by the President of the Arya Samaj in Lahore, given him by his
fellow-passenger. It is a vivid and interesting exposition. Andrews
regards the Arya Samaj as inadequate to the new circumstances because of
its members' uncritical reliance on the Vedas. These 'belong to the very
infancy of human thought and cannot possibly be practised literally by any
educated man today', while the the current practice of allegorizing the
Hindu scriptures, reminiscent of the Platonic Schools of Alexandria, is 'a
pathetic attempt to "pour new wine into old bottles"'. (9) At the same
time, he is sympathetic to many of the people involved in this movement, to
many of its leaders, who are 'active and earnest, not dead and
indifferent', and to others like the two hundred women members meeting
every week in Lahore 'for prayer to the One God'. This leads to his final
point, the observation - and he quotes extensively from the pamphlet to
substantiate this - that the Samaj had not only been deeply influenced by
Christianity, but also in some respects induced 'the highest anticipation
that it would lead on to Christianity'.

Throughout these earliest articles, in fact, we find a measure of sympathy
and respect for both Hinduism and Islam, but also, beside this, an
unequivocal affirmation that Christianity is 'the one universal religion',
and linking the two a vaguely adumbrated notion of fulfilment, 'the
Christian hope ... to retain and conserve these wonderful forces', giving
them a 'deeper, truer and more spiritual religious expression'. It was a
fulfilment which Andrews hoped would find embodiment in a Christian life in
community, for example in the Christian villages in the new canal colonies
of the Punjab.

Such Christian communities will escape many of the

evils of Western civilisation with its rush and
hurry and materialism. They will be living
examples, peculiarly Eastern, of some sides of the
Gospel which are not seen markedly on a large scale
in the West. 'Having food and raiment, to be
therewith content.'... Such words as these will
gather fresh emphasis if seen in the lives of Indian
village Christians.

Both the idea of a church peculiarly Eastern and the associated references
to the Sermon on the Mount are the beginnings of an important theme in
Andrews' thought.

There is a great deal more in these early articles that is revealing of
Andrews' first impressions, but enough has been touched on to illustrate
the wide-ranging and fresh vision which was to be the basis of his
attitudes, and the ground of their development. They were, however,
written for a readership in England. This was to be an important part of
his constituency as he sought to improve understanding of India among both
mission-supporters and the British public at large, but he has yet to find
a way into his mission to India's educated classes through literary work.

NOTES: Chapter Two

1. Introductory

1   Ind Int Oct 1909
2   Rudra TEW Jan 1906; SM Jan 1910
3   TEW Oct 1905

2. Orthodox and ardent

1   The Good Shepherd 1940, p. 162. The first record of his wearing Indian clothes, which he did only occasionally, was Tribune 29 Nov 1913.

2   St Clair Donaldson 'Varieties of Method of Missionary Work in India' TEW Jan 1904

3   DMN Jul 1904. Or about 165 including catechists, teachers, readers, bible women, nurses.

4   Brotherhood Minutes 9 Jul 1914 (Brotherhood, Delhi)

5   Oremus 1911

6   CC 1905. Biog p. 80 adds 'I kept in touch with him for many years'.

7   NI p. 173; Biog p. 80. For a picture of English social life in Simla, see Kipling 1890, originally published in C&MG Nov 1886 – Jun 1887, though both Andrews and a contemporary observer (Buck 1904, p. 68) thought that things had improved since Kipling had written, not least because of the influence of Curzon's stern attitude to duty.

8   'Report of a Visit to Rawalpindi' 13 Dec 1905 (SPG)

9   Andrews' Report 29 Sep 1906 (SPG); CMI Oct 1905

10   Stanton to Allnutt, 19 Sep 1905; Stanton to Andrews, 4 Apr 1905; Andrews to Stanton, 6 Apr 1905 (CMD)

11   CC 1906

12   Biog p. 100

13   SM Dec 1906; CMR Jan 1907

14   Rudra CC 1907

15   Biog p. 69

3. 'Things as they were'

1 Fraser 1903, p. 101
2 Edwardes 1965 (title)
3 Biog p. 51
4 J.C. Bannerjie in HR Sep 1904
5 TEW Oct 1912
6 Tribune 18 Jan 1907, 30 Jul 1907; St John Brodrick to Ampthill,
  8 Dec 1904 (Ampthill - NAI)
7 Pioneer 1 Jun 1904. 'The British fell into two quite distinct
  groups, those who belonged to the club and were invited to
  Government House, and the rest' Mason 1970, p. 96. The term
  'Anglo-Indian' is used here and throughout this study in its
  contemporary usage, to denote British residents in India.
8 G. Yazdani (Monk's file - S.S.C.)
9 HR Jan 1905
10 Andrews 1937, p. 44
11 'Lala Lajpat Rai' (typescript) (Chaturvedi - NAI)
12 Ellison and Walpole 1908, p. 81; NI p. 167
13 'Lala Lajpat Rai' (typescript) (Chaturvedi - NAI)
14 quoted in Barrier 1967, p. 377
15 NI p. 184
16 TEW Apr 1903
17 SSC Mag Nov 1908; NI p. 106
18 Biog p. 80
19 Darling 1966, p. 15
20 Andrews 1935, p. 72; NI pp. 167-8
21 CT 16 Dec 1910
22 Andrews 1930, p. 115

4. 'A dawn of hope'

1 WIOC p. 214
2 O'Dwyer 1925, pp. 56-7; Tribune 28 Nov 1906
3 TEW Oct 1905; HR Jan 1907; NI p. 191; IR Mar 1909.

A student of St Stephen's College, recalling various insults and violence by British officials against students of the College in the 1890's, remarked, 'In those days "natives" were treated like sheep ... aggressive methods of Europeans were taken ... meekly', while a teacher recalled of 1902-3 that 'the city trembled in its shoes at the sight of a man in a European hat .... There was no discontent of any sort or kind. Political thought was non-existent in the College .... Everybody spoke of us students and Indian staff in the College as "Natives", and we gladly called ourselves "Natives"' S.K. Gurtu and S.A.C. Ghose (Monk's file – S.S.C.).

4 Spear 1965, p. 174

5 Majumdar etc. 1964, p. 955; Hardinge to Morley, 11 May 1911 (Morley – IOL& R); TEW Oct 1905

6 MR Oct 1932; RI pp. 5, 42

7 A colleague of Andrews' in the Mission and the College, Hibbert-Ware, added further reasons, including 'the grinding poverty of the great masses of the people', and noted that 'the struggle of certain classes in Russia towards a fuller personal freedom has been followed with deep sympathy by educated men here' CC 1906.

8 Barrier 1967, p. 364

9 DMN Oct 1905; Barrier 1967, p. 363

10 Hindu Patriot quoted in Tribune 1 March 1904; quoted by Andrews in TEW Oct 1905; HR Sep 1904; MR Nov 1909; HR Jan 1907; RI p. 5

11 TEW Oct 1907, cf. Tribune 16 Feb 1909

12 e.g. 'A review of the Modern World' MR Nov 1909 – Apr 1910. If 'The striking boldness of thought which is singularly his' received some acknowledgement ("A Correspondent" CT 5 Dec 1913), it is important to note the rigour with which it was underpinned. He wrote in 1912 that 'all generalisations must be tenative and halting so long as the analysis of concrete situations remains unaccomplished' TEW Oct 1914.

13 HR Sept 1904

14 TEW Oct 1905

15 RI p. 4

5. 'An educated, scholarly English gentleman'

.1 Tribune 7 Apr 1914; Rudra CC 1915; Stephanian Jun 1939;
   'India and the Empire' 1921

2 e.g. NI pp. 193-4, RI pp. 45-6, 'The Claim for Independence'
   1921, Andrews 1930 pp. 95-6, Andrews 1935 p. 115

3 Speeches 1967, Vo. III, p. 193; Bombay Chronicle 14 Feb 1921
   (Chaturvedi - NAI)

4 Guardian 16 Dec 1908

5 Numbers nearly trebled between 1904 and 1914 (Monk 1935, pp.
   251-2). By 1912, the College was practically leading the Punjab
   University colleges in examination performance (DMN Oct 1913) cf.
   'The position which St Stephen's has won for itself is a very
   proud one' Lefroy to Montgomery, 19 Sept 1912 (CMD)

6 Hibbert-Ware to Stanton, 20 Oct 1904 (CMD)

7 Andrews to Stanton, 6 Apr 1905 (CMD). A gentle and unassuming
   man, of deep sensitivity and sympathy, Hibbert-Ware broke new
   ground by making systematic visits to the students in their homes
   (Monk 1935, p. 95).

8 An enthusiast for Westcott, Day's chief contribution as a young
   man at St Stephen's seems to have been in defying the prevailing
   racial aloofness, which led Hibbert-Ware, with characteristic
   self-effacement, to describe him as 'the first of a new type',
   while his students noted that his initials could be turned to
   'Jolly Good-Fellow Day' (Hartford 1940, pp. 55, 74, 92).

9 H. Tinker to D. O'Connor, 30 Jan 1975. Ghose was a man of great
   gifts; Andrews called him 'the ablest and most thoughtful
   Christian who has come under the SPG for many years' Andrews
   to Montgomery, 5 Nov 1909 (SPG). His career was marked by a
   series of crises as he struggled to reconcile his church
   membership with his nationalist sympathies. Throughout his time
   at Delhi, and beyond, Andrews was close to Ghose.

10 P.N.F. Young to D. O'Connor, 1 Jul 1974. Dayal was a Punjab
   delegate to the 1906 Congress (Report 1907, p. 91). He was host

at a reception for Keir Hardie, and at another for Lajpat Rai; he
and Ghose were in a deputation to the District Commissioner
regarding municipal taxes; in 1909, he organised a major swadeshi
event, the Delhi Arts and Industrial Exhibition, which was opened
by Lajpat Rai (Tribune 13 Oct 1907, 26 Jan 1908; 28 Jan 1908;
9 May 1909). He owned the Imperial Native Press in 1901 (Barrier
and Wallace 1970, p. 42).

11 Hibbert-Ware to Stanton, 20 Oct 1904 (CMD).

12 DMN Jan 1906

13 Directory 1919. The Directory lists 102 graduates from St
    Stephen's for the years 1905-14, and records the careers of 79 of
    them; 25 went into education, 23 into the legal profession, and
    21 into government service.

14 C.B. Young Stephanian Jun 1940; Andrews CC 1905; NI p. 169

15 Hartford 1940, p. 51; Royal Commission 1915, Vol. XX, p. 49;
    Andrews to Tatlow, 9 Feb 1908 (SCM)

16 CC 1905; SSC Mag Jul 1907

17 Tribune 21 Apr 1910

18 Staff Meeting Minutes 1 Nov 1904 (S.S.C.)

19 Hibbert-Ware CC 1906; Day CC 1906; DMN Jan 1906; Andrews CC
    1907

20 Biog p. 81

21 Gobind Behari Lal to D. O'Connor, 19 Dec 1974, cf. 'Andrews is a
    gentleman' Dunlop Smith (P.A. to Viceroy) to Godley, 30 Jan 1908
    (Minto - NAI)

6. 'The closest friend of all'

1 Andrews to Dunlop Smith, 1 Mar 1908, quoted in Gilbert 1966,
   p. 131. Andrews' non-Christian Bengali friends included Justice
   P.C. Chatterji, Vice-Chancellor of the University of Punjab (MR
   Nov 1908), and A.C. Majumdar and othe members of the Punjab
   Brahmo Samaj (Tribune 14 Feb 1909, 4 Jun 1911).

2 YMOI Dec 1925; NI pp. 87-8.

3 Andrews SSC Mag Easter 1923

4 Yazdani Stephanian Jun 1940

5 Sudhir Rudra on his father 13 Feb 1932 (Monk's file - S.S.C.).
   When Andrews was away from Delhi for some time in 1913, Rudra
   wrote to him nearly every day (Andrews to Munshi Ram, 17 May
   1913 - Chaturvedi - NAI). 'They were twins. Their
   relationship was a study in ideal friendship' Gandhi Young India
   9 Jul 1925

6 T.G.P. Spear Stephanian Jun 1940

7 MR Mar 1924; Andrews to Rudra, 1915 (Berkeley)

8 Andrews' intense friendships, invariably with men, are an
   interesting phenomenon. He admitted in a letter to Rudra that he
   had to share everything with him in his letters, and could not
   bear his distresses alone because he was 'too much of a "woman"
   by nature for that' Andrews to Rudra, 4 May 1915 (Berkeley).
   These friendships recall the world of Lytton Strachey, which
   was, of course, Andrews' world too - Cambridge around the turn of
   the century - cf. Holroyd 1967, Vo. I, p. 102.

9 SM Oct 1906, Apr 1907, Apr 1908

10 'The word "love" was ever on his lips and it never seemed forced
   or overstrained when uttered by him ... his personality cannot be
   summed up better than in the words of Christ, when he saw
   Nathaniel approaching in the distance: Behold an Israelite
   indeed, in whom there is no guile!' T.G.P. Spear Stephanian
   June 1940. Cf. Tagore's response to what he regarded as Andrews'
   excessive demonstrativeness, 'He is so sincere that I cannot take
   him to task for it' quoted in N.K. Mahalanobis to D. O'Connor,
   n.d.

11 SSC Mag Easter 1923

12 Young India 9 Jul 1925

13 SSC Mag Easter 1923

14 DMN Oct 1905; TEW Jan 1906

15 Andrews 1934, p. 130; Biog p. 81

16 SSC Mag Easter 1923

17 DMN Oct 1905

18 Sudhir Rudra on his father 13 Feb 1932 (Monk's file - S.S.C.).

19 M.M. Thomas also includes S.K. Datta, K.T. Paul, the Kumarappas
   and V.S. Azariah as 'responding positively to the national

renaissance ... for avowedly Christian reasons' Thomas 1970,
p. 247.

20 TEW Jan 1906; SSC Mag Easter 1923. Cf. Thomas op. cit., p. 247
'Andrews in his early writings shows almost the same pattern of
thought as that of S.K. Rudra, and quotes a great deal from him'.

21 MR Mar 1924; SSC Mag Easter 1923

22 e.g. Rudra quotes from Seeley 1883 in SM Jan 1910, a book to
which Andrews frequently refers (IR June 1908, CT 25 Nov 1910,
IR Dec 1910); Rudra uses the Pauline metaphor of the 'body' to
express the notion of national unity in YMOI Dec 1910, cf.
Andrews in TEW Jul 1910, Tribune 23 Aug 1910.

23 The only direct evidence is with regard to Rudra's most eloquent
paper of all, 'Christ and Modern India': Rudra delivered this as
an address at the Lahore Diocesan Conference in Nov 1909, and
Andrews subsequently asked the editor of SM to publish it, which
he did in Jan 1910.

24 Sudhir Rudra on his father 13 Feb 1932 (Monk's file - S.S.C.);
C.B. Young Stephanian Jun 1940

7. 'The vividness of a first impression'

1 Max Müller says that the Indian Civil Service was commonly looked
upon 'as a kind of moral exile' Müller 1883, p. 34. The
Secretary of SPG wrote that 'the Hindu is inherently
untruthful and lacks moral courage' Montgomery 1902, p. 35.

2 TEW Apr 1903

3 Raleigh 1906, pp. 489-99

4 Cf. 'How can we meet the new situation as statesmen of the
Church of Christ?' NMI Nov 1910

5 Cf. 'It has been those who are most interested in the Labour
Movement ... who have most appreciated India and have most ...
sympathy' MR Aug 1912.

6 Ellison and Walpole 1908, p. 57

7 TEW Oct 1907

8 Andrews saw the 'higher patriotism' exemplified in Rudra, 'an
Indian first and last .... He has been free from any slightest

taint of communal narrowness or credal bigotry' <u>SSC Mag</u>
Easter 1923

9 The analogy of Hindu philosophy with Neo-Platonism was not
uncommon, e.g. A.H. Ewing 'Christianity in India and in the Roman
Empire - An Analogy' <u>MCCM</u> Nov 1904.

CHAPTER THREE
BREAKTHROUGH TO MISSION 1906-7

1. Introductory

Andrews had noted remarkably quickly the new energy which was accruing to
the national movement around 1905, and how the movement was becoming a
question of over-riding concern throughout the educated classes for the
first time. His emerging theology of mission told him that, because this
was pre-eminently the issue which engaged people in their thoughts and
feelings, it was an important area of mission, and one in which new
formulations of Christian faith would be required. Because, however, it
was an area not in the geographical but in the sociological sense, and a
new area at that, appropriate new methods of mission would need to be
developed for it. The next year or more saw him developing these with
remarkable originality.

2. 'The iron of India's subjection'

In his article on the Japanese victories, written during the summer of
1905, Andrews had noted with regret that the tide seemed to be running
'towards the accentuation of racial differences'. Relationships had, of
course, been strained to varying degrees for long enough. While Western
claims to superiority in the eighteenth century had been based largely on
the arguments of higher civilization and greater knowledge, in the
nineteenth century they had shifted to a basis of superior racial and
inherent moral qualities, and for a number of reasons this had been
accompanied by an increasing social distance. The events of 1857 and, to a
lesser extent, of Lord Ripon's viceroyalty in the 1880's, and the
consequent growing awareness of the educated classes, had deepened the
sense of racial estrangement.

Evidence for the further deterioration of relationships which Andrews noted
in 1905 is varied and persuasive. The Head of the Cambridge Mission,
Allnutt, with more than a quarter of a century of experience in India, drew

attention in 1904 to 'the increasing distrust and suspiciousness which characterize the attitude of educated Indian gentlemen towards Anglo-Indians'. It was typical of Allnutt's own liberal position that he asked an Indian Christian friend, Kirthi Singh, a Small Court Judge, to write an article on 'The Relation of Indians to Europeans', and sent this, with an introductory note, for publication in the Delhi Mission News. (1) Kirthi Singh, forbearing to cite cases of violent personal abuse, quoted a series of telling examples to illustrate the 'solid fact' that educated Indians were despised. In explanation of this, he quoted the public statement of an Anglo-Indian official who doubted whether social intercourse between Europeans and Indians was in any way to be desired. For Kirthi Singh, the connection between social distance and racial contempt was obvious. This was a situation, Allnutt observed, in which the missionary had a duty of reconciliation, though he added that it was a duty too often neglected. Just over a year later, Allnutt noted that the increasing political agitation was affecting the relations of missionaries themselves with their Indian colleagues, and that time for 'self-adjustment and self-repression, so difficult always for us Westerners', was running out. (2)

If, as Kirthi Singh suggested, racial harmony depended on freer social intercourse, the times certainly seem to have been unpropitious. A young civil servant newly posted to Lahore in 1904 noted that it was a full year before he had his first talk with an educated Indian who was not an official, 'and even then it came by chance'. Things seem not to have been any better higher up in the government hierarchy; during his seven months as Acting Viceroy in 1904, Lord Ampthill did not come into personal contact with more than a dozen Indians. (3)

The deterioration of relations was exacerbated by a nervous apprehension among Anglo-Indians of the possibility of an uprising as the fiftieth anniversary of the rising of 1857 approached. This was so not least at Delhi, where in March 1906 a statue of the British general, John Nicholson, who had put down the 'mutiny' there, was erected near his grave. Andrews noted disapprovingly the 'drawn sword pointed towards the city'. (4) The erection of the statue was strongly deprecated by the leading nationalist newspaper in the Punjab as 'one of the imperialistic freaks of the ...

erratic' Curzon, the more irresponsible because 'relations are very much
strained at present'. Curzon had by then retired, of course; the statue
was unveiled by his successor, Lord Minto. Allnutt was relieved that 'not
a word was said which could give rise to any embittered feeling'. (5) The
apprehension, nevertheless, was widespread, and in a sermon at Westminster
Abbey on the fiftieth anniversary itself, Dr. Butler, the Master of
Trinity, even went so far as to wonder whether, with 'the dangers ... now
threatening the peace of India', it really was the will of God 'that those
countless millions of his Eastern children should be ruled by a race so
scanty, so unimaginative, so wholly different as ours'. (6)

The situation seems, indeed, to have been sufficiently serious throughout
India to prompt a demi-official query from Minto to the provincial
governors on the state of relations between Europeans and Indians. The
reply from Sir Denzil Ibbetson in the Punjab was the most gloomy of all, as
he noted that relations had changed very much for the worse during the past
five or ten years. He blamed this on 'the incessant stream of virulent and
malignant lies, misrepresentations and sedition, which is poured forth by
the greater portion of the native press without let or hindrance', and
which had, he claimed, exacerbated the feelings of the English community.
He was particularly concerned about the fresh wave of racial hostility of
the past year or two. 'I think', he added, 'that Lord Curzon's attitude
and policy in the matter began the change', and he noted that in the course
of 1906 things had become 'far more serious'. (7)

What made the situation so serious from the missionary point of view –
quite apart from the growing estrangements within the church, which Allnutt
had noted, – was that the victims of racial hostility insisted on regarding
their British rulers as the representatives of Christianity. Thus, the
nationalist newspaper, the Punjabee, presented the issue straightforwardly
in Hindu-Christian terms:

> It is seriously to be doubted whether the Hindus have
> ever learnt to hate an alien race with such intensity
> as they are beginning to display towards their
> present 'Christian' foreign rulers. And it is

equally doubtful whether any alien rulers have ever
hated the Hindus with a hatred so whole-hearted and
bitter as that entertained by the English now-a-days
towards them. (8)

We have seen already how there was a tendency to interpret the Russo-
Japanese war in religious terms. The racial question was, thus, open to a
similar interpretation.

This was a situation in which Andrews found himself implicated in a very
personal way. In March 1906, Bishop Lefroy invited him to act as Principal
of a large school for European children, the Lawrence Military Asylum at
Sanawar near Simla, during the hot weather of that year. (9) Andrews
accepted, and was there from April to early November, sharing a house with
the headmistress of the girl's establishment, a 'very refined and
cultivated English lady'. (10) During the summer, he invited Rudra to
stay, and also Rudra's son Sudhir, whom he prepared for confirmation during
the course of his stay. (11) The arrangement, however, did not meet with
the entire approval of the headmistress, who declared that she 'could not
sit at table with an Indian'. The seriousness of the racial division
between Indians and English came home to Andrews with the impact of a
revelation, the incident probably doing more than anything else to open his
eyes to the 'unchristian character' of the division. Touching, as it did,
his closest friend, he described how,

> The iron of India's subjection and humiliation
> entered into my very soul.

The incident illustrates well the importance of his friendship with Rudra
in enabling him 'so quickly to understand the difficulties of an Indian's
life as a member of a subject nation'. (12) It also served to intensify
his sense of the critical nature of the racial component in the relations
between Indians and Anglo-Indians, and this just at the moment when an
opportunity to make something of a public stand first presented itself to
him.

3. 'A Noble Englishman to the Rescue'

The Anglo-Indian press in the early twentieth century covered a fairly wide
spectrum of British attitudes with regard to current events, and the more
conservative element in the English presence was well represented. The
Civil and Military Gazette, with which the Kipling family had been
associated, was the leading Anglo-Indian newspaper in the Punjab, published
from Lahore, and it stood well to the right of the attitudinal spectrum.
To the vigorous nationalist daily, The Bengalee, it was 'the chartered
libertine of Lahore', while even the more temperate Statesman placed it
firmly in 'the Jingo section of the Anglo-Indian press'. (1)

There appeared in the Civil and Military Gazette on 24 August 1906, while
Andrews was at Sanawar, an extremely long letter deploring the 'Change of
Times in India', and signed 'Fifty Years in India'. It is a most
interesting revelation of attitudes.

> What is the one theme of conversation, of thought, of
> correspondence, among Europeans? The racial problem.
> What are Europeans asking one another - in offices,
> in clubs, in dining rooms? 'What is the country
> coming to? Where is all this anti-Britishism going
> to end?'

There is a sort of paternalistic sympathy in the writer's recollection of
'the courteous, respecful native gentleman of forty years ago', and even
the new swadeshi movement is 'a pleasure to encourage', and he is 'pleased
to see the people in homespun in their national costumes'. What upsets the
writer in the changing times of 1906 is the effect of the 'racial problem'
on the position of the Anglo-Indian, the 'loss of prestige'. This
situation is accompanied by a new phenomenon, 'the "Indian" gentleman of
today, with his English education, semi-European garb, decided air of
equality, and ... impudent, vicious stare'. The root of the trouble is
that the British in India have 'overdone education'.

Has education made the people any happier, more

contented, more loyal? This is, after all, the real
test of good government, and not the number of
frothy, truculent B.A.'s we turn out. A respected,
retired Civilian has said 'Show me an educated native
and I will show you a rebel!' And who will gainsay
the force of his epigram?

Amongst much more in a similar vein, the writer concludes by advocating
violent represssion:

When Swadeshism degenerates into ruffianism, unveiled
disloyalty and racial antagonism, I say ...
'Sjambok!'

The response to this letter was not confined to the columns of the Civil
and Military Gazette. The Punjab nationalist newspaper, the Tribune,
quickly reacted with an editorial, on 28 August, entitled 'Rip Van Winkle
to the Rescue'. Although this does not take the letter too seriously,
referring to its author as 'an old fossil', the promptness of the reaction
indicates that the letter had touched upon a sensitive issue. The bulk of
the immediate response, however, took the form of a series of a further
seventeen letters which appeared in the Civil and Military Gazette over the
following six weeks. Almost all of them are anonymous, and almost all of
them agree with the views of 'Fifty Years in India'. They fill out, in
fascinating ways, the position typified in the first letter.

Amongst these was a letter which appeared on 5 September, signed
'Sagittarius'. Noting that 'the greatest change in the demeanour of the
native began to show itself after the victory of the Japanese', the letter
is very much in the spirit of the first in the series, though more bitter
and hysterical in tone. The main point of it is the remedy proposed:

To get Indians back to their original callings, which
are trading and agriculture, only lower Government
appointments ... carrying a salary of Rs. 60 per
mensem or less, should, where necessary, be bestowed

upon natives. If Europeans or Eurasians are willing
to accept appointments carrying this low pay, ...
they should be given them; the natives receding
accordingly. (2)

This letter provoked a reply from Andrews, published on 8 September, a
spirited and vigorous response. It was uncharacteristically sarcastic. He
found Sagittarius' letter 'full of bitterness and reaction'. Its main
proposal would amount to 'treating Indians as serfs', and, apart from being
impracticable, would reflect upon Britain's 'boasted civilization', and
would disloyally negate Queen Victoria's 1858 Proclamation of racial
equality within the empire. Andrews then moved on to his main point, the
exposure of the fundamental error in Sagittarius' letter, that education
was the cause of the present situation. He argued that the real danger lay
in the alienation of the educated classes, who could easily become a class
of agitators who would prey upon 'the vast mass of ignorance and
superstition among the 260,000,000 of India who can neither read nor
write', and that in fact the present educated class were loyal. In the
circumstances two things were required: first, 'not less education but ...
a thousandfold more', through which 'the best ideals of our English life
can be understood and appreciated'; and second, the rejection of a policy
of 'social ostracism and a closing of all doors of sympathy and
friendship', which would be 'the most unpardonable and suicidal blunder', a
sure way of losing 'our most useful friends'.

In selecting as the main plank of his attack the question of education,
Andrews was taking up a recurring theme during this period. The following
year, for example, Curzon insisted in the House of Lords that the first and
foremost cause of political unrest in India was the education which Britain
had given. Even missionaries were liable to take this line. Under the
heading, 'Canon Ball's Balderdash on India', for example, the Tribune
reported that a 'Canon Ball of Calcutta who is now in Britain ... diagnoses
the cause of the present unrest with unerring instinct. First there is
education, and too much study of English literature'. (3) Andrews' attack
upon 'social ostracism and a closing of all doors of sympathy and
friendship' was also very central to his concern. Shortly afterwards, for

a Christian readership, noting that the Christian message was one of
'brotherhood and goodwill', he commented that one of the greatest stumbling
blocks to the message was 'the aloofness of the Englishman from the
Indian'. (4)

It is possible to detect in what we have quoted from Andrews' arguments the
assumption that Britain had a civilizing mission in India, and that loyalty
to the British government was a necessity for its accomplishment, but
beside this we need to note his acknowledgement, an eccentric one during
this period in missionary and civilian circles, that India was 'the home of
philosophers and thinkers when we ourselves were savages'. It needs also
to be noted that he was not merely making a personal statement, but
appealing to the Anglo-Indian community, lest Englishmen in India should
lose 'all sense of liberty and equity', and for a policy 'worthy of the
name of Englishmen'.

Andrews signed with his own name, and appended his Sanawar address, with
its suggestion of an official appointment. He avoids at this point any
hint of being a missionary, probably so as to appeal simply as Anglo-Indian
to Anglo-Indian. Certainly, an earlier letter in the sequence had
criticised mission schools and colleges, whose 'ill-adapted education ...
causes great unsettlement of mind and feeling'. (5)

Andrews' contribution evoked some response in the subsequent
correspondence. 'Sagittarius' himself replied, questioning Andrews'
interpretation of the Queen's Proclamation. Other critics included J.W.
Papworth of Lahore - one of the few correspondents who signed with their
own name - who claimed that it was an idle dream to hope that the
'manufacture of Babus' would lead to the amelioration of the condition of
the masses. '59 Years' complained that Andrews' letter was 'wanting in
those useful particulars as to the length of years of the author's
experience in India'. (6) This provoked a second letter from Andrews on 30
September. He reverted to the question of the Queen's Proclamation.

> Both the words and the spirit of that great charter
> are unambiguous.

He continued with a vigorous affirmation of his own loyalty and what that
implied:

> I am an Englishman in India who believes that my own
> King's pledged word to his people is a solemn promise
> and not a subtle fraud.

The correspondence continued for another two weeks in the Civil and
Military Gazette, with a number of letters contemptuous of the 'insolent'
educated Indian, insisting that the British were in India solely for their
own benefit, and, again, advocating violent repression of those who
questioned British rule. (7)

This correspondence cannot be regarded merely as a storm in a very
provincial teacup. Looking back a few months later for the causes of the
very serious unrest which erupted in 1907, Lajpat Rai, Punjab's leading
nationalist, argued that it had been brought about by the Anglo-Indians
themselves, the Civil and Military Gazette correspondence being,
chronologically, the first of the causes. (8) It was certainly taken very
seriously in a number of quarters. The Indian Association of Lahore on 5
November asked the Punjab Government to prosecute the paper, and, although
this proposal was rejected, the Chief Secretary admitted that the tone of
some of the letters was objectionable, and expressed the regrets of the
Lieutenant-Governor, Sir Charles Rivaz, that they had been published. The
Viceroy himself found the letters 'disgracefully low in tone' and admitted
to the Secretary of State, Morley, that it made his blood boil to know that
a leading English newspaper could publish such productions. Morley, in his
turn, had to fend off a demand from Sir Henry Cotton in the House of
Commons that steps be taken to discourage the publication of 'such
inflammatory utterances'. (9)

The correspondence was very important for Andrews. He says later that 'the
brutality of the Civil and Military articles ... roused ... (him) and made
... (him) more pro-Indian', and he adds the observation that he had
'advanced a long way between the autumn of 1905 and the autumn of 1906'.
Even more importantly, his letters were his 'very first introduction to the

Indian public'. (10) The response here was striking and immediate. On 13 September, the Tribune reproduced his letter of the 8th in full, and devoted an editorial to him under the heading, 'A Noble Englishman to the Rescue'. After rehearsing his 'crushing rejoinder', it continued:

> Men like Mr Andrews are the salt of the earth, and it
> is to the race of noble-minded sons of Mr Andrews'
> nature and foresight that England owes its greatness
> and glory.

This sentiment was echoed within the educated classes at the other end of the country, the Bengalee finding itself unable to express sufficiently its 'sense of deep obligation to Mr Andrews'. By the turn of the year, the Tribune is able to say that his name 'has almost become a household word in India on account of his profound sympathy with our aspirations'. The Tribune of 13 September had drawn attention in particular to Andrews' remarks about 'social ostracism' as indicative of his 'thorough insight into and deep acquaintance with the real situation'. Certainly, the Indian press's own striking response to his letter is some measure of the depth of the racial division at the time. The Tribune had welcomed his first letter 'as a weary and footsore traveller does an oasis in the sandy and barren desert'.

It is some indication of Andrews' sensitive perception of the circumstances and requirements of mission that he had reached such a position within some two and a half years of his arrival in India. And it is precisely with mission that we are here concerned. If the Tribune's reference to 'the salt of the earth' was little more than a figure of speech in the context, the Editor also acknowledged that 'here again the much derided Missionary has proved a benefactor to the people'. (11) His intervention in the columns of the Civil and Military Gazette was entirely within the terminological conventions of Anglo-India, but the motive was thoroughly missionary, in the sense in which Andrews understood the word, and in this respect it was highly successful.

4. 'The worthy Bishop'

Andrews was not alone in the Church in his consternation at the letters in the Civil and Military Gazette. His own diocesan, G.A. Lefroy, rose from a perusal of the majority of them 'with a sense of utter confusion and shame - almost of despair - for my country'. (1)

In the earlier years of the Cambridge Mission, prior to Andrews' arrival in India, Lefroy had been almost wholly concerned with evangelistic work among Muslims. From the very inception of the Mission's work, he had been uncomfortably aware of the hindrance to evangelism inherent in the association in people's minds of mission with British rule. Likewise, in the year of his consecration as Bishop of Lahore, 1899, he had expressed concern at the way relationships between Europeans and Indians in the church were deteriorating. If there is an air of complacency about his report to an English audience in 1904 that the civil administration was 'one of the glories of the Empire', and that Curzon was doing 'a magnificent work', by late 1906 he was acknowledging that developments noticed earlier had reached a critical point, 'a parting of the ways'. (2) The occasion of these remarks was Lefroy's third triennial charge to his diocese, delivered on 6 November 1906. It was on this public occasion that he expressed his confusion and shame at the letters in the Civil and Military Gazette, and was moved to a wide-ranging survey of the situation. He believed that, with substantial qualifications, the general trend and tendency of British rule had been in large measure the outcome of a true Christian instinct, 'the very reverse of ... the Roman or the Russian line'. The development of Indian nationalism was an inevitable consequence of the British presence.

> Would it not be madness to come with our English
> ideals, our ideals of personal freedom and equality
> of opportunity, of Local Self-Government established
> or aimed at, and of essential justice between man and
> man, ... and then expect nothing to happen; to expect
> that all things would continue as they had been from
> the beginning? ...England and England's spirit and

> genius being what it is - there <u>must</u> be movement,
> progress, growth, ... in this old land of India in
> which our own lot has been cast.

The failure of the bulk of Englishmen in India to appreciate this was a
matter of the utmost gravity, while their attitude to the educated classes
who had learned these ideals, an attitude of 'utter aloofness and
distance', 'a grim refusal of anything even approaching to a brotherly and
sympathetic bearing', would have far-reaching consequences. He went on to
insist that, with regard to the current deterioration in relationships,
'the English side' was largely responsible. It was, as Andrews had also
pointed out, a critical situation for the church: chaplains and
missionaries, in addition to their special obligation to try to reconcile
the two communities, must be 'on the right side in this question'.

> On the response which we as a community give ...
> depends the measure of further advance which we can
> make in the ... mission with which God ... has
> entrusted us.

In the discussion which followed the Bishop's charge, Rudra and other
Indians present confirmed and underlined both the seriousness of the
situation and also the need for improved inter-racial relations. (3) Their
views were echoed, interestingly, by the Secretary of State, John Morley,
but perhaps more importantly by the <u>Tribune</u>, which reported Lefroy's charge
at length over three issues, and followed this up with an editorial, on 15
December, entitled 'The Silver Lining'. Varying the metaphor slightly, the
editor likened Andrews' first letter, after the darkness shed around by the
earlier correspondence in the <u>Civil and Military Gazette</u>, to a first streak
of light, this being but a forerunner of the dawn represented by 'the
Bishop's solid effort ... to improve the relations between the two
communities'. (4)

This was the beginning of a period of very cordial relations between Lefroy
and the nationalist press, which was to last throughout the rest of his
Lahore episcopate. It was the beginning, also, of a series of

interventions within the ferment which these years represent, as he pressed
the more ebullient nationalists to 'knuckle under a bit', and the Anglo-
Indian community to a change of heart and attitude. During the very
serious disturbances in the Punjab in 1907, he had a number of meetings
with leading nationalists in Lahore, among them the Editor of the Tribune
and 'barristers, pleaders, or men of that ilk', and, among other things,
arranged for a deputation of them to meet the Lieutenant-Governor to
explain their position. (5)

Two months later, he took the opportunity of a sermon before the Viceroy to
reiterate some of the opinions that he had first publicised in his
episcopal charge, that the political awakening was the fruit of Western
education, and the situation called for 'a more generous and courteous
spirit' on the part of Anglo-Indians. Lord Minto agreed, and wrote to
Lefroy to say so, adding, however, that Anglo-Indian opinion on the whole
was quite unmoved, and that he had already heard lamentations over Lefroy's
views. (6)

A further opportunity to champion the educated classes occurred in August
1907. An article in the Civil and Military Gazette on 9 August, with the
contemptuous title, 'Babus and their Uses', attacked the 'literary class of
India' as a 'deadly legacy of Metcalf and Macaulay'. This prompted the
Bishop to imitate Andrews with a letter of protest, arguing the importance
of education for India. His letter was reprinted in full in the Tribune on
23 August, and this was followed two days later by an appreciative
editorial. There followed a response in the nationalist press right across
India, and the terms of it indicate, as in the case of Andrews, the
missionary significance of the entire episode. The Bengalee, for example,
referred to 'the worthy Bishop', and claimed that 'from myriad throats a
blessing will be pronounced upon ... the messenger of peace and good-will',
while the Indu Prakash carried an article entitled 'A Worthy Missionary of
Christ'. (7)

It was the seriousness of the situation from the point of view of mission
that Lefroy emphasised in some notes which he circulated to his brother
bishops in advance of the Episcopal Synod of 1908. He argued that 'the

educated classes' had 'a perfect right to insist' on the Bishops' declaring
their own attitude and feeling with regard to the national movement, and
that to be silent at such a time would be 'to repel and alienate'.

> I doubt whether any of the subjects which will come
> up for consideration at the Synod touches more
> vitally the question of the spread of Christianity in
> India during the next few years than this one ....
> It is certain that the attitude of educated Indians
> during the next decade will be profoundly influenced
> by the attitude which the Church adopts at this time
> towards the new movement, the new aspirations, of
> India. (8)

Lefroy continued to press this comparatively liberal and eccentric line
throughout his Lahore episcopate, a particularly notable intervention being
in support of the Transvaal Indians, which we shall touch upon later. He
carried on his campaign on other fronts also, for example to audiences of
mission supporters in England. (9) In 1908, his was a solitary voice, but
for Andrews' contribution promoting the same ideas, at the Pan-Anglican
Congress in London, and, again, in preparatory papers for the World
Missionary Conference at Edinburgh in 1910. (10)

A book published in preparation for the Congress and for the 1908 Lambeth
Conference, Church and Empire, to which he contributed the chapter on
India, gave Lefroy a further opportunity to express his views. There are a
number of indications here that he has reached a point where he hardly
wants to be associated with such a book at all. He says that it is
'useless ... to expect' of him 'enthusiasm about our empire', though he
concedes that 'a number of indirect influences, making ultimately for the
conversion of the land, are at work in consequence of our political
connection with it, which would be wanting in its absence'. He likewise
admits, echoing his 'great Cambridge teacher', Westcott's view of the
empire as a sacred trust, that he feels very deeply indeed 'the splendour -
unique in the world's history and solemn beyond words - of the position to
which, in the providence and by the guiding hand of God, the British Empire

has been called in the world today'. (11)

What was new, however, in Lefroy's theological understanding of the Indian missionary context, was his recognition that the national movement was so essential a consequence of British rule that 'for no such movement to have come sooner or late to the birth would have meant the utter failure of our country's and our Church's mission to India'. (12) It was not a large step from this - though a very significant one - for him to express in 1909 the conviction that 'the wave of a newly-awakened life ... passing over India' emanated 'ultimately and on the whole from the Spirit of God.' (13)

It is not entirely easy to be sure of the extent of Andrews' influence on Lefroy's views. Both the Bishop's Irish background and his long Indian experience helped to modify his view of the relation of church and empire. At the same time, we must note that his initial reponse to the 'Change of Times' correspondence followed closely on Andrews' intevention, and also that he seems to have been taking a leaf out of Andrews' book with regard to the later correspondence on 'Babus and their Uses'. Two years later, he drew attention to a statement of Andrews' on the changing circumstances of mission in India as 'quite the ablest and best I have seen anywhere', and one that had impressed him profoundly. That he regarded Andrews as having gone too far, there is a good deal of evidence, though he called this a 'generous ... failing'. He was not happy with his influence on S.A.C. Ghose, and in commenting on Andrews' published views, he expressed the opinion that he was 'never ... well-balanced'. His own summing-up of the relationship indicates, nevertheless, a measure of indebtedness:

> With all his limitations and faults he really is a
> splendid fellow, and has helped me more than I can
> possibly say. (14)

Bearing in mind his responsibility as Bishop for 'the most military of dioceses', and his constant necessary contact with the Anglo-Indian community, from Minto and Kitchener downwards, it is remarkable what an independent approach Lefroy was able to maintain. (15) If he really was, as Andrews held, 'very "Anglo-Indian" by instinct', he would seem to have

been an impressive example of that 'self-repression' for which Allnutt was
calling. (16) In determining his relative position during these years, one
bearing is provided by the impression that he made on the Liberal Secretary
of State, John Morley, who wrote to Minto:

> I found him one of the most attractive men I ever
> met. In the midst of a rather heavy day, he not only
> interested but excited me, and carried me for a while
> into the upper ether. Why did you not recommend him
> to be a Lieutenant-Governor? There's an experiment
> for you! His ideas delighted me. (17)

The other bearing is in relation to the Indian educated classes. The
Tribune, observing in 1908 that it was 'a matter of thankfulness that in
the ranks of Christian missionaries' there were to be found 'some good and
true friends of the cause of Indian Nationality', listed a select six such
friends. Andrews' name headed the list, but Lefroy's was also there, as
well as that of Allnutt. (18) These two bearings locate Lefroy very
clearly in the middle ground at a time of estrangement and conflict, and it
would probably be fair to say that the influence of Andrews had something
to do with this.

In connection with the question of Andrews' own changing point of view
during these years, this brief glance at Lefroy - and taking into account
that a study of Allnutt or of some of the other members of the Cambridge
Mission would disclose comparable responses - indicates that Andrews, while
he was to push the questions raised by the national movement much further
and make them the central plank of his missionary approach, did not work in
a situation of complete isolation.

5. 'Indian Nationality'

His foray into the correspondence columns of the Anglo-Indian press,
Andrews said, made him 'more pro-Indian', and also served to introduce him
to the Indian public. Encouraged, no doubt, by the warmth of the response
in the Tribune and elsewhere, he was quick to follow up this introduction.

During the cold weather of 1906-7, he became thoroughly caught up in the national movement, at a national level and, particularly, at this stage, in its political aspect.

It was a propitious moment for such an involvement. By 1900, the Indian National Congress, if still only 'an aspiration rather than a general dynamic', had spread all over India and was regarded by forward-looking members of the educated classes as the natural mouthpiece of their aspirations. What the Japanese victories, the partition of Bengal and the other developments around 1905 did was to radicalize the resolutions of Congress and draw the whole middle class into its sphere of influence. 'The pains of partition' - along with these other things - were 'the birth-pangs of Indian bourgeois nationalism', of which the Congress was the institutional expression. (1)

The December 1905 gathering of the Congress at Benares had gone so far as to give its blessing to the boycott movement in Bengal, arguing that a special grievance might warrant the use of special political techniques. On the whole, however, the Congress leadership, based in Bombay, and anxious to avoid too close an association with Bengal extremism because it hoped for sustantial reforms from the new Liberal government in Britain, had succeeded in keeping its resolutions relatively moderate. It was clear, though, that the 1906 gathering would be a critical one. It was to be held in Calcutta, and so was bound to be dominated by the political problems of a divided Bengal. With nothing yet to show, moreover, for Morley's liberalism, and so with the more radical elements making the running, everything pointed to its being what it indeed turned out to be, 'a notable landmark in the history of the Indian National Congress.' (2)

Just over a fortnight after his second intervention in the Civil and Military Gazette, Andrews published in the Tribune, on 17 October, a letter on 'The National Congress of 1906'. Acknowledging his limited knowledge of India, but hoping that his lifelong study of history and his love for the country would make up for this, he offered four suggestions for the forthcoming Congress, the times being critical and the dangers great. First, having heard W.T. Stead's name being mentioned in connection with the presidency, he urged that Dadabhai Naoroji or some other trusted Indian statesman should be approached.

On no account should an Englishman be approached....
It is essential that the outside world should clearly
see that India possesses statesmen of her own.

Secondly, he recommended the improvement of the organisation's constitution, with the provision of a permanent executive. Thirdly, he stressed the vital importance of retaining Muslim sympathy, the union of the Hindu and Muslim communities being 'the one final goal of national unity'. Finally, he pressed the point that, while 'political agitation ... (had) its place', emphasis on the social and industrial side of the Congress would 'unite the different communities, silence opposition, and win the respect of every Englishman worthy of the name'.

Andrews' four points were well chosen. All had current pertinence. For example, while certainly there can have been no causal connection, Naoroji was only finally approached eight days after Andrews' letter was published. Nor were any of his points controversial within the general parameters of nationalist thinking. (3) An interesting stylistic feature occurs in the letter: Andrews wrote that emphasis on social and industrial progress would prove to the outside world 'our' self-governing capacity. The pronoun has a slightly self-conscious air about it here, and, indeed, he was to use it rather self-consciously for some years to come. (4) It was nonetheless something of which none of his most liberal colleagues in the Cambridge Mission was either constitutionally or ideologically capable. It is a small pointer to the upheaval which was going on in Andrews' mind.

The Tribune drew the special attention of its readers to this 'remarkable letter', and, a few days later, on 4 November, pointing out that it had been reproduced and favourably noticed in other newspapers across the country, devoted two editorial columns to analysing and agreeing with it.

Andrews' time was not, of course, wholly taken up with these new concerns, although it is not surprising that he had to report in 1906 that his year's

work had been 'very broken', and that he was only able to act as a
supernumerary in College. (5) Early in November, he attended the Diocesan
Conference at Lahore, and read a paper on the subject of private prayer.
This may seem very remote from his more public concerns, but there may well
have been a connection. Although this paper has not survived, two articles
on prayer which Andrews wrote at Tissington Tatlow's request for the
Student Movement in England at this time, reproducing long passages from
Forbes Robinson's Letters to his Friends, are relevant. In the face of the
almost tragic drifting apart of Indian and English Christians, and the
creeping in of the 'official tone' even among missionaries, Andrews asks
whether Robinson's practice of prayer for his friends 'with the longing
prayer of love' is not what is required to bridge the widening gulf,
younger missionaries forming a 'true and deep Christian friendship with at
least one fellow Christian Communicant of another race', and pouring into
that friendship 'all the longing affection and intercession which God in
his great Love may bestow'. (6) In the second article, published in April
1907, he takes up the question of praying for Buddhist, Hindu and Muslim
friends, 'those in whom the potential Christ-life has not as yet been
quickened.' Quoting the parable of the sheep and goats, he suggests that
'we must see Christ in them', and 'bring them, by our very longing of love
potentially within the Body of Christ'.

If Andrews' paper at Lahore was on these lines, the connection with his
more public concerns is clear and congruous. A little later in November,
he conducted a three-day retreat at Lahore for women missionaries from the
Dioceses of Lahore and Lucknow. In the midst of his increasing involvement
in the national movement, it is interesting to catch a glimpse of another
side of Andrews here. One of the retreatants, very appreciative, wrote
home that he 'conducted the whole beautifully ... the Intercession Services
were wonderful ... either extempore, or with an adaptation or combination
of Prayers from the Prayer Book .... He spoke so slowly ... very quietly
and naturally'. (7)

Andrews' new concerns, however, seem to have all but dominated these last
months of 1906. In his letter to the Tribune about the forthcoming
congress he had described himself as 'an Englishman pledged to the cause of

Indian nationality'. Even during his visit to Lahore for the Diocesan
Conference, he took the opportunity of elaborating on this commitment,
delivering at Forman Christian College, in addition to an address to the
students, a public lecture on 'Indian Nationality'. He explained a few
weeks later that he had felt very keenly that the time had come, especially
in the face of much that had been written in the press that summer of an
opposite tendency, to declare publicly and openly, as a Christian and as an
Englishman, his 'intense sympathy with the higher national aspirations of
educated Indians'. (8) Certainly, he could not have made his sympathy much
more public. The lecture was delivered before 'the cream of the educated
Indian community of Lahore', under the chairmanship of the leading Punjab
'moderate', Harkishen Lal, and reproduced in full in the Tribune. At
Lahore Cathedral that Sunday, preaching at both morning and evening
services, he 'impressed on his English congregation the same views',
pleading for the recognition of 'Indian nationality'. (9)

Before the year was out, he had delivered variant versions of the same
lecture at Delhi, Allahabad and Calcutta. At Allahabad, 'pre-eminently a
city of the new professional man', one of the organisers was the leading
Congressman, Tej Bahadur Sapru, and the chairman, Pandit Madan Mohan
Malaviya, a 'patriarch of the Congress'. (10) So successful was this
occasion that he was asked to address two other meetings in the city,
'which he did with similar success'. (11) In every case, the text of his
lecture was published in full, and usually accompanied by an enthusiastic
editorial response. (12)

A scrutiny of Andrews' views on 'Indian nationality' at this time discloses
two main features. First, the position that he took was one of
considerable caution on the whole, aligning him with the more moderate
among the nationalists. With repeated assurances that 'the great heart of
the English Nation' guaranteed Indian progress, he laid great stress on the
need for 'a long period of settlement', because of the 'immense arrears in
political training and capacity still to be made good'. (13) The goal of
the process was a place 'beside the self-governing colonies' under the
Crown. (14) That such an approach should evoke loud cheers at Allahabad is
an indication of the frame of mind of many of Andrews' audience, and also

of how decisively he surpassed the usual nationalist expectations with
regard to English or missionary sympathy. (15) In retrospect, in the early
1920's, that is how he himself saw things.

> It is curious now to see how very cautious I was at
> that time, but all the same it was regarded as
> remarkable as coming from an Englishman. (16)

The point was made at the time, by a correspondent in the Hindustan Review,
Parmeshwar Lal. 'Somehow', he wrote, 'I had been led to expect even more
from what I had read about the reverend gentleman'. Though he is prepared
to call Andrews' sympathy 'remarkable ... in these days of bitter racial
jealousies', and is 'always grateful for such little sympathies as we can
get from the British race', he nevertheless comments that 'the superb self-
complacency so characteristic of the English people never seems to desert
him'. (17) To the extent that Andrews' views were close to those of many
moderate nationalists, this is possibly a slightly unfair comment, although
he himself looked back on his early writing and speaking as done in 'the
evil patronizing way'. (18) Parmeshawar Lal certainly represented a
minority viewpoint in the nationalist press. His comment does, however,
help us to see precisely where Andrews stood.

The second aspect of his views at this time is the insistence that he
derives his attitude to Indian nationalism from his Christian faith. For
example, his lectures were almost invariably prefaced with the phrase, 'As
a Christian missionary ...'. He claimed that 'to give others .. that
Nationality which we ourselves prize', is a necessary concomitant of the
belief that we should do to others as we would have them do to us.
Similarly, the demand that each nation should receive its highest and
fullest and best development, which meant development 'on national lines',
was a direct outcome of belief in 'the Brotherhood of Man', which, with
that in the Fatherhood of God, is the basis of 'the whole Christian
religion'. (19) Here, again, there was a dissenting voice. Madan Mohan
Malaviya at Allahabad pointed out that people in India had their own 'Gita
and other sacred books', and needed only to turn to these with
understanding to find that inspiration which Christians drew from the

Bible. More typical, however, was the response of Harkishen Lal at Lahore, who remarked at the end of the lecture, 'Blessed are the peacemakers', and of the Tribune's editor who wrote in this context, 'Verily, Mr. Andrews is a true soldier of the Cross and champion of justice and righteousness for all mankind'. (20)

Andrews was clearly a very effective public speaker. (21) He was fortunate, also, that among the educated classes there was a virtual cult of the public lecture for him to utilize. And yet, he was to penetrate even deeper into the mission territory represented by the educated classes before the year was out.

It is not entirely clear when, in spite of the misgivings of Allnutt, the Head of the Mission, he decided to attend the 1906 meeting of the Indian National Congress in Calcutta in the December. Perhaps the thought was in his mind when he wrote his letter to the Tribune of 17 October. Possibly the idea came from a meeting with the veteran Bengali Congressman, Surendranath Bannerjee. (22) It seems as likely, however, that his close association at St Stephen's College with the young lecturer, Raghubar Dayal, who was to attend the Congress as a Punjab delegate, suggested the idea to him. Certainly there was an unprecedented interest in the Congress in the Punjab that year. (23) Andrews went as a visitor, staying at the Oxford Mission, and attended all the sessions, accompanied by the Head of the community, Canon Brown, and enjoying a front seat through the good offices of Bannerjee. (24)

It was, as has been noted, a more than usually important meeting of the Congress. Under the influence of the more radical elements in the movement, whom Andrews called 'the younger party', and who were represented most significantly in the speeches of B.C. Pal and Tilak, 'the Mendicant Policy', as it was called, was thrown over, and major resolutions were endorsed on self-government, boycott, swadeshi, and national education. (25) With regard to the first of these, the President, Naoroji, had concluded his address by saying that Congressmen had before them 'a clear goal, a clear star ... of Self-Government or Swaraj'. (26) Andrews was deeply impressed with Naoroji's contribution.

> He looked like one who had come to fulfil a mission
> at all cost and would go through with it, though it
> cost him all he had left of life. ... He looked like
> an aged warrior battling determinedly to claim
> self-government for India.

There were, of course, to be many definitions of self-government in the
debates that followed, but for Andrews the significant thing was that, 'for
the first time, in such a place, ... the form and nature of India's demand
was expressed by an Indian word ... easily understood throughout ... India
by the simplest villager as well as the educated classes'. (27) Andrews
was interested in many aspects of the debates. He recorded something of
this in an article, 'An Englishman's Impression of the National Congress',
in Bannerjee's newspaper, the <u>Bengalee</u>, on 28 December, and other comments
in some notes appended to a published version of his 'Indian Nationality'
lecture. (28) He expressed concern that social questions seemed to be
subordinated to the political issue, and hoped that Annie Besant's phrase,
'Nation Building' would 'remain in the memory of Indians at the present
time'. On the whole, the tenor of his remarks confirms his own later
comment:

> I came away from the Congress deeply impressed by
> the greatness of the National Movement. But I was
> still as strongly as possible an Imperialist and a
> believer in the British Empire. I was also what may
> now be called a Moderate in my ideas on Nationalism,
> ... thinking ... only Mr. Gokhale was safe as a
> leader. (29)

There had been valuable opportunities to meet the nationalist leaders,
including Gopal Krishna Gokhale, and the veteran Christian Congressman,
Kali Charan Banerji, to whom he would often in future allude. His meeting
with Gokhale he regarded as particularly important, as a letter which he
wrote on his return to Delhi indicates.

> If at any time there is any way you can suggest

in which I can help the national cause, you know
how glad I shall be to do so if it is within my
power. (30)

The Congress was not to loom so large again in Andrews' concerns for most
of the remainder of his missionary years. One reason was that, after the
very divisive meeting of the following year at Surat, 'listless, fragmented
and without leadership, the Punjab nationalist party – like its parent
organisation, the Indian National Congress – fell asleep'. (31) Another
was the effect of the Indian Councils Act of 1909, usually known as the
Minto-Morley reforms, a small but clear step in the direction of
representative and responsible self-government, which led to a 'Congress-
government honeymoon' which was to last for some five years. (32) A third
reason may have been the 'very great anxiety' in the Cambridge Mission
about his activities, which he discovered on his return from Calcutta, and
which he saw would lead, despite the liberality of the Mission and the
great sympathy of Allnutt, to an ultimately intolerable situation. (33)
The second half of 1906 and early 1907 represented, nevertheless, an
extraordinary venture by a missionary, affirming his Christian motivation
openly, into the heartland of the 'political nation'.

6. 'A true Christian opportunity'

Andrews' hope of making a literary career the main end of his missionary
work, which he had expressed to Allnutt and Stanton in 1905, was on the way
to fulfilment with remarkable rapidity. There were to be several aspects
to this career, though he himself saw that reaching 'the rapidly rising
Native Christian Church' and 'the rapidly growing educated Native
Community' were the most pressing needs. His success in relation to these
groups, the latter in particular, is one of the most interesting features
of his missionary years.

Throughout the nineteenth century, the press had been a vital and
dramatically expanding factor in the creation of the educated classes and
in their growing political awareness. By 1905, it was reported that 1,539
newspapers and journals reached an estimated two million subscribers

throughout India, among the most influential being the 285 published in English. (1) Every region had a network of such publications, and the convention, deriving from an earlier period when the gathering of news was very difficult, whereby a paper would reprint items from contemporary publications in other regions, contributed to the India-wide dissemination of information and ideas.

The Punjab reflected the general pattern, with its own distinctive features. The new educated classes were much involved in journalism and publishing. Several of Andrews' early Punjab friends and acquaintances had such interests. His Urdu teacher, Shams-ud-Din, had for a time edited the Panjabi Akhbar, owned by his father in Lahore; his colleague at St Stephen's College, Raghubar Dayal, at one time owned the Imperial Native Press, while a temporary teacher at the College, Syed Haidar Raza, produced a journal, Aftab. Another acquaintance, Amir Chand, a former student of the College and a teacher at St Stephen's School, published books and, at various times, the Imperial Fortnightly Advertiser, an Urdu weekly, a religious journal called Thundering Dawn, and, with Raghubar Dayal, a weekly, Akash. (2)

All this was part of the considerable increase in newspaper and journal production which took place in the Punjab around the turn of the century. In the 1880's, some forty newspapers were published in the province annually, while in the first three or four years of the twentieth century, the number had risen to one hundred and forty. More important, of course, was circulation. Most publications had a very small readership, and only a very few reached a circulation of above 2,000. Quite the most influential 'Anglo-Vernacular' newspaper in the Punjab was the Tribune, with a circulation in 1903 of 1,700. (3) Although founded in 1881 by a wealthy Punjabi, Sirdar Dayal Singh Majeetia, it had been taken over before Andrews' time by Surendranath Banerjee of Calcutta, and was dominated editorially by the Bengali élite and their Brahmo associates. The founding in 1904 of the Panjabee, edited by a Maratha disciple of Tilak, and with most important editorials in the early years written by Lajpat Rai, created an energetic alternative to the Tribune, the two representing respectively the 'extremist' and 'moderate' positions in the national movement. (4)

We have already seen how warmly the Tribune responded to Andrews' letters on the changing times in the Civil and Military Gazette. Andrews took immediate advantage of this. The Tribune's first editorial approval of his stand appeared on 13 September. By the issue of 17 September, he had his first submitted contribution published, a letter on 'The Education of our Children', a discussion of an earlier correspondent's proposal to found a public school in the hills. (5)

This was the beginning of a very special relationship with the Tribune, which was to continue right through Andrews' missionary decade in the Punjab. Perhaps he was particularly fortunate that the editorship had been assumed in the preceding April by Alfred Nundy, who, as a former assistant secretary of the Indian National Congress known for his moderate opinions, produced a newspaper with whose views Andrews would be particularly content to be associated. Nundy must also, as a Christian, have warmed to the sympathetic interest of a missionary co-religionist. (6) Certainly, some such rather exceptional explanation is required for a relationship that was to be so close. Andrews was to contribute over the next eight years some forty-five items, from brief letters to articles extending through several issues, from pieces reproduced from other publications to specially commissioned and signed leaders. As a further measure of his influence in and through the Tribune, there occur during the same period at least one hundred and thirty-three news items or editorial comments alluding to him.

If Andrews had confined his writing to the Tribune, he would have achieved a breakthrough to an engagement with the educated classes in itself quite unique. No contemporary missionary achieved a position remotely comparable. Bishop Lefroy, who certainly enjoyed a position second only to that of Andrews in the eyes of the Tribune, contributed nothing directly to the paper, and is quoted or referred to less than forty times during the same period.

But his place in the Tribune represented only one part of Andrews' journalistic enterprise. Although he did not write anything like so extensively for other Indian newspapers, there were also the monthly journals which were another very significant medium for him. 'Three

reviews of distinction voice Indian Nationalism', Ramsay MacDonald reported
in 1910, citing The Indian Review of Madras, The Hindustan Review of
Allahabad, 'the most severely political and moderate', and The Modern
Review of Calcutta, 'the most literary of the three, which shows all the
characteristics of the Bengal spirit and is most in sympathy with the left
wing'. (7)

In these substantial publications also, Andrews rapidly established a
strong position. His first entry into this area was, like his first in the
Tribune, a modest enough contribution, a poem, earnest and not very
distinguished, on 'The New Indian Nation', which appeared in the December
1906 issue of Saccidananda Sinha's Hindustan Review. This was immediately
followed the next month by his long article on 'Indian Nationality'. The
Modern Review was first published that month, January 1907, under the
editorship of Ramananda Chatterji, whose friendship was to become for
Andrews 'one of the greatest gifts which God has given me in my life'. (8)
His first contribution appeared in the July issue that year. He wrote for
all three reviews throughout the rest of his missionary years, a total of
some fifty-nine items, occasionally poems but mostly articles. To the
Modern Review in particular he became a leading contributor, with some
forty-five entries in the course of the next seven years, and, as in the
case of the Tribune, there are frequent news items and editorial comments
referring to him. Even more than in the newspaper, Andrews' place dwarfs
any other Christian and missionary presence. (9)

In seeking to quantify Andrews' penetration of the educated classes in this
way, we must also take into account three other points. First, the
widespread reproduction of his articles, or summaries of them, and of the
texts of his public lectures and addresses, in every major regional centre,
so that, for example, an item which he wrote for a Madras publication would
be reproduced in full in a Punjab newspaper, one for an Allahabad newspaper
in a Bengal journal. Bearing in mind, of course, that the reference is to
the English-speaking classes, the Bengalee's editor was not exaggerating
when he claimed in 1909 that 'When ... Andrews ... speaks, the whole
country listens'. (10) Second, his influence was extended through the
reprinting of some of his articles as separate pamphlets. (11) Third,

there was the extensive correspondence which ensued, as he wrote in 1909.

> I now have a large correspondence with educated
> Hindus throughout the country arising out of literary
> work. This correspondence, which has been singularly
> frank and open, is one of my chief means of gaining
> the Indian point of view.

The following year, he referred to his correspondents as 'hundreds of the best educated Indians from all parts of India', while in his annual report of 1911, he wrote of 'young educated Indians ... eagerly seeking help and advice', and added that this correspondence now took up a daily portion of his time. (12) This feed-back from his writing was important both as a source of information and understanding, and also as a ground for claiming to speak with authority on what Indian people thought. (13)

There were other important strands to Andrews' literary career during these years. The 'rapidly rising Native Christian Church', which he had also seen the need to serve through literature, received his attention. In addition to editorial work, which we shall note later, thirty items, from brief letters to such weighty contributions as his Occasional Paper on 'Ordination Study in India', were written up to mid-1914. He wrote most often, on some fourteen occasions, for the Oxford Mission to Calcutta's Epiphany, a weekly religious paper with the remarkably high output of 12,000 copies. He was impressed with the hold that the Epiphany had obtained 'in the educated mind of India' and his articles are addressed as much to the educated classes at large as to the Christian community. (14) The same was true of the Indian Interpreter, for which he wrote occasionally. Produced by two Scottish missionaries, Macnicol and Robertson, it was addressed, from an explicitly Christian standpoint, just as much at people of other faiths as at Christians, aiming to be at Poona a Christian equivalent of what the other reviews were in their cities.

Addressed more exclusively to a Christian readership were his contributions to the National Missionary Society's National Missionary Intelligencer, the Methodist Indian Witness, the Occasional Papers of his own mission, and the

Y.M.C.A.'s Young Men of India, to this last of which he contributed several
particularly substantial articles. This aspect of Andrews' work was on a
much smaller scale than his writing for the educated classes at large, in
these last four publications a total of only fourteen contributions.

Following his first three articles, published in the English journals of
the missionary societies, he continued to address the supporters in England
of foreign missions. He wrote nine articles for the Delhi Mission News,
and nine for S.P.G.'s The East and the West. In a similar category were
his articles and letters in two English church weeklies, the Church Times
and the Guardian. Clearly, Andrews saw the task of interpreting Indian
aspirations, and the church's work in that context, as an important one.
His two books published during the period, North India (1908) and The
Renaissance in India (1912), had the same object. So, too, had some of
his twelve contributions to the S.C.M.'s Student Movement, though writing
for this had an additional advantage, since he noted that it was
'constantly seen by educated Hindus in India', especially those who had
leanings towards the Christian faith. (15)

Andrews did not make much use of the Anglo-Indian press. Perhaps his early
experience of the Civil and Military Gazette led him to a conclusion like
that of Lord Minto, who found the Lahore paper's Allahabad contemporary,
the Pioneer, 'past praying for'. (16) One or two items were reproduced in
these newspapers, and he did, as we shall see, intervene on one further
occasion, in the Pioneer, to champion Indian interests in the face of
Anglo-Indian attitudes. In a somewhat similar category was a letter he
wrote to the London Spectator.

The only other significant literary work during these years was the St
Stephen's College Magazine, which he founded in 1907, and edited for six
years, himself contributing numerous editorials and thirteen signed
articles. His personality and outlook pervade the whole magazine, and his
own interests and commitments are reflected in many of the articles written
by the students.

Altogether, it will be seen that Andrews' literary output during his

missionary years was as prodigious as it was to remain for the rest of his
life. (17) The course of events in 1906, therefore, through which he found
himself a champion of Indian interests and moved quickly to exploit the
opening that this presented, created a remarkable breakthrough to the
literary career which, a year or so earlier, had been no more than an idea.
As a career, it was not without its early problems. An observation of
Allnutt's in February 1907 suggests a measure of irritation at a missionary
exercise that did not fit into the usual Delhi pattern.

> Andrews is quite an uncertain member of the staff,
> and in point of fact destined himself for literary
> work.

The situation seems never to have been resolved wholly satisfactorily. Two
years after Allnutt's comment, the observation of a visitor from England
was passed on to the Secretary of S.P.G., Bishop Montgomery, by B.K.
Cunningham.

> Andrews should be relieved of his College work ...
> because of the position he has won for himself in
> India. He has entry to the Indian Press.

In the following year, Rudra was calling for an additional permanent member
of the college staff, 'to permit Mr Andrews to devote more of his energies
to literary ... work'. (18) The surprising thing was the energy Andrews
was able to find for this work while still teaching at St Stephen's.

Inevitably, such an output had its dangers. To be made as welcome as he
was by the Indian press tempted him into writing too much, and there are
signs of a tendency to give utterance on every conceivable occasion and
every conceivable topic. (19) The overall impression of these early
writings is of freshness and vigour, but the prolixity and wooliness, with
a tendency to lapse stylistically into something like the complacent
authoritativeness of the Victorian sage with the confident certainty that
everything he said would be well received, which was to spoil some of his
later work, is already something that it is possible to envisage. (20)

Many missionaries, of course, wrote and published a good deal as part of
their work. In an earlier generation, John Murdoch, with immense industry,
had written and published scores of tracts, establishing his own system of
distribution. Another contemporary approach was that of J.N. Farquhar,
whose work appeared in the form of books and tracts, or in the relatively
enclosed world of Christian journals, and only very occasionally in the
established Indian press. (21) Another was that of the Oxford Mission with
their Epiphany, and Macnicol and Robertson with the Indian Interpreter, two
slightly different, and in their way successful attempts to penetrate the
mission field of the educated classes. What distinguished Andrews'
approach, at least in its most impressive and distinctive aspect, is what
might be called an 'incarnational' approach, whereby he worked in and
through the existing and accepted secular channels created by the educated
classes themselves.

There can be no doubt that he saw his literary venture, especially with
regard to the 'educated native Community', as essentially a missionary
enterprise. Certainly, writing for that particular readership, he used its
own language. Thus, in the Tribune, he called for 'every energy of the
Press, the pen', to advance social reform, insisting that public opinion
had to be instructed, the whole attitude of society changed. The entire
employment of the press, 'probably ... the greatest formative power in
India today', was to accomplish the 'making of India'. (22) Indeed,
Andrews subsequently went so far as to suggest that 'the intellectual
thought about the National movement ... grew in some measure' from his own
writings in this period. (23) Writing, however, for a Christian audience,
he called his literary work 'a true Christian opportunity', an attempt,
'outside the Christian fold, in the great mission field of the
non-Christian world ... to reach and influence the centres of thought and
movement in the East', and 'to keep the Christian ideal before the minds of
educated men'. (24) The content and significance of this venture, we must
now proceed to consider.

95

NOTES: Chapter Three

2. 'The iron of India's subjection'

1 DMN Oct 1904
2 DMN Jan 1906
3 Darling 1966, p. 38; Mudford 1974, p. 215
4 Andrews' footnote to his poem 'Nicholson', Andrews 1916
5 Tribune 11 Apr 1906; DMN Jan 1907
6 DMN Jul 1907, also published as a pamphlet (SPG, n.d.)
7 Ibbetson to Minto, 23 Mar 1907 (Minto - NLS)
8 Punjabee 2 June 1906 (PNNR - IOL & R)
9 Andrews proposed that his earnings at Sanawar should go towards salary increases for two Hindu members of the College staff - Andrews to Allnutt, 10 May 1906 (CMD)
10 Allnutt CC 1907, Biog pp. 83-4
11 Andrews' Report 29 Sept 1906 (SPG)
12 Biog pp. 81, 84. This was not Rudra's only experience of this sort. His daughter 'was not allowed to go to our Diocesan Hill School, because she was not a Eurasian, but an Indian Christian, and she was obliged, therefore, to go the Roman Catholic Convent, which does not make such distinctions' Andrews to Montgomery, 24 Jan 1912 (SPG)

3. 'A Noble Englishman to the Rescue'

1 Quoted in Tribune 29 Aug 1907, 12 Nov 1907. Barrier (thesis) shows that the C&MG had previously been in complicity with the Punjab Government, intentionally intensifying Hindu-Muslim disagreements in order to keep the latter out of the Congress (p. 52).
2 The irrationality of the proposal is clear when it is recognised that a quarter of a century previously, in 1881, there were already some 1500 Punjabis in government employment at salaries above the proposed ceiling, Barrier (thesis) Appendix B.
3 MR Aug 1908: Tribune 1 Aug 1907

4 SM Dec 1906

5 Signed 'An Englishman', C&MG 4 Sept 1906

6 C&MG 16, 19 Sep 1906

7 C&MG 2, 3, 4, 5, 12 Oct 1906 - this last, from a missionary,
   J.L. Pennell, supported Andrews' position.

8 Rai 1908, p.. 237-8

9 Tribune 29 Nov 1906; Mary, Countess of Minto 1935, p. 123
   Parliamentary Debates 1907, 1228 (11 Mar 1907)

10 Biog pp. 84-5

11 Tribune 23 Sept 1906, 22 Jan 1907, 14 Sep 1906, 14 Sep 1906

4. 'The worthy Bishop'

1 Lefroy's charge to the Diocese of Lahore, 6 Nov 1906. The full
   text was printed in the Tribune 11, 12, 13 Dec 1906.

2 CT 13 May 1904

3 DMN Jan 1907

4 Lefroy sent Morley a copy of his charge, and received a highly
   appreciative reply, Montgomery 1920, p. 189. The Tribune
   continued to acclaim him as 'a true friend and sincere well-
   wisher of ours' (15 Jan 1910), and to attribute to him 'Christian
   charity and benignity' (18 Feb 1913).

5 Montgomery 1920, pp. 189-90, 91; Barrier (thesis) p. 283

6 Minto to Lefroy, 15 July 1907 (Lefroy's reply, 17 Jul 1907)
   (Minto - NLS)

7 Quoted in Tribune 25, 29, 30 August 1907

8 Montgomery 1920, pp. 174-5

9 CT 29 May 1908

10 Pan-Anglican Congress 1908, Vol V, Sect D, and Preparatory
   Paper for Commission 1 (WMC)

11 Ellison and Walpole 1908, pp. 67-69

12 Montgomery 1920, p. 175

13 Preparatory Paper for Commission 1 (WMC)

14 Preparatory Paper for Commission 1 (WMC); Lefroy to Montgomery,
   22 Feb 1906 (SPG); Lefroy to Montgomery, 1 Dec 1913 (CMD)

15 Montgomery 1920, p. 131

16 Andrews to Tagore, 12 Dec 1912 (Santiniketan)

17 Mary, Countess of Minto 1935, p. 407

18 Tribune 2 Jun 1908; the other three on the original list of five
    were E. Greaves of Benares (London Missionary Society), R.A. Hume
    of Ahmedabad (American Board of Missions) and William Miller,
    former Principal of Madras Christian College (United Free Church
    of Scotland); Allnutt's name was added to the list in Tribune
    16 Jul 1908

5. 'Indian Nationality'

1 Spear 1965, pp. 174-6, 7

2 G. Johnson in Gallagher etc. 1973, p. 267

3 Andrews' fourth point is more finely balanced as between
   'moderates' and 'extremists' than might appear, in that social
   and industrial development, usually a 'moderate' theme, was
   strongly emphasised by the Punjab 'extremists' - Barrier (thesis)
   pp. 103-7, 111, 123.

4 In a letter to the Oxford Mission's Epiphany just a few days
   earlier, on 6 Oct 1906, he had introduced the pronoun more
   carefully, 'our nation - I use that pronoun "our" of the land of
   my adoption'.

5 CC 1907

6 SM Oct 1906

7 Hayes 1909, p. 123. There are notes on the retreat (pp. 124-5).
   Based on the Book of Revelation, Andrews touched in parallels
   between the Indian Church, 'so tiny, insignificant', pressed down
   by 'great world powers of darkness, ... idolatry more active,
   feverish than ever', and the Church at the close of the first
   century; he depicts this latter oppressed by 'the great world-
   power of Rome, a mighty engine of precision', but the parallels,
   at least in these notes, are very lightly suggested.

8 Bengalee 28 Dec 1906

9 Tribune 13 Nov 1906. Harkishen Lal was a trustee of the
   Tribune, leader of the Brahmo faction in the Lahore Indian
   Association, a banker and industrialist - Barrier (thesis)

pp. 55-6, 80, 93

10 C.A. Bayly in Gallagher etc. 1973, p. 31; Sitaramayya 1935, p. 169

11 Tribune 25 Dec 1906

12 Lahore lecture: Tribune 13 Nov 1906; Delhi lecture: Tribune 16 Dec 1906; Allahabad lectures: Tribune 25 Dec 1906 and 25 Jan 1907, and HR Jan 1907 (this seems to have been a specially commissioned version; it was reproduced in full in Tribune 22 Feb 1907, and 'published and very widely circulated in the form of a pamphlet' Biog p. 85); Calcutta lecture: Bengalee 28 Dec 1906

13 Tribune 13 Nov 1906; 25 Jan 1907; HR Jan 1907. Cf. 'Even when criticizing the British, the Tribune generally defended the proposition that the rulers had the interests of India at heart' Barrier (thesis) p. 126.

14 HR Jan 1907. This was Gokhale's line at the 1905 Congress, 'a self-governing colony in the Empire'.

15 Tribune 25 Dec 1906

16 Biog p. 85

17 HR Apr 1907

18 Andrews to Tagore, 11 Feb 1914 (Santiniketan)

19 Tribune 16 Dec 1906; 25 Jan 1907; 25 Dec 1906

20 Tribune 25 Jan 1907; 13 Nov 1906

21 A fellow-missionary wrote of his 'remarkable ease of diction' DMN Jan 1912; cf. a colleague at St Stephen's: 'he gave a talk to the College about some, probably Government injustice and he put the case so eloquently that I said to myself that were I an Indian I would want to knife the first Englishman I saw!' P.N.F. Young to D. O'Connor 7 May 1974

22 Bengalee 28 Dec 1906 indicates that he had met Bannerjee before the Congress.

23 After sending no delegates in 1902, the number rose to 28 in 1904, and by 1906, when 'Punjabi politicians had moved from disillusionment with the Congress and political apathy to partnership in the Congress and militant agitation', there were 138 delegates - Barrier (thesis) p. 111.

24 For a description of his first visit to Calcutta, NI p. 98. A
   few days after the Congress, Brown, at the annual meeting of the
   Mission, expressed warm sympathy with Indian 'strivings after
   political freedom', and called on the Church to take 'a firm
   stand against racial antipathy' - 'A Notable Pronouncement'
   Tribune 15 Jan 1907.

25 Andrews and Mookherjee 1938, p. 211; HR Jan 1907

26 Quoted in Gallagher etc. 1973, p. 267

27 Bengalee 28 Dec 1906; Andrews and Mookherjee 1938, p. 211

28 HR Jan 1907

29 Biog pp. 86-7, though he later said that Gokhale 'stood at this
   time between the old and the new' Andrews and Mookherjee 1938,
   p. 184.

30 Andrews to Gokhale, 24 Jan 1907. He repeated the offer in
   Andrews to Gokhale, 24 June 1907 (Gokhale - NAI).

31 Barrier (thesis) p. 314

32 Spear 1965, p. 180. The SSC Mag for Jan 1910 carries the text of
   a speech by S.A.C. Ghose at the Annual Reunion of the College,
   but omitting his usual 'political harangue and tirades'. He has
   'abjured politics ... now that the pains and sacrifices of the
   last three or four years have begun to bear some kind of fruit'.

33 Biog pp. 87-8. In CC 1907, he reported that he had been severely
   criticised, and that Allnutt had asked him to write an occasional
   paper on the subject - which he seems not to have done, unless
   his 'India in Transition' of 1910 was this.

6. 'A true Christian opportunity'

1 Barrier 1974, pp. 9-10.

2 Barrier and Wallace 1970, pp. 42, 57, 104; Stephanian Spring
  1973; Tribune 28 Apr 1914; Sangat Singh 1972, p. 133

3 Barrier and Wallace 1970, p. 149

4 Barrier (thesis) pp. 125-6, 129

5 In the ensuing correspondence on the topic, it was indicated that
  the original proposer intended to name the school 'King
  Edward's', after Andrews' old school in Birmingham - Tribune

5 Dec 1906.

6 Nundy's Christian allegiance was certainly a matter of note in the Punjab. The Tribune's new rival, the Panjabee, on 14 Apr 1906, the day after Nundy's first edition, warned that the Tribune would eventually champion Christianity and end up as a tool of government – Barrier (thesis), p. 150.

7 MacDonald 1910, p. 192

8 Biog p. 116

9 MR carried one article by an Indian Christian (May 1910), and one by another missionary, Andrews' friend, J.S. Hoyland (Jun 1913) during the period. Two much lesser reviews of the period, the Indian World and East and West (Bombay) carried occasional appreciative references to Andrews, but nothing of great significance, e.g. Indian World Dec 1907, Jun 1909, Feb-Mar 1911, East and West Aug 1909.

10 Tribune 20 Feb 1909

11 E.g. the article on 'Indian Nationality'; his 'Christianity and Patriotism', NMI Feb 1910, was circulated as a pamphlet by the Young Liberals' League – MR Sept 1910.

12 Preparatory Paper for Commission 4 (WMC); YMOI Jan 1910; CC 1912

13 'No Englishman has a better right to speak from the Indian point of view, and ... no one has a better knowledge of the Indian national consciousness' Garfield Williams in YMOI May 1909

14 NI pp. 95-6

15 SM Jun 1913. Of his work at building bridges of understanding between British and Indian people, 'no one did more' – Tinker 1976, p. 10.

16 Mary, Countess of Minto 1935, p. 315. Minto's successor, Hardinge, observed that 'if the angel Gabriel came down from heaven, the Anglo-Indian press would see in him a Mephistopheles' Hardinge to Harcourt Butler, 3 Feb 1912 (Hardinge – C.U.L.).

17 His literary output during these years, and excluding the books published in 1908 and 1912, moved to a peak in 1910, for which year we have 42 published items, including 30 major articles.

18 Allnutt to Stanton, 28 Feb 1907 (CMD); B.K. Cunningham to

Montgomery, 27 Feb 1909 (SPG); Rudra <u>CC</u> 1911

19 He felt qualified by 1906 to publish a leaflet, 'Hints to Missionaries' for circulation in Britain through SPG - SPG Standing Committee Minutes, 11 Oct 1906 (leaflet missing).

20 But, for his continuing journalistic power, note Nehru's comments on a 1921 pamphlet, 'This was a brilliant essay ... and it seemed to me not only to make out an unanswerable case for independence, but also to mirror the inmost recesses of our hearts. The deep urge that moved us and our half-formed desires seemed to take clear shape in his simple and earnest language' Nehru 1936, p. 66.

21 Sharpe 1965, p. 368, cites only three articles in the Indian reviews.

22 <u>Tribune</u> 23 Aug 1910; 13 May 1910; <u>SSC Mag</u> Jul 1909

23 <u>Biog</u> p. 110. This 'incarnational' approach did not convince everyone. An Indian writer claimed that it was looked upon as 'barefaced bribery' (<u>Tribune</u> 30 Oct 1909), but this view seems not to have been widely expressed.

24 <u>CC</u> 1909; <u>TEW</u> Oct 1907; <u>YMOI</u> Apr 1911. An English critic complained of some of his articles in <u>MR</u>, with 'never an allusion in them to Christ or the Gospel' (C.R.N. Blakiston <u>CT</u> 12 Dec 1913); the following week, B.K. Cunningham argued that the Indian response to Andrews left no room for doubt that he was held to be 'beyond question and primarily a great Christian' <u>CT</u> 19 Dec 1913.

CHAPTER FOUR
TOWARDS A THEOLOGY OF NATIONAL RENAISSANCE

1. Introductory

The object of the Cambridge Mission, to be a new Alexandria, meant an
engagement with the Indian people in that which most deeply moved and
concerned them. In his first two or three years in India, Andrews had
discovered that from one end of Asia to the other, a vast process of change
was under way, taking in India the form of a national movement, and that
this was the deepest source of thought and feeling amongst those from among
the educated classes whom he met, and with whom he had so quickly
established himself. It was to remain close to the centre of his attention
throughout his time in Delhi.

His first two or three years in India had coincided with an historic stage
in the development of Indian nationalism. After the 'awakening' of 1905-6,
the next really serious development had to wait upon the 1914-18 war and
its effects, and upon Gandhi's rise to power, but the 'surging, heaving
ferment' continued throughout Andrews' missionary decade. Around 1907 and
1908, it was known as 'the Indian Unrest', and in this unrest the Punjab
and Delhi had their own singular part as 'storm centres of the seditious
movement'. (1) Andrews wrote later of 'the wounds of those terrible
years'. (2) Thereafter, the tempo relaxed for a time and in some respects.
In 1909, 'after a long and serious delay', the Indian Councils Act, usually
known as the Morley-Minto reforms, was passed, 'a great step', Andrews
believed, towards representative and responsible government. (3) The royal
visit at the end of 1911 can only have been undertaken on the assumption
that all was serene, or at least under firm control. (4) The respite was,
however, only short-lived, and Gandhi's return to India at the end of
Andrews' missionary decade meant that the national movement would soon move
into a higher gear.

Throughout these years, Andrews continued, to an observer, 'a radical in
politics and an enthusiast by temperament, ... advanced in his ideas',

although he was not again caught up so closely as in 1906 in the more
directly political side of the national movement until the very last year
or so and his visit to South Africa and the beginning of his association
with Gandhi. (5) These were, nevertheless, years of prodigious activity in
his new-found journalistic vocation, as he pursued the opportunities opened
up by the sequence of events in his first two years in India, and sought
'to reach and influence the centres of thought and movement in the East',
and, in so doing, developed what we may call a theology of national
renaissance. (6)

2. 'Imperialism and its ethics'

If there existed in Anglican circles any sort of theological interpretation
of the situation in India at the beginning of Andrews' missionary decade,
it could be summed up in what he himself later called 'a Church and Empire
creed'. (1) This is hardly surprising, bearing in mind both the special
character of 'the Church of England in India' as an Ecclesiastical
Establishment closely tied to the Government of India, and also the fact
that the British empire, extending over more than one-fourth of the globe,
and in direct influence over nearly one-third of the people of the world,
was still expanding and reached its greatest extent only in the 1920's.
The fact of British rule had long attracted theological appraisal by
Anglicans. In the late nineteenth century, the views of Westcott on
'Imperial duty' became for many the classic Christian version of liberal
imperialism. These views continued to find expression in church circles
during Andrews' missionary years, for example, in the symposium, Church and
Empire, published in preparation for the Pan-Anglican Congress of 1908
(itself described as 'the "Imperial Conference" of the Church'). (2) The
book's subtitle, 'Responsibilities of Empire', conveys broadly the attitude
of the contributors.

At the same time, these years also witnessed, in the judgement of Lefroy,
'the spread ... amongst Englishmen of thoughts and phrases connected with
the Empire and Imperialism' which filled him with the utmost apprehension
for their revelation of 'low and selfish purposes'. (3) Accompanying these
was a view among Christians which was more than complacent about the fact

of empire, and which spoke of 'imperial Christianity', and of the Church's
role as to 'sanctify the spirit of Imperialism'. (4)   In the <u>Church and
Empire</u> essays, this view is represented in the claim that the British
empire was 'internal to Christianity', 'an expression of the Christianity
which the Church has to guard'. (5)   A contemporary Liberal critic, J.A.
Hobson, accused the Church of 'mystification', saying that language of this
kind enabled imperialism to escape general recognition for 'the narrow and
sordid thing' that it was. (6)   Such criticism, however, found no echoes at
the Pan-Anglican Congress.

Where did Andrews, who was later to be identified as one of a very small
band of 'atheists of empire', stand with regard to the empire during these
years? (7)   We can begin to answer this question by looking at his
treatment of the commonplace idea of the providential nature of British
rule. We have seen how Lefroy acknowledged, if with substantial
qualifications, the place of the British empire within the divine
providence: he yielded to none in recognising 'the vast benefits that on
the whole, in the Providence of God', had accrued to India from her
connection with 'England'. (8)   Allnutt, no more complacent than Lefroy,
took a similar line, acclaiming the imperial beneficence 'the most unique
and noble spectacle the world has ever seen, ... a Christ-like enterprise'
upon which, he was sure, 'the divine blessing must rest'. (9)   This sort of
view continued to be reiterated throughout the period, even by moderate
Indian nationalists, such as the President of the 1911 Congress, Bishan
Narayan Dar, for whom British rule was 'still the greatest gift of
Providence to my race'. (10)

Andrews seems to have been reticent and cautious in this matter. In a
paper on 'Missionary Service', written in 1911, he makes use of the analogy
of the Roman empire, pointing out how St Paul 'used quite fearlessly in
laying down the lines of advance ... its organisation, its great roads of
commerce, its imperial functions and authorities, its language and
literature', but he calls these 'world forces', and justifies Paul's use of
them by saying that 'All belong by right to Christ, and all may be made a
part of the great citizenship of the Church, for all are Christ's, and
Christ is God's'. This view is more reserved than that of the

'Providentialists', suggesting a concern to define rather cautiously the
way in which the British empire might be viewed as a gift of God, that is,
only as an opportunity for Christian mission. The same qualified approach
is evident in his sermon, 'Imperial Responsibilities', preached at
Cambridge the following year. Elsewhere, he appears to have referred only
once to the empire's being 'committed to us for direction', but this is so
isolated a reference as to be quite untypical, and its tone, even so, is
much more restrained than that of Lefroy, with his reference to 'the
splendour of the position to which ... the British Empire has been called
in the world'. (11)

In spite of this evident unwillingness to justify the British empire
theologically, Andrews clearly had in many respects at this time a very
positive attitude towards it. This comes out particularly in reflections
which he shared with his Indian readers. Thus, his view of the history of
the British period in India – and he frequently alluded to the question 'as
a student of history' – was that it had followed upon a situation in which,
'to a people sunk in anarchy and disorder, ... reform from within had
become impossible', so that 'the needs of peace and settlement and strong
central control were primary'. If the process had begun with the
'intolerable commercial rapacity ... and corruption of the East India
Company', nineteenth-century India had witnessed, with many lapses, 'a slow
but steady advance in just and tolerable government'.

Particularly when addressing this Indian readership, he expressed a marked
satisfaction with the way things had developed. He pointed out that there
had been built up 'the outward fabric of a new civilization, ... framed and
elaborated with all the talent that intellect could command'. The British,
moved by the 'great ideals of the great Victorians – men such as Canning
and Lawrence, Edwards and Outram, our great and good Queen Victoria', were
'tolerant conquerors', imposing a 'mild subjection' as the necessary price
for slow but steady advance. He did not, however, envisage this advance,
even when it led to 'the fullest expansion of nationality', as ever being
incompatible with loyalty to the British crown. (12) Indeed, he was
remembered by one of his students at this time as 'a staunch believer in
British rule', and this would certainly appear to be the view which he

intended to convey to Indian people during most of this period. (13)

Andrews subsequently recalled that it was about 1909 that he became inescapably aware of a contrast between 'the free life of a nation ... and the sham life of an Empire', but this is certainly not reflected unambiguously in his writing. (14) The occasion of the royal visit to India in the winter of 1911-12 furnishes an instructive illustration of his attitude. The main public event of the visit, at which important policy decisions were announced - regarding the reunification of Bengal and the transfer of the capital from Calcutta to Delhi - was the durbar which was held in Delhi. St Stephen's College was involved in a small way, with the playing fields taken over for a visitors' camp, and the students employed as stewards. To one former student whom Andrews knew well, Har Dayal, the event disclosed nothing more clearly than 'the sham life of an Empire'. To him, these were 'dark days of shame', concerned quite specifically with the fostering of an illusion:

> The jaded King of England was trotted out to Delhi
> ... to impress the grandeur of the 'Empire' on the
> minds of the assembled hosts of Hindustan. (15)

Har Dayal was certainly correct in seeing the transfer of the capital as 'the final culmination of the empire-building process in India' for that was precisely what it had represented to the man who had first put the idea to the Viceroy, and he too had spoken in terms of appearances, of 'the outward and visible sign that the British Raj' was there '(humanly speaking) for ever'. (16) Others at St Stephen's College saw things very differently from Har Dayal. The royal visit made them, one student wrote, 'the happiest and noblest of men'. (17) Certainly, there is nothing to suggest that Andrews' colleagues were among those, who, after the King and Queen had left the durbar, 'made obeisance to the thrones', although to Rudra the durbar was an occasion to offer 'homage and love', and it deepened Raghubar Dayal's 'love to the British Throne'. (18) Andrews shared this enthusiasm, and, while his mind was also on the practical implications for mission strategy of the transfer of the capital, he saw the presence of the King and Queen as 'the triumph of goodness and

simplicity and love', doing much to dispel the bitterness and resentment
among educated Indians which lay behind the 'Indian Unrest'. He was even
moved to write an article for Indian readers on the royal visit as
exemplifying the virtue of imperial duty. (19) The contrast in his mind
between the free life of a nation and the sham life of an empire is, then,
far from evident in his writing about the royal visit.

If Andrews developed any sort of critique of the empire as such at this
time, it was with regard to the economic base. This he addressed to an
audience in Britain, through a paper, submitted for consideration at the
Pan-Anglican Congress, on 'India and England: Some Moral Aspects of the
Economic Relation'. (20) It is, in some respects, surprising, in view of
his own earlier work in Britain on the conflict between capital and labour,
and in view also of the acknowledged influence of Rudra who was an economic
historian, that he did not make more in his writing of the fundamental
economic structure of the imperial system. This one essay was,
nevertheless, very notable. With extensive quotation from the Indian
'economic nationalists', Naoroji, Ranade, Dutt and Gokhale, he deals with
the 'moral aspects' of the economic relationship in four ways. (21) He
deals with 'English predominance' as deterring Indian initiative and so
forcing 'a steady contraction of innate powers', the 'drain' of wealth from
India to Britain, tariffs such as the Cotton Excise Duty, and the system of
land revenues, and he finds them, respectively, 'evil', 'unjust',
'iniquitous' and creative of 'immense ... possibilities of human
suffering'. He concludes by drawing attention to 'a new school of Indian
economists, sometimes called by the name of "Extremists"', with their chief
doctrine summed up in the word 'Boycott'. Andrews is cautious in his
judgement of this movement, but concludes with a speculation that the
Swadeshi movement as a whole may prove in certain directions 'the economic
salvation' of India. The entire exercise was an extremely radical
departure, not least when seen alongside the otherwise absolute complacency
of the Pan-Anglican Congress with regard to the economic basis of the
empire. (22)

How are we to interpret the co-existence of this criticism, for a British
audience, of economic imperialism, with Andrews' positive assessment of

British rule for an Indian readership? One way is by saying that he seems
to have seen his role at this time – as indeed he did throughout the rest
of his life – as to build bridges of understanding between Britain and
India, and so to promote the slow evolution of the latter within the
empire. We see him pursuing such an aim quite explicitly in 1908 in a
correspondence with the Viceroy's Private Secretary, Dunlop Smith. Andrews
wrote to Dunlop Smith thrice at this time, as one 'in a peculiarly
favourable position to hear daily from the inside what the Moderates ...
(were) saying'. He was concerned to 'stiffen the backs of the Moderates
against the Extremists', and, to this end, urged upon the Viceroy both the
principle of consultation, and the notion of 'a really warm and kind-
hearted pronouncement of sympathy', which would 'make them patient and
cheerful'. (23) A similar interpretation can be placed upon his
correspondence with the succeeding Viceroy, Lord Hardinge, in 1913, with
regard both to the role of the Arya Samaj and also to the plight of Indians
in South Africa. Andrews was, then, by no means a revolutionary in his
attitude to the empire during most of his missionary decade, any more than
were most of the Indian nationalists, and in some respects, like them, he
was a vigorous collaborator. In this respect, a visitor from England at
the time made an interesting observation.

> Men who were inclined to criticize British methods
> always ended up by saying that Englishmen of Mr.
> Andrews' type were doing more to bring about a
> true and deep Imperialism, founded upon trust
> and affection, than people in England usually
> understood. (24)

Certainly, he himself said that 'an imperialism which proceeds through
conquest and protection, to uplift to a level of equality either backward
or decaying nations' could be wholly Christian in its 'spirit and purpose',
though he nowhere identifies this theoretical imperialism with British
practice in India, and several times, speaking of 'imperialism and its
ethics', he said that it was essential to work out 'the whole question of
... "empire" ... de novo from the Christian standpoint'. (25)

Another way of interpreting Andrews' ambivalence, however, is to say that
his critique of empire was only developing gradually and unevenly – that in
some ways during this period he continued to voice the Westcottian ideals
of liberal imperialism, though never with any enthusiastic affirmation of a
'Church and Empire creed', while in others he began to be attracted by the
sharper criticism of the 'Extremists'. This perspective makes room for a
marked shift in the balance of his views from about 1912.

He had often quoted a remark of J.R. Seeley's in The Expansion of England
to the effect that 'subjection for a long time to a foreign yoke is one of
the most potent causes of national deterioration'. (26) At the end of
1912, he alluded to this idea in a letter to Tagore:

> My thoughts turn more and more to a longing for an
> India that shall be altogether independent, and yet
> one knows this can hardly be at present. Only how to
> get out of the vicious circle of subjection leading
> to demoralisation (both of rulers and ruled) and
> demoralisation leading to further subjection – that
> is the eternal problem! (27)

In discussions with Gokhale in March 1914, he came to the conclusion that
this process had to be halted, and that 'it was no use working round and
round in a vicious circle – producing semi-independent Indians through
entering the Government system and so perpetuating the present dependent
system'. While he agreed that India was 'not ripe' for political
independence, nevertheless, unlike Gokhale, he had reached the conviction
that 'Indians who were patriots' needed to work 'outside the present
system', because only outside it could 'independent character' be formed,
and only this independent character could be 'the ultimate emancipator of
India'. (28) Behind these convictions lay Andrews' experience of working
with an Indian of just such independent character, Gandhi, in South Africa
in January and February 1914, though the convictions were decidedly
Andrews' own. They did not amount to anything like the repudiation of the
imperial relationship that he was to make by about 1920-1, and which Gandhi
himself only came to in 1929, but they mark the direction of his changing

ideas unmistakably. (29)

If a 'Church and Empire creed' had ever made any sense to Andrews, it had
ceased to do so before the end of his missionary decade, and any
theologizing on what was going on in India would have to have, for him, a
quite different starting point. Before we turn to Andrews' thinking about
Indian nationalism, however, there is one aspect of the imperial phenomenon
that troubled him more than all the others, racialism, and to this we must
first turn.

3. 'The Ethics of Race'

We have seen how racial feeling was an acute and increasingly bitter
problem in India in the early years of the century, accentuated no doubt by
the growing self-awareness of the educated classes. For Andrews, the
question of race was, though distinct, closely associated with the question
of 'imperialism and its ethics', and he sometimes referred to 'the ethics
of "race" and the ethics of "empire"' together. (1) Although sympathy for
Indian friends like Rudra lay behind his concern, he was also responding to
a great deal of public evidence of a 'rapidly developing colour prejudice'
at the time, to the 'bad, wicked race dominance, ... the perpetual social
insolence of the military Anglo-Indian' which he saw embodied in the
Commander-in-Chief, Kitchener, attitudes which were indeed recognised by
both the Viceroy and the Secretary of State as 'one of the potent causes of
the Indian unrest'. (2) The 'race-problem' would be, Andrews claimed, 'the
most serious difficulty for the church of the twentieth century to meet and
overcome'. (3)

In every aspect of the question 'an ultimate moral principle' was involved
and a Christian attitude needed, and there was required of the Church's
leaders and thinkers 'something of the same kind of work' which had been
undertaken of late with regard to 'the home social problem'. Andrews
suggested, therefore, that 'the work of raising the Christian standard with
regard to the treatment of races' required 'a Christian literature of its
own'. (4) His own writings in this field, addressed largely to a
readership among the 'dominant race', represent a pioneering effort in

this matter, a uniquely early effort to initiate such a Christian literature. (5)

In his earliest writing on the subject, Andrews suggested cautiously that the Christian commentator should not enter into details but simply define and boldly declare principles. Soon, however, so critical did he judge the matter to be, he was advocating 'a careful analysis ... of concrete modern instances' where the problem was acute. (6) His own most elaborate analysis of what he called 'the Sahib spirit' occurs in his North India of 1908, which Lefroy called 'quite the ablest and best ... statement ... I have seen anywhere'. (7) With vivid illustration from his own Punjab experience, he examines 'the position of a "Sahib", with all the dominance which that name implies', treating systematically of the 'sahib' as '(i) a foreigner, (ii) influential, (iii) overbearing, (iv) patronizing'. He did not confine his concern to the Punjab, or even to India, but drew attention, as indeed did 'thoughtful Hindus' to 'colour prejudice ... gathering ... alarming volume in Africa, Australia, America, and even in Europe itself'. (8)

Andrews was clearly aware of the theorizing on race that had gone on in the nineteenth century. His own opinion on aspects of it was most elaborately expressed in his WSCF paper of 1911.

> The early theory of the nineteenth century
> nationalists, that 'race' and 'state' must always
> exactly correspond, is contrary to the Christian idea
> of liberty and progress. There are no 'natural
> rights', with a divine sanction, by which races may
> claim to remain always separate. The fallacy is of
> the same kind as that which Rousseau propounded
> concerning the 'natural rights' of individuals.
> Humanity is an organism in which both individuals and
> races are closely and intimately inter-connected.
> It is also a growing organism, which does not look
> back to the past for its ideals, but looks forward to
> the future. The 'noble savage' is no more an ideal

> for humanity than the pure, unadulterated race. The
> theory of the 'natural rights' of races, if carried
> to its extreme form, would justify the stratification
> of caste, which was racial in origin. The argument
> on which it is based becomes, from the Christian
> standpoint, a <u>reductio ad absurdum</u>, a contradiction
> of all the Christian postulates. Indeed, the
> Christian argument works entirely in the opposite
> direction. It involves racial contact and
> intermingling, leading on to a brotherhood of
> Christian nations, leading on to a commonwealth of
> man.

Here are several of the 'Christian postulates' which he made so much of
during these years, the 'Christian idea of liberty' and of 'progress', and,
more importantly, his notion of human solidarity, of humanity as an
'organism'.

Andrews worked out the 'Christian argument' in several places. His fullest
treatment of it was in his address on 'Racial Unity', given at the YMCA
Triennial Convention at Calcutta in 1907. (9) This is largely a reading of
St Paul, who, starting as 'a Pharisee of the Pharisees, prouder than the
proudest Brahmin of his religious position, more keen than the keenest
Englishman on his race superiority', became 'the great unifier of races',
for whom 'the mystery of racial unity in Christ' was the 'great life-
principle', its fulfilment 'the object of his apostolate'. Andrews'
procedure is to trace through the Epistles the course of 'the great
struggle', and the arguments deployed in securing the recognition of Jew
and Greek as 'fellow-heirs, fellow-citizens, of the same Body'. He was
conscious that his approach might seem an eccentric reading, and, in the
course of anticipating that criticism, he reviewed some of the main points
of his argument, and went on to place the issue in a wider context.

> Was it simply a question of racial unity on which St
> Paul was ready to stake, as it were, the whole
> Christian position? Yes, in a sense, it was all; for

in that one principle, Christianity did really stand
or fall ... to admit privilege was to deny that one
foundation, 'Christ crucified'; to give up the one
ground of acceptance, 'By grace ye are saved'. Yes,
in a sense, when Jew and Greek partook of the one
Bread and shared the one Cup, and gave each to each
the kiss of Peace, it was all, the mystery was
revealed; for all the marvellous and glorious future
of Christianity was included, was foreshadowed in
that one act. Yet in another and wider sense it was
not all, but was only the beginning. It was to St
Paul a pledge and foretaste of a unity which should
never cease developing, until in wider and wider
circles all were 'one Man in Christ'; until the many
races of mankind became one humanity.

The application of this to contemporary India, to the relationship between
'the proud Englishman and the sensitive Indian', Andrews did not find
difficult, although he limited the full expression of racial unity to those
who shared the Christian faith, who, as Christ's body, 'redeemed and
unified humanity', were 'the nucleus of that Unity'. We shall look later
at Andrews' treatment of this aspect of the question.

In this early paper, Andrews makes a point that is to recur hereafter, that
the racial division in India was not only between Indians and Europeans, but
also within Indian society, itself 'divided into a thousand separate
communities'. The caste system was itself a sacralizing of racial
dominance, and as such a warning as to how racial injustice can be given
almost permanent form, with a history 'written over the whole of India in
letters of untold suffering and hopeless misery', and lying still 'like an
incubus in the land'.

What was most crucially at stake, however, was the implication for mission
of the racial question as raised by the conduct of British people in India,
and of 'the white Governments'. Because of the identification of British
people with Christianity, this question was 'the most pressing missionary

problem in India', as he stated in virtually every publication with a
British readership to which he had access. He conceded that a debate such
as that which Farquhar had initiated in the Contemporary Review on the
divinity of Christ and its challenge to the position of 'the Hindu
enlightenment' was deeply interesting, but insisted that it paled into
insignificance beside 'the glaring contradiction between Christian theory
and public practice' in the matter of race. Younger Indians saw
Christianity going 'hand in hand with acts of oppression and cruelty to the
coloured races of mankind', and acts of this kind practically filled the
picture. (10)

> Men may go on for ever arguing about the comparative
> value of the Vedantist or Christian conception of the
> universe. I do not wish to minimize the importance
> of such philosophic speculations .... But the bulk
> of thinking, struggling, feeling, sensitive men and
> women, who have their own difficult, practical
> problems to face day by day, will look, and rightly
> look, not to philosophy but life. If the moral
> supremacy of the Christian faith is constantly
> lowered in their eyes by what they see around them in
> practical Christian conduct, then all the philosophic
> argument in the world will not convince them that
> Christianity is the One True Religion for the whole
> human race. (11)

It was time for 'Missionary Statesmen, those who try to gauge the real
situation', to take cognizance of this fact. (12)

In this cause, Andrews persistently gathered and presented evidence of 'the
real situation', pointing out, for example, how in a single week in 1908 he
had counted in the Indian press as many as twelve allusions to the failure
of Christian public morality, the failure in racial relations. However
impressive the exceptions, his assessment was that the 'prevailing'
Anglo-Indian spirit of domination was shared by 'the bulk of the English
laity'. (13) To illustrate the effect of this, he quoted at length, on

several occasions, a Hindu writer in the journal <u>Indian World</u>, pointing out
that the sting of the quotation lay in the repetition of the word
'Christian'.

> What can we think of the Christian missionary who
> never cares to raise his voice against the failure of
> Christian justice, against Christian tyranny, against
> Christian high-handedness and repression? When we
> study the heartless, and sometimes shameless, way in
> which independent states and people are brought under
> subjection by Christian nations; when we glance at
> the treatment accorded to coloured people all over
> the world, and, above all, when we consider the
> supreme contempt with which all subject peoples are
> looked upon by their Christian conquerors, we not
> only begin to lose faith in Christian civilization,
> but we almost begin to have a lurking antipathy
> against Christianity itself. (14)

This particular aspect of British rule in India, then, undermined the
Christian mission in a very damaging way.

The Bishop of Madras, preaching before the king at the Delhi Durbar in
1911, affirmed that the permanent value of any empire lay in 'its power of
making real and effective in the world the ideal of brotherhood'. (15)
Andrews had seen enough of 'another imperialism' which implied 'the
perpetual subjection of one race to another', to convince him that the
situation in India was 'wholly contrary to the Christian ideal', and dealt
'a deadly wound at the humanity which Christ came to save'. While he
continued to acknowledge the necessity of empire as such throughout these
years, it is clear that the racial factor, because it offended against
Christianity's 'central doctrine' of 'the unity of mankind in Christ', and
so undermined the Church's mission in a very fundamental way, was
particularly important to Andrews. (16)

4. 'The great giver of emancipation'

Imperialism and racialism represented, for Andrews, a very serious obstacle
to mission. The emerging national movement, on the other hand, presented
only 'problems', though indeed 'a whole new series of problems'. Prominent
among these was how far nationalism could be welcomed 'without trenching
upon spheres which ... (were) purely political'. That it was to be
welcomed, and 'bought up' by the missionary, he had no doubt. (1)

The need for a Christian witness within the intellectual processes of the
national movement was expressed at this time by a young Indian Christian,
N.C. Mukerji, in an article in the Indian Interpreter.

> What we need is a body of teaching which would do for
> our nationalist movement what Christian Socialism has
> done for the Labour Movement in England, and thus
> harness it to the service of Christianity instead of
> letting it run amuck. (2)

Andrews' own background, 'Christian Socialism ... in England', was not a
bad qualification for this task. Certainly, it was precisely in these
terms that an English visitor to St Stephen's College saw his work.

> It has been encouraging ... to observe in him and his
> colleagues how universal in their range are the
> principles of the Christian Social Union as formed in
> England. In India, perhaps even more than in
> England, the Religion of the Incarnation has to
> justify itself in its social aspects and by its
> practical bearing upon the reorganization and
> reconstruction of human society. (3)

In a wide-ranging series of articles during these years, Andrews provided,
almost single-handed, the 'body of teaching' for which Mukerjii was
calling.

He seems to have first become aware that the movement was far more than a
'purely political' phenomenon when he saw 'the varied forces of national
life' embodied in the 'social, temperance, industrial and religious
conferences gathered round the Calcutta Congress', and he was soon
questioning whether the movement was 'even mainly "political"', these
aspects of the movement, 'simple, wholesome reform' having 'the element of
permanency which is lacking in party politics'. (4) In his preference at
this time for 'simple, wholesome reform' over 'heroics or revolutionary
measures', Andrews was identifying with the line of the 'moderate'
nationalists, with what has subsequently been described as 'liberal
nationalism', a tradition shaped significantly in the late nineteenth
century by M.G. Ranade, and then embodied in the work of Gokhale, to whom
Andrews had offered his services after the Calcutta Congress. (5) His
writing during these years discloses an interest in many features of this
tradition, and he did much to aid its development, as well as to relate it
to the 'Religion of the Incarnation'. At one time or another, he took the
opportunity of writing or speaking on almost every imaginable aspect of the
'varied forces of national life'.

We have already seen how in his paper for the Pan-Anglican Congress, he
introduced the ideas of the Indian economic nationalists to wider circles.
The debate about the extent of the 'exploitation of Indian resources ...
under the conditions of British supremacy' was one which went on in
Andrews' own circle. Lefroy regarded the idea of 'the drain' of Indian
wealth to Britain as false, and he urged the Viceroy to refute it publicly.
Rudra, on the other hand, taught Andrews that the 'economic drain' upon the
masses was 'steadily increasing'. (6) Andrews soon accepted the latter
position. His concern, however, was with the moral and social effect, and
he shared with Ghose a conviction that the consequence of British supremacy
in this field was a people 'sinking lower and lower in pauperizing
subjection'. It is not surprising, therefore, that he not only supported
the swadeshi movement in general, as other missionaries did, but went well
beyond the liberal position by also supporting the boycott of English
manufactures. (7) Andrews made various practical proposals on the economic
front, but not much relating them to his thinking about the Christian
faith. (8) In some respects, though, he must have accepted, since he wrote

an enthusiastic introduction, Ghose's radical thoughts in the <u>Student Movement</u> on 'subjection for trade purposes'.

> If Christianity is ever to become acceptable to the
> fallen Indian population, it must show its power in
> breaking the chains of the oppressors. (9)

For Ghose, this subjection indicated 'the magnitude and gravity of the problem before the missionary and the Church'. Such terms echo Andrews' own opinions at this time.

Andrews wrote about <u>swadeshi</u> on a number of occasions. While not understating the economic aspect, he set about widening the concept, claiming that 'true Swadeshi is a spirit'. This spirit, in those who had it, made for a 'spiritual purpose, namely the achievement of national self-consciousness', and this involved breaking through 'denationalizing caste prejudices', forsaking 'customs which separate Indian from Indian', uplifting 'the submerged and depressed classes', meeting with and treating one's fellow countrymen 'on equal and brotherly terms'. Presented in these categories, <u>swadeshi</u> was none other than 'the constructive power of love and brotherhood'. The Christian dimensions of this exercise are clear enough, and indeed, Andrews went on to develop the notion in the familiar categories of Westcottian theology, claiming that to promote 'the highest and the best in India for the benefit of mankind' would transform <u>swadeshi</u> into 'a spiritual principle which God himself ... (would) bless, for it ... (would) be in the line of the divine order of the progress of the world'. (10) Significantly, the <u>Tribune</u> identified Andrews' 'all embracing Swadeshi' as 'a new gospel'. Even more significantly, however, and it is a measure of his success in communicating as a missionary with the nationalists, the <u>Tribune</u> did so in a special leading article which welcomed his reflections as certain to make for 'the highest ideal of Indian nationality'. (11)

Important for an all-embracing <u>swadeshi</u> was the question of caste. Andrews occasionally refers to the system in objective terms, commending its scientific study. Occasionally he acknowledges it as 'a living and growing

system', representing to Hindus 'the social side of life and the social
moral code', and with, in the past at least, a 'protective' value. (12)
Usually, however, he is highly critical. His sharpest criticism he
reserved for his readership in Britain, representing it as, in origin, 'the
most imposing experiment in race-aloofness that the world has ever seen',
and pointing out 'the insidious nature of the evil and its blighting
effects', the 'untold suffering and hopeless misery' that it created, 'as
destructive in its moral effect on the higher as it ... (was) degrading on
the lower castes', a system of 'bondage, ... slavery'. (13) Lest this be
dismissed as the prejudiced view of a foreigner, he pointed out that the
evils of the system were being felt 'in educated India' with 'a bitterness
never experienced in earlier times', and he several times quoted Tagore's
assessment of 'the hypnotic hold which this gigantic system of cold-blooded
repression has taken on the minds of our people.' (14) To cap his
criticism for a Christian readership, Andrews pronounced it 'a hopeless
contradiction in practice of the equality and brotherhood of man'. (15)
For his nationalist readers the issue of caste is always stated in the
context of nationalism. Thus, the system is 'a standing weakness to
national unification', its very existence 'de-nationalizing', while, in a
Calcutta journal, he called its 'partitions ... even more disastrous' and
'far more artificial than that of Bengal'. (16)

A closely related area of concern was regarding the outcastes, known in
offical parlance as the Depressed Classes. Andrews expressed from time to
time, mingled with his prayers for 'the unheeded poor ... lifting dumb
hands against the oppressor's wrong', a general concern for 'the awakening
... of the masses'. While he believed that the destiny of the country was
in the hands of the educated classes, he warned that the postponement of
'the education of the masses in the very elements of Nationalism and self-
development' would place 'the most fatal weapon in the hand of those who
would wish to keep India in subjugation'. (17) It is, however, his
particular concern for the most oppressed layers, the Depressed Classes,
which concerns us here. This large sector of Indian society, 'one fifth of
the whole nation', was refused the benefits of education and enlightenment,
and regarded as unclean by the other classes of society. (18) Although the
Christian missions, including the Cambridge Mission, had been working in

this sector for many years, the outcastes were virtually ignored by the
educated classes. (19) Farquhar noted that this began to change around
1903, but in fact the first editorial reference to the 'untouchables' in
the Tribune occurs as late as 1910. (20) Andrews reported to S.P.G. the
following year that the desire to help the outcastes was perhaps the most
significant factor in the increasing momentum of the national movement.(21)
From the beginning, he drew attention to the importance of the Depressed
Classes for the movement, and, although he wrote only one article
specifically on the subject, a short contribution to a nationalist
symposium in 1912, he made frequent allusions to the question in the
nationalist press. Thus, we have seen how his concept of swadeshi
incorporated 'a genuine longing to see the submerged and depressed classes
... upraised'. Here was 'the most vulnerable point in India politics', a
matter so crucial that on it 'the whole future of Indian nationalism'
depended.

> Until Brahmin and Sudra can unite in terms of mutual
> love for their motherland, Indian nationality cannot
> be achieved. (22)

At the end of this period, he had come to see that the liberation of the
Depressed Classes might involve a 'bitter and prolonged ... struggle', and
that this would not necessarily have the support of the 'leisured
classes'. (23) His general position, however, was usually expressed in
terms of a more idealistic unitary view, whereby the Depressed Classes
would find their place in a body politic which he depicted under the
Pauline metaphor of the body.

> It must be shown in practice that ... the depressed
> classes ... are ... members of the Indian nation ...
> (and) that 'where one member suffers, all the members
> suffer with it, and where one member rejoices, all
> the members rejoice with it'. (24)

It is very interesting for our uncovering of Andrews' theology of the
national awakening that he saw Christian involvement in the service of the

Depressed Classes as presenting a challenge to Hindu India because it took place on the basis of 'consciousness of sin and the unutterable love of God's forgiveness'. (25) We will examine this later, and at this point simply note that he insisted on placing the question of the Depressed Classes on the agenda of the national movement.

One of the most striking features of the Calcutta National Congress, for Andrews, had been 'the assembly of Bengali ladies who led the singing of the songs of new Bengal'. (26) In missionary work, belief in the importance of reaching India's women, as a key both to evangelism and to social progress, was a commonplace, and the large number of women from Britain in this work – and there were more women than men among the expatriate staff of the Delhi Mission in our decade – as well as telling us something about Britain's social conditions, underlines the seriousness of this belief. Andrews took note of this, and in a chapter on 'Indian Womanhood' in The Renaissance in India examined the 'remarkable transformation in modern India' which the education of women represented.

In many respects, his picture is conventional enough. What is distinctive, however, both in this chapter and elsewhere, is how he relates this to emergent nationalism. Thus, one of the most important outcomes of the general stir and upheaval of the national movement was that it had 'penetrated the Zenanas'. Thus also he noted the active involvement of women, not only in religious and social reform movements, but also in the passing of resolutions during the 'unrest' at pardah meetings often numbering many hundreds of the most influential women, in Delhi itself and in every city of Upper India. (27) Thus, too, when two of his former students, on going to Oxford, took their wives with them, he applauded their 'patriotism'. (28) The publication of the Minto-Morley reform proposals, omitting any reference to women's suffrage, prompted him in 1909 to look ahead to the time when 'the women of India, educated and enlightened, will pour their own treasures of self-sacrifice and devotion into the common cause of the nation'. (29)

A further issue that Andrews saw as essential to the development of an authentic national movement was that of Hindu-Muslim relations. The formation of the Muslim League in 1906 as a counter to growing Hindu influences marked an important stage in a relationship of growing significance. One of Andrews' closest friends in Delhi, Hakim Ajmal Khan, was a founder-member of the League. (30) As early as 1906, Andrews was saying that at the forthcoming Congress at Calcutta it was imperative that the sympathy of the Muslim community should be retained, because 'the union of the two great communities ... (was) the one final goal of national unity', and because, indeed, without that union there could be no nation. (31) Throughout these years, he continued to draw attention to this question, to appeal for sympathy, and to suggest practical measures to improve the relationship. He applied himself most substantially to the question in 1911, when the mater was at 'an acute stage', in two articles in the <u>Hindustan Review</u>, 'The Evolution of Liberty in Europe', and 'Lord Acton on Nationality'. (32)

> Has the Muhammadan invasion and settlement produced a living organism which may, in the long run, be assimilated, without loss of its own identity, in the greater living organism of India herself, or will the Muhammadan Community always remain an unassimilated factor?

Drawing on Acton's <u>History of Freedom</u>, Andrews' argument was undoubtedly more sophisticated than his usual simple advocacy of unity in the national movement.

> If 'liberty for the realisation of moral duties' is the chief end of politics, then those states are substantially the most advanced which include various distinct nationalities without oppressing them. Those in which no mixture of races has occurred are imperfect, and those in which the effects of mixture have disappeared are decrepit.

The principle could be applied in various ways to the Indian situation, and he dealt with both caste and the Depressed Classes before turning to

criticise Hindu nationalism and to a concluding consideration of the
question of Hindu-Muslim relations as 'the final problem of Indian
nationality, more difficult of solution than all that have gone before.
... History is being made concerning it with amazing rapidity, and .. with
far too little serious thinking'. That Andrews contributed significantly
to the nationalists' thinking on this subject is indicated by the very
positive nation-wide response to his two articles, with appreciative
comments in Indian World, the Tribune, Leader, Madras Standard, Morning
Post of India, Indian Social Reformer, Hindu and Mahratta. (33)

There were further aspects to his wide-ranging interest in the national
movement. He wrote a number of articles on the arts and nationalism,
highlighting in particular 'the delicate tender Eastern painting of
Abanindra, the music and poetry of Rabindranath Tagore', his efforts to
articulate the connection being unique but for the work of the young art
critic, A.K. Coomaraswamy in his Art and Swadeshi. (34) He also wrote a
number of articles on questions of public health, indicating its relevance
for national development, and creating a strikingly original and
progressive alternative argument to that of the social-Darwinists, who were
still at this time considering the necessities of 'an Imperial Race'. (35)
A third aspect was his advocacy of rationality, of acting in 'a scientific
way', in which he identified himself with the line of the moderate
nationalists, the school of Ranade. (36)

During these years, then, Andrews responded positively to many aspects of
the national movement, drawing out the importance for the movement of
'utilizing every material circumstance which makes for progress', and
promoting these with sustained energy. (37) With regard to both the range
and the force of his advocacy, he was quite alone. For all the originality
of their ventures, Macnicol and Robertson, with their Indian Interpreter,
and the Oxford Mission with their Epiphany, the only other significant
missionary enterprises in the field at all, achieved a much more modest
break-through into the world of the educated classes. Amongst all the
reprinting of and reference to articles from one nationalist journal in the
others, there is not a single reference in any of the major journals for
the years 1904 to 1914 to either of these publications, while Andrews

dominates them as no one even among the Indian nationalists did at the time.

Just as he had seen the general strategy of literary work among the educated classes as a missionary venture, so, too, did he regard his advocacy of the particular, diverse strands of the national movement. Thus in concluding a lecture on 'The Spiritual Awakening of the East', which he delivered at the Brahmo Mandir in Lahore in February 1909, he specifically alluded to his vocation in this connection.

> I have spoken of these movements in the East - I, who
> am a Padre, a Christian Missionary, a man whose
> calling is to teach religion - I have done this,
> because I firmly believe that these forces, these
> movements, in their ultimate analysis are spiritual,
> not material, are religious in their bearing, not
> secular. They are forces which will, I believe,
> uplift from apathy and even from degradation millions
> of the human race. As such, they cannot be without
> supreme significance to me in my vocation. I believe
> that now, in this our day, as at the beginning, the
> Spirit of God is moving on the face of the waters -
> the troubled waters of humanity, and is speaking the
> word of power, 'Let there be light', and there shall
> be light.

The Tribune reported this lecture very enthusiastically, calling it 'great and inspiring' and added an illuminating gloss.

> He sees divine providence in all this, he considers
> the awakening as the work of the Spirit of the Lord
> filling the whole Orient. (38)

In at least two other places, addressing a Christian readership, he said the same thing, using not these generalized categories of theism, Spirit and creation, but the more characteristic ones deriving from the synoptics and St John.

> It is possible ... to ... call these national
> movements purely secular; yet I cannot see how this
> can be done by anyone who holds intelligently the
> faith of the Incarnation, and who believes that Jesus
> is the Son of Man. Movements of spirit which are
> taking place in an area including 800,000,000 of the
> human race cannot be without religious significance
> to the believer in Him who is 'the Light that
> lighteneth every man coming into the world'. (39)

He went on from such statements to express the belief that the most potent
source of the new spirit in India was 'the message that centres in the One
Supreme Personality of Christ, ... Christ, the great giver of emancipation
... who has revealed the light of progress to India'. (40)

Here, then, from within the national movement, rather than from the
imperial angle, Andrews was inspired to make Christian sense of what he saw
going on, in a process that was both a disclosure of his own expansive
theology and also an act of witness.

5. 'Furious devotion'

In what is still 'the classic account' of modern religious movements in
India, J.N. Farquhar devoted a chapter, dealing with the years 1895 to
1913, to 'a new nationalism', which he tentatively called 'Religious
Nationalism'. (1) He identified two strands, corresponding more or less to
the positions of the 'extremist' and 'moderate' tendencies in the national
movement, whose emergence Andrews had witnessed at the 1906 meeting of the
Congress.

> Full proof of the depths to which the Indian mind has
> been stirred may be seen in this, that in all the
> best minds, the new feeling and the fresh thought are
> fired by religion, either a furious devotion to some

divinity of hate and blood, or a self-consecration to
God and India which promises to bear good fruit. (2)

We find a response to both strands in Andrews' thinking, to the former a
very negative response, to the latter a very positive.

With regard to the former, 'extremist' Hindu nationalism, there was in fact
a most interesting development beneath, as it were, Andrews' very nose,
that is, among his own colleagues and students in Delhi. Nor was this a
merely local matter, for it involved, in the words of the official
governmental record of the period, 'the two most sinister figures in the
modern history of Indian sedition', one of whom went on to initiate what
was 'by far the most serious attempt to subvert British rule in India'. (3)

The sequence of events in these matters is complicated and somewhat
obscure, but some picture of the sequence, and of the chief protagonists
and their motivation is possible. There were two main but inter-related
phases, one from about 1906 to 1909, an aspect of the 'Indian Unrest', and
a second culminating in the near-fatal bomb attack on the Viceroy in 1912.

The first phase began with the enrolment during 1906-7 of '50 or more' St
Stephen's College students - approximately half the College - into 'a
secret society to spread agitation on Bengali lines'. (4) Prominent
initially was a Muslim, Haidar Raza, 'the new leader of the Delhi public'.
He was a graduate of the College who had returned to teach there
temporarily in 1905, and who subsequently edited a new Delhi newspaper,
Aftab. (5) Haidar Raza's lieutenant was one of Andrews' own students,
Ishwar Das. (6) Haidar Raza attempted to unite Hindus and Muslims in order
that they might 'triumphantly march together hand-in-hand in the paths of
progress and self-government'.

The attempt appears to have been frustrated by the setting of 'the whole
Hindu community against him and Muhammadans in general', a development in
which another of Andrews' students, 'one of the most seditious members of
St Stephen's College', Gobind Bihari Lal, was involved. (7) At this time,
two of Andrews' colleagues, Raghubar Dayal, teacher of Sanskrit in the

College, and Amir Chand, a teacher in the Delhi Mission's school, who was
to be a delegate at the critical Surat meeting of Congress, appear to have
taken an increasing part in the leadership of the group. (8) Certainly,
they were prominent during the following year, 1908, organizing large
public meetings to felicitate Lajpat Rai, the Punjab nationalist, on his
return from a period of deportation, holding protest meetings about
taxation, other speakers including S.A.C. Ghose, Haidar Raza and Behari
Lal, and leading a deputation to the Deputy Commissioner. (9) Not
surprisingly in the atmosphere of the times, the Political Department of
the Government filed a report in June 1908 on the 'Attendance of members of
the educational staff of the Cambridge Missionary Society, Delhi, at
political meetings held in Delhi', and Allnutt, under pressure from the
Punjab Government, persuaded Amir Chand to sever his connection with the
school. (10) S.A.C. Ghose's public abandonment of the political arena on
the announcement of the Minto-Morley reforms, with their promise of
constitutional advance, may be a pointer to at least one reason for the
subsidence of this first phase. (11)

Throughout these years, another graduate of the College, whose name was to
be closely associated with the second phase, was much in evidence in the
reports of the Director of Criminal Intelligence. This was Har Dayal, soon
to win 'legendary popularity as an uncompromising revolutionary
nationalist'. (12) Har Dayal had already graduated from St Stephen's when
Andrews arrived in 1904, and was initially thereafter studying at
Government College, Lahore, where he secured the first First Class M.A. in
English ever awarded in the University. He often returned to Delhi, where
his parents lived, and actually taught at St Stephen's in Rudra's place
when the latter was visiting Britain in 1905. Andrews got to know him, and
when Har Dayal went to Oxford on a government scholarship later that year,
Andrews, by then on sick-leave, visited him there. On his return from
Oxford in 1908, Har Dayal was much in contact with the extremist students
around Amir Chand, whose house had become for them 'a kind of Jacobin
club'. (13) There is no record of further contact with Andrews until
several years later, although there is a story of Rudra's unsuccessful
attempt at this time to dissuade him from his deepening involvement with
extremism. (14) Har Dayal remained in India for only a few months, his

name much associated at this time with that of Lajpat Rai, and then,
branded by the Political Department 'one of the most violent members of
the revolutionary party', he left, to live the remainder of his life in
exile. (15) Andrews saw, in retrospect, the tragedy of this sensitive
young man, 'one of India's noblest children, ... his character true and
pure, ... (who) in happier times would have done wonders with his giant
intellectual powers'. (16)

The second phase of Delhi's extremist politics during these years was
overtly and actually violent, culminating in 1912 in two bomb-throwings, a
fatal one in Lahore, and, in Delhi, a near-fatal attack on the Viceroy,
Lord Hardinge. These led on to the Delhi Conspiracy Trial of 1914, and the
hanging of four men, including Amir Chand and another former student of St
Stephen's College, Awadh Behari. (17) The attempt to inculpate Har Dayal,
in self-imposed exile in America, failed, although his influence 'as a
power of evil' was much stressed during the proceedings. (18)

The religious ideas of this group of nationalists, in which three strands
can be identified, are interesting, though more complicated than the
'furious devotion' described by Farquhar. First, there is an equation of
India with Hinduism. This is represented in a picture found with the books
of the conspirators, representing a 'divinity of hate and blood', the
goddess Kali with a festoon of European heads round her neck. (19) A
modification of this lay in part in Awadh Behari's vision of 'a great
United Nation - apart from Hindu or Islamic Kingdoms', although this view
was not shared by Har Dayal, in whose opinion 'holy ... virgin soil' had
been originally 'desecrated' by the Muslims, 'the irreverent idol-breakers'.
The religious element is found also in Behari's reference to the teaching
of Krishna, 'the Lord himself', that 'the Kshatrya must slay the foes of
his Motherland ... as his duty, and he does it without sin' - although,
again, Behari makes the point that not only the Hindu scriptures, 'the
Gita, the Vedas', but also the Qur'an 'all advocate assassination'. (20)
The inner resources for a patriotism of this sort were supplied by one of
the leaders of the group, Rash Behari Bose, in his teaching on yoga in his
book, Yogi Sadhan. (21) In this, the ideal of renunciation of the world is
equated with the willingness to die for a noble cause, sustained by the

teachings of the <u>Bhagavad Gita</u>. Perhaps the most independent and striking expression of this Hindu nationalism is in Awadh Behari's reference to the actual bomb-attack on the Viceroy.

> The special manifestation of the Divine Force at
> Delhi in December last has proved beyond doubt that
> the destiny of India is being moulded by God himself.
> ...The thrower of the bomb on the representative of
> the tyrannical Government at Delhi was none else
> but the spirit of the Dispenser of all things
> Himself. (22)

There was also among the group some small indication of Christian concepts and influences. Thus, Awadh Behari's allusion to 'penance and sufferings which equip nations to be fit instruments to carry out His Will', and Har Dayal's call to 'bring back the age of St Francis and St Bernard', an age, as he saw it, of heroic self-sacrifice. (23) We find more of this second element in the latter's <u>Yugantar Circular</u>, put out at this time, though it has a rhetorical ring to it, perhaps no more than a borrowing of Christian terminology. Thus, in seeking to describe the 'moral power of the (Delhi) bomb', Har Dayal calls it 'our resurrection' because it seems to open up 'a new epoch in the history of the Revolutionary movement in India'. The 'beloved hero' who threw the bomb is acclaimed in the cadences of Christian liturgy.

> His is the wisdom and the glory and the power.

There is talk of the British rulers as 'the wicked ones of the earth', and 'When "Caesar" calls himself the "Son of God", the bomb answers that he is but "the Son of Man"'. The Christian component in Har Dayal's complicated intellectual make-up is further seen in a letter at this time in which he commended for a young man's education not only <u>The Gospel of Buddha</u> but also Thomas à Kempis' <u>The Imitation of Christ</u>, 'a book of the highest value for the formation of character'. (24)

A third element in the thinking of the Delhi conspirators derived from

contemporary Western democratic and libertarian movements. We find
indications of this in the list of books seized as evidence by the police,
with titles like Underground Russia and Conspiracy under the Terror,
Michael Davitt's Career of a Nihilist and Tavernier's Making of a Patriot,
as well as books on Mazzini and Garibaldi. (25) It is also evidenced in
Har Dayal's own writing.

> Deep down in the human heart ... lies hidden the
> yearning for justice, equality and brotherhood, ...
> (therefore) we instinctively honour those who make
> war on inequality and injustice by any means in their
> power.... On such occasions, we should recount the
> deeds and repeat the words of Rousseau and Voltaire,
> Marx and Bakunin, Vera Vassulitch and Sophie
> Petrovskie, and all our beloved comrades who have
> lived and died for the Ideal that we cherish. (26)

- a reminder of the attraction of the theory of philosophical anarchism to
Har Dayal, and also that he had already published the first Indian study of
Marx. (27)

That these three elements, Hindu, Christian and secular, could to some
extent co-exist in the thinking of the group is some measure of the
intellectual and religious ferment to which the educated classes were
subject.

It is not entirely obvious how much Andrews knew of the 'secret society'
among the College students, with many of whom he must have been in frequent
contact as a teacher, or about the Delhi conspirators. He must have been
in friendly touch with Amir Chand as late as 1910, and he said that the
C.I.D. had circulated rumours about his own close connections with this
leading conspirator, although he claimed in 1914 that in fact Amir Chand
had 'cut' him for the previous three or four years. He also said that he
was himself spied upon by students in the pay of the government. (28) In
the earlier phase of the Delhi extremist movement, in 1907, he expressed
'very strongly indeed' to his own senior students his indignation at the

deportation of Lajpat Rai. (29) In his considered assessment, he laid the
blame for this whole development on 'police tyranny and espionage of the
worst type, ... the ruthlessness of the police', to which the 'underground
plots' and 'the violence of the conspirators' were only a response. (30)

At the same time, he very clearly disapproved of this response. He
reported with satisfaction that on two separate occasions when anarchist
pamphlets had been sent to members of the College, those who received them
had immediately brought them to Rudra, who had himself passed them on to
the civil authorities. He joined with his College colleagues in a formal
expression of abhorrence of another political murder by a student from the
Punjab. He also voiced the College's 'horror and detestation' and
'condemnation' of 'anarchist propaganda', and, at the time of the Delhi
conspiracy, was 'thankful beyond words' at the unearthing of the
conspirators. (31)

To do this while abating 'not one jot of ... earnest appreciation for all
that ... (was) good and wholesome in the National Movement' was to walk
something of a tightrope. (32) He did not walk it entirely alone. Both
Rudra and Allnutt, with distinct courage, spoke up for Amir Chand at his
trial. (33) Nevertheless, it was Andrews who was singled out in the
Hindustan Review and praised for his discrimination and courage, as 'one of
those few Europeans who did not allow their vision to be blurred even
during the darkness of the bomb outrages, and who had the courage and the
insight to realize the meaning of the struggle, even while the struggle had
assumed an ugly shape'. (34)

Andrews' sympathy, however, was clearly qualified not only with regard to
the extremists' violent methods but also in regard to their religious
ideas. He drew attention to these latter chiefly in two places, in his
book of 1908, North India (both in the chapter on 'The National Movement'
and in an appendix on 'Modern Krishna Worship'), and in an article on
'Nationalism and Religion' in the Indian Review. Nowhere does he seem to
have said much about the secular influences which we have seen among the
Delhi extremists. The nearest he got was to criticize what he called
'religious nihilism', as it had been held by Derozio and the early Bengal

reformers, because it failed to utilize 'the enormous forces of good which
are inherent in religion', and he noted with approval, of the students
involved in the contemporary Calcutta conspiracy case, that 'religion was
with them a supreme interest', and that their disgust with British rule was
not due to 'any lawless atheism', (35) On the Hindu elements in the
extremists' thinking he had more to say. Pointing out how the 'Neo-Hindu
revival ... (was) at present adding to its strength by its absorption under
religious forms, of the national ideal', he illustrated the point by
quoting from a variety of nationalist speeches and newspaper articles. His
account, when compared with those of other missionaries and Western
observers, Nicol Macnicol, for example, and Ramsay MacDonald and Vincent
Chirol, is strikingly complacent.

> The emotional side is prominent in the new Krishna
> cult. The passion of self-surrender is encouraged,
> and devotion to country is made equivalent to
> devotion to Krishna himself. (36)

Only Farquhar, in his pamphlet, Gita and Gospel, shared this sympathetic
understanding of the neo-Krishna literature as an expression of the
national spirit. But, although Andrews detected in this literature 'an
echo of what ... (was) most dear and precious to the Christian', his
response on the whole was negative. Thus a nationalism which equated
patriotic sentiment with devotion to Krishna as a 'national Avatar' had 'an
unsubstantial basis'. It was irrational, and, 'looked at from the higher
ground of truth', could not be 'justified or countenanced', being
impossible to reconcile with 'progress and enlightenment'. At the same
time, the past association of Krishna worship with 'evil legends and
practices' posed the threat of 'national degeneration', while he warned
that a cynical playing upon the 'superstitions, bigotries and fanaticisms'
of 'the ignorant masses' by the 'emancipated' was a tool that could turn
back on the hand of the user. (37)

A letter he wrote to the Viceroy indicated the political dimension of his
concern, lest 'the rapid Hinduising of "national" ideals going on among the
younger men' should 'reach the masses' to the advantage of the

extremists. (38) A further objection that he pointed out to this sort of
religious nationalism was that it was 'reactionary' because of its
exclusion of Muslims, Parsees and Christians. Were they all to be
'boycotted and driven out of the country before anything "national" could
be accomplished?' (39) This last point was a particularly important one.
In North India, Andrews described an incident which had taken place early
in 1908, which 'would have been absolutely incredible' a short time
previously.

> A large meeting was held to hear a lecture on Bhakti
> (devotion), at which nearly 3,000 were present, and
> Mr Tilak took the chair. Dr Garde, an elderly and
> highly-respected and learned Hindu, a friend of Mr
> Tilak's, got up to speak, and traced the doctrine of
> Bhakti in Hinduism from Vedic down to modern times.
> He mentioned, while doing so, the name of Christ as a
> great Western saint who practised Bhakti. The name
> ... was received with such shouts and hisses that the
> speaker was obliged to sit down, and in spite of the
> chairman's efforts to keep order the meeting had to
> be closed. As I have said, this would have been
> quite incredible in India only a short time ago, and
> in a great part of India it would be impossible
> still. Yet it shows us what may be expected if the
> anti-foreign movement becomes anti-Christian.

Andrews saw the 'new Krishna cult' as a further aspect of this development,
offering salvation to the multitude by the grace of the legendary Krishna,
and representing, because of its obvious appeal in conjunction with
nationalism, 'the most serious rival of Christianity in the near
future'. (40)

Here, then, was an aspect of the national movement as it was developing,
and as it was developing even among his own students, to which he could not
give his support. His role as a Christian missionary committed to reaching
the centres of thought and movement in the East, demanded, therefore, the

identification and energetic promotion of an alternative religious basis
for Indian nationalism.

6. 'Self-consecration to God and India'

If the neo-Hinduism of the extremists offered the Christian missionary
little scope for a theological accommodation, there was another strand in
Indian religious nationalism which, at least to Andrews, did. Farquhar
called this 'a self-consecration to God and India', and it corresponded
with what Andrews noted as the religion of 'those who believe in one God
and who love India with a passionate devotion'. (1) From the perspective
of his emerging theology, and in particular as this represented a
development of the 'Religion of the Incarnation' of 'Maurice and the
Cambridge School', Andrews gave a great deal of attention to this aspect of
the religion of the nationalists, and in very positive ways. He did so
chiefly, but not exclusively, in a series of articles in the nationalist
press, 'The Religious Basis of a National Movement', 'Religion and
Patriotism', 'First Principles of a National Movement', 'The Awakening of
the East: Its Meaning and Significance', and 'Nationalism and Religion'.
(2) He tended to reserve some of his more explicitly Christian reflections
for Christian journals and the College magazine, in articles such as 'The
Spiritual Force of Christianity', 'Christianity in Japan', 'Christianity
and Patriotism', and 'Christianity and the Test of Vitality'. (3) Very
significantly, however, as we shall see, an article on 'The Doctrine of the
Atonement', highly pertinent in this context, appeared in the nationalist
Indian Review.

Of the inevitability of a religious dimension to a national movement in
India, Andrews had no doubt, for religion was 'the strongest indigenous
instinct of Indian nature', and this not only among the more conservative.

> Young India, in spite of all temptation to accept a
> materialist solution of her problems and throw aside
> her spiritual yearnings, remains today irrevocably,
> incorrigibly idealist, and refuses to lower her
> standard.

To Andrews, it was as desirable as it was inevitable. Thus, he welcomed
what he called a 'spiritual' factor as good in itself.

> Nationality, when it touches the heart of a great
> people, is itself a spiritual thing. (4)

Elsewhere, he stressed the importance of religion from another angle,
making much of Acton's theory that a balance between the religious and
civil states was a guarantee of political freedom, while a subordination of
religion to politics amounted to a position of 'great national danger'. At
the same time, only 'some spiritual force' could have the power to 'raise
the masses of the people' and effect a permanent regeneration. The lack of
a religious basis of the sort that he envisaged would be a weakness in a
national movement; his remarks on this in a Christian publication were
enthusiastically endorsed in the Tribune. (5)

Behind all this, however, there clearly lay the perception that this
'spiritual' factor was a point of contact for him as a missionary.

> In all that is happening, ... the thoughtful
> Christian ... can recognise the transplanting of
> Christian thought in Eastern soil. Nationality,
> liberty, enlightenment, the raising of the
> multitudes, these are seeds which have hitherto only
> struck deep and permanent root in Christendom. They
> have come to the East from the Christian West. They
> have touched the anima naturaliter Christiana in
> India, ... and have begun to fertilize. (6)

This reference to a 'natural Christian soul' in the context of Indian
nationalism had real substance for Andrews. It was also to be discerned,
he maintained, through a study of Indian history, and his discussion of
this represents a particularly interesting and original contribution to the
thought of the national movement. He first began to develop this idea in
his early lecture on 'Indian Nationality', where he pointed out that 'the
civilization of Ashoka and Akbar ... (with its) ideals of tolerance and

peaceful development', ideals which were at the time 'unimagined in the West', demonstrated the possibility of 'a united India and a progressive development on Eastern lines'. His most deliberate exercise in this direction was a lecture which he published in the Modern Review and elsewhere in 1908, 'Indian History: Its Lessons for Today', in which he appealed to Indian people to recognise what, at least in the Buddhist era, Indian genius could accomplish 'without extraneous aid or interference'.

> Here, as it were, we are mining in the very bed-rock
> of Indian mother earth, to see what treasures we can
> find, and 'the gold of that land is good'. (7)

This line in Andrews' thinking, in marked contrast to the denigrating line taken by contemporary British historians of India, and unique in missionary circles, was welcomed in the Tribune as 'remarkable' in a leading article. (8) Such a view of Indian history, then, made it the more possible to take account of contemporary nationalism within a missiology inescapably reminiscent of the approach of the Alexandrian apologists.

Nationalism could also be accommodated in terms of the sort of 'fulfilment' theory which Farquhar was making popular in some Christian circles. Rudra did this quite explicitly.

> We believe that in ... welcoming ... the new national
> spirit ... we are acting in accordance with the
> example of Him 'who came not to destroy but to
> fulfil'.

Andrews seems not to have done so in just such terms, although he clearly took a similar line, saying that Indians involved in the national movement were, 'though not owning our Master's allegiance, .. yet doing His work'. (9)

A particularly important concern was with regard to theism. Farquhar claimed that Christianity had made people in India feel that 'the only possible religion is monotheism'. Much that Andrews wrote during this period was clearly intended to establish this as a common ground in the context of nationalism, and so he drew attention to 'the truly remarkable trend of Hindu thought towards Theism', a trend in which he felt the current was running more strongly than it had done for many generations. (10) He frequently presented this in terms of the need for reformation.

> Patriotism is not to be cultivated by a depreciation
> of religion, but rather by a purification of religion
> itself. (11)

His most explicit intervention was in an early attack on 'idolatry', which he said would lead inevitably to the 'degradation' of the nation, and in an accompanying proposal.

> Would it not be possible for those who believe in one
> God and who love India with a passionate devotion to
> take a vow, not merely to buy swadeshi articles ...
> but, what is infinitely more important, that he will,
> under no circumstances and on no occasion take any
> part in, or be present at, ceremonies or festivals in
> which idolatry is practised? (12)

His approach was usually, however, by a positive advocacy of a reformed religion. Most explicit was his public support for the All-India Theistic Conference, for the Brahmo Samaj, with its re-accreditation of Hinduism's own theistic teachings, and for the Prarthana Samaj, with its 'theistic principle and rejection of idolatry'. (13) He pointed out that these theistic forms of Hinduism were important in relation to nationalism because they represented a real common ground with Islam and Christianity: thus, the trend within Hinduism was itself the result of Christian influence, while the unity of God in both Islam and Hindu theism represented lines of convergence which gave 'solid ground for a great hope'. (14) His usual line, however, was straightforward advocacy of a theistic faith as, in itself, a service to nationalism. In several places he held up the example of Mazzini, a great favourite among the nationalists, as an exponent of the primacy of a belief in 'God and truth'

for a sound nationalism, a sound national fabric depending upon moral and
spiritual character, itself 'the great reward offered to every true and
worthy seeker after God'. (15)

In his contributions to the nationalist reviews and newspapers in the
middle years of his missionary decade, Andrews' discussion of religion and
nationalism did not often take up overtly Christian, as distinct from these
generalised 'spiritual' and theistic themes, except in one or two
particular respects. There are occasional references in the reviews to the
role of Christianity in the West as being among the 'factors which made for
nationality', while in the College magazine he claimed that it was
Christianity that had 'evoked the self-conscious manhood of the younger
nations'. (16) An article on 'The Christian Moral Standard' in the
Epiphany illustrates one of the ways in which his understanding of the
Incarnation functions in his reflection on nationalism. Thus, 'the
perfect moral character of Christ', being 'complete for all time' and
'morally universal', slowly but surely takes its place as 'the one
arbiter of nations' and goes 'deep into the moral conscience of modern
nations'. (17) In Christ's moral universality, he wrote in the Epiphany a
year later, 'Indian national thinkers and workers may find a quarry open
for them ... from which to hew the stones of the great social fabric of the
New India'. (18) The claim was a large one, but so too was his own
achievement in holding this objective before the nationalists.

Chiefly in Christian journals, we find Andrews adopting and developing a
way of referring to Christ which he was to carry over in a small way into
the nationalist publications, that is, of Christ as 'the Son of Man'. (19)
In this latter context, he clearly uses the title to express the sense of
Christ's universal significance and his solidarity with the human race,
very much as it was used in the incarnational theology of contemporary
Anglicanism. (20) Thus, in a developed expression of the idea in the
Modern Review, we come across the phrase in a discussion of Christian
attitudes to the national movement.

> When we come to ... the national movement, we go for
> our direct teaching to St Paul's ideal of the body of

> humanity, of which Christ, the Son of Man, is the
> head, - 'Whether one member suffer, all the members
> suffer with it; or one member rejoice, all the
> members rejoice with it.'. In this ideal of the Body
> of Humanity, there is the fullest possible scope for
> national development. It is, indeed, the charter of
> national rights and liberties. (21)

This passage, however, opens up a theme in which Andrews much more
consistently and overtly applied Christian concepts and terminology, though
in an uncommonly universalist way, in discussion of the national movement,
that is, the theme of human solidarity. This was one of the central
elements in his thought, as it had been for both Maurice and Westcott. It
was a theme which, in both secular and theological spheres, was very much
alive at the time: Rudra's son called it 'the most vital ... discovery ...
ever made, ... (that) man has discovered man', and we regularly come across
it in the nationalist journals and newspapers. (22) It is in this context
that we have to see Andrews' series of six substantial articles, 'A Review
of the Modern World', in the Modern Review, in which he discusses the
leading contemporary social and political features of each continent in
turn, in relation to India, the underlying presupposition being that
'mankind makes up today one corporate whole to a degree that was never
realised in past ages'. (23) He was familiar enough, of course, with the
secular, political categories, including the Marxist, of the discussion -
in fact, he talked them over during these years with Ramsay MacDonald when
the latter was visiting Delhi - but his own line was almost invariably to
emphasise what he saw as a Christian intepretation of current developments.
(24) He expressed this usually in terms of the Pauline metaphor of the
body. This is so from his very earliest reflections on the national
movement. Thus, in his address to a nationalist audience in Calcutta at
the end of December 1906, he applied the Pauline terminology to a specific
problem in nationalism.

> To quote the words of St Paul, 'If one member of the
> body suffer, all the members suffer with it ...'.
> The great bulk of your fellow-countrymen are

> uneducated, unenlightened and very poor .... The
> national idea can never be realised until the masses
> are raised and enlightened.

Hereafter, throughout these years, this notion and terminology are a
striking feature of his writing for the nationalists. (25) It is no
surprise to find them being taken up and used by Indians, and not only
Christians, in his immediate circle. (26) It is noteworthy, however, that
we should find a Hindu at the Congress just five years after that address,
speaking of the Indian people as 'belonging to one another, ... being
members of one body'. (27) Nothing can be proved about the origin of this,
but no one other than Andrews was promoting such thinking within the
national movement in these years.

We find a fuller and more careful development of this theme in his writing
for a Christian readership, where it assumes a universalism strongly
reminiscent of that of Maurice.

> To paraphrase St Paul's words in this wider
> connection, 'When one member of humanity suffers all
> the members suffer with it, ... And one race or
> nation cannot say to another, "I have no need of
> thee". For the body of humanity is not one member,
> but many. And even the races which seem to be more
> feeble are necessary: and those peoples which we
> think to be less honourable, upon them we need to
> bestow more abundant honour. For God has tempered
> this body of mankind together, giving more abundant
> honour to the part which lacked, that there should be
> no schism in the body, but the members should have
> the same care one for another'.

Elsewhere, he called this 'the larger catholic position', that 'humanity is
one brotherhood in Christ'. (28) It is in this context that he developed
the most distinctive and original concept in his theology of national
renaissance, the notion of what he called 'the Body of humanity', which was

for him the 'commanding vision, ... at the very centre of the New
Testament'. This unity of humankind was 'the true Christian ideal', because
'to the Christian, this body of humanity is informed and inspired by the
divine life, and the divine life, though infinite in its working and
expression, is ever one.' (29) The concept is reminiscent of at least one
of the Fathers, and of the holistic vision of Maurice and Westcott, but
Andrews made it very much his own. (30)

At first, while human unity was already important for him, as his Burney
Prize Essay indicates, he used the language of 'the body' in a more
restricted way, so that it was the Christians who were 'his Body', though,
as such, 'the nucleus of that unity'. Two or three years later, however,
his vision of 'the body of humanity' has become itself the emerging
'spiritual humanity, the Church Catholic'. Nevertheless, he continued to
the end of the decade to regard the Church, as usually understood, as
having a special, indeed a crucial role.

> This brotherhood, ... this body of humanity, ... (we
> Christians) expect to be built up in its spiritual
> ideal by means of the Christian Church.

For this reason, the church is called to 'represent' the commanding vision
of the body of humanity 'before the eyes of men'. (31)

Elsewhere, he expressed his conviction that Christianity's role in this
regard was unique. In doing so, he had behind him Rudra's arguments in his
remarkable paper, 'Christ and Modern India', where he showed that neither
Hinduism nor Islam was capable of providing a basis for an authentic Indian
nationhood because they lacked appropriate universal principles. Quoting
Rudra at length, he claimed that Hinduism and Islam, having been put to the
test of experience, had 'only proved their own impotence as nation-building
forces'. Thus, he felt able to speak of the Church's special calling
within the context of Indian nationalism, because only the vision of the
body of humanity growing up into the fulness of Christ, the Son of Man,
'satisfies the aspirations of mankind for a unity and a goal'. (32)

We have seen that, by and large, when Andrews addressed Indian nationalists
directly, his Christian convictions were expressed relatively discretely,
and that it was chiefly in addressing a Christian readership that there was
much overt reference to Christian ideas. One very interesting exception
was an article that he wrote for G.A. Natesan's Madras journal, the Indian
Review, a substantial presentation and discussion of 'The Doctrine of the
Atonement', printed prominently as the opening article in the issue of June
1912. Andrews' article stands out, however, not only in that issue, but as
a quite unique phenomenon in the whole spectrum of the journalistic
literature of the educated classes in the period, a carrying of the
preaching of the cross into the very heartland of Indian nationalism.

As we would expect, Andrews' exposition falls very much within the category
of moral theories of the atonement, and is unmistakably a product of the
catholic movement in Anglican theology. From the point of view of his own
emerging theology, it has to be seen in the context of a tendency, common
in the Anglican theology of the period, to stress the Incarnation as the
central principle in theology, to the neglect of the doctrine of the
Atonement. To understand the full significance of this article in the
development of his thought, then, it is helpful to turn to his review of
his position as he understood it in 1909.

> I find the whole prospect of Christian doctrine
> widening out in certain directions. I do not now
> almost exclusively concentrate my thoughts upon the
> death of Christ as consequent upon the fall of man.
> I do not view human history, as it were, as one great
> failure, with nothing else but sin in the foreground,
> or my missionary work as wholly and solely concerned
> with sin and its removal. I find that this is not
> the true balance of the Gospel narrative itself. For
> I see in that record now more clearly than before the
> immense, unlimited work which Christ came to
> accomplish as the Head of humanity, in building up
> the 'good'; and that this is in no way inferior to
> His work of removing the 'bad'. Redemption now

implies to me both aspects, not one only. (33)

In spite of this, it is not obvious that 'both aspects' of the work of Christ received equal emphasis in Andrews' writing during these years, and the Indian Review article appears to register a corrective within his own reflection. It was certainly intended, and this he makes explicit, as a corrective to the trend of contemporary liberal theology as this was assimilated to the religion of the educated classes.

> There has been ... going on now for more than a century an assimilation of central Christian thoughts, especially the great commmanding and correlative thoughts of the Fatherhood of God and the Brotherhood of Man. Life is being fashioned on every side upon a more directly theistic basis. Both Islam and Hinduism have felt the power of this impact of thought. The stern monotheism of the former has been made more tender; the vague and uncertain theistic ideas of the latter have been made more defined. But although this great advance has been made, it has hitherto remained in a great measure ineffective as a social power, transforming human society, because the vision of God's Holiness has not gone side by side with the vision of His Tenderness and Love. The danger is that this modern attenuated creed accepting the Fatherhood of God without the awe of His Holiness, and declaring the Brotherhood of Man in theory rather than in practice – may produce a religion which is a mere comfortable and indulgent sentiment, with no passionate longing for inward purity, no striving after fruits of a true repentance, no spiritual agony for the sin of the world. (34)

Hence, his exposition of the doctrine of the Atonement. At one point, he summarises the doctrine as he is presenting it, and one sees how skilfully

the 'manward' emphasis of late nineteenth-century Anglican atonement theory
is accommodated to the theism of educated non-Christian Indians.

> We seem to learn three lessons which form the three
> parts of the one Sacrifice of God. First, that the
> Divine Purity shrinks back with unutterable shrinking
> from contact with human sin. Secondly, that the
> Divine Love is so infinite as to overpass that awful
> barrier of moral evil in order to come close to us,
> to redeem us. Thirdly, that the contact of Divine
> Purity and Love with human sin involves suffering and
> sacrifice even in God Himself. The life and death of
> Christ, who is God Incarnate, is thus the measure and
> the symbol, in time, of the eternal sacrifice which
> flows from the Divine Love.

The doctrine is presented largely, however, in psychological terms, as the
source of a 'mighty, quickening spiritual impulse, which will stir to the
very depths the hearts of men'. As such, the doctrine is presented to
'thoughtful Indians, who see their own need and the needs of their
country', offering them 'some glimpse of the potentiality of this Christian
doctrine of the Atonement, which, when believed with heart and soul, has
power to change the lives of men and send them forth to spend and be spent
in unselfish service'.

There are no indications in the newspapers and journals of the nationalists
of the response to 'The Doctrine of the Atonement', but its publication is
none the less a remarkable thing, a measure not only of the balance of
Andrews' own theology of national renaissance at the end of the main phase
of his missionary years, but also of the seriousness of his missionary
penetration of the national movement.

The years 1904 to 1914 saw a considerable development in Andrews' views
about Indian nationalism, as he came into contact with and thought about
many aspects of the movement. By his own later standards, his views were
in many respects very cautious at this time, and, indeed, he retained

throughout the period a sort of residual respect for some features of
British rule, not least, perhaps, because of the liberality of some of the
officials that he got to know, Sir John Meston, Sir Guy Fleetwood-Wilson,
and Lord Hardinge among them. That he should have held positive and
constructive views of the movement at all, though, and that he should have
taken it so seriously as to develop something of a theology of national
renaissance, was strikingly original. The World Missionary Conference in
Edinburgh in 1910, in it Commission on 'Missions and Governments', under
the chairmanship of Lord Balfour, after taking soundings in India, found no
case being made, least of all by missionaries, for any such thing.

> Missionaries in India ... are on the whole agreed
> that a transfer of power to the natives of the soil
> should proceed pari passu with their advance in
> enlightenment and moral stability. But very few
> indeed consider it part of their duty to spend any
> part of their time and thought in propagating this
> idea. (35)

That provides us with a measure of Andrews' originality, though he had some
support among his colleagues in the Delhi Mission in general, and from
Allnutt in particular. For Andrews, as we have seen, the devotion of time
and thought to the national movement was central to his whole understanding
of his missionary vocation, for it was there precisely that he found common
ground as a Christian with 'the bulk of thinking, struggling, feeling,
sensitive men and women' among the educated classes, discerning indeed
among them and their concerns that anima naturaliter Christiana to the
uncovering of which the Cambridge Mission to Delhi was committed.

<u>NOTES</u>: Chapter Four

1. <u>Introductory</u>

1 This is how Keir Hardie put it after his visit to Delhi and the
  Punjab in 1907 - Hardie 1909, p. 57. He met several of Andrews'
  nationalist friends while in Delhi and Lahore, but there is no
  indication that he and Andrews met - <u>Tribune</u> 13, 24 Oct 1907.

2 Andrews to Lady Hardinge, 5 Feb 1913 (Hardinge - CUL)

3 <u>TEW</u> Oct 1912; <u>MR</u> Nov 1909

4 <u>TEW</u> Oct 1912. Andrews made a number of references to the
  pacificatory effect of the visit, e.g. <u>YMOI</u> Jan 1912, <u>RI</u> p. iii.

5 Dunlop Smith to Lady Minto, 21 Feb 1908, quoted in Gilbert 1966,
  p. 127.

6 The phrase is taken from a chapter-heading in Thomas 1970;
  Andrews figures largely in this chapter.

2. <u>'Imperialism and its ethics'</u>

1 Andrews 1930, p. 115

2 J.E.C. Welldon <u>The Nineteenth Century and After</u> Jun 1908

3 Ellison and Walpole 1908, p. 67

4 Hobson 1902, pp. 214, 228. Hobson was quoting Lord Hugh Cecil,
  speaking at the 1900 annual meeting of SPG

5 Ellison and Walpole 1908, p. 11

6 Hobson 1902, pp. 207, 210. Hobson was well aware that 'most
  British missionaries' did not take this mystificatory line,
  though he found some striking examples of those who did (p. 214).

7 Kiernan 1972, p. xxxiii

8 Preparatory Paper for Commission 1 (WMC)

9 In a sermon preached at Simla <u>DMN</u>⁄Oct 1914

10 <u>Tribune</u> 27 Dec 1911

11 (SCM); <u>MR</u> May 1913; 'India in Transition' 1910

12 Tribune 17 Oct 1906; <u>CT</u> 25 Nov 1910; <u>HR</u> Jan 1907; <u>Tribune</u> 4 May
  1910; <u>IR</u> Dec 1910; <u>RI</u> p. 102; <u>HR</u> Jan 1907; <u>MR</u> May 1913;
  <u>HR</u> Jan 1907; <u>Tribune</u> 7 Jan 1913

13 Gobind Behari Lal to D. O'Connor, 9 Dec 1974

14 _Biog_ pp. 102-3

15 Dayal 1913

16 G. Fleetwood-Wilson to Hardinge, 22 Jun 1911 (Meston – IOL & R)

17 _SSC Mag_ Mar 1912

18 _Tribune_ 9 Jan 1912; Rudra _CC_ 1912; _SSC Mag_ Mar 1912

19 _RI_ p. 11; _YMOI_ Jan 1912

20 _Pan-Anglican Congress_ 1908, Vol. 2, also in _IR_ Jun 1908

21 For the importance of these four economic nationalists, see Chandra 1966.

22 The papers in Vol. 2, Part 2 of the Report dealt with 'Morality in Commercial and Social Life'. There were no other papers on international or imperial aspects of the question. Part 1, 'Speeches and Discussions on Capital', got no closer than R.M. Burrows' reference to the 'never-failing flow of dividends' from India, etc., 'while no one cares, no one sends back that tithe of Christian charity that is their very certain due'. The Chairman, the Bishop of Columbia, summing up, hoped that all who had investments in the colonies would make some return by supporting the religious work there.

23 Andrews to Dunlop Smith, 28 Jan 1908 (Minto – NLS)

24 _CT_ 5 Dec 1913

25 _WSCF_ 1911. Andrews' paper, 'Students and the Application of Christ's Teaching to International and Racial Relations', was read for him at the 1911 Conference of the World Student Christian Federation in Constantinople, as he was not able to attend, and subsequently printed in the Report. It is an important landmark, bringing the questions of racism and imperialism onto the agenda of the emerging ecumenical movement.

26 _IR_ Jun 1908, _CT_ 25 Nov 1910

27 Andrews to Tagore, 12 Dec 1912 (Santiniketan)

28 Andrews to Gandhi, 5 Apr 1914 (Gandhi SSS)

29 Pamphlet 'How India Can Be Free' (1921), cf. Gandhi in _Young India_ 20 Mar 1930

3. 'The Ethics of Race'

1 CT 25 Nov 1910

2 TEW Oct 1914; Andrews to Montgomery, 1907 (quoted in Tinker 1979, pp. 39–40); Tribune 1 Sep 1908

3 WSCF 1911

4 TEW Oct 1914; WSCF 1911

5 J.H. Oldham's Christianity and the Race Problem of 1924 is generally regarded as the pioneer work in this field, but Andrews, in a series of important articles, preceded Oldham by nearly twenty years. Oldham acknowledged Andrews' 'unique knowledge' of aspects of the subject (p. 129).

6 SM Apr 1908; TEW Oct 1914

7 Preparatory Paper for Commission 1 (WMC)

8 CT 16 Dec 1910; NI, pp. 161 ff.; TEW Jul 1910, also DMN Jan 1909. WSCF 1911

9 SM Apr 1908. For a very favourable account of Andrews' paper, YMOI Oct 1907

10 DMN Jan 1909; SM May 1907, also NI p. 21, TEW Jul 1910, CT Nov 1910, WSCF 1911, RI p. 171; DMN Jan 1909 – for the Farquhar debate, see Sharpe 1965, pp. 244 ff.

11 CT 25 Nov 1910

12 DMN Jan 1909

13 DMN Jan 1909; NI p. 21

14 Quoted in WSCF 1911, TEW Oct 1912, RI pp. 169–70

15 Tribune 12 Dec 1911

16 WSCF 1911; TEW Jul 1910

4. 'The great giver of emancipation'

1 TEW Oct 1907

2 Ind Int Apr 1909

3 J. Carter in DMN Apr 1907, cf. A.S. Duncan-Jones' of NI in DMN

Apr 1909, 'It is not our fancy, surely, to see ... the widening
influence of Maurice and the Cambridge School'.

4 HR Jan 1907; YMOI Sep 1908

5 Tribune 27 Apr 1910

6 IW 6 Sep 1901; Minto to Ibbetson, 7 Dec 1907 (Minto - NLS);
   Biog p. 102

7 IR June 1908

8 E.g. his articles on 'India's Death Rate', Tribune 18, 20, 23 Aug
   1910. His proposal in Tribune 27 Sep 1907, for utilizing 'the
   spare time of 25,000,000 tillers of the soil', not by 'building
   huge town factories and herding the people together', but with
   'machinery which can be worked by hand', anticipates a main theme
   of Gandhian economics.

9 SM May 1907

10 Tribune 16 Aug 1907

11 Tribune 23 Aug 1907

12 NI p. 235, CT 2 Dec 1910, 'India in Transition' 1910; Preparatory
   Paper for Commission 4 (WMC)

13 TEW Jul 1910; The Day of Opportunity 1912, p. 68

14 'India in Transition' 1910, CT 2 Dec 1910, etc.

15 TEW Jul 1910, CT 2 Dec 1910

16 Tribune 16 Aug 1907; MR Apr 1910. N.b. Forrester 1980, p. 149,
   on Andrews' 'challengingly relevant Christian analysis of Indian
   society'.

17 Poem 'The Famine Year' (i.e. 1908) in Andrews 1916; MR Dec 1907;
   RI p. 15; Tribune 25 Dec 1906

18 Tribune 13 May 1910

19 For the Cambridge Mission's work in this sector, see Lefroy 1884.
   Earlier nationalist attitudes are well exemplifed in Banerjee's
   remark in 1895, 'I was not aware that any responsible Congressman
   had ever asked for representative institutions ... for the
   masses', quoted in Andrews and Mookherjee 1938, p. 160.

20 Farquhar 1915, pp. 370-4; Tribune 27 Aug 1910, the language being
   very much the sort Andrews was using, 'the beginning of nation-
   building from the deepest foundations upwards'.

21 CC 1912

22 The Depressed Classes 1912; Tribune 16 Aug 1907; 13 May 1910; 23
    Aug 1910, also SSC Mag Feb 1908; 25 Dec 1906

23 MR Aug 1912

24 Tribune 23 Aug 1910

25 IR Jun 1912

26 RI p. 210

27 RI pp. 231; 207, 210; MR Feb 1911

28 SSC Mag Dec 1907, cf. two articles in Tribune 27 Apr, 13 May
    1910, on 'How to serve my country', where he calls for the social
    emancipation of women from the restrictions of life in the zenana.

29 IR Jan 1909

30 Singh, S. 1972, p. 116

31 Tribune 17 Oct 1906, 25 Jan 1907

32 HR Jan 1911, Feb 1911

33 Indian World Feb-Mar 1911, Tribune 18 Feb 1911. HR, between
    Feb and May 1911, carried appreciative comments from the other
    publications. Andrews' willingness to apply Acton's ideas to the
    Indian situation contrasts with J.S. Mill's earlier insistence
    that his views in On Liberty and Representative Government were
    not applicable to India (see Said 1978, p. 14).

34 Andrews' articles include 'Shakespeare and Nationality' SSC Mag
    Jul 1907, 'National Literature and Art' MR Jul 1907, also Tribune
    27 Apr 1910, MR Feb 1911, SSC Mag Feb 1911, MR Aug 1912, Mar
    1913. The Tribune commented editorially on Coomaraswamy's book
    on 20 May 1909, and reviewed it on 28 Jul 1912.

35 Among the social-Darwinists, n.b. Lord Rosebery, quoted in Hyam
    1976, p. 131. In Andrews, malaria needed to be attacked because it
    'did more than any other thing to destroy the national vitality'
    SSC Mag Nov 1908; the heavy death-rate was a serious economic
    'drain' and a loss to the nation of 'moral and spiritual wealth'
    Tribune 18 Aug 1910; hill schools were necessary to counter the
    enervating effects of the heat of the plains, because
    these were a 'hindrance to the national movement', a 'National
    cause' being taken up with great enthusiasm and then fading,
    while walking in the Simla Hills was a stimulus to those
    essential virtues of a national movement, 'character and courage'

<u>HR</u> Jan 1907, <u>Tribune</u> 16 Dec 1906, <u>MR</u> Nov 1911; thus, too, an
important aim of education was to build up 'a strong, healthy,
manly character' so that the national movement would gain 'new
force and activity' <u>Tribune</u> 17 Sep 1906, <u>HR</u> Jan 1907; the
eradication of 'the Drink Problem' would 'make the sobriety of
the Indian people ... notable among the nations of the world' <u>MR</u>
Nov 1910.

36 E.g. 'Only as we intelligently meet the facts and study them in a
scientific manner can we hope to deal rightly with ... the
scourge of the Punjab (malaria)' <u>SSC Mag</u> Dec 1911; similarly, the
prospect of effectively combating climatic conditions was
improving because humanity was 'beginning to act in a scientific
way' <u>HR</u> May 1907; also <u>SSC Mag</u> Nov 1908.

37 <u>MR</u> Dec 1907

38 <u>Tribune</u> 20, 16 Feb 1909

39 <u>TEW</u> Oct 1907, <u>NI</u> pp. 190–1

40 <u>YMOI</u> Jan 1910

5. 'Furious devotion'

1 Low 1973, p. 144; Farquhar 1915, pp. 354 ff.

2 Farquhar 1915, p. 355

3 <u>Summmary</u> 1916, p. 17. The 'two' are Har Dayal and Amir Chand.

4 D.C.I. 5 Oct 1907 (NAI)

5 <u>Akhbar-i-Am</u> May 1907 (PNNR – IOL& R); <u>Tribune</u> 11 Aug 1907

6 D.C.I. 21 Sep 1907 (NAI); <u>SSC Mag</u> May 1907

7 <u>Tribune</u> 18 Aug 1907; DCI 5 Oct 1907 (NAI); <u>SSC Mag</u> May 1907

8 D.C.I. 21 Sep 1907 (NAI). 'They were ably assisted by a good
sprinkling of lawyers, cloth merchants and other local leaders'
Singh S. 1972 p. 118

9 D.C.I. 4 Jan 1908 (NAI); <u>Tribune</u> 26 Jan 1908; 28 Jan, 2 Feb
1908; 8 Feb 1908. Later, Lajpat Rai was to become one of
Andrews''greatest friends' (Andrews <u>True India</u> 1939, p. 156),
'more than a brother' (Articles. 16 – Chaturvedi – NAI).

10 Included in the Index of the Home. Political files (NAI), the
report is missing; <u>Tribune</u> 11 Apr 1914.

11 SSC Mag Jan 1910. Har Dayal took a different view of the
    reforms. 'Then the tyrants ... decided to conciliate the people
    by offering "reforms" and "concessions". Jobs were created for
    "educated parasites"; councils were enlarged and expanded for the
    benefit of ambitious politicians and lawyers. These futile and
    deceptive measures served to rally the "moderates" to the side of
    the government, as dogs are silenced with a bone thrown among
    them' Dayal 1913.

12 M.N. Roy, quoted in Brown 1975, p. 226

13 Gobind Behari Lal, quoted in Brown 1975, p. 49

14 Dharmavira in Har Dayal 1960, p. 349

15 'Memo on the doings of Lajpat Rai since his release' Home.
    Political Nov 1908 (NAI)

16 'Lala Har Dayal. A Noble Patriot and Truth Lover' (handwritten.
    Articles 15 – Chaturvedi – NAI). Cf. Spear: 'a rudderless
    individual, with a passion for liberation but an unorganised
    though powerful mind' (JRAS 1976, p. 173).

17 Awadh Behari had joined St Stephen's in 1904; his tutor was the
    Sanskrit teacher, Raghubar Dayal – SSC Mag May 1907.

18 DCI 1 Jul 1913 (NAI), also Summary 1916, p. 17

19 Tribune 3 Apr, 28 May 1914. For a missionary criticism of Kali
    in this role, Macnicol 1909.

20 Behari 1913; Har Dayal quoted by Andrews in HR Jan 1909

21 The press reports of the Delhi Conspiracy Trial describe this as
    an unpublished manuscript Tribune 1, 3 Apr 1914.

22 Behari 1913

23 Behari 1913; Dayal 1913

24 Har Dayal to Rana, 19 May 1910 (Har Dayal Papers, NL)

25 Tribune 2, 18, 25 Apr 1914

26 Dayal 1913

27 As a further illustration of Dayal's complicated intellectual
    make-up, n.b. under the title of his MR article on Marx, from
    St Matthew, 'And unto the poor, The Gospel is preached'.

28 Andrews to Munshi Ram, 22 May 1914 (NAI); Amrita Bazar Patrika
    1 Apr 1919

29 Pamphlet 'National Education' c. 1921

30 Andrews and Mookherjee 1938, p. 206

31 CC 1910; SSC Staff Minutes, 5 Jul 1909; SSC Mag Jul 1909; Andrews
    to Hardinge, 23 Nov 1913 (Hardinge - CUL). Moderate
    nationalists were no less vocal in their dissociation from the
    violence: the Tribune (24 Dec 1912) said the Delhi Bomb throwing
    was 'as outrageous as sacrilege ... the dastardly attempt, which
    an all-benign Providence has averted'.

32 CC 1910

33 Tribune 14 Jul 1914; 11, 12, 14, Jul 1914. In a sermon at Simla,
    Allnutt referrred to Amir Chand as one of his oldest friends,
    DMN Oct 1914.

34 In an anonymous review of RI, HR Feb - Mar 1913

35 IR Jan 1910; Guardian 16 Dec 1908

36 NI p. 198. Cf. Macnicol 1909, MacDonald 1910, p. 189, Chirol
    1910

37 NI pp. 203, 209; IR Jan 1910

38 Andrews to Dunlop Smith, 1 Mar 1908, in Gilbert 1966, p. 131

39 IR Jan 1910; HR Jan 1909. Cf. his comment that neo-Hinduism of
    this sort 'shows no signs' of providing a basis for national
    unity NI p. 229.

40 NI pp. 210, 230. Cf. Allnutt's conclusion that this emerging
    popular religion was 'not simply anti-British, but in the main
    anti-Christian in its ideals, its objects , and its methods of
    action' DMN Jan 1911.

6. 'Self-consecration to God and India'

1 Farquhar 1915, p. 355; Ep 6 Oct 1906

2 Ep 17 Aug 1907, Tribune 15 Jan 1908; SSC Mag May 1908; Tribune
   20 Feb 1909; IR Jan 1910

3 Ep 20 Apr 1907; SSC Mag Dec 1907; NMI Feb 1910; Ep 28 Oct 1911

4 IR Jan 1910; MR Jul 1907

5 HR Jan 1911; SSC Mag May 1907; Tribune 2 Oct, 15 Nov 1907

6 TEW Oct 1907, cf. NI p. 190. Andrews' terms in these two places,
   'nationality, liberty, enlightenment, the raising of the
   multitudes, ... emancipation, progress', make a striking cluster

of what might be termed 'modernization ideals', subsequently to become very important for India's development philosophy – see Myrdal 1968, Vo. 1 _passim_, also my discussion of this in 'Study of Religion and Social Reality', Singh H. n.d.

7   MR Sep 1908, reprinted in _Tribune_ 20 Sep 1908, _Dawn_ Sep, Oct 1908, SSC Mag Nov 1908

8   _Tribune_ 8 Sep 1908. Andrews himself particularly criticised Vincent Smith in this regard MR Nov 1908.

9   Rudra CC 1909; YMOI Sep 1908

10 Farquhar 1915, p. 434. Perhaps Farquhar had noted Andrews' own observation that 'the influence of Christian Missionary enterprise has been among the greatest causes ... (of) the truly remarkable trend of Hindu thought towards Theism' _Tribune_ 20 Feb 1909; IR Mar 1909.

11 SSC Mag Feb 1908

12 Ep 6 Oct 1906

13 _Tribune_ 16; 20 Feb 1909; RI p. 136

14 _Tribune_ 20 Feb 1909

15 SSC Mag Feb, May 1908, IR Jan 1910

16 MR Dec 1907, also HR Jan 1907; SSC Mag May 1907

17 Ep 25 Nov and 2 Dec 1911. This is very close to Westcott on 'the universality of Christ's character' in a sermon on 'the Unity of Humanity in Christ' Westcott 1888, pp. 39–54.

18 Ep 18 Jan 1913

19 The chief passage is in _Ind Int_ Oct 1909.

20 E.g., Westcott 1888, p. 44, and Scott Holland in SM Dec 1909

21 MR May 1913

22 Sudhir Rudra in YMOI Jan 1914; Kalinath Ray IW Aug 1908, Hiralal Halder MR Nov 1909, E. Willis MR Sep 1910, _Tribune_ 31 Dec 1911

23 MR Nov 1909 to Apr 1910

24 MacDonald stayed with Andrews in Delhi in Oct–Nov 1909 and Dec 1913, and explained his 'economic and social ideas'. Andrews wrote an account of their discussions 'J. Ramsay MacDonald. A Reminiscence' _Indian Daily Mail_ 2 Feb 1924 (Chaturvedi – NAI).

25 _Bengalee_ 28 Dec 1906; e.g. MR Nov 1909, _Tribune_ 23 Aug 1910

26 Rudra in YMOI Dec 1910; Sudhir Rudra in YMOI Jan 1914; a Hindu

teacher at St Stephen's in <u>SSC Mag</u> Nov 1908

27 Bhupendra Nath Basu <u>Tribune</u> 31 Dec 1911

28 <u>TEW</u> Oct 1914; <u>NMI</u> Feb 1910

29 <u>TEW</u> Oct 1914, cf. <u>WSCF</u> 1911

30 R.C. Walls has indicated to me a patristic use of the term, in
    Hilary of Poitiers <u>De Trinitate</u> 2.24 'He was made man of a virgin
    so that he might receive the nature of flesh: that the body of
    humanity as a whole might be sanctified by association with this
    mixture' cf. Maurice 1892, Vol IV p. 9 'It was the business of
    Christ's ministers to proclaim that there could have been no
    families, no nations, no social impulses, no laws ... if there
    had not been one living centre of the whole body of Humanity, one
    Head of everyman'. Westcott may not have used the phrase, but
    the idea is very important for him. e.g. Westcott 1887,
    pp. 9, 57.

31 <u>SM</u> Apr 1908; <u>WSCF</u> 1911; <u>TEW</u> Oct 1914

32 Rudra <u>SM</u> Jan 1910; <u>RI</u> p. 248; <u>TEW</u> Oct 1914

33 <u>Ind Int</u> Oct 1909, with a variant in Preparatory Paper for
    Commission 4 (WMC).

34 <u>Tribune</u> 22 Nov 1910 contained a good illustration of the position
    that Andrews was seeking to correct, with an explicit rejection
    of the Atonement. T.L. Vaswani of Karachi, speaking in London to
    the Liberal Christian league (founded by R.J. Campbell) of the
    Hindu's 'own interpretation of the life of Christ – his pure
    humanity, his perception of the divine in all things natural ...
    the full brotherhood of Man', maintained that 'there was no room
    in India for the doctrine of blood'.

35 <u>Missions and Governments</u> (Report of Commission 7) 1910, p. 34

CHAPTER FIVE
TOWARDS AN INDIAN CHURCH

1. Introductory

Andrews' penetration of the national movement was a striking feature of his
early, missionary years in India, the Christian witness that he bore within
it a unique achievement, and the development of his theology in the context
of nationalism of considerable interest. If these had represented the sum
of his work during these years, they would have marked a prodigiously
creative ministry. But, in addition to reaching 'the rapidly growing
educated Native Community', he had from the beginning set out to reach also
'the rapidly rising Native Christian Church'. This, too, he did in
interesting ways.

His activity in the church included participation in its ordinary
institutions, parish and religious community, mission and diocese, in the
preparation of candidates for baptism and confirmation, and the training of
ordinands, as also in the conducting of retreats and quiet days, and in
such movements as the YMCA. We also come across him in connection with
a number of newly emerging institutions and movements, the formation and
development of the Student Volunteer Missionary Union's short-service
scheme, the training of missionaries in an 'Indian School of Study', the
Indian student movement which was to become the SCM of India, a new
religious community known as the Brotherhood of the Imitation, and the
National Missionary Society. He was also involved in international
movements and meetings in a small but highly significant way, in the world
convention of the Christian Endeavour movement, and, through the
contribution of papers, in the Pan-Anglican Congress of 1908, the
Constantinople assembly of the World Student Christian Federation, and the
World Missionary Conference at Edinburgh in 1910.

As with regard to the national movement, his interest and concern were
reflected in his writing. His two books written during these years were
both essentially about the church, North India in a series called

'Handbooks of English Church Expansion', and The Renaissance in India, subtitled 'Its Missionary Aspect', written for mission-study circles in Britain. He also wrote a certain amount for journals such as the Oxford Mission's Epiphany, the YMCA's Young Men of India, the National Missionary Society's National Missionary Intelligencer, and his own Cambridge Mission's series of Occasional Papers, as well as missionary-society magazines in Britain, the two leading Church of England newspapers, the Church Times and the Guardian, and the SCM's Student Movement. In addition, he did a considerable amount of editorial work, publishing two collections of prayers, preparing with Allnutt and two CMS missionaries a new lectionary, and - a major exercise running from 1906 to 1913 - serving as General Editor for a series of 'Indian Church Commentaries' on the New Testament.

In the course of all this, Andrews' own theological understanding developed and acquired greater definition, well beyond the question of a 'theology of national renaissance'. At the same time, the influence which he exercised on the thinking and activity of others in the church was widespread. In addition to his own immediate circle, Rudra and Ghose, the members of the Brotherhood and Bishop Lefroy, we find him cooperating in one way or another with many leading Indian Christians of what he called 'the more "national" type', V.S. Azariah, P. Chenchiah and K.T. Paul, for example. Such Christians held that no one expressed better than Andrews 'the general opinion that prevails in the New India on matters of vital importance that affect the spread of the Gospel'. (1) There was also much substance in the observation of a Bengali visitor to Delhi, that he had 'succeeded in indoctrinating a noble band of youthful English missionaries with his own ideals', though his influence in the church spread far more widely. (2) His editorial work, both informal, as in his assistance of the Scottish missionary, J.N. Farquhar with his Crown of Hinduism, and formal on the 'Indian Church Commentaries' earned expressions of deep thankfulness for 'unwearied help and counsel'. (3)

In many ways then, Andrews made a lively and influential contribution to the development of the Indian Church.

2. 'Indian Christians and the National Movement'

From the day after his first arrival in Delhi, Andrews had been aware of
weaknesses in the Indian Church, not least among these its foreign
appearance and connections. In the context of the new wave of the national
movement from 1905 onwards, these weaknesses appeared to him dangerously
accentuated. The 'foreign aspect' of Indian Christianity was closely
linked with 'ideas of subjection to a foreign yoke'. (1)

One particularly serious effect, which Westcott had indicated many years
before, and which Andrews often pointed out, was that the Christian
community appeared to be largely 'denationalized'. (2) In the new context,
he plainly had in mind Christian sympathy, or lack of it, for the national
movement in its more strictly political sense, noting no doubt a Bengali's
comments in the Modern Review that 'Indian Christians are for the most part
non-patriotic, if not unpatriotic'. He illustrated this on one occasion by
quoting the remarks of a representative of the older generation of Indian
Christians in the Punjab, who looked upon the very word 'national' as
anathema, and described the fruits of the national movement as 'rebellion,
bloodshed, disobedience', a movement which, if it was ever granted its
rights, would destroy the church. This position was certainly disputed by
other Christians in the Punjab, but one of them admitted that 'there are
only 5% amongst us who have a love for their country and do earnestly
discuss its political situation'. (3)

While Andrews recognised the historical reasons for these denationalizing
tendencies, he pointed out that, in the context of the new national spirit,
they were a serious impediment to the church's life and mission, inhibiting
the growth of a 'true Christian character ... in indigenous ways'. He
noted too that they were driving many of the most independent thinkers
among the Indian Christians, men like Rudra and Ghose, in the direction of
'a kind of unattached Christianity'. (4) To the nationalists who were not
Christians, however attractive they might find the more progressive
features of Christianity, the church was 'an enemy to be avoided', and they
shrank from becoming Christians because this represented 'a rejection of
their Indian aspiration' and 'a death blow to their Indian life'. (5)

It is not, therefore, surprising, that Andrews sought to influence the development of the Indian Church in a number of ways during these years in relation to the national movement.

One small way in which he did so was through directly challenging the assumption among non-Christians that Christianity was inherently denationalizing. He did this briefly in a letter to the Epiphany, and more substantially in an address given at the College on 3 December, 1907, by drawing attention to the current enthusiasm among Indian nationalists for Japan and by going on to illustrate the current enthusiasm for Christianity in Japan, the rejection of Buddhism, and the acknowledgement that Christianity had been 'one of the most vital factors ... in the National Movement'. (6) If the Indian situation was very different, at least the point was made that Christianity in an Asian context was not inherently denationalizing.

A second way in which Andrews set about this was by making the case for Indian Christian involvement in the movement. His approach was sometimes simply a matter of exhortation, to 'Love India with Christ's love', but he also argued that patriotism was a Christian duty with a spiritual basis. His most careful case was made in an article, 'Indian Christians and the National Movement', in the Indian YMCA's Young Men of India. (7) A lesson was to be learnt from the Church of England, which, by allowing itself to be 'too fast-bound to the governing classes' and standing aloof from the Labour Movement in its early, struggling days, had alienated itself from the mass of the people. In the same way in India a great opportunity would be lost and a like fate befall the Indian Church if it stood aside from the national movement and failed to assist in the creation of a casteless nation. If it did this, it would set a premium on retrograde forces and itself become merely a new caste. The issue was urgent, a 'great and noble opportunity' was presented, to 'direct, guide, restrain, inspire', while the movement was still at a formative stage, but this would be lost in one or more generations. Some of the characteristic stresses of his emerging theology are disclosed as the case is made. A 'deep love of country' is 'worthy of the Master who loved his own city, Jerusalem, and wept over her', and is 'divinely implanted in the human heart'. For this reason, non-Christian nationalists, though not owning the Master's allegiance, are 'yet doing His work', and Christians ought to be working alongside them. Indeed, if the 'new movements of humanity' all over Asia had in them elements which made for a 'higher humanity', then Indian Christians had a special part to play with respect to 'the fallen, ... the weak, ... the depressed, ... the masses', whom they had been taught to look upon as 'neighbour, ... brother, and ... friend'. Christians particularly, therefore, represented 'the forces of enlightenment and progress', and had been 'trained, as it were, as engineers to cut the channels for fallen humanity', and held in the Bible 'the guiding construction plans for human progress'.

The article had a mixed reception. A Bengali Christian, J.J. Ghose, replying in the same journal, reiterated the commonplace fear that Indian Christians could expect from national rule dominated by non-Christians only 'humiliation, indignities and even persecution'. The same note was struck at the Lahore Diocesan Conference the following year by Canon Ali Bakhsh, who, however, sought to make a virtue of the Indian Christian predicament by suggesting that the community might have a mediatorial role to play between the imperial government and the nationalists. Others, however, responded more favourably. Rudra, at the same Conference, claimed that a truly Indian Church would only find its goal in 'a completely independent India'. K.T. Paul, representing a younger generation, defended Andrews. Long after Britain's 'political mission to India' was finished, the Indian Christians would still be Indians. The movement presented 'a Divinely appointed opportunity to demonstrate to ... (their) non-Christian compatriots' that Christianity had made them not less but even more patriotic than everyone else. (8)

A third way in which Andrews sought to relate the Church to the national movement was in the matter of mission strategy. The most remarkable growth of the Church in India, and not least in the Punjab, had been, and continued to be during the first few years of the century, through the mass movements among Hindus of the lowest castes and those right outside the caste system. (9) The success of the movement raised a question about

mission strategy, and this was put challengingly, early in 1907, by
H.A. Whitehead, the Bishop of Madras, in whose diocese the mass movements
were also particularly strong.

> The Church seems always to be about twenty years
> behind its opportunities, largely because we persist
> in spending our best energies year after year in
> preaching the gospel to people who show no readiness
> to accept it. The present disposition of our forces
> in India is a striking illustration of this policy.
> Four of our strongest and best equipped missions are
> established in Calcutta, Cawnpore, Delhi and Poona
> ... and in all these four places the Christian
> community has been almost entirely unprogressive for
> the last thirty years .... But what a contrast this
> presents to the state of the S.P.G. mission in the
> Telegu country. Here we have a really remarkable
> movement among the pariahs of Hindu society. (10)

Whitehead went on to argue that such a situation demanded a radical change
of policy, and a shifting of the church's resources from education in the
city centres to evangelism in the country districts. He called for a full
public discussion of the question, and to this Andrews and his colleagues
in Delhi responded. (11) Not surprisingly, all of them opposed the main
proposal. Lefroy, whose episcopal oversight comprehended the mass-movement
areas of the Punjab, had much sympathy with Whitehead's position, but
insisted, nevertheless, at both the Pan-Anglican Congress and the World
Missionary Conference, on putting education first 'as that which ... has
probably contributed the largest share of the influences and elements which
are at present operative on behalf of the spread of the Gospel, ...
remembering ... the wave of life and movement ... which is passing over the
country'. (12)

It is this last point that Rudra emphasised. Because those who sought
higher education, from the higher castes, represented the progressive
forces at a time when a 'new India' was coming to birth, 'missionary

colleges should exist in the fulness of intellectual, moral and spiritual
efficiency, so as to set before youthful India the perfect Image of the
Divine'. (13) This was Andrews' line also. The context of mission was,
and would be 'for the next thirty years', nationalism, and higher
educational work, as every leading Indian Christian whom he met told him,
was 'the key to unlock the future'. In this context, and especially in the
climate of the 'Indian unrest', the witness of the Christian Church as it
was did not really help, but, rather repelled, because it remained 'outside
the new movement'. This was not the case, however, with the missionary
colleges, which, in the face of a distinct reaction against Christianity,
held their place in the esteem and respect of the people because they were
seen to be sympathetic to all that was best in the new spirit.

> There is ... a good prospect that if we hold strongly
> the almost commanding position we have obtained in
> the Universities, we may still keep the National
> Movement in touch, and even in sympathy with
> progressive Christian thought, until the witness of
> the Christian Church itself grows stronger, her
> foreign dress is shaken off, and her contribution to
> the life of the nation is recognised.

Andrews was by no means uninterested in or disparaging of the church's
mass-movement work, and he included in <u>North India</u> a sympathetic chapter on
the subject. His criticism of Whitehead's position, however, was that it
was 'short-sighted' and failed to 'discern the signs of the times'.

> In the long run, as the National Movement advances,
> and ideals of social service advance at the same
> time, the witness of such a Church of the poor ...
> will tell among the more thoughtful educated Indians.
> But this can hardly happen in the North for another
> thirty years.

Meanwhile, to stem and reverse the deepening 'estrangement from the
church', the latter's work in higher education, 'the link of connection ...

(with) the new forces' needed to be strengthened. (14)

Whitehead had pointed out that the church's work in higher education had
produced very few baptisms, and he specifically cited the case of the Delhi
Mission. (15) This point was taken very seriously, and over the ensuing
years, Andrews and Rudra and several of their colleagues enunciated in
reply their own theology of mission. Andrews did so himself in many
places, but perhaps most substantially in a preparatory paper for the World
Missionary Conference, and in an article in the Indian Interpreter.

> I am led more and more, by my missionary experience,
> to regard the conversion of India, not as an
> aggregate of so many individual conversions, but far
> rather as a gradual process of growth and change in
> thought, idea, feeling, temperament, conduct - a
> process which half-creates and half-reconstructs a
> truly Christian religious atmosphere, Indian at its
> best and Christian at its best. In such an
> atmosphere, once formed, the spiritual growth of the
> countless millions of India may go forward and fresh
> fields of spiritual victory may be won. (16)

He called this process 'assimilative', and, following Rudra, found a
warrant for it in the parables of the leaven and of the seed growing
secretly. It amounted to a praeparatio evangelica among the educated
classes as remarkable as that represented by the faith of the Jews of the
Diaspora in the Roman Empire, and a chief instrument of it was the church's
higher educational work, which set forth 'her highest and noblest moral and
spiritual ideals .. to the rising generation'. (17)

Andrews and Rudra were alive to the danger of simply creating 'a vague and
ill-defined Christian atmosphere'. Rudra claimed that educational missions
had effected 'a most remarkable baptism of thought', but this was not
enough. If India was to reconstruct herself on a stable basis, 'a strong
Indian Church' would be needed to counter 'the forces of inertia and
conservatism'. (18) Andrews, too, thought that 'the assimilative ideal'

was becoming 'alarmingly popular'. There was a place also for
confrontation and challenge, and for carrying college-teaching forward 'up
to the highest point, where Christianity alone provides the remedy for sin
and the life-giving power for good'. (19) In terms of mission strategy,
however, the church would have to be content during the current political
ferment to sustain its colleges as homes of a new spiritual life which was
not yet wholly Christian, but which was, nevertheless, 'poles apart from
the old Brahmanical system with its superstitions and idolatries', and
pointed forward to the time when India would find its fulfilment 'within
the Church of Christ, the Son of Man'. (20)

Bishop Whitehead's argument was by no means conclusive. Montgomery, the
Secretary of S.P.G., after visiting North India, was persuaded that the
church there had to 'hold on to the positions which they ... already
occupied and await the course of events'. (21) The issue came up
substantively at the Pan-Anglican Congress the following year under the
heading, 'Strategic Problems. Village Populations versus Educated
Classes', with Whitehead continuing to press 'a gospel to the poor', but
the case for a mission to the educated classes was made equally strongly.
(22) The World Missionary Conference, in the Report of Commission III,
chaired by Charles Gore and significantly entitled Education in relation to
the Christianisation of National Life, deplored the 'waves of anti-
educational sentiment which ... (had) in times past checked or undone the
educational work of missions', and concluded that the missionary colleges
and the mass movements were together the two great forces compensating for
'the evil of an exotic non-national Christianity'. The key chapter carries
two approving references to Westcott and his advocacy of 'Alexandrian
Christianity as the type of Christianity most akin to the Indian mind', and
Andrews is quoted at length, on a far greater scale than any other
missionary correspondent. (23) If Whitehead's challenge, significant as it
was, never looked like carrying the day, it at least served to draw Andrews
and others into the debate and led to a sharper definition of the issues
involved.

Reviewing these years in 1912, Andrews was prepared to acknowledge that,
'since the great national revival, ... both missionaries and congregations

... (had) been inspired with a new spirit', though he was also painfully conscious of lost opportunities which the church might have siezed 'if she had been more prepared'. (24) No one had done more than Andrews to foster this inspiration and alert the church to its opportunities.

3. 'Religious Swadeshism'

If it is true, as Latourette has argued, that the primary prerequisite for the transplanting of Christianity and its taking firm rootage is the achievement of an indigenous leadership and a maximum of self-government, the church situation in India during the early years of the century called for urgent changes. The massive preponderance of foreign missionaries in all positions of leadership in the non-Oriental churches was a striking feature of the situation. Andrews was quick to notice this and to draw attention to it.

> No Indian bishop or even archdeacon, ... after a hundred
> years of missionary effort! (1)

This contrasted unfavourably with the early church's practice of encouraging indigenous leadership and initiative from the outset, as he demonstrated in a substantial article, 'The Indigenous Expression of Christian Truth'. (2) It was particularly damaging, as Rudra pointed out, in the context of the new national aspirations, the 'present foreign ecclesiastical jurisdiction' being 'widely interpreted as further political subjection', and so repelling 'the more independent Indians who love their country'. (3) There were also the unfortunate effects deriving from the fact that the missionary was, as Andrews put it, 'not only a Western but a Sahib, ... linked in a hundred ways with the ruling class'. Attitudes of superiority and contempt were carried over into the treatment even of 'the noblest and highest Indian Christians'. The 'continual subordination' to which they were subjected, was, moreover, 'not a good soil for the growth of originating and governing powers', and change was called for among missionaries.

> To decrease that the Indian may increase ... must ...

be ... an integral part of missionary principle. (4)

Not surprisingly, in the new circumstances from 1905, the call went up from within the Indian Christian community for 'religious or missionary Swadeshism'. (5) We find this reflected in Andrews' circle, in papers presented by two of his colleagues at the Lahore Diocesan Conference of 1906, on 'Self-Support, Self-Government, and Self-Propagation'. It was also being said that the time was coming when the English missionaries should gradually withdraw themselves from positions of leadership - though such views were, as Lefroy pointed out, still distinctly heterodox among missionaries, restricted to 'a very few of the very best'. (6)

Andrews was active on this question in a number of ways, one of which was with regard to the development of synodical government. This was a particularly necessary matter for Anglicans, with their 'Church of England in India', as it was known. Its overarching organisation, the Indian Ecclesiastical Establishment, was an increasing embarrassment, in Andrews' judgement, 'with the great proportion of its clergy in the pay of a foreign Government', and that, as an Indian friend pointed out, at the Indian tax-payer's expense, and 'acting as State officials'. For Andrews, the State Establishment would have to go because it was an anachronism and an offence, 'the position of bishops and priests as paid government servants ... becoming more and more liable to hopeless misunderstanding' as the Indian national spirit advanced. (7) For Rudra, the witness of the church was 'compromised, ... almost desperately compromised ... by these fetters'. Not surprisingly, Lefroy, quoting Andrews, was soon himself saying that the gravity of the position could hardly be exaggerated. (8)

The Anglican bishops had for some quarter of a century been committed, at least in theory, to modifying these arrangements through the development of synodical government, but it was only with the Episcopal Synod of 1908 that the first definite moves were made, and then not least because of the reinforcement of the Synod by 'two staunch advocates of reform', Foss Westcott of Chota Nagpur, and Lefroy. (9) Andrews, as we have seen, and perhaps some of his circle, clearly influenced Lefroy. Four years later, as the Provincial Synod moved towards dissociating the Church from the imperial government and towards autonomy, Rudra played a unique part, pleading for the title, 'The Church of India'. (10)

A second important aspect of the development of indigenous initiative at this time was the formation of the National Missionary Society. This had originated in the south under the inspiration of two Y.M.C.A. secretaries, V.S. Azariah, who had two years earlier founded the Indian Missionary Society of Tinnevelly, and G.S. Eddy, an American. The first meeting was held at Serampore on Christmas Day, 1905, the object of the Society being 'to evangelize unoccupied fields in India and adjacent countries, and to lay on Indian Christians the burden of responsibility for the evangelisation of their own country and neighbouring lands'. Andrews was appointed, with ten other missionaries, to the original Advisory Board, which was 'wholly and solely' to maintain a link with the foreign missionary societies. Although he was to report 'but a cold welcome' to the Society in many mission stations, his own colleagues, and in particular Lefroy and Allnutt, welcomed it with great enthusiasm and admiration. Both were soon to report, with equal enthusiasm, that many of the younger Indian Christians of Delhi were interested and had formed a local branch. Lefroy, almost overwhelmed at the immensity of the missionary task in his diocese, 'grotesque, if ... not so appallingly sad and humiliating', told the World Missionary Conference that he found its formation 'a true cause for thankfulness'. (11)

Andrews was soon involved in an almost unique way for a non-Indian. He went with Eddy to intercede with Lefroy for the recognition of the Society in the Punjab, and when the Punjab provided 'the first Missionary and the first Mission-field', Andrews, as a member of the Advisory Board, was called in to discuss the question of the young man's ordination. Although he found that his membership of the Board brought him 'a considerable amount of interesting work and correspondence', he was always emphatic that the Society and its work should be entirely in the hands of Indian Christians. (12) A criticism in the Gwalior Mission Journal that the Society was over-centralised and 'all engineered on European lines', drew him to its defence to point out that if it was to be national, some organization was essential. The 'immense power' which a Hindu movement

like the Arya Samaj derived from good organization indicated that
organization was in itself 'neither Eastern nor Western'. (13)

Andrews was present as the only European participant in the first
conference of the Society, held in Delhi at Easter, 1912. Not only did he
speak, but he also took the chair when the chairman, K.T. Paul, General
Secretary of the Society, spoke. It is some measure of his own place in
the emerging Indian Church that the 'swadeshi' principle was overlooked in
his case.

A third area in which Andrews was involved in the question of indigenous
leadership in the church was with regard to the Principalship of St
Stephen's College, 'the most honourable office in the Mission'. (14)
Hibbert-Ware had gone on furlough early in 1906, and the thought had
occurred to some of appointing the recently-arrived Andrews temporarily in
his place, or even the much younger F.J. Western. However, the Mission
Council in Delhi, made up of the members of the Brotherhood, had little
difficulty in agreeing to the acting appointment of Rudra, who had been on
the staff for twenty years and Vice-Principal for several. This worked
extremely well, and Allnutt reported with pride and satisfaction that the
appointment was an unqualified success. Andrews added that the new
context, 'national enthusiasm', had made the appointment of a 'loyal and
patriotic Indian' the more significant. (15) With Hibbert-Ware's decision,
however, later that year, to leave educational for village work, the
question arose of the permanent Principalship, and here the issue appeared
more difficult.

The Cambridge Committee were unanimously in favour of Rudra's appointment,
but wished to leave the decision to the people on the spot. Among the
latter, a vigorous debate ensued. The first step was that the members of
the Brotherhood agreed to submit memoranda on the issue for common
consideration. Of the ten who did so, in January 1907, five were
unequivocally in favour of Rudra's appointment, or, in principle, of the
appointment of an Indian Christian, two were uncertain, and three strongly
opposed.

The general issue of the appointment of an Indian was complicated by a
sense that the College was 'a distinctive gift of Cambridge to Delhi', and
that therefore the link with Cambridge should be embodied in the Principal.
Four of the supporters, G.A. Purton, N.C. Marsh, Western and Andrews,
regarded the Cambridge link as a subordinate issue. Western, indeed,
suggested that that the issue was the leadership of an 'Indian College', so
that insistence on the Cambridge factor was indefensible, while Marsh and
Purton argued that 'the liberal lines' of the work and method at Delhi,
deriving from the 'Cambridge ethos', themselves required that leadership
opportunities be given to Indians, Marsh's only condition being that 'the
Missionary work and Religious Influence in the College' should be a
paramount concern of the Principal. B.P.W. French maintained that it was
precisely and primarily the effect which Christianity had produced, 'the
influence of Christianity on a man's whole personality', which had produced
distinguished Indian candidates.

French's note was, in some respects, the most radical of all, with his
observation, extraordinary for 1907, that 'it may well be the case that the
time has not come for a general exodus of all European missionaries', but
that 'to continue to hold the inhabitants of a country in subjection is
opposed to the basis of Christianity', so that those who laid stress on the
religious aspect of politics had a duty to do all in their power to
encourage the movement for self-development. If Andrews, in his note, took
the matter any further, it was by pressing the question to the point of
action by insisting that it was 'not a principle' of the Mission that a
Cambridge man should be the head of the College, but that 'the appointment
of Indians to responsible positions' as soon as possible was a principle of
all the Mission's work, and a principle so vital that his whole position in
the Brotherhood would need to be reconsidered if there was any departure
from it.

Of the two who wrote ambivalent memoranda, one said that for him the only
significant factor was Rudra's attitude towards 'intending converts' - was
he going to encourage them? The other, Allnutt, felt that the pros and
cons of appointing an Indian were so nearly balanced that he could only
take 'an opportunist position': while Andrews had to be discounted as a

candidate because his 'intense sympathy with the nationalist movement' would alienate Government, source of important grants for the College, Rudra, on the other hand, had given proof of possessing remarkable qualifications for the position, so that the policy of appointing him was by no means one of despair. Allnutt added, in a letter to Stanton at Cambridge, that Rudra was so eminently fitted for the post in every way, that not to appoint him would be 'a slur on the Indians'. (16)

Opposition to the appointment came from three of the oldest and, apart from Allnutt, most senior members of the Mission. W.S. Kelley's objections were the most mild. Apart from a reservation about 'the uncertain tone of the Indian religious mind at the present', he could see the value of showing 'a legitimate sympathy with a National movement', but feared that Rudra, though as nearly ideal a Vice-Principal as could be hoped for at the time, would fail generally in his dealing with government officials. H.C. Carlyon made the point about government grants, and the link with Cambridge, and indeed saw nothing wrong with appointing 'a young man fresh from Cambridge when an experienced Indian ... (was) at hand'. He claimed that under Indian leadership, work had 'a tendency to stagnate'. The nationalist factor was a ground for not appointing an Indian.

> I consider that the present time of feverish
> excitement is most inopportune for making any radical
> change. ... Let us strive by all legitimate ways in
> our power to hasten the spread of the Gospel but let
> us remember that men are continually hindering it by
> not exercising sufficient patience.

Finally, Lefroy, recognising 'very great force indeed' in some of Carlyon's arguments, wrote a lengthy note. Affirming that the special aim of the College was to bring to bear on the great problem of the evangelisation of India the thought and devotion of the Christian Church 'in the particular form, with the particular ethos, which Cambridge ... (had) gradually made their own', he believed that, 'at any rate from this point of view', the ideal Principal would be an Indian graduate from Cambridge. But there were other points of view, and Lefroy admitted to 'an old-fashioned belief in a

Western effectiveness and energy and grit and grip', which was far ahead of anything that India could supply at that time. Also, he very greatly regretted that 'a fiercely political, and in large measure anti-English, spirit' had been allowed to supplant the missionary motive in the College, and having intimate opportunities of knowing how very seriously the authorities viewed this as characterising St Stephen's 'in quite special – and, as they would hold, objectionable – measure', he feared that 'the attitude of the Punjab Government towards the College would be ... most injuriously affected' by the appointment of a permanent Indian principal. In the circumstances, until a suitable Englishman could be found, Rudra, – whom Lefroy liked as much as possible and wholly believed in as a true Christian man, though he was nothing like a born leader – should be asked to continue as acting Principal.

> It might seem almost ungracious to ask this of him,
> if not intending to let him have the substantive
> post, but I believe his genuine Christianity could
> respond to the test.

With the circulation of these memoranda as a preliminary to a Brotherhood meeting, a further stage in the debate was introduced. Western and Andrews each produced a second paper, commenting on those of Carlyon and Lefroy. Western's was a careful refutation of their arguments. Andrews' paper, quite the longest in the entire exercise, was equally systematic. With regard to the special link with Cambridge, the Bishop's position was a dangerous half-truth, the other and equally important half being the need to evoke 'an Indian Christianity, a College imbued with an Indian Christian spirit and not Anglicised'.

> We have in Rudra a man who is steeped in Cambridge
> traditions. The whole trend of his thought is
> Westcottian: he reveres Westcott our Founder.... At
> the same time he has that which is still more
> important from our point of view, viz. a passionate
> love for his country. He combines Cambridge with
> India, India with Cambridge.

Westcott and Hort would surely have welcomed the appointment of an Indian
as Principal, and this would, indeed, be an answer to 'the prayers and
longings of our pious Founders'. As to the Bishop's concern for vigorous
and effective leadership, Rudra had startling qualities and was strong
where many of his countrymen were weak, in discipline, firmness and powers
of hard work; these had developed remarkably during his acting
principalship, and latent qualities had appeared which the Bishop had not
had the opportunity to see. As to the Bishop's remarks about the College
being 'fiercely political', these only showed how out of touch Lefroy was
with both St Stephen's and the student world as a whole.

> When most of the colleges are seething with
> discontent and smothered disloyalty, our students are
> almost to a man strong and loyal nationalists.

- and this was due in large measure to Rudra's influence. Andrews was sure
that Rudra's Christianity would stand the test of an extension of his
acting position at the end of which he would step down, but, he added
sharply, 'would ours?' He concluded by throwing back at Lefroy his own
words at the Diocesan Conference, that it would be madness to come to India
with 'our ideals of personal freedom, ... and then expect nothing to
happen', and by repeating that a vital principle was at issue for him, and
that if Rudra was passed over at this point, 'the whole idea of ... (his)
missionary work would be shattered'. This was a spirited and challenging
paper, and a powerful contribution to the debate. Throughout, we find his
characteristic point about relating mission to nationalism, his conviction
that the spread of the Gospel would be hastened by sympathy with the Indian
point of view and the exercise of the principles of equality and
brotherhood. The question was one of profound significance for 'the whole
Church of India', a matter of Christian principle but also of 'Christian
... statesmanship'. Rudra's confirmation would be a demonstration of a
genuine desire to build up 'an Indian Church with Indian leaders', and
would thus represent 'a new and important step forward' for the church.

Allnutt, at least, seems to have found that Andrews' and Western's second
memoranda answered his own uncertaintiies, and when the Brotherhood came to

vote on the question, he joined Rudra's supporters and the matter was substantially carried. (17)

It should be added that Lefroy made the most public confession possible of his mistaken judgement of Rudra, in a preparatory paper for the World Missionary Conference, while he spoke at Church House, Westminster, on how splendidly the experiment had succeeded, and how important this was in the context of the 'Indian Unrest'. (18)

The mechanics of Rudra's confirmation went ahead, and Allnutt wrote to him on 2 June 1907, confirming the appointment, in a moving and enthusiastic letter, expressing pleasure both personal, and at the principle acted upon, 'the one called for by the growth of the Indian Church'. (19)

The principle was one to which Andrews would frequently refer over the coming years, almost invariably citing the case of Rudra's appointment and his subsequent statesmanlike and brilliant leadership in its vindication. (20)

4. 'The Eastern Ideal'

To the extent that the 'Sahib spirit' characterised the ministry, the church was dangerously, if not fatally compromised, and, indeed, Ghose went so far as to say that it rendered the missionary's work quite useless.

> The young missionary ... imperceptibly enters into
> the possession of a vast heritage of accumulated
> prejudice against the Indian as such. ... I could
> point to many missionaries in this sad plight -
> living a sort of withered existence, unloving and
> unloved. ... This official tone ... turns him into a
> stone. It is a blight which touches hearts once
> active, living, liberal and makes them barren, hard
> and fruitless. (1)

It was essential, therefore, that an alternative model should be found for

the Christian ministry in India. Rudra put this into words which T.V.
French might well have used in his thinking about the needs of the Indian
Church.

> We need a body of spiritual Christian men eminently
> fitted by learning and temperament to pursue a life
> of study and contemplation, to be like swamis and
> paramhansas, fitted to set a new standard of
> Christian holiness which shall appeal to the New
> India of the future. Such men would have a Mission
> to Indian Christians as well as non-Christians. They
> would supply an indigenous centre of authority and an
> indigenous interpretation of the Christ-life, based
> on their own true Indian Christian character and
> learning and wisdom. If they formed a true Christian
> asram, their title would not be derived from foreign
> churches, but from their own intrinsic spirituality.
> It would be a title bestowed upon them by Christ
> Himself and His Spirit. Imagine a Christian
> Chaitanya or a Christian Vivekananda! (2)

During these years, some interesting developments in this direction took
place in the Punjab, and with these Andrews was closely associated.

In the summer of 1907, while staying at Simla, he visited, with Lefroy, the
small village congregation at Kotgarh, where the latter was to administer
confirmation. Among the candidates was a seventeen-year old Sikh convert
who had been baptised two years previously. Andrews noted that, though
'very humble and quiet', his face was 'gloriously aflame with his first
love for Christ'. This was Sundar Singh, later to become 'perhaps the most
famous Indian Christian who has yet lived'. (3)

In September 1905, Sundar Singh had been sent up from Ludhiana to get him
away from the excitement which his conversion had aroused there, in the
care of a young American 'free-lance' missionary, Samuel E. Stokes, and
Stokes had arranged for his baptism by John Redman, a CMS missionary at

Simla. Thereafter, in the summer of 1906, under the influence of Stokes, he had donned the saffron robe of the sadhu and begun to develop his distinctive ministry, which was to have such a unique impact, both in India and in the Western world.

While Acting Principal at the Military School at Sanawar during the hot weather of 1906, Andrews had heard of Sundar Singh, who was at that time working with Stokes among lepers in nearby Sabathu, but did not meet him then. A first proper meeting had to wait until some months after Sundar Singh's confirmation, when Andrews visited him while he was working in the plague camp near Lahore in about November 1907. Over the next four years, he and Rudra spent their summer vacations in the Simla hills, and met Sundar Singh often between his evangelistic itinerations in the Indo-Tibet border areas. In the winter they welcomed him at the College. Andrews also visited him whenever possible while Sundar Singh was at the Divinity School at Lahore, between December 1909 and August 1910. He was thus able to write of a 'growing friendship', and even of their becoming 'like brothers together'. (4)

Sundar Singh was clearly already capable of profoundly influencing those whom he met. Thus, Rudra wrote his fine paper, 'Christ and Modern India', with its vision of an authentic Indian Church centred on 'devotion to a Supreme Person ... without any obscuring medium, ... in keeping with the natural bent of Indian and Eastern character', when he was, Andrews noted, 'in almost daily touch with Sadhu Sundar Singh'. Similarly, the Christian students at St Stephen's College, who sat up with him far into the night, were more deeply influenced as Christians by him, Andrews recalled, than by the 'conventional lives' of Rudra and himself, and the course of life of several of them was dramatically changed. He also clearly made a deep personal impression on Andrews himself, bringing him 'nearer to Christ', and he wrote many years later that when he was with him during these early years, 'he strengthened my own faith and helped me to keep the pure flame of Christ's love burning bright'.

Andrews used to talk about him frequently with Rudra, and discuss his way of life, and he saw from the first how very highly significant Sundar Singh

was as a sign for the Indian Church in his development of the ministry of a
Christian sadhu.

> The whole future of the Christian faith in India
> seemed to centre in the ideal he put before us.

It has been suggested that Sundar Singh's theology was even more important
than his style of ministry, but this had at that time hardly begun to
develop. Andrews only took serious account of this, his 'creative power of
thought', many years later. What mattered at this time was the adoption of
an Indian form of consecrated life in the service of Christian ministry and
evangelism.

> Sundar Singh, by his creative personality, set
> forward a true type for Indian Christians to follow.
> ... To the East the Sadhu brings the message that
> Christ belongs to them no less than to the West; that
> it is their function to express Him truly as
> belonging to the East. It is theirs to offer to the
> West a new vision of Christ as He walks the Eastern
> road and dwells among the Eastern village folk in
> lowly poverty, simplicity and self-denial. (5)

After the middle years of his missionary decade, Andrews saw much less of
Sundar Singh, but his estimate of his significance for the Indian Church
remained high, surviving a public campaign denigrating his integrity. Well
over twenty years later, he wrote his <u>Sadhu Sundar Singh: A Personal
Memoir</u> to sustain interest in what Sundar Singh had achieved and
represented, based largely on these early years in his Christian life, 'the
greatest and the best years'. (6)

During these same years, and closely linked with the ministry of Sundar
Singh, there were other novel developments in Christian mission in the
Punjab. These relate to the work of the young American, Samuel Stokes,
who had come in India at the age of twenty-two early in 1904, had worked
for a short time 'in connection with the SPG mission in Delhi', and had

then moved on to the Simla hills. There, in August 1906, he distributed
his possessions and, after three days alone in prayer, assumed 'the
Friar's robe and the obligations of a Friar's life' as he understood
these, 'the life of poverty and conformation to the earthly life of our
Lord', believing that if this could be 'applied to the life of this land,
and lived here, men could not but believe in Jesus Christ'. (7) It was
not the first time that the Franciscan life had been regarded as specially
significant for India, nor was it to be the last.

Stokes and Sundar Singh, who met in the summer of 1906, worked in close
association over the next few years, tending the sick in leper and plague
camps, and, 'barefooted and bareheaded, wearing the ochre-coloured sadhu's
dress', on evangelistic tours towards Tibet, when they were invariably
'received and listened to with reverence'.

At this stage - presumably during the hot weather of 1907 - Andrews had
'long and intimate talks' with Stokes, and lived with him for 'more than a
month'. (8)

Stokes' own account of his and Sundar Singh's work during this phase is
interesting and also intensely moving. He describes in detail his work in
a plague-infected village in the plains in the spring of 1907, his gradual
acceptance by the villagers being the more remarkable in that this was at
the height of the Punjab's agrarian unrest, when feelings against
foreigners were especially bitter. In his own understanding, Stokes was a
friar, trying to conform his life to his vision of 'the perfect friar', to
the vision of 'the homeless, suffering, serving Christ'. It is some
measure of the effectiveness of this Franciscan approach that in the eyes
of the villagers he was a true 'Bhagat of God', and even 'their' bhagat,
and 'Maharaj'. (9) That Stokes was not romanticising his ministry and its
effectiveness is made clear by Lefroy, who was filled with 'thankfulness
and hope' at Stokes' work. He referred to him at the World Missionary
Conference, to his 'personal holiness and nearness to Christ', to his
ministry, its 'love and ... practical good sense and brightness', and to
its 'priceless value' as a witness to Christ, which appealed 'directly and
in the strongest way possible to the religious instincts of the East and

realises their ideals'. (10)

Stokes discovered that 'a thousand doors which had remained closed to him
as a Sahib' opened gladly before him 'as a poor Religious'. 'That barrier
which all earnest missionaries in India keenly feel', which had formerly
been his despair, had been removed. This encouraged him to propose an
extension of this ministry. He travelled to England and the USA in 1908,
speaking and writing of his experiences and of his plans for a Franciscan
Brotherhood, or, as he came to call it, a Brotherhood of the Imitation of
Jesus. He also discussed the question with Lefroy, who agreed to support
the venture. With the latter's approval, he published in SPG's The East
and the West specific proposals, that, for example, the Brotherhood should
be devoted to the service of 'all who are afflicted', and that it should do
educational work in existing institutions. (11)

In the next year or two, the Brotherhood of the Imitation began to take
shape. A recruit from England came out under the auspices of the CMS in
November 1909. (12) More significantly, perhaps, two Brahmin sanyasis who
had become Christians under Stokes' influence, Swami Isananda and Swami
Dhar Tirath, came to be associated with the community. (13) Stokes' chief
and only full associate, however, was F.J. Western, who had joined the
Cambridge Brotherhood, like Andrews, in 1904, and in September 1909 moved
over into the Brotherhood of the Imitation, of which he was to remain a
member for just over two years, before returning to full membership of the
Cambridge Brotherhood. His move into the Brotherhood of the Imitation was
noted respectfully by the Tribune, in a news item entitled 'True
Self-Sacrifice', a further indication of the missionary significance of
Stokes' approach. He is described as having left 'his fashionable rooms in
the SPG Mission House', and 'turned a sanyasi,... living in a very small
room in the School Boarding House, ... a dhoti, a long over-garment, a rug
and a matting, form the necessities of his daily life, ... maintaining
himself on 6 rs. a month', and it is all seen as 'an eye-opener to most of
our Indians'. (14) Others were associated with the community. (15) Among
these, Sundar Singh remained 'entirely a free-lance', but 'retained the
most friendly relations' with the Brotherhood. (16) Andrews described
himself as 'an Associate Member' and 'Chaplain of the Order', and clearly

saw himself as closely connected, though not formally admitted as a member. Poor health kept him from what he later saw would have been, for him, a 'false move ... for while Stokes was clearly called to the villages, I was as clearly called to the English-Educated'. (17)

Although Stokes preferred to continue with his work among the lepers and in the plague camps, he did himself also, in fact, pursue a very interesting line in educational work. As early as 1907, the Tribune reported him as wishing to establish 'a Christian Gurukula', that is, a school centred on a guru, a religious teacher. (18) In pursuance of this, he published a prospectus, 'A Scheme for a Christian Gurukula', setting the need for such a school in the context of the emerging nation, never more in need of 'true men, with high ideals and earnest purpose, consecrated body and soul to the service of God and their motherland'. The proposal is very much a mixture of East and West, with its call for an institution for the sons of Indian gentlemen, which may combine 'all the advantages of the ancient gurukula of the Aryans with those of a first-class modern boarding school', in which 'each instructor will aim to live Christ in the midst of the boys, and to do it in such a simple and manly manner, that the Lord may become for all within the walls of the Gurukula, a living Personality, and the figure of all that is noble, manly, bold and to be desired'. (19) In June 1909, he submitted proposals to the CMS in London to take over and reshape the Society's Primary School at Kotgarh, with F.J. Western in charge, the enterprise to be modelled on the Arya Samaj's institution. The scheme was approved, and, though Western did not remain long in charge, Stokes was able in 1910 to report its establishment as part of the 'work accomplished' in the previous year. The Tribune followed this development also with interest. (20)

Another aspect of the activities of the Brotherhood of the Imitation was a small amount of publishing, under the imprint of the Christian Literature Society. This included an anonymous study, Divine Incarnation, in which the Christian doctrine is compared and contrasted with Hindu beliefs, and, by Stokes himself, The Historical Character of the Gospel, an anthology of Jewish, Roman and Greek background texts for the origins of Christianity. Andrews contributed to this latter a short preface, emphasising that 'Christ was no mythical figure, but stood forth in the broad daylight of history', in this respect 'differing altogether from the Krishna Legend'. The Modern Review gave this last an enthusiastic welcome, adding that Indians would 'always reverence those among the followers of Jesus who, like Mr. Andrews ... himself, try to mould their lives after him'. (21)

The Brotherhood of the Imitation did not last very long. In August 1911, Stokes announced that he was to marry a wife from within the Kotgarh Christian community. This he did in the autumn of 1912. In explaining his decision, he disclosed developments in his thinking which represented a criticism of the Brotherhood, for he made it clear that it was not simply a matter of his leaving the community, but rather of his conviction that 'the Brotherhood as such must go.' While he acknowledged that the ideal of the Brotherhood expressed 'a very real side of the Gospel message', it was open to misunderstanding, particularly in India, because it confirmed the mistaken Eastern conception that the truly religious life was to be attained only by freeing oneself from the 'net' of worldly affairs, including 'all the relationships of normal life, home, family and friends'. The 'Gospel of the Incarnation', on the other hand, that 'in Jesus of Nazareth the Son of God became not only a man but Man', represented a call 'to grow not super-human, but more human', and to work for the consecration of these 'relationships of normal life'. The 'principle of the Incarnation' could also be applied in another sense, in that by uniting himself by marriage with the Indian community, he might reverse the conventional missionary approach of working 'from without inward', a method which weakened and pauperized. Stokes added a third point, that an inter-racial marriage represented his 'fierce protest' against the 'ancient racial prejudices' that he discerned in the church. (22)

Stokes' decision effectively brought the Brotherhood of the Imitation to an end. In November 1911, Western told Lefroy that he did not feel capable of carrying the work on. He returned to the Cambridge Brotherhood, retaining his belief in what he called 'Franciscanism', and insisting on continuing in his new style of life. It would be, though, as

Andrews noted, 'something much less naturally visible to the world ...
but keeping closely to the inner spirit of poverty and devotion to the
poor'. (23)

It remains to say something on Andrews' own reflections on these
developments to which he was so close. The early and most informal phase
of Stokes' ministry gave Andrews more food for thought than anything else
that he had seen in India.

> It was all Christianity pure and simple, expressed in
> a language 'understanded of the people'.

He wrote at some length in <u>North India</u> on Stokes' approach, and of what he
called 'the Franciscan ideal', the 'full life of holy poverty and
renunciation', because it seemed both to represent, as the missionary-as-
sahib never could, 'the life of the Crucified', and also to reflect
'perhaps the strongest religious instinct ... among educated and uneducated
Indians of all creeds', that is, renunciation. (24) This was a point which
he made frequently over the next few years with his Indian Christian
readers. (25) He sometimes qualified his advocacy, however, suggesting,
for example, that 'Eastern Christianity .. will have ... its ascetic,
mystical, formless side; but it will also clothe itself in beautiful
garments of its own, and appeal to the home, the family, the people, as
well as to the solitary idealist'. (26) It is notable that Andrews was
saying this in November 1909, when the Brotherhood was just being formed,
two years before Stokes was expressing his own similar reservations. At
the same time, Stokes' ascetic line certainly chimed in with one of
Andrews' own deepest impulses, and he sought to exemplify in his own life
'the laying stress on the literal imitation'. As a friend from these early
years later recalled, Andrews himself 'imbibed to a wonderful degree the
Eastern ideal of a religious life, and was content to live a life of
simplicity and poverty, ... in order to be easily accessible to ... our
country and all her people'. (27)

On the Brotherhood of the Imitation, his most extended consideration occurs
in an article, 'The Indian Missionary Ideal', published early in 1911 and

based on a letter which he wrote to 'a Scotch missionary' who had sought
his opinion as to whether he considered the Brotherhood suited to
contemporary India. (28) In this, he considers three possible missionary
methods. The first of these, the transmission of all that is precious to
the missionary in his own personal Western experience of Christianity, what
he called elsewhere, quoting Sir George Birdwood, 'egotistical religious
proselytism', the manufacture of 'exotic' or 'hybrid' Christians, 'out of
touch with their own countrymen and their country's ideals', he takes
little time over. (29) The second he calls the assimilative ideal, 'I must
become an Indian to the Indian in order to win the Indian'. This, he says,
had proved immensely attractive to younger missionaries two or three years
earlier.

Then had come the third approach, 'a life which went deeper', the ideal of
the literal imitation of Jesus, 'not the Western model, not the Eastern
model, but the primitive model of the earliest Christian days, when love
and sacrifice and renunciation were the very salt of the Christian life'.
The strength of this approach is that it places the cross at the centre,
rousing the church from an over-trust in the busy activity of organisations
and institutions, and pointing to 'the one final power of Christianity upon
the lives and hearts of men', in contrast with the assimilative ideal which
is liable to bypass the cross. For this reason, 'the biggest truth of all
for India at the present time' lay in this imitative ideal. To start with
'assimilation to Hindu ideals' and possibly bypassing the cross would
create the risk of 'Christianity being merged with Hinduism'.

> Christ is indeed the Fulfiller of each world
> religion, yet He is something infinitely more. He is
> the Crucified ... (and so) Hinduism, great and lofty
> as it is, must die and be reborn before it can live
> to Christ. (30)

Assimilation, nevertheless, as 'the fuller catholic ideal', must follow,
and in due time 'the young and vigorous Church of India will build up its
own living fabric out of those very truths of Hinduism which are today
showing signs of decay and death'. The Brotherhood of the Imitation was

correct for that particular time in setting forward 'the path of that renunciation which must precede the new birth in India'.

Andrews was more sad than he could say about Stokes' 'hasty withdrawal', as he regarded it, from the Brotherhood of the Imitation, though he agreed with him that 'the Hindu ideal ... had crept in in certain ways'. (31) Indeed, he was soon publicly stating again, at the first conference of the National Missionary Society, his reservations about what he called on that occasion 'the sadhu ideal', namely that it did not recognise the worth of the domestic ideal, and that it created the false impression that there is 'merit' in renunciation, and that inaction is necessary for greater spiritual development. (32)

Andrews' enthusiasm, nevertheless, for the sort of developments represented in the person and ministry of Sundar Singh, and of Stokes, and in the Brotherhood of the Imitation, and his publicising of them, are clear indications of the general direction in which he wished to see the church moving with regard to modes of ministry and common life. It was a direction in which there were subsequent developments, not least in the Christa Seva Sangh at Poona, where Andrews' advocacy may well have been influential. (33)

5. 'One Body'

During the middle years of his missionary decade, Andrews' theology of national renaissance ran over into a conception of an emergent Body of Humanity, of which Christ as Son of Man was Head. Throughout these years, however, although he was led to affirm his belief in the actuality of a 'church' far wider than the company of the baptised, he held on to the conviction that Christianity was 'the one final religion of universal brotherhood and the one unifying religion of the whole human race', and that the church was 'the nucleus of that unity'. It is not, therefore, surprising that within such a strongly holistic perspective, he saw, or came to see the question of church unity as very important, and was 'continually thinking and working towards a unity that is infinitely varied, Catholic, all-embracing'. (1)

The decade preceding Andrews' own arrival in India had seen the beginning
of the movement towards church union in India and Asia generally. In this,
the Anglicans had been in a small way involved. Andrews' own involvement
in the student community, in which so largely the ecumenical movement
began, provided him with 'a living inspiration', the World Student
Christian Federation recovering for him and many others 'the sense of the
unity of Christendom'. (2)

Anglicanism itself presented a not entirely united front, so that in the
Diocese of Lahore the work of SPG and CMS went on in comparative
independence. While it is clear that other members of the two societies
were anxious to co-ordinate their work, and even see the societies
disappear, 'and the Church to appear to be what it is, a real organic
whole', it is noteworthy that moves in this direction were at Andrews'
instigation. (3) With other Christians, likewise, the Baptists in Delhi,
and the Presbyterians in other parts of the Punjab, cooperation was
developing. Allnutt in particular among the members of the Delhi Mission
was vigorous in the promotion of practical union with the local Baptists.
Andrews' chief contribution, in addition to a series of practical ventures,
was in the promotion of the new movement and thought about it through his
writings.

He dealt with two aspects of the matter of church unity. First, he gave
some consideration, though rarely at great length, to the theological
problems of church union as usually understood. His views on this were
never the chief subject of a major article, but we are able to build
up something of a picture of his position as it developed during these
years. (4)

In matters of church unity, he claimed to be 'a High Churchman', and was
indeed so regarded, and warned the W.S.C.F. against any suggestion that
'the Reformed Churches in the West' represented the whole of active
Christendom. His Indian experience in a sense reinforced his position,
giving him 'an intense passionate longing ... for corporate organic unity',
and leading him to advocate 'close and effective co-operation between the
different missions'. (5) With regard to this, making much of the

cooperation already achieved in Delhi with the Baptists, he worked out and proposed a theory of 'practical union'. Characteristically, he prefaced this with a discussion of what has more recently been called a wider ecumenism, which he called 'outer co-operation', that is, 'work among non-Christians of a very close and spiritual character'. 'Inner co-operation', that is, cooperation among Christian groups, he believed to be possible for Anglicans with other Christian bodies, provided that these fulfilled three conditions. They must be such as '(i) Recognise order and discipline and membership in a Church as essential. (ii) Regard the sacrament of baptism as imperative for converts. (iii) Are orthodox concerning the Person of our Blessed Lord and Saviour'. More important, perhaps, was his enunciaton of a principle which, many years later, at Lund, was to become a guiding criterion for the ecumenical movement.

> Practical union in work and prayer up to the point
> where in practice our principles are seen to diverge.

He added, 'If I had written "where in _theory_", I am afraid we should have made very little progress; for we all imagine our own theories to cover far more ground than they really do'. (6)

On this question of cooperation, he acknowledged that his proposed principle could be held in conjunction with 'a strictly denominational position', beyond which he did not believe that Anglicans were at that time prepared to go. He himself, however, admitted in 1909 that, though 'more a sacramentalist, ... more a "Churchman" than ever', he had moved far from a narrowly 'denominational position', a development which clearly parallels his developing thought about human solidarity, 'the Body of Humanity'.

> I could not now speak of ... Episcopacy as of the
> 'Esse' of the Church, or regard a Quaker who had
> conscientious scruples as to Baptism as not belonging
> to the 'Body of Christ', or consider a Presbyterian
> or Congregational Sacrament of Holy Communion as _ipso_
> _facto_ invalid, or speak as I used to do of
> nonconformity as outside or half outside the

> covenant. The world of the Mission-field has made me
> long for corporate organic unity with an intense
> passionate longing, but it has made me also realise
> that the pathway to Corporate Unity is not so narrow
> and exactly defined as I had imagined and that the
> variety in the One Body is as important as the
> unity. (7)

Andrews spelt out this new position in a preparatory paper for the World
Missionary Conference. Some measure of where he stood may be seen when one
compares this with the attitude of the large number of SPG supporters in
England who presented a 'Remonstrance' in July 1910, against formal
recognition of the Conference, in order to check any further association on
the part of the Society 'with the principles of Inter-Denominationalism'.
The shift in Andrews' position is fairly typical of missionaries in India
at this period. Inevitably, in his case, the national movement was a
significant factor. 'We are beginning to feel', he told the National
Missionary Society, 'the enormity' of imposing Western divisions on Indian
Christians. (8) A few months later, he pointed to the way the early church
had developed, 'an Alexandrian Christianity distinct in tone and colour
from that of Ephesus or Antioch, ... Rome or Carthage', the church in each
great racial or national area having its own autonomous life, the meeting
together of these autonomous churches on an equal footing being 'the
highest conception of Church Unity and Catholicity that has ever been
presented to the world'. (9)

It was, in fact, essentially Indian conditions which shaped Andrews'
developing viewpoint about church unity. This does not mean that he was
prepared to abandon important Anglican principles. Indeed, he affirmed in
1912 his conviction that the Anglican contribution was 'a vital one, for
the Indian Church', and he urged non-Anglicans to deal directly with
controversial subjects, the question of 'valid Ordination and valid
Sacraments', and to 'meet each other's real difficulties'. (10)
Interestingly, he spelt out, if briefly, the significance of these two
particular issues for the Church in India. Thus, he suggested that, as in
no other country in the world, 'the supreme value of the episcopate' stood

out in India.

> Loyalty to a central person is an instinct among
> India's great unlettered rural population.
> Furthermore, India is a land of traditions, a land in
> which the past counts for more than the present. To
> be linked with the Church of all the ages, to be in a
> distinct historical succession from the Apostles
> themselves ... - these are ideas singularly vivid to
> the Indian mind.

In this, Andrews was anticipating by more than a decade a view which was to
gain recognition at the conference on church union at Tranquebar in 1919, a
meeting so crucial in the history of ecumenism. 'The Tranquebar men seemed
to say', Sundkler has written, '... Episcopacy is in accordance with the
genius of India'. (11) He found, similarly, an Indian solution to the
ecumenical problem of sacraments. In an article for a Presbyterian
publication, observing that in Europe 'Form' and 'Spirit', the sacramental
and the non-sacramental views, had been set one against the other 'and
division rather than harmony' had ensued, he suggested that what was needed
was 'a people of spiritual genius and intense religious fervour' who might
in future be able to harmonize these two positions, and that India might be
the setting for such a synthesis, for the two positions appeared already to
exist in harmony in Hindu life. He went on to explain that they were to be
seen in 'the India of the devout Brahman, every act of whose daily
household life is a sacrament leading to the unseen', and 'the India of the
homeless sanyasin, who has left all earthly ties to follow his ideal, and
has laid aside all ceremonies and forms in the free life of the Spirit'.
Against such a background, it might be possible to look forward to 'an
Indian Church harmonizing the sacramental and the mystical'. (12)

At another level, however, Andrews saw that 'the reunion of the Church'
would not merely mirror existing Indian phenomena, but would provide a
saving alternative and answer, that is, to India's 'inherited communal
instincts and its pathetic longing for unity'. Over against this, there
had to be posed a visible unity, 'simplicity of doctrine combined with a

clear visible expression of the Christ-life of unity and love shown forth
to the world in an organized society'. In this respect, reunion lay 'at
the very heart of the Indian missionary problem', and was the essential
precondition of 'Indian acceptance of the Faith'.

> The ideal of a United Christendom would mean more to
> India than to any other country. (13)

Significantly, among the many reviews of The Renaissance in India, in which
this passage occurs, it was a Hindu, writing in the Indian Review, who
acknowledged the cogency of this particular argument. (14)

The second, and to Andrews more important aspect of church unity which
concerned him was with regard to what he called the 'social expression of
Christianity', and to a very specific social issue. It is indicated in
the observation of a Church Times correspondent, who drew attention to
his devotion to 'the great and worthier ideal of a united Catholicism
which shall gather East and West together and shall have no race
distinctions'. (15)

We have already seen how important the question of 'the ethics of race' in
the public sphere was for him. If the Church's mission was critically
damaged by the conduct of 'the white Governments', its own internal
handling of the racial question was also very important, was, indeed, 'the
greatest moral problem before the Indian Church, ... - the union of the two
divided races, Indian and English, within One Body'. (16)

Andrews alluded to this question throughout the period, cited numerous
instances of racial division within the church, and wrote several
substantial articles on the subject, in particular, in addition to his
early paper on 'Racial Unity', a series on 'Race Within the Church'. (17)
In the earlier paper, delivered in late 1907, he had traced through St
Paul's letters his 'life struggle' for racial unity in the church.
Although he had applied the principle universally through his figure of
'the Body of Humanity', he also showed how for St Paul it was in the church
that the struggle had first to be won, so that the unity of the church

might be 'a pledge and foretaste of a unity ... to embrace all creation'.
This struggle had now to be fought within the Indian Church, the struggle
for a 'Christian unity ... which makes no distinction of race or colour or
caste', and which would drive out 'our miserable privileges, our worldly
prejudices, our wretched superiorities' and reveal to the world 'the
"mystery" which has never been realized before in this land'. (18) Andrews
made a complementary point in his North India of 1908. There he draws
attention to examples of racial unity, such as the collaboration of the
Brahmin convert, Goreh, and the English religious, O'Neill, 'one of the
most beautiful things ever witnessed in the Indian mission-field - European
and Indian, of one heart and one soul in Christ, living as brothers
together'. This is a recurring theme in the book, and indeed, gives it its
basic structure. The concluding paragraph brings the issue back to the
centre of attention.

> Ultimately, the present difficulties and perplexities
> of the Indian Church resolve themselves into the one
> great problem of the intermingling of races within
> one Body.

The solution of this 'problem' at the same time defines the mission of the
Church in India, to be 'the true nursing mother of the Indian nation'.

> For that which neo-Hinduism shows no sign of
> accomplishing, the Christian Church, coming
> victorious out of her own internal struggle, may at
> last achieve. She may first learn within herself,
> then give to India, the spirit of unity. (19)

In his early paper on 'Racial Unity', Andrews had drawn attention to the
importance in 'the Pauline Churches' of the Lord's Supper, as the place
where the unity of Jew and Greek was most fully expressed, as they
acknowledged one another in the Kiss of Peace and in the sacrament itself.
In the January 1910 issue of The East and the West, there appeared an
article by R.F. Callaway, 'Colour Antipathies: A Study of Conditions of
Church Life in South Africa', in which the author argued that 'whatever

fellowship is desirable within the sphere of religious life may
legitimately be kept within that sphere and not intruded into the domain of
social life'. His reason for this was his belief that the profound racial
antipathies experienced in South Africa, however indefensible 'in the
sphere of religious life', were such that they seemed only surmountable
under the impulse of 'lust'.

> Does not this suggest to us the thought that within
> the sphere of social life there is a limit beyond
> which fellowship is neither desirable nor good?

In other words, as Andrews characterised Callaway's position, 'the races
should part, as it were, at the church door'. Andrews recognised that this
position was an advance on 'those terrible portents of our time,
race-churches and race-sacraments', but insisted that it did not go nearly
far enough. Thus he was led in the first of his articles on 'Race Within
the Church' to a careful but unequivocal advocacy of inter-racial marriage,
'whenever and wherever it is the natural outcome of Christian sympathy and
pure Christian love', reminding his readers that 'the Holy Communion was
intended to cover the whole of life, ... to symbolise and lead on to the
most intimate human friendship and affection between the members of
Christ's Body'. Pointing to the caste system as 'the most imposing
experiment in race-aloofness' that the world had ever seen, he noted that
most missionaries were agreed that the overthrow of the system was only
finally effected when Christians of different castes intermarried. The
Indian experience, then, underlined the error of Callaway's position, and
exposed it as 'hypocrisy and cant', and pointed to a contrary conclusion.

At a time when the social distance between British and Indian was in its
worst period, the advocacy of inter-racial marriage was a bold and
provocative thing. The editor of The East and the West nevertheless took
his arguments very seriously.

> Those who have been accustomed to shudder at the
> suggestion which ... (this article) contains will
> feel, after carefully perusing the arguments of its

> writer, that the question cannot be settled by a
> shrug of the shoulders, or by any of the stock
> arguments which have done service in the past.

This response was echoed in other places, in both India and Britain, in Christian publications. The general reaction, however, was very different, and Andrews later recalled that the article 'probably brought upon myself more odium among Europeans in India and even in England than even my political views'. (20) Certainly, when he raised the issue again two years later, at an S.P.G. Summer School in England, Bishop Montgomery vigorously attacked his position, and 'the summer school was in a hubub'. It was some consolation to Andrews that Charles Gore suppported him. (21)

During these years, Andrews wrote a further two articles with the same title, taking up again the now familiar theme of the racial division between Indian and British in the Indian Church, and going so far as to wonder whether St Paul, if he had been present, would have recognised 'we Anglicans in India ... as Churchmen at all'. On a number of specific issues, he was criticised by European correspondents and praised by the Modern Review, but neither article was as radical or attracted as much attention as the first in the series. Both are valuable, nevertheless, for their continuing insistence on the importance of what were to come to be known as 'non-theological', or, more correctly, 'cultural and social factors' in the ecumenical movement. (22) Nowhere else in the missionary literature of the period do we come across any such serious and sustained handling of 'this strange and portentous phenomenon in Christendom', which so offended against the fundamental principles of Andrews' thinking on the human race and the unity of the Body of Christ.

6. 'Theology from the Eastern point of view'

Before he ever came to India, Andrews had been encouraged by Westcott to expect the emergence of a distinctive Indian theology, for, 'as Greece had been the leader of Europe, India would always be the leader of Asia.... These, he said, were the two great thinking nations of the world'. (1) Andrews' earliest impressions, however, as we have seen, were of 'spiritual

usurpation' in the church, and he alluded several times to the theological
and doctrinal aspect of this. In this, he appears to have been influenced
by Rudra, who often referred to an 'intervening Western medium' in
theology, and to India's need to go direct to 'Christ the fountain head of
inspiration and new life, ... not further down the stream, where human
controversies have disturbed the clear waters'. Rudra clearly felt very
strongly about this.

> The Indian Christian community, in the expression of
> its deepest thoughts, has been taught to learn
> foreign formularies, and foreign systems of theology,
> ... elaborated and recast, renovated, elaborated and
> recast again. The indigenous mind naturally loses
> all freshness, elasticity and vitality under this
> ecclesiastical schooling. ... This lack of vitality,
> the half-dead and half-alive spirituality, which is
> the present characteristic of the Indian Church, is
> due to enforced conformity to Western standards. ...
> Indian Christianity ... is not the true expression of
> Indian thought and aspiration. (2)

Nor did this particular criticism come only from within the church. The
editor of the Modern Review pointed to a contrast between the achievements
of Christian converts, to which Andrews had drawn attention, and the lack
of creativity among later generations of Indian Christians, born and
brought up within the church, and so out of touch with those springs of
vitality in the non-Christian community on which the first-generation
converts had drawn. (3) Andrews took this criticism very seriously. It is
not surprising, therefore, that he should have turned his attention to the
promotion of what he called 'Indian Christian Theology', or, in terms more
reminiscent of Westcott, 'the contribution which Indian Christianity may
make towards the interpretation of the great Catholic Doctrines of the
Church'. (4)

One way in which he did so was by publicising such Indian theology as he
knew to have been written at the time. Rudra, who himself made a modest

but striking contribution, on 'The Christian Idea of the Incarnation', reported in 1909 that there was so far very little indigenous Christian thought known to him, and he went on to mention the work of Krishna Mohan Banerjea, Nehemiah Goreh, and Brahmabandhab Upadhyaya. (5) Andrews also knew of these, and introduced them to a wider public. He devoted some space to Banerjea and Goreh in North India. (6) Important as he saw them to be, however, he regarded them as much less constructive and important than Brahmabandhab, to whom he devoted a substantial article in the Church Times, later reproduced in part in The Renaissance in India. Andrews made the point that he had himself lived 'in close contact with' one of Brahmabandhab's most intimate disciples, though it is not clear who this can have been. The article is made up largely of extracts from the writings of Brahmabandhab, including translations of his two Sanskrit hymns, to the Blessed Trinity and to the Word Incarnate, which Andrews calls respectively 'A Hymn of Adoration' and 'a canticle of the Incarnation'. While pointing out that the author was 'ready to go further than most of us would regard as the bounds of the Christian intellectual and social ideal in his approximation to Hinduism', he conceded that he made very careful distinctions between Hindu and Christian doctrines, for example, 'between the Hindu doctrine of the Avatar and the Christian doctrine of the Incarnation'. He concludes that Brahmabandhab's work is evidence that, 'when the period of Western imitation is over and Europeanizing tendencies have ceased, the Indian Church may have an important contribution to make to Catholic theology'. (7) To have introduced this work, still regarded as 'the most successful example of a true adaptation or incarnation of the faith in India', to a wide audience in the West so early is an indication of Andrews' perspicacity in the matter of Indian Christian theology. (8)

It has been suggested that in Brahmabandhab's work, for all its brilliance, 'Aquinas looms too large and the Bible too small'. (9) Certainly, Andrews himself regarded the Bible as of central importance as a basis for an Indian theology, and he was involved in a sustained effort over a number of years to make it, and the best modern interpretation of it, accessible to Indian Christians. This he had an opportunity to do through his appointment in 1906 as General Editor, under 'the general Episcopal supervision' of Lefroy, for a series of 'Indian Church Commentaries', which were published in accordance with a resolution of the Synod of Anglican bishops in India of 1900. Andrews appears to have been responsible in this way for the general editing of some six commentaries published over the next seven years, and it is clear from the prefatory acknowledgements of the editors of the individual volumes that he had an important and often indispensable part in their making. (10) The aim was that these commentaries, 'while presenting a direct and scholarly interpretation of the New Testament based upon the work of the great English Commentaries', should at the same time include 'references to Indian religious thought and life', to make them serviceable to both Christians and non-Christians in India. (11) In this latter respect, these commentaries are lively and colourful and highly successful, and it is not surprising that they were well received. Lefroy found the first of them 'most fascinating and valuable', and supplying 'a _great_ need'. McLeod Campbell reported from India that the reception of the first volume indicated 'the felt need for such literature', and Eugene Stock, reviewing the first five of them for the Church Missionary Review, found them 'very impressive' and 'valuable'. (12)

Andrews' most energetic attempt, however, to encourage the development of an Indian theology was with regard to the training of ordinands. At the end of 1908, he had noted of ordinands in India that they spent a great proportion of their time in studying matters that to them were 'almost valueless'.

> They cram up the various sixteenth-century heresies
> mentioned in the English Thirty-Nine Articles, they
> labour at the Gallican and Sarum Uses for their
> English Prayer-book paper, they learn by heart the
> names of early Saxon saints and Puritan divines.

He had also earlier noted that the tendency of a past generation of missionaries to undervalue Hindu philosophy and literature meant that a theological method like that of the early church, as described in Harnack's Expansion of Christianity, had hardly begun to be attempted. He feared

that without urgent development of ordination training, church life in
India would 'drift into a backwater, away from the main current of newly-
awakened national consciousness'. (13)

His opportunity to do something about this came at the beginning of 1909,
when Lefroy initiated an enquiry among the clergy about the ordination
subjects of examination in his diocese. The syllabus current at this time
at the Divinity School at Lahore indicates the general approach. The
doctrine course for deacons, for example, was based entirely on the
Thirty-Nine Articles, while for priests was added an exclusively English
reading list, Hooker, Butler, Wace, Liddon, Moule, etc. 'Other Religions'
were taught in the course for senior catechists, and the approach is clear
from the recommended texts, the essentially controversial Christianity
compared with Hinduism and Islam by W. Hooper, and Pfander's Mizan u'l
Haqq. By late January or early February 1909, Andrews had sent to Lefroy a
lengthy letter and a rough outline of a new syllabus for deacons and
priests.

For want of a body of theology written 'from the Eastern point of view' by
either Westerners of the stature of Westcott or Indians not caught up, as
Imad-ud-Din and Goreh had been, in passing controversies, Andrews proposed
that the Bible should be the basis of study, being 'a truly Eastern book',
every one of whose writers was an Asiatic. As a possible supplement, he
recommended the theology and history of the first four centuries, which
show 'the mode of general interpretation when thought was nearest to the
East and nearest also to the source'. He included also the study of
'living Hinduism and living Islam' - 'Hindu Theism and true Mohammedan
religious earnestness' - these, rather than English church history, the
Articles and the Prayer Book, being the 'rock whence ... Indian deacons
were hewn'. Amongst a great deal of specific argument, he makes the point,
so close to T.V. French's original hope for the Delhi Mission of
'attempting to introduce the Alexandrian School system and programme', that
those who teach ordinands are 'what Socrates would have called "midwives",
not parents - helping to bring to the birth the seed in them', an exercise
in which Indian teachers in the diocese, Ali Bakhsh of Lahore, and Ghose,
should have a very special part to play. Some idea of the main thrust of

his proposed syllabus itself can be seen in four recommendations, namely
that there be reference to i) Hindu and Muslim traditions and conceptions,
with a special study of the theme of 'Christus Consummator, with reference
to the fulfilment in Christ of Hinduism and Islam', ii) 'the great Eastern
Fathers of the Church', iii) 'modern Indian missionary conditions', and
iv) questions of 'national and social righteousness'.

Lefroy clearly liked Andrews' proposals. While he considered that they
went 'too far in the direction of excluding Western theology and
influence', he was clear that they were in the right direction. He
consequently circulated them for comment to representative bishops and
clergy in India, China, Japan, Africa, Britain and Ireland, and, more
importantly to Andrews, to a number of Indian Christian correspondents.
Lefroy noted, in the responses he received, 'a remarkable consensus in the
acceptance' of Andrews' general approach. There was criticism of his
application of the Socratic principle, which evoked an elucidation from
Andrews. The principle was, he suggested, plainly vindicated in St John's
description of the Logos enlightening every person, as also in Christ's own
method, for Christ 'looked for the light, ... for the faith', and found
them already present in 'the heathen Syro-Phoenician woman' and the 'pagan
Roman centurion'. He also responded to this criticism from another angle.
Noting that the influence of the 'anglicizing' process in theology was so
overpowering as to threaten to put a stop to all 'truly indigenous,
original Indian Christian thought', he observed that several correspondents
had assumed that the introduction of frequent references to Hinduism and
Islam in his draft syllabus was for 'a kind of controversial artillery'.

> Nothing was further from my thoughts. It was rather
> in order that Indian Christianity should become
> deep-rooted in the soil of all the good religious
> instincts already existing among the Indian peoples.
> Those to whom such a thought of Christian
> assimilation is still unfamiliar should read
> Harnack's Expansion, and see what happened in the
> first four centuries. If we regard, and rightly
> regard, these centuries as models, if, as Anglicans,

> we take our ideals from them, then we must be
> prepared to follow the early Church in this, perhaps
> the greatest mark of her Catholicity, and not refuse
> to allow an entrance of the 'glory and honour' of the
> 'nations' into the Holy City.

In July 1909, Andrews sent a second, revised syllabus to Lefroy, together
with these comments on the correspondence. The revision did not
significantly change the thrust of the first draft. It is most
interesting, indeed, in its elaboration of the earlier version and its more
precise disclosure of Andrews' objectives. The proposals, revised
proposals and correspondence between Andrews and Lefroy, were then put
together and published in 1910 as an Occasional Paper of the Delhi Mission.
This clearly aroused great interest as being 'so poignant for the future of
Indian Christianity'. (14) That the future which he envisaged was still,
until recently, largely awaiting its realization is a comment on his
exceptional foresight in this matter. (15)

Behind such an enterprise as Andrews' work on ordination study in India,
lies, of course, the sort of presupposition that we find in the thinking of
a number of missionaries in India at this time, that the other religions
will find their fulfilment in Christ. Andrews' proposals went further,
however, in seeking to create the sort of space in which an Indian theology
might emerge, 'conserving all that is good in Indian religious tradition
and looking for an indigenous development of the Christian faith on Indian
soil'. (16) He was never under any illusion that he, or indeed any Western
Christian, was qualified to work this out.

> All that we foreigners can do is to dig the ground
> and put up some useful scaffolding. We cannot
> ourselves erect the final building.

It nevertheless appears to be the case that some of his own insights and
reflections were of some service in this respect.

In 1911, Andrews spelt out the necessities of this theological task in a pamphlet, <u>The Indigenous Expression of Christian Truth</u>, in which he suggested that among the tasks awaiting completion was the careful separation of 'that which is purely Western in the Christian message (and therefore not binding upon India) from that which is universal'.

> This does not mean a vague, undogmatic, invertebrate
> Christianity, with no backbone of belief, but it does
> mean an essential Christianity, which can take as
> soon as possible local colour from its surroundings,
> and thus become, at one and the same time, indigenous
> and catholic. (17)

This 'essential Christianity'was something that Andrews was himself searching for in a very personal way during these years, as if his own inner quest corresponded with what he believed to be the general requirement. His fullest disclosure of this occurs in a paper entitled 'A Missionary's Experience', where he set out to answer the question, 'What difference has the complete change of environment from England to India made in your outlook upon Christianity?' Some of his answers to the Commission IV questionnaire for the World Missionary Conference, which must have been written at about the same time, cover the same ground and supplement the picture. Although he called his answer 'fragmentary and inconclusive', the editors of the <u>Indian Interpreter</u>, who printed it, found it 'stimulating ... valuable and important'. (18) Certainly, there is nothing to compare with it for its open and thorough self-scrutiny in the answers of other correspondents to the World Missionary Conference.

The most distinctive feature of these two papers is the testimony to 'a widening of the idea of Christ's work and presence in the world'.

> I now look at all human life and human history more
> from the central standpoint of the Incarnation. I
> think more of the extension of the Incarnate life in
> wider and wider reaches of humanity, till all is
> summed up in Christ himself. (19)

A handful of other missionaries were noting at this time a similar
development in their thought. Andrews' elaboration of it is not only much
fuller than that of the other correspondents, but also much more
distinctive. There are a number of strands in his Christological
reflection. First, and 'deepest of all', there is the importance for him
of the person and teaching of Christ in the Synoptic Gospels, and
particularly the Sermon on the Mount, Andrews' 'daily companion'. These
sources appear to him increasingly 'elemental, universal, simple', in their
presentation of Jesus as 'the Son of Man, ... the Head and Representative
of the human race'. In the light of this understanding of Jesus, 'every
spiritual gift, ... every noble act, every deed of service to mankind' build
up 'that larger Church, the Church of aspiring Humanity, the Church of Him
who is the Son of Man'. Another main strand derives from the Johannine
writings, to which he turned 'continually'. He calls this 'a deeper
appreciation of the work and Person of Christ, the Eternal Word, the Light
and Life of all mankind'. This way of understanding Christ leads him to
declare himself, in India, 'as often a learner as a teacher', discovering
in Hindu experiences of 'Christ, the Eternal Word', much that is 'very
beautiful indeed and full of illumination'. In his college work, likewise,
he finds himself having to learn a new approach, though it is, of course,
an old one, and the one that the founders of the Delhi Mission had had in
mind.

> I find myself dwelling more and more on the
> underlying thought of St Clement of Alexandria,
> namely, that Christ the Word is Himself the Teacher,
> who teaches in His own inward way, through the innate
> instincts, and traditions, of all those His children
> who have been feeling after Him if haply they might
> find Him.

In some further reflections in his Commission IV paper, he spoke of how the
Epistle to the Ephesians, along with the Johannine writings, had become for
him 'more and more luminous and inspiring'. Perhaps it is in this
perspective of a cosmic Christology that we have to understand his
reflections on the Eucharist, and especially his reference to 'the

consecration of ... Christian friends and ... Hindu friends ... (with their
own special gifts and treasures) to Christ, to make up His Completeness'.
Not surprisingly, Andrews went on in this paper to speak of his conscious
desire 'to stretch all dogmas to their widest limits, the Sacraments, the
Church, the Incarnation itself, the Atonement', though in his Indian
Interpreter version of it, he went back to 'the supreme need of reducing
Western religious experience to its simplest forms, in order to make it
intelligible to Indian minds', and suggested that in this simplification it
was desirable that 'even the idea of the Church' should be 'germinal rather
than mature', and 'the fully developed sacramental form of Christianity'
must give way, for the time being, to 'a more elementary type'.

It is this 'more elementary type' then, a faith centred upon 'the
simplicity of the primitive Gospel' and upon the Son of Man who is also
'the Light of all mankind, ... the Eternal Word', which stood out 'with
some distinctness' as the starting point for 'an eastern embodiment of
Christianity'. If Andrews derived this to some extent from the 'liberal
catholic' incarnational theology of Westcott and others, as undoubtedly he
did, it equally points forward, and to some extent helped to shape, one of
the most distinctive developments in Indian Christian theology to date, the
important theme of 'the humanity of Christ and the new humanity' which we
find in the work of Chenchiah and Chakkarai, Devanandan and M.M.
Thomas. (20)

A central feature of the dream of French and Westcott of a new 'Alexandria'
in India, was the emergence of a truly Indian Church, something far
greater, Westcott had said, 'than collecting scattered congregations round
English clergy who may reflect to our eye faint and imperfect images of
ourselves'. This would be 'an organization of the Faith' which would
preserve and not destroy all that was 'precious in the past experience of
the native peoples', hallowing to the service of that Faith every possible
'mode of influence ... - the asceticism - the endurance - the learning,
which are indigenous to the country'. While, over thirty years later,
Rudra was still lamenting that the Christian Church in India had so far had
'little scope to develop its own organic life', Andrews' labours during his
missionary decade represented a brilliant contribution towards that end.

In the last months of the decade, the <u>Church Times</u> hailed him as 'the arch-representative of the Catholic Christianity which would put into the background the essentially English features of the Christianity which we present to India, and would lead our Indian brethren to look towards their own form of Catholic Christianity'. (21) The assessment was judicious.

NOTES: Chapter Five

1. Introductory

1 Preparatory Paper for Commission 4 (WMC); <u>NMI</u> Mar 1910
2 <u>MR</u> Feb 1912
3 Waller 1909, p. viii, cf. Walker 1909, p. viii

2. 'Indian Christians and the National Movement'

1 Preparatory Paper for Commission 4 (WMC)
2 Westcott 1873, pp. 37-8, cf. Andrews in <u>TEW</u> Oct 1907, <u>NI</u> p. 179,
   <u>YMOI</u> Apr 1911
3 <u>MR</u> Dec 1908; <u>CT</u> 21 Oct 1910; <u>Tribune</u> 21 Aug 1906
4 <u>IR</u> Dec 1910; <u>CT</u> 16 Dec 1910. N.b. Rudra's vision of an Indian
   Church with 'no rigid hard-bound system, ... no regulations of a
   Book' <u>SM</u> Jan 1910. Ghose was among those almost lost to the
   institutional church: 'We sent him to Bishop's College at one of
   its feeblest epochs and he came back disgusted, fed up with
   westernisms and having no word for his own country' Andrews to
   Montgomery, 5 Nov 1909 (SPG).
5 <u>MR</u> Dec 1908; <u>NI</u> p. 216; <u>YMOI</u> Jan 1910
6 <u>Ep</u> 9 Nov 1907; <u>SSC Mag</u> Dec 1907. V.S. Azariah spoke at the
   College at about the same time, about Japan, which he had just
   visited for the 1907 WSCF Conference - <u>DMN</u> Jan 1908.
7 <u>NMI</u> Jan 1908, cf. <u>YMOI</u> Jan 1910; <u>YMOI</u> Sep 1908
8 <u>YMOI</u> Nov 1908; <u>DMN</u> Oct 1910 - F.J. Western, reporting on the
   Conference in <u>DMN</u> Jan 1910, indicated that Bakhsh was expressing
   the majority view among Indian Christians; Rudra <u>SM</u> Jan 1910;
   Paul <u>YMOI</u> Jan 1909.
9 Phillips 1912, p. 34 shows that in the Punjab in the first decade
   of the twentieth century, the Christian population grew by
   431.6%, almost entirely through the mass movements.
10 <u>TEW</u> Jan 1907. Whitehead argued his case also in the <u>Guardian</u>,
    <u>The Nineteenth Century and After</u>, etc.
11 In addition to Andrews, Rudra and Lefroy, dealt with in the text,

Allnutt, Day, Hibbert—Ware and G.A. Purton also went into print on the subject.

12 Preparatory Paper for Commission 1 (WMC)

13 'Indian Students' 1910, also <u>CC</u> 1907, 'Missionary Education' 1908

14 'Conishead and India' 1908 (SCM); Andrews to B.K. Cunningham, 11 Feb 1908 (SCM); <u>NI</u> pp. 218-9, 35-60, 215; <u>TEW</u> Oct 1907

15 <u>Guardian</u> 4 Sep 1907. He quoted Hibbert—Ware's report, 'we cannot record a single conversion sealed by baptism among the students' <u>CC</u> 1905. Hibbert—Ware had already faced up to this very constructively in 'The Place of Education in Missionary Work' 1904.

16 <u>Ind Int</u> Oct 1909, cf. his Preparatory Paper for Commission 4 (WMC) on the growing appeal to him of 'the Catholic side of Christianity', 'not a single narrow scheme or plan of salvation dominating my thoughts as in times past - a salvation concerned solely and entirely with individual souls, as so many atoms or isolated units, but a redemption, a reconstruction, a consecration of all life, of society as well as the individual'.

17 <u>DMN</u> Apr 1908; <u>YMOI</u> Mar 1911. He cited the case of K.C. Sen as an example of an acknowledged assimilation of Christianity <u>YMOI</u> Jan 1910. He also saw in the poet Tagore's call for an 'overwhelming influx of higher social ideals', a call 'not to come over to India merely to count up converts by statistics, or proselytize by any and every means, fishing in troubled waters, but rather to come over in Christ's name to help a whole people in distress and anguish of spirit; to be content to sow the good seed of Christian thoughts of brotherhood and fellowship, of freedom and enlightenment, of service and sacrifice, and thus fulfil Christ's words, "... ye did it unto me"' <u>CT</u> 2 Dec 1910. Cf. Rudra on the Christian Colleges 'The work they are doing for the future of Indian Christianity is of inestimable worth. Their work is like that of leaven, slowly but surely altering the thoughts and ideals of the country. Leaven cannot be measured statistically. There is now a mighty movement of intellect going on in India. If the Christian Church were to withdraw at such a time from the work of higher education, it would be almost

suicidal' <u>CC</u> 1907.

18 <u>RI</u> p. 53; 'Missionary Education' 1908; <u>DMN</u> Jan 1911

19 <u>TEW</u> Jan 1911; <u>CC</u> 1911. In this connection, he welcomed the
English translation of Schweitzer's <u>Quest for the Historical
Jesus</u> in 1910 as a providential antidote to an overemphasis on
the idea of assimilation, the picture given in that 'strange last
chapter' being 'the very reverse of evolution, assimilation' <u>TEW</u>
Jan 1911. The whole of this article is important for the complex
dialectic of his thought at this time.

20 <u>RI</u> p. 259.

21 <u>TEW</u> Jul 1907

22 <u>Pan-Anglican Congress</u> 1908, Vol. V, pp. 151-9. Lefroy and Foss
Westcott took a middle position, while Copleston of Calcutta
favoured the mission to the educated classes.

23 The Commission presented their Chapter 7 as central. The most
extensive quotations from missionary correspondents are extracts
from <u>NI</u>, while Andrews' proposals regarding Ordination training
in India are also cited. The only other missionary correspondent
named in the Indian section is A.G. Fraser. Bigg 1905, of which
Andrews, as we shall see, had already made considerable use, is
treated as an important authority. Westcott's advocacy of
'Alexandrian Christianity as the type of Christianity most akin
to the Indian mind' is twice quoted.

24 <u>RI</u> pp. 176-8. This account of the Church's response to the
national movement takes little account of developments in south
India around Chakkarai, K.T. Paul and others, though the latter's
support for Andrews provides a connection.

3. 'Religious Swadeshism'

1 <u>TEW</u> Oct 1907, also <u>NI</u> pp. 29, 227-8. <u>Guardian</u> 30 Dec 1908,
<u>YMOI</u> Apr 1911, <u>RI</u> p. 256. V.S. Azariah was consecrated in 1912,
the first Indian bishop of the Latin rite in 1921.

2 <u>YMOI</u> Mar 1911. If Chapter 7 of Commission 3's report at the
WMC derived much from Andrews, he, in turn, seems to have
taken a good deal from it for this article.

3   'Missionary Education' 1908

4   NI pp. 29, 160, 163, 225-6

5   D.L. Joshi CMI Mar 1906

6   DMN Jan 1907, cf. Jan 1906; Lefroy's Preparatory Paper for
     Commission 1 (WMC)

7   NI pp. 185-6, 226; TEW Oct 1907. A correspondent pointed out
     that though the Anglican Church was, as he put it, the smallest
     Christian body in India, the Bishop of Calcutta received annually
     Rs. 72,620, 'nearly twice as much as all Roman Catholic
     Archbishops, Bishops, Priests, together' Tribune 26 Jul 1913.
     Andrews later pointed out that 'practically the first political
     document of constructive statesmanship emanating from an Indian
     public body' was a petition to Parliament in 1852 which included
     an objection to supporting Anglican bishops and others out of
     the general revenues of the country - Andrews and Mookherjee
     1938, pp. 103-4. In NI, p. 186, he quotes an Indian Christian
     friend to the effect that the sight of 'a chaplain travelling at
     double-first class fare at the tax-payer's expense, and living in
     every way like a Sahib', led to inevitable conclusions about
     missionaries, because 'the Church is one and the clergy are one'.

8   'Missionary Education' 1908; Preparatory Paper for Commission 1
     (WMC)

9   Grimes 1946, pp. 107, 9.

10   Rudra's speech is the only verbatim quotation in the minutes of
     the Synod - Grimes 1946, p. 115.

11   Abraham 1947, p. 28; NMI Feb 1908; NI p. 172; Allnutt CC 1907,8;
     Lefroy - Preparatory Paper for Commission 1 (WMC)

12   Eddy 1935, p. 216, NMI Feb 1908; CC 1908

13   NMI Feb 1908. Nevertheless, slightly later 'We have ... a very
     delicate and tender plant to rear and foster in the Indian
     Christian life .... It may be that their "method" of the
     spiritual life differs materially from our own, and depends far
     more on personal affinities and attractions, as its connecting
     bonds, than on defined organization such as we seem to need ....
     Would not organization come much better - in a much more living
     way - if it grew up from within, in Indian ways, not Anglo-Saxon?

Would it not then have much more missionary power and attractiveness' <u>SM</u> May 1909.

14 Allnutt <u>CC</u> 1908. Except where otherwise stated, the data for the rest of this section is drawn from the correspondence and memoranda in the file 'Principal of St Stephen's College'. (CMD)

15 Stanton to Allnutt, 19 Sept 1905 (CMD); Allnutt <u>CC</u> 1907; Andrews <u>CC</u> 1907

16 Allnutt to Stanton, 3 Jan 1907 (CMD)

17 This account may go some way to dispel a myth that still has currency in India, that Rudra's appointment was the work of Andrews alone, in the face of the united opposition of his missionary colleagues, e.g. S.K. Bose <u>Stephanian</u> Jun 1971, also Hollis 1962, p. 50.

18 Preparatory Paper for Commission 1 (WMC); <u>CT</u> 29 May 1908.

19 Monk's file - SSC

20 <u>TEW</u> Oct 1907, <u>NI</u> pp. 217-8, <u>DMN</u> Jul 1909, also his evidence given in November 1913 to the Royal Commission on the Public Services in India <u>Royal Commission</u> 1915, Vo. XX, pp. 26-50. The example of Rudra's appointment was also cited in the Report of Commission 3 <u>World Missionary Conference</u> 1910, pp. 32-3.

4. 'The Eastern Ideal'

1 <u>SM</u> May 1907. Ghose wrote this article at the request of Andrews, who, in some prefatory remarks, claimed that it represented 'the suppressed feeling of a very large and growing number of earnest Indian Christians'.

2 <u>YMOI</u> Dec 1910

3 <u>NI</u> pp. 153-5; Andrews 1933, p. 18; Boyd 1969, p. 92

4 Andrews 1934, pp. 109, 114

5 Andrews 1934 <u>passim</u>. For a student's recollections, Singha n.d., p. 164.

6 Sundar Singh's later over-exposure as a celebrity may well have had a damaging effect upon him, but there is no reason to doubt the authenticity of Andrews' picture of his obscure early years

as a Christian, substantiated as it is by Stokes' recollection of 'his very manifest sincerity' in those days – Stokes to Hosten, 22 Sept 1923, also Redman to Heiler, 25 May 1925 (Hosten Papers).

7 Hosten 'Some facts and dates in the life of Mr Samuel E Stokes Jr.' (Hosten Papers); TEW Apr 1908; Stokes to Western, summer 1911, quoted in Stokes 1908, p. xxxvii

8 NI pp. 155, 180

9 TEW Apr 1908. He also, however, used the term 'sadhu' of himself (Stokes 1908, p. 29), while Sundar Singh referred to Stokes' assuming the 'life of a faqir' Nur Afshan 21 Jul 1916 (quoted in translation in Hosten Papers).

10 Preparatory Paper for Commission 1 (WMC)

11 TEW Apr 1908. Proposals in TEW Jul 1908. Also while in England, Stokes had discussions with CMS, and on 16 Sep 1908 was appointed a missionary of the Society with 'a Roving Commission' (CMS Punjab and Sindh Précis, 10 Mar 1909).

12 CMS Punjab and Sindh Précis, 15 Dec 1909, also 21 Sep 1910

13 W.E.S. Holland CMI May 1910; Stokes' printed letter to friends in America, 3 Feb 1910 (Hosten Papers); DMN Jan 1908. Andrews later published a piece on Dhar Tirath, 'a translation of the aged Swami's words dictated by him in his room at Kotgarh' Ind Int Oct 1911.

14 Tribune 30 Oct 1909

15 In addition to Western and the CMS recruit, 'Mr. Branch', Sundar Singh refers to 'Mr. MacMillan, Mr. Jacob' Nur Afshan 21 Jul 1916 (Hosten Papers).

16 Western to Hosten, 23 May 1925 (Hosten Papers)

17 Biog p. 101; Andrews to E.S. Talbot, 1914 (Berkeley)

18 This was reported, interestingly, by Munshi Ram (see Ch. 6 below), at the Arya Samaj Anniversary at Lahore Tribune 5 Dec 1907. Had Stokes consulted Munshi Ram, head of the Arya Samaj Gurukula?

19 The pamphlet is anonymous, but parts correspond to passages in a printed letter from Stokes to friends in America, 3 Feb 1910 (Hosten Papers).

20 CMS Punjab and Sindh Précis, 7 Jun 1909, etc.; DMN Jul 1909;

Printed letter to friends in America, 3 Feb 1910 (Hosten Papers);
Tribune 30 Oct 1909

21 _MR_ Nov 1913

22 Stokes to Bardsley, 28 Aug 1911; Stokes to Western, n.d. (both
    published in Stokes 1908)

23 Western to Allnutt, 22 Aug 1912 (CMD); Andrews to Montgomery,
    27 Oct 1911 (SPG)

24 _NI_ pp. 162-4, 180-2

25 _NMI_ Feb 1908, _YMOI_ Jan 1910, _NMI_ Nov 1910

26 _SM_ Nov 1909

27 Andrews to E.S. Talbot, 1914 (Berkeley); S.N. Mukarji _Stephanian_
    Jun 1940

28 _TEW_ Jan 1911

29 _Guardian_ 30 Dec 1908

30 The background to this is important: 'The Apostles ... discussed
    the Logos doctrine and the doctrine of the Universal Church long
    before the period of assimilation began in the first Christian
    centuries; and we may try even now to define Christian lines of
    contact with Hinduism, though we may not be able to adopt Hindu
    ritual or accept Hindu social organisation. For the present
    generation at least there must be, instead of this, a readiness to
    "give up all", which is the first test of discipleship. There
    must be the complete break with idolatry and caste and all their
    intricate and complex associations. Christ the Fulfiller of
    Hinduism is also the Lord and Master who said: "I came not to
    bring peace but a sword"' _TEW_ Jan 1911. Cf. Farquhar 1913
    'Hinduism must die in order to live. It must die into
    Christianity' (p. 51).

31 Andrews to Montgomery, 27 Oct 1911 (SPG)

32 _NMI_ May-Jun 1912. Andrews was sympathetic enough about Stokes'
    desire to marry across the racial divide; indeed, probably before
    the latter had begun to think on these lines, Andrews' had
    advocated inter-race marriage (_TEW_ Jul 1910). Nor was Andrews
    the first Punjab missionary to do so. H.U. Weitbrecht had
    described it a year earlier as 'the most powerful source of
    influence' which a missionary could exert on social and national

life - Preparatory Paper for Commission 4 (WMC).

33   The founder of the Christa Seva Sangh in 1921, J.C. Winslow, said that the impulse 'to become an Indian to the Indians' came to him from Andrews, from his life and writings - Winslow 1954, pp. 74-75. Winslow first met Andrews in 1906 - Winslow to O'Connor, 6 Feb 1973.

5. 'One Body'

1   Ind Int Oct 1909; SM Apr 1908; Preparatory Paper for Commission 4 (WMC)

2   WSCF 1911

3   Allnutt CT 10 Jun 1910. 'We are ..., at Mr Andrews' instigation, trying to come into closer touch with CMS workers in the diocese' G.A. Purton DMN Jul 1909.

4   Only two articles were concerned especially with the question, IW 7 Mar 1911, TEW Jan 1912.

5   IW 6 Sep 1910; IW 16 Aug 1910; WSCF 1911; Preparatory Paper for Commission 4 (WMC)

6   TEW Jul 1912

7   Preparatory Paper for Commission 4 (WMC)

8   NMI Nov 1910

9   YMOI Mar 1911

10   TEW Jul 1912; IW 7 Mar 1911

11   NI pp. 45-6; Sundkler 1954, p. 133

12   Ind Int Oct 1909

13   RI p. 265; Ep 12 Jul 1913; RI p. 265

14   T. Rajagopalachari IR Mar 1914

15   Ep 12 Jul 1913; CT 19 Dec 1913

16   SM Nov 1909

17   TEW Jul 1910, Oct 1912, Oct 1914, also YMOI Feb 1908, Ind Int Oct 1909, 'India in Transition' 1910, YMOI Mar 1911

18   SM Apr 1908

19   NI pp. 69, 228-9. Other inter-racial 'pairings' in NI are Abdul Masih and Daniel Corrie (p. 11), Imad-ud-Din and Bishop French (pp. 126-7), Bhola Nath Ghose and Rowland Bateman (p. 144),

Sundar Singh and Stokes (p. 154). Was another implied in the
Dedication of the book 'To my friend Susil Kumar Rudra' (p.ix)?

20 Biog p. 107

21 Montgomery to Stanton, 24 Jul 1912 (CMD); Biog p. 107

22 It is interesting that it was while in South Africa that Andrews
related his concern for unity in regard to race to those other
aspects of unity which were so preoccupying Anglicans at the time
in the Kikuyu controversy 'It may be that when we have seriously
and penitently endeavoured to remedy this growing schism of race
which exists, almost unchecked, inside our own community today,
that God in His great mercy will open the way by which we may
remedy those schisms of faith which divide and distract us' CT
6 Mar 1914.

6. 'Theology from the Eastern point of view'

1 Biog p. 47

2 TEW Jul 1913; SM Jan 1910; YMOI Dec 1910

3 Review of NI in MR Jul 1909

4 NI p. 72; CT 4 Nov 1910

5 'The Christian Idea of the Incarnation' was a paper which Rudra
read at a 'Convention of Religions' at Allahabad, which he and
Andrews attended in Jan 1911. It was reproduced in full in the
local nationalist newspaper, the Leader 31 Jan 1911, and as a
CLS pamphlet, 1911, and in a shortened version in SM Jun
1912. There are indications of the influence of Brahmabandhab,
and echoes of Westcott in this important paper. Rudra's 1909
comments are from his Preparatory Paper for Commission 3
(WMC). He also referred in this to two European contributors
to Indian theology, W.A. Mill, and George Westcott.

6 NI p. 72

7 CT 4 Nov 1910. A much shorter version of this, in which he
equates Brahmabandhab's work with that of Tertullian, Athanasius
and Basil, is in an appendix to RI, pp. 289-91.

8 G. Gispert-Sauch 1972. The only known early reference in Britain,
in addition to Andrews', is that of A.M. Fairbairn who, presumably

during Brahmabandhab's visit to Oxford in 1902-3, prophesied the
victory of his ideas - Heiler ed 1970, pp. 244-5.

9 Boyd 1969, p. 77

10 Walker 1909; Waller 1909; Pakenham-Walsh 1910; Walker 1912;
Weitbrecht 1912; Crosthwaite 1916.

11 General Preface by Lefroy

12 Lefroy to Allnutt, 6 Dec 1909, quoted in Montgomery 1920, p. 186;
quoted in B.K. Cunningham to Montgomery, 27 Feb 1909 (SPG);
CMR Jan, Feb 1913

13 Guardian 30 Dec 1908; NI p. 199; 'Ordination Study in India'
1910. Unless otherwise stated, all the information in the next
four paragraphs is taken from this paper.

14 This was the conclusion of a meeting of Indian and English
clergy, convened by their bishop, at a CMS Conference at Agra
in March 1910 - CMI May 1910.

15 N.b. Boyd 1969, pp. 1-2, 'The teaching given in theological
colleges throughout India has been, and still is, dominated by
western theology, as a glance at any syllabus will show'. Boyd
was writing particularly of the churches of the reformed
tradition. The same seems to have been still the case with the
Roman Catholic Church at about the same time - e.g.
Abhishiktananda 1970, especially the section 'Ministers'
Training'.

16 Ind Int Oct 1909

17 YMOI Mar, Apr 1911

18 Ind Int Oct 1909; Jul, Oct 1909

19 Preparatory Paper for Commission 4

20 The phrase is the sub-title of an article about these four Indian
theologians by F.J. Whaling, in S.J.T.. Andrews' influence is
acknowledged only in the case of Thomas. He was in touch with
Chenchiah at this time, as we have seen, and there is much in the
latter's writing that is very close to Andrews' theology, not
least his remark that 'India will not be afraid of claiming Jesus
as belonging to our race as the head of humanity, as the Son of
Man' (Sudarisanam 1938, p. 27). Andrews' stress upon 'a more
elementary type of Christianity ... in which even the idea of the

Church is yet germinal rather than mature', is a main theme in
Chakkarai – see especially his article 'The Church' in
Sudarisanam 1938, pp. 101-123, also T.V. Phillip on 'Chakkarai
and the Indian Church' in Taylor 1976, pp. 153-65. Thomas has
clearly been much attracted to Andrews' thinking, see especially
Thomas 1970, _passim_, where he states that Andrews 'has carried
the idea of the Divine Humanity of Christ to a new stage of
development' (p. 143). Boyd 1969, pp. 324, 330, notes that of
all the Christian writers whom Thomas discusses, the two whom he
commends with least reservation are Rudra and Andrews, and he
concludes his examination of Thomas' 'massive and consistent
theological statement', by observing that in its central features
it 'comes close to the view ... of C.F. Andrews'.

21 Westcott 1873, pp. 38-9; Rudra 'Missionary Education' 1908; _CT_
5 Dec 1913

CHAPTER SIX
PEOPLE OF OTHER FAITHS

1. Introductory

Andrews' capacity for deep friendships across the racial divide was by no
means limited to people, like Rudra and Ghose, within the church. From the
very beginning of his missionary decade, we find him entering into
comparable friendships with people of other faiths, relationships deep,
emotional and unreserved. In these, the religious component was always of
great interest and significance to him, and this in its turn determined
considerably his evaluation of other faiths, and his own developing
theological understanding of them.

His interest in other religions was not, of course, limited to that derived
from these friendships, and we find him in several other ways during these
years seeking to understand them better, and to encourage mutual
understanding, appreciation and sympathy.

Andrews learned a certain amount from literary sources. Thus, we find him
commending classical Hindu texts such as the Vedanta-sara, as well as
serious Western expositions such as those of Deussen on the Vedanta and
Risley on caste and religion. (1) He also took people's own definitions of
their faith seriously. Thus, among his notes there survives a life of the
prophet Muhammad, carefully transcribed from the narration of a Muslim
friend, while, similarly, he turned to such Hindu expositions of Hinduism
as Lala Baij Nath's Hinduism Ancient and Modern. (2) One aspect of his
interest in Hindu literature was with regard to a work called In Woods of
God-Realization, the collected English writings of a neo-Vedantist from the
Punjab, Swami Ram Tirath (1873-1906). The first four volumes were
published at Delhi by Amir Chand, whom we have met as one of the Delhi
'Conspirators'. At his request, Andrews wrote the introduction to the
first volume. Though confessing to 'only a faint and distant sympathy ...
with the philosophy of the Advaita Vedanta', and making some sharp
criticisms of its 'illegitimate short cut to the simplification of the

problem of existence', he was appreciative of 'the poetic spirit of Swami
Rama'. (3) Amir Chand was delighted with Andrews' introduction. It was
reproduced as an article in the Arya Samaj's journal, the Vedic Magazine
and Gurukula Samachar, and was also fulsomely praised in two nationalist
journals. (4)

St Stephen's College provided the setting in which to develop some of his
ideas about religions. Rudra reported in 1908 that he himself wished to
encourage among the students 'a serious study of comparative religion',
this to be based on Westcott's The Gospel of Life, and a little later we
find Andrews delivering a course of lectures in college on 'The Religious
History of India'. He reported at about the same time 'a term's work on
the fundamental principles of Christianity, showing wherein it differed
from all the other religions of the world'. (5)

A similar title, 'Indian Religious History', was given to his series of
lectures at the Indian Missionary School of Study. At about the same time,
a visitor to Delhi observed that his 'methods of missionary work and ...
intelligent appreciation of Hindu and Mohammedan thought ... (were)
exhibited in the life and work of ... the numerous body of younger
missionaries who (were) inspired by his brave and hopeful spirit'. (6)

Andrews also did a great deal to introduce developments in Hinduism to
people in Britain. Thus, he wrote a number of articles, 'A Hindu
Apologetic', 'A Modern Hindu Apologetic', 'What is Hinduism?', and some on
contemporary movements such as the Dev Samaj and the Prem Sangat. In
addition, there were his notes on 'Modern Krishna Worship' in North India,
while his series for the Church Times, 'Indian Church Problems', included a
substantial amount of description and illustration of contemporary
Hinduism. (7) His most masterly survey, however, was in The Renaissance in
India. Though he himself came to feel that the editorial committee in
Britain had pressed upon him a view of some features of Hinduism that
lacked proper sympathy, the book was very widely welcomed. One or two
reviews in Britain found it too sympathetic. (8) Its reception by
reviewers in India, however, was uniformly enthusiastic. Among missionary
reviewers were Farquhar and Macnicol, the latter of whom said that it was

'an amazingly complete and luminous account of the Hindu situation, written with a knowledge that perhaps no other observer could command'. The Indian Christian community was also very positive. Very significant was its warm welcome in nationalist circles, the Hindustan Review making the quite remarkable observation that much of it might have been written 'by an Indian thinker of the Reform School'. (9)

This last point is important, that Andrews' appreciation was at this time largely of the reforming movements within the Indian religions. One reviewer of The Renaissance in India pointed out that Andrews represented 'modern English-educated Indians', and that it was plain that he did not know much of 'the ways of thinking of some of the old Pundits in Benares and Muttra'. (10) That was so, and, indeed, his whole approach to missionary strategy rested on the significance which he attributed to the former class. It may also, however, help to explain why Andrews' very positive approach to Indian religions was not wholly appreciated by those who saw more of the latter class. An S.C.M. visitor to India, Nathaniel Micklem, struck by 'the unspeakable vileness and degradation of heathenism', was emphatic that Andrews' views in The Renaissance in India did not represent Hinduism 'as Hinduism appears to most of the missionaries working there.' (11) Of the religion of the educated classes, however, he clearly had a unique understanding.

Within that highly significant sphere, it was his friendship with individuals that was perhaps his most unusual achievement during these years, an achievement the more remarkable in the light of a contemporary comment that 'few Indian Christians were in real touch with non-Christians'. (12) To these friendships we now turn.

2. 'The New Islam'

Although Islam represented only the second largest religious community in India as a whole, during Andrews' missionary decade it was quite the largest in the Punjab, with more than half the province's population among its adherents. This made the Punjab, as a contemporary study said, 'the most important Mohammedan diocese in India'. Delhi itself had only a

slightly smaller proportion, and visually was still the city of the great
Mughuls, its largest building, the mosque, Jama Masjid, 'a great epitome of
Indo-Saracenic art', while the Delhi Mission was described as 'one of the
greatest of Moslem mission enterprises'. (1) It is not, therefore,
surprising that Andrews' first sustained encounter with people of other
faiths was with Muslims.

As a result of the British imperial presence and 'the stimulus of Christian
assault', a unique feature of Indian Islam was a modernizing movement,
which Andrews called 'the New Islam', and which could be described as a
renaissance or reformation. (2) The leading figure in this movement had
been Sir Syed Ahmad Khan (1817-98), the 'Erasmus of Delhi', who had
exercised a considerable influence both as an individual and through the
reforming institutions which he established. Because much of his work
centred on Aligarh, where he founded the Muhammadan Anglo-Oriental College
in 1877, his principal followers came to be known as the Aligarh School.
(3) During his missionary decade, Andrews got to know some of this group,
his first meetings going back to his very first year in Delhi. Among them
was Hakim Ajmal Khan, an expert in Yunani medicine. Andrews visited him
'constantly' during these years, though there is little record of what
passed between them at this time. (4) Particularly, however, he got to
know two elderly Delhi Muslims, Nazir Ahmad (c. 1832-1912) and Zaka Ullah
(1832-1910).

These last two had been friends from their earliest years in pre-Mutiny
Delhi. Nazir Ahmad was the leading Urdu prose-writer and novelist of the
nineteenth century, while his translation of the Qur'an into literary Urdu,
the first such translation, and his theological commentary on it, were very
influential. Zaka Ullah, who had been Professor of Vernacular Learning and
Science at Allahabad for thirty-seven years, was perhaps most important for
his work in translating scientific text-books into Urdu. Both had attended
the old Delhi College in the 1840's, when it was the centre of the
remarkable Delhi Renaissance, in which Western scientific learning had
played such an important part. Both had been close friends, supporters and
'passionate disciples' of Syed Ahmad Khan, Zaka Ullah being on the board of
his M.A.O. College at Aligarh from its foundation to the day of his

death. (5) Both had also had long associations with St Stephen's College, publicly associating themselves with the College's work, and helping with the teaching when possible. By 1907, he was able to say that they had shown him, 'a missionary', every kindness and courtesy, and had given him their 'confidence and friendship'. A little later, he wrote of their treating him 'as a son rather than as a foreigner and alien', and until their deaths in the later part of the decade, he was 'constantly in their company, sharing their affection'. (6)

Nazir Ahmad, Zaka Ullah, and 'a small group of intellectual companions', the 'leading men of Old Delhi', used to meet for discussion in the evening in the Public Library, and there Andrews would come and join in, his own latest article being often the subject for consideration. 'It would have been difficult', he wrote later, 'to find in the North of India a more distinguished intellectual circle than these courtly old men, ... members of all creeds, ... who used to gather round ... Zaka Ullah ... each evening.' In Zaka Ullah's last illness, in 1910, Andrews visited him daily, and also conveyed messages from him to his ailing friend, Nazir Ahmad. Zaka Ullah's last words were prayers to God, 'and along with them' - addressed to Andrews - 'the one word of human affection, "Beta, Beta!" - "My son, my son!".'

In the few months remaining to Nazir Ahmad, whom Andrews called 'the greatest of all the learned men of Old Delhi', he wrote for Andrews, in Urdu, a memoir of his 'oldest and most intimate friend', Zaka Ullah, whom he called 'a model of true Islamic culture'. The sense of Delhi's past which this memoir conveyed was one of the things which Andrews greatly valued also in these friendships, for Zaka Ullah personified for him 'the ancient courtesy of his own ancestral house and also of the Moghul Court of Delhi' in which he had been brought up, and Nazir Ahmad 'the old high culture of this ancient capital of India'. Andrews was sad to see 'the old beautiful Moghul art of Delhi' passing away before his eyes under commercial pressure, and 'the old beautiful poetry and music perishing unheeded'. (7) Zaka Ullah, whose family had been for many generations teachers of the royal princes of the House of Timur, and who could remember Delhi as a purely Oriental city almost untouched by Western influences, and

who himself 'revered the past with its glorious traditions of Arabic
learning and Persian culture', talked with Andrews for hours about these
things.

Andrews' first significant encounter, then, with people of other faiths was
with these reforming Muslims. It was from them that he derived his
understanding of Islam. Central to this was his acknowledgement that,
however much in the Qur'an was derivative, 'Islam in itself is a new
creation, a new spirit in religion, ... one of those startling and
momentous births in the religious history of mankind'. Of the central
place of the Qur'an he also learned from Zaka Ullah, who often recited
passages to him, and told him that there was never music in the world 'like
the music of the Arabic of the Quran Sharif'. (8) Andrews also drew
attention to other normative features of Islam, its 'hard, clear-cut
Deism', its 'rough-hewn moral ideal, massive and simple', its power, 'at
its best in moulding character and creating an atmosphere of reverence'.
(9) Andrews' appreciation of Islam, thus briefly outlined, is much more
positive than even that of Lefroy, for whom Islam's moral ambivalence was
always inescapable - the conclusion that 'nowhere have light and darkness
been so interwoven the one with the other'. At only one point was Andrews
sharply critical, that is, with regard to the 'subjection of womanhood',
which carried 'countless evils in its train'. Characteristically, this
placed 'an insurmountable obstacle in the way of national development'.
(10)

It is not difficult to identify some of the distinctive characteristics of
the Aligarh movement in Andrews' portrait of his friends, particularly Zaka
Ullah, for whom Syed Ahmad Khan had been his 'greatest living hero'. It
was, for example, a movement favouring contemporary British culture, and
Zaka Ullah had 'frankly accepted western science and a great deal of
western thought. He recognised that a new age had come, the age of the
West. ... he recognised that the effete Moghul dynasty was not capable of
ushering it in successfully; therefore a change of dynasty was natural'.
In the light of these views, he had written <u>Victoria Namah</u>, in which he
portrayed 'the imperial house of Victoria' as 'continuing the traditions
and the glories of the great house of Timur'. The more political side of

this, again reflecting the Syed's position, was that, though he favoured
improved relations with Hindus, and 'disbelieved entirely in any policy of
Muhammadan isolation', he 'could look forward to no period ... when the
mediating influence of a third and neutral factor such as the English,
would be rendered unnecessary'.

At the same time, personal loyalty to the Syed necessarily involved
acceptance of the old British Liberals' position, so that, to Andrews'
surprise, Gladstone and John Bright were still much admired in Zaka Ullah's
circle. Most importantly, however, if Syed Ahmad Khan's greatest life work
was his insistence that his community must learn modern scientific methods,
then Zaka Ullah was indeed an important and typical disciple, for he
devoted nearly fifty years of his life to one literary pursuit, the
preparation of science text-books in Urdu. Andrews recorded that 'his were
the books that were most widely read as text books in schools', and that he
thus 'exercised an extraordinarily powerful influence in Urdu writing at a
most critical time of transition'. (11)

Zaka Ullah was, nevertheless, in one respect, an independent reformer, that
is, in his attitude to Hindu-Muslim relations. The usual line of the
Aligarh School, following Syed Ahmad Khan's opposition to any sort of
political alliance with the Hindus, was, by the turn of the century, to
look upon the Muslim community as a separate entity. Thus the first
foundation of Muslim nationalism was laid in India. At the same time,
British policy during Andrews' missionary decade was designed to accentuate
'the antagonism of ... Hindus and Mohammedans'. (12) Zaka Ullah, however,
through an early Christian influence during his student days, was
consistently opposed to any policy of 'Muhammadan isolation'. He 'held
firmly the view that harmony and reconciliation were always possible'.
This attitude was reciprocated among Delhi's Hindus, and Andrews even heard
of one Hindu household where 'every evening, when they lighted the lamps as
an act of worship in their ancestral home, they included the name of ...
Zaka Ullah, in the prayer that is repeated at that time'. Andrews was
clearly much attracted by this side of his old friend, for it chimed in
with his own vision of 'India's greater unity', and he went so far as to
say, on Zaka Ullah's death, that he chiefly associated his memory with

Christ's beatitude on the peacemakers. (13)

In his North India, Andrews noted that there was in India 'an entirely new development in the faith of the Prophet, which eagerly embraces modern science and modern social ideals, and aims at the highest Western culture, combined with a simplified creed and doctrine'. (14) This last, in Zaka Ullah's case, was accompanied by an abandonment for the greater part of his life of many of the outward observances of his religion, though he remained in many respects a conservative figure, indeed, in Nazir Ahmad's estimate, 'outwardly the most conservative man in Delhi'. His position earned Zaka Ullah, Andrews says, the reputation in Delhi of being a 'free-thinker'. The latter seized upon this term of disparagement, and made of it a virtue, and in the process gives us an extremely illuminating religious portrait of Zaka Ullah.

> If the phrase 'free-thinker' means that he thought
> freely and sincerely and with an open mind about
> Religion, and regarded the spirit of his Islamic
> faith to be more important than the letter, then the
> phrase is nobly true concerning Zaka Ullah, and he
> well deserves the title. For it would have been hard
> to find a man more free from formalism and bigotry,
> more open-minded and tolerant. ... He venerated,
> indeed, and openly respected those, like his father
> and grandfather, with whom the formal side of
> religion was a living reality, which clearly helped
> to sustain the spiritual life. ... With his own
> hard-earned money he sent his parents to perform the
> pilgrimage to Mecca and Medina, prescribed by Islam
> in its formal code, and he rejoiced in their
> devotion. ... But his own nature, in this respect, was
> different. He lived a life of simplicity and
> comparative poverty, with the consciousness of God's
> presence ever about him; and he left off during the
> greater part of his life many of the outward
> observances which were connected with his Islamic

faith. Yet never by any word that passed from his
lips in my presence (and we talked freely and
intimately about these very things) did I gather that
he regarded himself as anything else than a true
Muslim.

Andrews' estimate, therefore, was that his life 'was all of one piece', and
that, despite his 'changed ... mind', he had 'kept his own soul'. In this,
he represented in typical form what has been called 'the working faith of
modern India, ... the solution of synthesis'. (15) This Andrews
recognised, claiming that Zaka Ullah deserved a place among the great
Indians of the nineteenth century as 'a singular and beautiful example of
the combination of the past and the present, of the East and West', and
also, for this reason, in Andrews' judgement, as 'a true prophet of the
future'. (16)

Before Zaka Ullah's death in 1910, Andrews had already made some literary
reference to him, both in North India and in a rather slight article in the
Student Movement, in which he wrote appreciatively of Islam as he had
learned of it from Zaka Ullah. Within the months following his death, he
wrote a tribute for the Tribune, and, for the Modern Review a much more
thorough evaluation of the importance of his educational work for the
renaissance of Islam. (17) More importantly, he responded to a wish that
Zaka Ullah had himself expressed, that he should write a memoir based on
their conversations over the years, and thus publicise views that Zaka
Ullah was convinced remained valid. For this, Andrews gathered information
over the next two years, although it was not until the 1920's that this
found final form, in a series of articles on 'Old Delhi' in the Modern
Review, and as the book, Zaka Ullah of Delhi. (18) This last is important
in reflecting the scope and nature of Andrews' first sustained approach to
people of other faiths, while the Introductory Memoir, by Nazir Ahmad,
carries, as we shall see, a valuable external testimony to its
significance.

In writing about Islam in the Student Movement article, Andrews proposed
that the only appropriate Christian response to the continuing vitality of

Islam was 'a Living Church, filled with the Holy Spirit of Love'. On two
occasions during these years, Andrews' concern and affection for the Indian
Muslim community took an active public form. The first was relatively
slight, when, early in 1908, he accompanied Zaka Ullah and Nazir Ahmad to
Aligarh, at their request, to help in the resolution of a conflict between
the students and the European Principal of the M.A.O. College. (19) The
other, though a trivial incident in itself, involving a dispute between the
Muslim community and the imperial authorities with regard to a road-
building scheme which threatened a building related to the Machhli Bazar
Mosque in Cawnpore, came to assume, in 1913, in the Viceroy's judgement,
'an Imperial rather than a provincial aspect', and was, in fact, the first
Muslim issue in India with an avowedly nationalist significance. (20)

Andrews' part in this was to represent to Sir John Meston, the Lieutenant
Governor of the United Provinces, the views of 'moderate' Muslims, as he
learned of these in particular from a new friend, Sir Ali Imam, the Law
Member of the Viceroy's Council. (21) More 'extreme' elements in the
Muslim community expressed something of the new Pan-Islamic sentiment, and
a growing disaffection with British rule. Andrews was in touch with them
also. (22) However, he clearly took the older, Aligarh line, for he
proposed that the Government should receive sympathetically a deputation of
'thinking Mohammedans', and so strengthen 'their power and willingness to
work with' the Government. This would be a proper response to the
'incredible amount of genuine religious feeling, widespread and deep',
which had been aroused. It would also, as Meston interpreted the
proposals, isolate the 'extremists'. (23) Andrews' intervention, as he
himself recognised a few days later, 'did very little good', and it took a
personal visit of the Viceroy to Cawnpore to effect the necessary
compromise. (24) Meston's comment, however, that Andrews was 'such a good
fellow' and so sincerely anxious that justice and righteousness should
prevail that the utmost respect had to be paid to his suggestions,
indicates how energetically Andrews was prepared to promote the interests,
as he saw them, of a religious community other than his own. (25)

These interesting forays into public affairs serve to illustrate how
Andrews was moved to put into practice in the public sphere his conviction

about the Christian response of 'love' to Islam. In a sense, the ground
for such an approach was already prepared in the Delhi Mission. Although
the older missionary approach through formal, public disputation, still
continued, and although elements in contemporary Indian Islam could still
speak of the Church's 'implacable hatred towards Islam', Lefroy had already
dispensed with what he called 'the old, hard, knock-you-down-with-a-brick
style of controversy', and developed 'a better and more Christian type',
which he saw, not as the confrontation of an enemy, but as the winning of
'the disguised friend'. This was an approach built on a theory of
fulfilment, and it acknowledged that Islam had a 'most definite and
valuable' contribution to make to the life of the church. (26) Andrews'
approach went a great deal further than this, however, as he sought to
express his solidarity with his Muslim friends, and the gap between what
Lefroy was saying and what Andrews was doing in these two small episodes is
a measure of the originality of his approach to people of other faiths.

How Andrews thus moved the Christian-Muslim encounter onto a quite new
plane is even clearer in his personal relationship with his old Delhi
friends. The testimony to this and its importance we find in the
observations of Nazir Ahmad.

> We, Musalmans, have been accustomed from our
> childhood to read in our sacred books the different
> accounts of the friendly relations between the early
> followers of Islam and their Christian neighbours,
> especially in the neighbouring kingdom of Abyssinia.
> Now, lately, we have seen with our own eyes, in the
> city of Delhi, a living example of the same kind of
> cordiality existing between Musalman and Christian.
> For the friendship between Munshi Zaka Ullah and ...
> Mr Andrews, is of this character. Neither of them
> had any worldly object to pursue in cementing their
> devoted friendship. Their love for each other was
> pure and disinterested. Both of them had penetrated
> deep down into the inner fundamental truth of
> religion itself, apart from creeds and dogmas. Their

mutual affection, which was so profound and sincere,
was really love for the sake of God. It did not
depend on man .... If Musalmans and Christians in
India could learn to love one another as these two
friends have already done, then the time would soon
arrive when the followers of both religions would
begin to chant the following lines of the poet,

> I should become one with you,
> And you would become one with me:
> I should be the body,
> And you would be the soul.
> Then no one would be able to say
> That I am different from you,
> Or that you are different from me. (27)

If this was a fulfiment of Syed Ahmad Khan's 'principle of friendliness',
it also represented a new discovery for Andrews, a confirmation in
experience of what he was saying about the work of Christ the Eternal Word.
Later, he was to write of how Zaka Ullah had shown him, by the beauty of
his life, 'what Christ's own character must have been like in its meekness
and humility'. (28) Even at the time, some four months after Zaka Ullah's
death, there were already intimations of this later conviction.

> As I recall his pure and beautiful character, so
> simple, so transparent, so gentle, another beatitude
> comes before me, the most sacred of all, – 'Blessed
> are the pure in heart, for they shall see God'. (29)

Andrews and Nazir Ahmad were both equally clear that there was never any
question of Zaka Ullah changing his religion and becoming a Christian.
This did not mean that Andrews abandoned any idea of proclamation. 'We
need to tell', he insisted, 'with the passion and fire of Christian love,
our Beautiful Names of God'. This was to be done, however, only in a
context such as that which had been established and shown to be possible in
this case, a relationship of friendship and mutual acceptance. Zaka
Ullah's own words describe the terms of mission to people of other faiths,

as Andrews was beginning to identify them.

> 'What is the use', my old Musalman friend once said to
> me, 'what is the use of argument and controversy? Let us
> speak together of the Attributes of God. Tell me your
> "Beautiful Names" of God and I will tell you mine'. (30)

3. 'The Divine Preceptor'

Of the nineteenth-century movements favouring vigorous reform within
Hinduism, undoubtedly the most influential was the Brahmo Samaj, centred on
Bengal, its founder, Ram Mohan Roy being himself 'the pioneer of all living
advance, religious, social and educational, in the Hindu community during
the century'. (1) By the beginning of the twentieth century, the Brahmo
Samaj was, like the other more radical reforming movements which demanded
complete separation from caste, either stationary or declining.
Nevertheless, it still attracted, in Andrews' judgement, 'some of the
choicest souls in all India', people who were doing 'the noblest
constructive work'. (2) It was within this community that Andrews entered
into his second friendship with someone of another faith.

Visiting Bengal only briefly and infrequently in the earlier years of the
decade, Andrews had not at first been much aware of the significance of the
Brahmo Samaj. His first contacts of any note were through the Bengali
dispersion in the Punjab, amongst whom, as we have seen, he had a number of
friends. His lecturing in the Brahma Mandir in Lahore in 1909 is an
indication that he must by then have known something of the Samaj. His
evaluation of the movement during these middle years was, unlike that of a
number of earlier Christian observers, very positive. He saw it as the
product of Christian missionary enterprise, crossed, as it were, with an
ancient Indian theistic tradition, and he commended it to his readership in
Britain for the help that it rendered to 'the spread of Christian ideas'.
At the same time, he claimed that no religious body in India represented 'a
nobler zeal for social reform and moral and spiritual progress'. (3)

No single individual at this time was more representative of the Brahmo

Samaj than Rabindranath Tagore, whose father had succeeded Ram Mohan Roy as
leader of the movement and had done so much to consolidate its force as a
movement for reform of religion and society. Some ten years older than
Andrews, Tagore was, by the first decade of the twentieth century, an
established Bengali poet and dramatist, indeed, 'the acknowledged king of
Bengali literature'. (4) He was also an educationalist, a committed
supporter of the national movement, and an energetic leader in the Brahmo
Samaj.

We have already found Andrews quoting with approval Tagore's heterodox
views on caste. Before meeting him, he went so far as to call him 'perhaps
the greatest living Indian thinker'. He also noted the impact of Tagore's
poetry and songs, and read what few translations were then available. On
this basis, he hailed him in some verses early in 1912 as 'lord of a new
world of song', sent to give his nation birth. (5) It was only in the
month of the publication of these verses of Andrews', March 1912, that
Tagore began the translations which were to make up the collection known as
Gitanjali, 'Song Offerings'. These were to lead to his discovery by the
West, and to his winning the Nobel Prize for Literature. It was at the
point of Tagore's discovery in the West that Andrews first met him.

Tagore visited England in the second half of 1912. He took with him,
adding to them on the voyage, translations of some of the poems which he
had written originally between 1900 and 1910, an intensely religious phase
of his life. Although he told his niece after the publication of these in
November 1912, under the title Gitanjali, that writing in English seemed a
delusion to him, they were immediately taken up in London, initially by the
painter, William Rothenstein, and W.B. Yeats, and then by 'all the literary
lions of the day'. (6) Andrews, visiting England in the summer of the same
year, partly to see his parents, partly on College business with Rudra, was
taken to Rothenstein's by the journalist, W.H. Nevinson, whom he had met
during the latter's tour of India in 1907. There he met Tagore, on the
notable occasion when Yeats first read the poems to the assembled guests.

This meeting was to mark the beginning of a lifelong relationship, and one
which was soon to influence very markedly the course of Andrews' life. His

account of the evening and of some of his subsequent meetings with Tagore, he detailed in two articles sent back to the Modern Review in India, 'An Evening with Rabindra' and 'With Rabindra in England'. (7) These reflect, as do even more his many letters to Tagore from this time onwards, in their mixture of enthusiasm and an almost cloying emotion, both the depth and the unsatisfactoriness of this relationship. On Tagore's side, he clearly already knew of Andrews, no doubt from the unique place which he had secured in the nationalist press, for, at Rothenstein's, he crossed the room, clasped his hand, and said, 'Oh! Mr Andrews, I have so longed to see you'. To this was soon added a reciprocated affection, so that, a little over a year later, Tagore was able to say, in phrases which Andrews himself might have used, that the latter was more than a brother to him, and his love one of the most precious gifts that had fallen to his share in this world. (8) It was a friendship that was to last, with its own particular vicissitudes, through the remainder of Andrews' life.

Andrews saw as much as possible of Tagore during the last two months of his leave, visiting him often in London and taking him for a holiday to a country vicarage in Staffordshire. During these two months, he read the proofs of Gitanjali, learned a great deal about the Bengal renaissance in general and Tagore in particular, and began to form a determination to visit his school at Santiniketan as soon as possible after his return to India. Each of these had its consequence.

One consequence was that to a large extent he took over Tagore's business and literary affairs with his publisher in the West, Macmillan, a task which he continued to perform for many years. While he probably did this very badly, there are indications that Tagore came to rely on Andrews' judgement with regard to his writings in English. (9) Certainly, however, Andrews' interest in Tagore's literary work provided a starting point for their relationship.

During their conversations at this time, Tagore told Andrews much about his own life, and about the history of the literature of Bengal. The latter made remarkable use of this information. There was an article for readers in Britain, in the Contemporary Review, but, more particularly, a lecture

delivered over the next two years on various interesting occasions, in a
deliberate attempt to underline contemporary Indian cultural achievement
and so to challenge attitudes of racial contempt. First, and perhaps most
remarkably, he took this challenge to the centre of imperial power, when in
May 1913 he delivered the lecture at the Viceregal Lodge at Simla before
one hundred invited guest, the Viceroy, Lord Hardinge, presiding. In the
aftermath of the Delhi extremists' bomb attack, in which Hardinge was
injured during a state procession in Delhi in December 1912, Andrews had
found himself in an exceptionally close friendship with the Viceroy and
Lady Hardinge. Throughout 1913, he took advantage of this in the promotion
of a variety of causes. His aim in this lecture was to improve
understanding between 'poor, sun-dried, fossilised Anglo-India' and the
Indian people by evoking respect and understanding for Tagore's
achievement. Though the whole event seemed to him, he told Tagore,
'strangely unreal', he was heard with 'rapt attention' by what the
Anglo-Indian Pioneer called 'a large and most interested audience'. (10)   A
Bengali commentator concluded that the lecture would 'rehabilitate the
Bengalis in the opinion of the rulers of the land'. (11)

He went on, characteristically, to deliver the lecture elsewhere in Simla
also, in the Arya Samaj Mandir, at the Bengali Kari-bari Club, and at the
Brahma Mandir. (12) The most interesting subsequent presentation of it,
however, was in South Africa some months later, where he had gone to
support Indian interests. There he gave the lecture in the City Hall in
Cape Town, 'before the Members of the Parliament' and others. The effect
was such that the chairman of the meeting, Lord Gladstone, concluded that
it would 'do much to induce a feeling which would help to a solution of the
troubles which had stood in the way of good relations between India and
South Africa'. (13)

Andrews was greatly attracted by all that he heard from Tagore about his
school at Santiniketan. Located at the ashram founded there by his father,
Maharshi Devendranath Tagore, it seemed to represent, as indeed was its
aim, the best in the movement for 'National Education', as this had been
propounded in recent years, particularly in Bengal. It was also a place,
he noted, where 'music and song ... (had) been made, as in Plato's

"Republic", the very warp and woof of the texture of education'. (14) A
new English friend, W.W. Pearson, had sailed back to India with Andrews, to
take up private tuition work in Delhi. Caught up with the same enthusiasm,
Pearson paid an immediate visit to the school, and on his return helped to
confirm Andrews' determination to visit Santiniketan. What attracted
Andrews about it was that it sounded to be such a successful synthesis of
the Hindu educational tradition and the requirements of an emerging nation
in the modern world, or, as he put it a couple of years later, a successful
attempt 'to get behind that vandal and iconoclast, Macaulay, and be truly
conservative (while progressing) in this conservative country'. (15) He
paid a first short visit in March 1913, and a longer one four months later.

Most important of all, however, was Andrews' discovery of Tagore himself as
a religious man, his understanding of Tagore's position, and his attitude
to him. The basis of all this lay in their friendship. For both of them,
this had, from the earliest days, a religious significance. Thus, Tagore
told Andrews that he needed his friendship, but he also explained that he
saw this as a religious 'realization in love', which contrasted with the
sort of inter-religious encounter that was no more than 'the triumph of
dogma or sect'. In reply, Andrews claimed that the 'harmony' that they had
discovered in the matter of religious faith was the 'deepest root' of
friendship, though he went further to suggest that 'the love of friendship'
was itself the path along which he had 'found the way to God'. (16)

What was the basis of this harmony? Andrews admitted that the deepest joy
of his friendship with Tagore derived from the latter's 'appreciation of
the Christian spirit in its purest form', and its profound influence on his
work. At the same time, he was concerned to acknowledge that the source of
Tagore's appreciation of Christianity lay in his 'deep study of the
Upanishads, in the Buddhist ideal, in the Vaishnava Hymns, and the sayings
of Kabir'. Even a poem so 'wholly Christian in spirit' as the well-known
Gitanjali 10, which sees God especially present 'among the poorest, the
lowliest, and the lost', could be paralleled, 'symbolically expressed, ...
in a hundred passages in the early Vaishnava hymns'. In other words, the
highest values which Andrews knew as a Christian, he identified and
acknowledged as present within Tagore's Hinduism itself. He deprecated the

tendency of some Christian commentators like Evelyn Underhill, who were
'obsessed by the arrogant thought' that everything in Hinduism which had a
Christian ring about it had been derived from the Syrian or Nestorian
Church, and therefore was 'non-Hindu'. In the same way, there were central
features of Tagore's religious outlook, his 'realization of the spiritual
in and through the material', and his 'leading idea of the <u>Jivan-Devata</u>',
which he called 'the glory and the wonder of Rabindranath, ... great and
noble conceptions', for which he suggested no Christian equivalents. (17)

Other particular features of Tagore's religion were very significant for
Andrews. He regarded his 'love of nature, ... glorious optimism, ... grasp
of the fulness of life' as an important corrective to 'popular Hinduism',
with its stress on renunciation. We may recall here Andrews' reservations
about what he regarded as the over-emphasis on asceticism in the
Brotherhood of the Imitation as unwisely reinforcing this. Here, in
Tagore, was a Hinduism which, however alien to contemporary Hindu values,
was 'not foreign to ... ancient Hindu thought', was in harmony with the
Christian affirmation of the goodness of creation and a 'true pathway to
salvation'. (18) Indeed, it sent Andrews back to read Christ's life 'over
and over again' in the light of his new vision from Tagore's eyes, and to
find there 'something really optimistic, not pessimistic, ... His joy in
little children, in married life, in home friendship, in the beauty of the
world of birds and flowers and trees', all of which made 'joy, pure
innocent joy, the end, not suffering'. (19)

Tagore had not, however, stopped at that point. Andrews pointed out that
the poet had 'passed on from the period of sheer unbounded delight in
nature and physical beauty, to enter into the mystery of the sorrow and
suffering of the world'. A letter of Andrews' at this time thanked Tagore
for writing to him 'so fully about suffering in God', in a way which made
him feel that he had himself 'held the old Christian beliefs ... far too
crudely'. Although the rest of the letter is not entirely clear, it is
remarkable that, in acknowledging the way in which he had been led to
modify his understanding of Christ's teaching, he says to his Hindu friend,
'you have set me free'. (20)

There was, then, a clear sense that his own faith was enriched in this encounter with someone of another faith. There were a number of other aspects to this. In the first place, there was a very personal element, whereby Andrews was soon able to ask Tagore to pray for him, and to ask for his 'spiritual help and counsel'. By the end of 1913, he was able to say that through his love for Tagore, he had found 'a new confidence and a new assurance'. Through sitting at his feet, he was confident that increasingly he would see the truth and the truth would make him free. (21)

In addition, he shared, in a measure, in the religious practices of his friend. This is the easier to understand in the light of Tagore's father's instructions for worship in the temple at Santiniketan.

> The one invisible God is to be worshipped, and such
> instructions are to be given as are consistent with
> the worship, the praise and the contemplation of the
> Creator and Maintainer of the world, and as are
> productive of good morals, religious life, and
> universal brotherhood. (22)

After his first visit, he referred to 'our prayers in the Mandir', and his friends said that he had looked like a 'Pandit' sitting in the Mandir in Indian dress. After returning to Delhi, he said that he continued, in spirit, to join with the members of the ashram in their prayers so that he felt that it had all become a part of his inner life, the ashram with its mandir 'a sanctuary and a shrine' to him. More surprisingly, on one occasion, we find him using an explicitly Hindu category, when, shortly after his mother's death, he wrote that he found her 'presence' in the ashram, and he exclaimed to Tagore, 'The goodness of the Shivam is unutterable, and ever meets us in the hour of our deepest need'. Whatever was in Andrews' mind at this point – he appears to be using an attribute, goodness, of the divinity – he had written to Tagore a few months previously that through his love for him, he had 'entered into the spiritual heritage of India herself, and been made one with her spiritual experience and felt its depth and power'. (23)

The third aspect was, as we have seen, that he claimed that he had been
granted a new vision of Christ from Tagore's eyes. Much of what he wrote
to Tagore at this time certainly had a new ring about it, as he spoke of
the 'Universal Compassion' and the 'Universal Charity' of Christ, which was
so contradicted by 'the old conventional Christianity' of the 'dominant
races and rulers'. (24) More significant, however, was his new conviction
that this 'Christ of the Gospels' stood in 'a spiritual relationship' with
what he called 'the Hindu-Buddhist ideal'. He expressed this publicly at
the time in his lecture at Viceregal Lodge, in broader terms.

> May it not come to pass that, in the higher ranges of
> ancient Hindu thought on the one hand, and in the
> higher ranges of primitive Christianity on the other,
> there will be found a great mountain chain which,
> when fully explored, will unite the East and West
> together, and offer at length an unbroken highway for
> the great onward march whereby humanity shall reach
> those shining tablelands 'to which our God Himself is
> Moon and Sun'. (25)

Andrews sensed a certain extravagance in such speculations when he came to
develop them in his private letters of early 1914 on the possible
historical links between Jesus and 'the Hindu-Buddhist stream', although
they were probably more substantially based than the position which he had
criticised in Evelyn Underhill. What led him into these speculations was
the profound impression made upon him by some of his new neo-Hindu friends,
among them Tagore himself. (26) Tagore was a Hindu, drawing his
inspiration, as Andrews acknowledged and insisted, from his own Hindu
heritage. In spite of this, he was capable of evoking from Andrews a most
remarkable affirmation.

> The strongest belief I have in the world is that
> which you have put into poetry for all time in 10 and
> 11 of Gitanjali. (27)

He refused to explain this in terms that he had found adequate only months previously, in <u>The Renaissance in India</u>.

> I have been obsessed by a piece of theological
> jugglery (I can call it now by no other name) which
> made out that Christ, as the Logos, was the Logos of
> the Buddha, etc. But my conscience, as well as my
> reason, has stood up in revolt at last against such
> shuffling. It is disingenuous; it isn't honest. It
> tames Jesus into an artificial, theological figure,
> not the true Son of Man. As the latter I can worship
> him, not as the former. (28)

If we can begin to sense here the religious difficulties of Andrews' middle
years in India, there is also to be noted the strong testimony about Christ
as 'the true Son of Man', a phrase which indicated for him the universal
significance of the Incarnation. It finds a striking echo in Tagore's
lines in <u>Gitanjali</u> 11.

> Our master himself has joyfully taken upon him the
> bonds of creation; he is bound with us all for
> ever. (29)

By any estimate, Tagore is a major figure in modern Hinduism. In calling
him 'the great sentinel', Gandhi was recognising the unique role he played
as the guardian of the moral integrity of the national movement. (30)
Gandhi also, however, with many others, called him 'Gurudev', the divine
preceptor, for the specific values which he maintained were significant
beyond the questions raised by that movement, and were, indeed, pertinent
to 'the greatest of all the problems in India, ... the cultural problem,
the great <u>quo vadis?</u> of the Indian spirit'. His solution, as in the
case of Andrews' Muslim friends, has been called the solution of
'synthesis'. (31) In his case, this took an extremely subtle form. It is
true that 'he more than anyone else has captured and expressed in words
that even Western man can understand, if he will, the subtle flavour that
pervades the whole majestic fabric of Hinduism'. (32) Nevertheless, he did
not see himself as an orthodox Hindu, and his neo-Hinduism in fact took the

form of a most 'radical challenge to the traditional spirituality' through
its support for 'personal values'. (33) It was this that Andrews
recognised and hailed, his own expansive and expanding Christology finding
fresh vindication precisely in that which distinguished the religion of
Tagore.

4. 'In the Heart of the Universal Mother'

As the Brahmo Samaj was essentially a Bengali movement, so the Arya Samaj
belonged in particular to the Punjab. Both movements represented responses
within the Hindu community to the Western, and more specifically Christian
presence in India, so that, inevitably, they had much in common - their
organizational structure and approach to worship, their monotheism and
opposition to caste. At the same time, there were distinct differences.
The overt and extreme syncretism of the former, exemplified in its earliest
phase in Ram Mohun Roy's The Precepts of Jesus, severely restricted its
appeal. The latter, with its insistence on the authority of the Hindu
scriptures - however much these might be re-read to legitimise radical
religious and social reform, as in Dayananda's Satyarth Prakash of 1875 -
had a much more conservative appearance than its Bengali counterpart, and a
much more extensive appeal.

From the founding of a branch at Lahore in 1877, the Arya Samaj grew
dramatically in numbers, activity and influence, so that, by the census of
1911, there were some quarter of a million members, making it quite the
largest and most dynamic movement within the Hindu community in India in
this period. (1) A number of factors, over and above its conservative
appearance, account for this remarkably impressive development, but for us
the most important is the challenge represented by the nexus of imperialism
and Christianity to which it was a response. This challenge was felt in
the Punjab particularly strongly, where the harsh tradition of the imperial
administration was accompanied by a remarkable expansion of Christianity,
inescapably evident both on the ground and in the figures published in the
decennial census. (2)

If the Arya Samaj's numbers were a response, so was its style. Just as

Dayananda's 'aggressive and uncompromising ... faith fitted the
mid-Victorian atmosphere of dogmatic Christianity and imperial arrogance',
so the Samaj's reputation and practice as militantly anti-Christian had its
origins in that same nexus, and was one of its most striking features at
this period. (3) Western and Christian religious and social values were
undoubtedly assimilated, but they were invariably presented as 'Vedic' in
contradistinction from a demonic Christianity.

The normal view of the Arya Samaj among missionaries at this time appears
to have been unremittingly hostile, and a number of them specialized in
anti-Arya literature, much of it characterized by aggressiveness and
contempt. From the beginning, the response within the Delhi Mission was
more mixed. The Samaj had established itself in Delhi during the 1880's,
and, as it attracted numbers of St Stephen's students, it was felt that it
could not be ignored. (4) Curiously, it was an S.P.G. missionary
associated with the Delhi Mission during the last two decades of the
nineteenth century, R.T. Williams, who was the 'sharpest and most bitter'
of all the Samaj's missionary antagonists. (5) Others, however, among them
Bickersteth, Allnutt, Lefroy and Rudra, recognised and acknowledged some of
the reformed and progressive features of the movement, while a young member
of the College staff, Colin Sharp, took a party of students to visit one of
the Samaj's institutions, the Gurukula at Hardwar, in 1910. (6) No one
before Andrews, however, could be said to have taken to heart the call in
the Delhi Mission News to adopt the approach of 'the great Alexandrian
teachers of the Early Church' in dealing with the Arya Samaj. (7)

Perhaps it was Sharp's visit to Hardwar that activated Andrews' interest.
Certainly, it was at the Gurukula that he was to take the Christian
encounter with the Arya Samaj to new and still unique levels of intimacy
and reciprocity. He had, of course, been aware of the Samaj's journal, the
Vedic Magazine. It also has to be noted that the Samaj made its presence
felt in Delhi with fresh vigour in the early years of the century, Allnutt
reporting, for example, that the movement was '"booming" largely' in the
city in 1909. (8) Most of Andrews' comments during the middle years were
sympathetic. He was critical of the intellectual basis of the Arya Samaj's
apologetic, several times repeating that it could not possibly stand 'the

light of modern criticism and historical research', though, even on this
point, he believed that Dayananda was right on the main issue for which he
contended, because 'the Vedic religion, though it might be very far from
all that he described, was infinitely purer and nobler than popular
Hinduism'. (9) He had even fewer reservations about the Samaj's practical
aims and achievements in the fields of religious and social reform, and
education, seeing these as clearing the ground for a great moral and
religious advance. This he regarded as far more significant from a
Christian point of view than the 'bitterly hostile' anti-Christian
propaganda, because it provided the basis for a possible convergence.

> The more the Samaj proceeds on modern lines and meets
> with modern social and educational difficulties, the
> more nearly will it approach that Faith which has
> shaped those lines of progress. (10)

All this was before Andrews had made any significant personal contact with
the Samaj. This, when it came, was within the more militant wing of the
movement, which had developed from the late 1880's in response to very
specific Christian challenges. In contradistinction from the moderate
wing, which was more rational and secular in its ideals, the militant wing,
deeply committed to attacking caste and ritual, saw the movement primarily
in religious terms and pioneered such developments as preaching missions,
the publication of tracts, and the practice of shuddhi, whereby Muslims and
Christians were re-converted and the depressed classes found a place within
the radically reformed Hindu community which the militant Aryas sought to
create. The moderates retained control of the Samaj's first major higher
educational institution, the Dayananda Anglo-Vedic College at Lahore,
affiliated to the University of Lahore, while militant hopes came to be
focussed in the Gurukula at Hardwar, opened in 1902 and teaching English
and Science only as secondary and subordinate to Sanskrit and Hindi, and
'Vedic truth', its promoters despising the current University system as
incompatible with 'sound scholarship in Vedic learning'. (11) The Gurukula
established itself rapidly, so that the anniversary celebrations in 1908
were reported as attracting sixty to seventy thousand visitors, while the
following year the Tribune could claim that 'the eyes of the whole country'

were fixed upon it. By 1913, it had three hundred Brahmacharis, or
students. (12) Andrews wrote appreciatively of the Gurukula on the basis
of what he heard about it, of its 'high religious ideal of education'. (13)

The dominant figure in the militant wing was Munshi Ram (1857-1926), later
known as Swami Shraddhanand, a convert of Dayananda, and head of the
Gurukula from its inception. It is not clear when Andrews first met him,
but it was in January 1913 that he was able to pay a first short visit to
the Gurukula. There ensued further visits. (14) There also ensued a
variety of involvements for Andrews with the Arya Samaj, and, above all, a
profound friendship with this leader of militant Aryanism, reflected most
vividly in a series of letters written between them in that first year of
their friendship. (15)

The various aspects of Andrews' involvement with the Arya Samaj are in
themselves very interesting. To start with, Andrews, as both a teacher and
supporter of the movement for National Education (and already looking
forward to visiting Tagore's school at Santiniketan), was interested in the
Gurukula as 'the only Institution in India', as Munshi Ram claimed, 'where
an earnest effort is being made to ... impart education on ... truly
Dharmic lines'. (16) In an article for the Tribune, 'The Gurukula and Its
Ideals', in which Munshi Ram had asked him to include whatever criticisms
he felt to be necessary, he found it possible to write with unqualified
enthusiasm about the emphasis on physical health, on the practice of
brahmacharya, or 'chastity', as he translates it, on the use of the
vernacular, on the emphasis on 'Vedic Literature' and Sanskrit. His only
substantial criticism was of the claim that the actual 'applications of
modern knowledge' were to be found in Vedic literature, 'instead of the
principles which underlie modern knowledge'. If, at this point, he found
'a final divergence of opinion' with his new Arya friends, his
acknowledgement of what he calls 'the fresh and vital ... principles of the
great Vedic past' (though he nowhere defines these) helped to soften his
criticism and ensure that the divergence did not impair friendship, 'or
cause a loss of spiritual sympathy' between them. (17) The important
thing, as Andrews saw it, was that the Arya Samaj appeared to have created
in the Gurukula an institution in which 'the impulse from the West' could

be assimilated 'in harmony with the genius of the country, not against it'. The Gurukula, thus, disclosed, in the terminology of Andrews' increasingly expansive theology, 'the hand of the great Artificer, making all things new'. (18) He was not the first missionary to make a positive evaluation of this institution. His friend, W.E.S. Holland, after visiting the Gurukula six years previously, had concluded that the Arya Samaj was 'a schoolmaster to bring this people to Christ'. (19) No one else, though, followed through the implications of such a conclusion as Andrews was to do.

One of the barriers that prevented missionaries and others from a sympathetic view of the Arya Samaj was the reputation that it had acquired of being actively seditious, the Gurukula producing, as one admirer, Ramsay MacDonald, sarcastically observed, 'yellow-robed sedition-mongers ... available to roam over the country, nominally as Samaj propagandists'. (20) Munshi Ram was particularly energetic in opposing Arya involvement in nationalist politics. He blamed the reputation for sedition on missionary propaganda. Andrews found himself caught up in this aspect of things in several ways. Thus, in 1912, there had appeared a novel, Siri Ram, Revolutionist: A Transcript from Life 1907-11, about a young Punjab student involved in sedition, with the Gurukula at the centre of the trouble, harbouring 'budding anarchists'. In response to a very favourable review in the Anglo-Indian Pioneer, Andrews, at the request of Munshi Ram and his colleagues, wrote to the newspaper to repudiate the novel's 'utterly false representation' of the Gurukula. (21) His spirited defence of the Samaj and the Gurukula not only elicited an apology from the author, but also won much admiration from the nationalist press as the action of a 'high-souled' Englishman, and, most notably, votes of thanks from branches of the Arya Samaj at Ambala, Gurdaspur, Sargodha and Delhi. (22)

More remarkable was what he made of the relationship that he had established with the Viceroy and Lady Hardinge following the assassination attempt of December, on behalf of the Arya Samaj. Throughout 1913, he exploited the relationship to the full to promote the cause, as he saw it, of the Samaj and the Gurukula with the imperial authorities. This cause he understood to be the dissociation of the Samaj from extremist nationalism

in the mind of the authorities, and the official recognition of the
movement as essentially religious and at the same time 'loyal'. To this
end, he involved Munshi Ram as fully as he could in the organization of
Lady Hardinge's 'Children's Day', an all-India event which Andrews helped
to arrange as a thanksgiving for the Viceroy's survival of the attempt upon
his life. Andrews subsequently told the Viceroy that Munshi Ram had called
it 'the best day in India since the King's visit'. (23) Similarly, he
secured three hundred copies of a picture of the Viceroy and Lady Hardinge
'specially for the Gurukula Brahmacharis', and arranged a meeting between
Munshi Ram and the Viceroy. (24)

What are we to make of all this? The liberal Lieutenant Governor of the
United Provinces, Sir John Meston, identifying 'the growing importance of
the Arya Samaj as a moral force', recommended consulting it whenever
possible, so as to 'win over the more moderate elements to our side'.
Munshi Ram himself seems to have been happy to go along with a
rapprochement of this sort, and made his own gesture of loyalty by turning
in to the imperial authorities several extremist leaflets by the Delhi
conspirators that he had received, calling them 'un-Aryan'. (25) Andrews'
own position would appear to have been that he regarded collaboration
between the Arya Samaj and the government as serving Indian interests. To
secure the sympathy of the Viceroy, 'our noble raj-rishi', and so to
frustrate 'the forces of reaction' in government, which were so hostile to
the Samaj, while preserving the educational independence of institutions
like the Gurukula, was to promote these interests. So convinced was he of
this that he saw the bridge-building that he was doing as a work to which
God had called him, and he felt, as he told Munshi Ram, that 'the hand of
the Divine Master' was in all that he was doing. It was also 'an
opportunity such as never was given .. (him) before of witnessing for the
Motherland and helping forward the cause ... of this dear country'. (26)

That Andrews regarded himself as witnessing not only for 'the Motherland',
but also for Christ, becomes evident, however discreetly, in the intimacy
of his friendship with Munshi Ram. Of considerable interest in this
respect is a recollection of Andrews and Munshi Ram together at the
Gurukula, written by a Quaker missionary friend, J.S. Hoyland.

Munshi Ram was a magnificent figure of a man, with a
thin ascetic face, and a huge hooked nose. He looked
like an Afghan. Many, indeed most, of his ideas were
poles asunder from those of C.F.A. He was very
emphatic, sometimes definitely dogmatic, in his
statement of his views. But C.F.A. listened
patiently, made no comment on what was repellent but
took pains to bring out by further questioning and
discussion what was of permanent value. In those
conversations one could see 'that of God' in the
intellectual outfit of Mahatma Munshi Ram being
reached, emphasised, developed, by the quiet and
humble fashion in which C.F.A., ignoring the less
worthy aspects of his friend's views, asked for
further information on and implied his deep interest
in the more worthy parts. The two personalities
acted and re-acted on each other in a remarkable way.
Munshi Ram's personality was by far the more striking
and in a sense 'effective'. C.F.A. was content to
take a very secondary place, to sit back and listen
most of the time, now and then throwing in a
suggestion or asking a question which strengthened
'truth' in his friend. (27)

The basis for this exchange, and for all that was to follow, was plainly,
it is important to say, friendship. What Rudra called 'this meeting of
truly kindred spirits' was, for Munshi Ram and Andrews, a joining of hearts
together, comparable with the relationships with Rudra and Tagore, but more
intimate, Andrews felt, than with the latter at least. (28) It involved,
as with Tagore, a complete openness about his increasing discomfort with
his missionary role. (29) In connection with this, there were requests for
Munshi Ram's prayers and 'spiritual advice'. Human affection, of which
there is a great deal in the correspondence, is almost invariably expressed
in close association with expressions of a sense of religious communion.
Thus, the more 'close and human' the relationship, so 'perhaps ... the ...

more divine'. Andrews goes so far as to suggest that this experience
represents for him the fulfilment of the process begun at his conversion in
1890, 'a crown and completion of my heart's longing ... the yearning for
the nearer presence of God'.

> I found that fulfilled during those days at the
> Gurukula, and it came through you, my dearest friend.
> God has used you and your work as His spiritual
> temple, and I was treading, all unworthy, in its
> courts.

Dialogue at this level meant for Andrews not merely an exchange of ideas,
but an expectation of new things to be learned from his Hindu friend in the
sphere of religious experience, and this entailed a corrective to his
previously exclusively Christianity-centred perspective.

> I had (before I came to India) a kind of sense that
> from Palestine (which we call the Holy Land) the
> light had gone forth and spread in wider and wider
> circles. I had left out of account (strange as it
> may seem to you) in my view of history the vast
> spiritual expanse which has been going on developing,
> all the while, on the other side of the world, in
> Asia itself. Here, on this side, I see clearly now,
> there was one Holy Land, one sacred soil, from which
> all the deepest religion sprang - the Holy Land of
> India Herself. It is that which I am now as it were
> exploring and finding every day in its fresh beauty.
> It is, as it were, a fresh world to me, with beauties
> all its own, and I long, my dearest friend, more and
> more to join hands with you and walk together through
> it; for you who are sprung from the very soil of this
> sacred land itself can explain it to me and teach me
> more than all books, for you can give me the living
> spirit. That is what I shall claim from your love
> and I know I shall not ask in vain.

If this is somewhat vague, a slightly later letter indicated what Andrews hoped to gain from this encounter, that is, a corroboration of his conviction about the significance of Christ which yet found place for a proper valuation of Hindu faith, and in particular of the Vedas, so important to the Arya Samaj.

> Shall I tell you what is becoming more and more the
> longing of my life and the goal I am dimly striving
> towards? You must have guessed it already, but now I
> can express it more clearly .... It is to relate the
> figure of the meek and gentle Christ, yet withal so
> brave and fearless and true, with the teaching of the
> Hindu Shastras. I do not find this picture as yet in
> the Vedas so clearly - you may help me there - but I
> do find it in the Upanishads and in all the ideal of
> Hindu India which flowed out of them, and out of
> Buddhism, and out of the character of Rama and Sita
> and the teaching of Krishna as revealed in the Gita.
> I can see how Indian has preserved this ideal,
> wonderfully preserved it for mankind; and that it can
> be quickened again in these new ages of the world.
> And in the union of spirit which is contained in this
> unity of teaching, East and West may become truly
> one. (30)

There are moments in this profound encounter when Andrews' enthusiasm carried him beyond orthodox Christian categories, as, for example, when he agreed with Munshi Ram that it was 'indeed .. the Loving Mother Herself' who had drawn them together. He spoke similarly of the experience of prayer.

> I ... join with you in the early morning quiet and my
> heart meets your heart in the Heart of the Universal
> Mother who has bound us Her children together in
> love. (31)

Throughout, however, he continued to affirm the centrality of Christ for
his own faith.

> It is the Christ of the Gospels who draws me and
> fills my life and has filled it from my youth up.

Because he always presented his own Christian position in an irenic mode,
he was in a position to openly question some aspects of Hinduism, and even
to confront and challenge his Arya friends about the more abrasive anti-
Christian polemic which was a feature of the Samaj. Thus, when Ram Deva,
one of Munshi Ram's assistants, published in the <u>Vedic Magazine</u> an attack
on the Bible, Andrews, referring to Rudra's son, Shuddhir, wrote, 'If I
were to tell Ram Deva that such a careless, unthinking statement made by
him (whom Shuddhir respects and loves) might sow a poisonous seed in
Shuddhir's heart and destroy his fresh young faith in Christ which has made
him the beautiful character he is, he would be horrified and indignantly
deny any such intention.' (32) It would be interesting to know the effect
of this sort of challenge.

We do know, however, something of Munshi Ram's response to Andrews. It is
unfortunate that so few of his letters to Andrews have survived, but one in
particular is very important in indicating the reciprocal character of the
relationship.

> Your letter of the 21st instant has made me feel what
> I have not felt for the last 28 years. I had been an
> atheist of some 9 years standing when the vision came
> to me which poured a balm into my lacerated soul. I
> had laid my doubts before the great Dayananda thrice
> and had been silenced in discussion, but I was not
> convinced. And when I repeated this a third time the
> great Yogi said 'You asked questions and I replied to
> them. I never had the presumption to say that I
> would convince you. It is <u>He</u> alone who can convince
> you of <u>His</u> reality'. And the time came and I was not
> only convinced but felt the Presence and a calm which

> I cannot describe. And then I had to struggle and
> struggle in the Arya Samaj. Ah! The Divine Mother
> alone knows how many times this heart of mine has
> been hit hard during the last 28 years. But the balm
> has come again. As I read your account of the
> unsophisticated pure young heart's true conversion,
> all the wounds which I had received were healed at
> once and I again had a taste of the pure joy after
> 28 years. I thanked the Divine Mother for this new
> blessing for I felt that I had not lived in vain.

Proceeding, Munshi Ram commented on Andrews' developing disagreement with
some of his missionary colleagues; in doing so, he thanked the 'Divine
Mother' for giving Andrews 'the strength to act with true Aryan (in other
words Christ-like) patience'. (33) This open and perceptive
acknowledgement of Christ at the heart of the Arya Samaj is, especially in
the light of the treatment of Christ in Dayananada's <u>Satyarth Prakash</u>,
truly remarkable. It is some measure, not only of Munshi Ram's liberality,
but also of the significance of the inter-religious dialogue which Andrews
was developing.

5. 'A saint of action'

If the middle years of Andrews' missionary decade were comparatively
uneventful after his initial dramatic entry as a missionary into the
political nation, the last twelve months found him involved in this sphere
as never before, in what he later called 'in certain ways the most exciting
time in all my life'. (1) In the course of this, he established a further
extremely interesting friendship beyond the Christian fold, in the
neo-Hindu community, with M.K. Gandhi.

The context of this was the struggle of the Indian community in South
Africa, to which Gandhi had belonged for some twenty years. The community
was made up of two elements. There was, first, a large number of labourers
who had been taken to South Africa, as to many other British colonies,
under the indenture system, a form of virtual slavery operated by the

British authorities to provide cheap labour for British colonial commercial
enterprises. A smaller element consisted of traders and professional
people, known increasingly inappropriately as the 'free Indians'. The lot
of the former group had always been wretched, and was becoming a cause of
increasing concern to the nationalists, a concern reflected in the columns
of the Tribune. (2) Deepeningly oppressive legislation against the 'free
Indians' had attracted resolutions in the Indian National Congress from the
early 1890's, further discriminatory legislation in 1906 and 1913 arousing
much anxiety. (3) Partly in consequence, the issue was also of concern to
the Government of India. (4) While economic factors were very important,
race-hatred was 'the vital driving force' behind the legislation against
the 'free Indians'. (5) As white oppression increased, and with it the
South African Indian resistance, so, too, did the stature of Gandhi as
leader of that resistance. This was noted in India, not least through
Gandhi's enlistment of Gokhale as spokesman in India for the community's
cause. Gandhi's development of a distinctive form of organised resistance,
which he called satyagraha, was followed with admiration in the nationalist
press. (6)

Because of the identification of the white element in South Africa with
Christianity, the treatment of the Indian community there appeared to have
very serious implications for the Church's mission in India. Thus, a Hindu
acquaintance of Andrews, G.A. Natesan, speaking at the 1909 Congress,
suggested that Jesus Christ himself, as an Asiatic, would have been turned
away from the Transvaal by 'the white Christian plutocracy'. (7) The
course of events was followed with concern in the Delhi Mission. (8)
Lefroy spoke on the subject while visiting Britain, and wrote a very
substantial article for The East and the West, 'British Indians in the
Transvaal: An Empire Problem', in which he traced with indignation the
deepening degradation of the community at the hands of the white colonists,
particularly following the incorporation of South Africa into the British
empire. His 'brave words' were noted among the Indian nationalists, and
the Tribune announced that the Punjab was grateful. (9) Rudra made his
concern public in a letter to the Times, and Allnutt noted the 'appalling
effects' in India of events in South Africa. (10) From early in his
missionary decade, Andrews was alive to the issue and its implications. At

the meeting of the Indian National Congress that he had attended in 1906, there was a resolution about the South African situation, and another about indenture there and elsewhere, and a debate which must have enabled him to judge the intensity of feeling which the issue aroused. He noted, too, how every offensive episode in South Africa was reported in the nationalist press. This, he claimed, was leading the educated classes in India to conclude that 'the Christian talk about the brotherhood of man is hypocrisy and cant', and was affecting every mission station in India where higher educational work was going on. (11)

As well as publicising such views among church people, Andrews made a number of efforts to have pressure put upon the South African authorities. Twice, for example, he tried to do this through the Viceroy. On the first occasion, in January 1908, when indignation was running particularly high in India at developments in the Transvaal, he wrote an open letter to Lord Minto. He followed this with a private appeal, asking him to make 'a really warm and kind-hearted pronouncement of sympathy with the suffering and difficulties of the Transvaal Indians, and a very strong and almost indignant declaration that Government is not indifferent'. (12) One difficulty in this matter was that, as Ramsay MacDonald explained in the St Stephen's College Magazine, the Government of India had no constitutional rights in regard to it. (13) The Viceroy, nevertheless, took Andrews' letter seriously, and it may have helped to inspire the 'strong representations' which the Government was reported to be making somewhat later during Minto's viceroyalty. (14) Andrews' intervention was welcomed by the Tribune as truly voicing the feelings of the Indian public. (15)

He made a further attempt to persuade the Viceroy, in this case Lord Hardinge, in 1913, to champion the cause of the South African Indians, and other indentured workers in other colonies, 'directly, immediately, drastically and publicly'. This Hardinge did a few months later, in a speech in Madras. Andrews' appeal had no doubt played its part, for Hardinge had told him that he valued his views on the question, and was very grateful for them. (16)

Similarly, Andrews tried during the later months of 1913 to mobilise the

Anglican bishops in India, through Lefroy, by this time Metropolitan, to
exert pressure on their opposite numbers in South Africa to intervene in
the 'very terrible situation' there. This would help to overcome the
'terrible ... effect' on Indian educated thought of 'the silence of the
Church'. (17) Lefroy was sympathetic, and in fact sent a contribution to
Gokhale's campaign fund. He accepted Andrew' proposed draft letter to
South Africa without amendment, but failed to get agreement among his
colleagues about the wording, and had to be content with a private letter
to the Anglican Archbishop of Cape Town, to which he got a rather frosty
reply.

By the time the Indian bishops' involvement in the question had run its
largely ineffectual course, Andrews was making his own most remarkable
contribution by actually going to South Africa to meet and associate
himself with Gandhi in the struggle of the Indian community. His first
significant information about Gandhi and his activities must have come from
the latter's close associate, Henry Polak, whom Andrews met while Polak was
touring India in 1909 and 1910 to publicise the cause of the Transvaal
Indians. (18) Polak's interpretation of the significance of satyagraha,
with its combination of 'meekness ... and steel-like courage', as a putting
into practice of Christ's teaching about returning good for evil, which
made the Transvaal Indians better Christians than their persecutors, cannot
have escaped Andrews' notice, and perhaps helped him to make his initial
assessment of Gandhi, before actually meeting him, as 'the most saintly and
heroic Indian of modern times'. (19)

It was, however, through again meeting Gokhale, Gandhi's political guru,
while Gokhale was campaigning on the South African issue in the later part
of 1913, that Andrews was persuaded to visit South Africa. Early in
November, Gokhale had appealed throughout India for funds. Andrews'
response was immediate, both in persuading Gokhale to visit St Stephen's
College to launch the appeal there personally, 'the first public one among
the students', Andrews was proud to note, and also in placing at Gokhale's
disposal anything he personally had to give, 'time, money - everything'.
(20) This offer was accepted, and Gokhale asked him, 'as one of the
best-known and most respected Englishmen in India', to go to South Africa

as his representative 'to report on the situation'. (21) At the last minute, his new English friend, W.W. Pearson, a private tutor in Delhi, offered to go with Andrews, and the latter agreed. Andrews' decision to go was criticised, though not universally, in European circles, while the nationalists saw it as a 'unique ... act of loving self-sacrifice' which had 'laid the country under obligation'. (22)

A delay in the passage of the steamer to Natal provided Andrews with an opportunity for further reflection on the issues involved, and he wrote an article for the <u>Tribune</u> and the <u>Modern Review</u> advocating a strenuous campaign to halt the recruitment of indentured labourers.

> The ground taken should be the highest, namely that it is unworthy of a civilised country to allow its citizens to sell themselves into virtual slavery. (23)

Although he had agreed with Pearson that the latter should concentrate on indenture questions during their visit to South Africa, this article, nevertheless, marks the beginning of a phenomenal endeavour whereby 'virtually on his own, Charlie Andrews ... carried through a reform almost equal to the abolition of slavery'. (24)

Andrews was in South Africa from 2 January 1914 to mid-February, and wrote in great detail on every aspect of his time there in telegrams and letters to Gokhale, numerous letters to Tagore and Munshi Ram, and a series of articles for the nationalist and other publications in India, South Africa and Britain. (25) It was a time of prodigious activity, which included, in addition to much writing, public addresses to both the white and Indian communities, including the lecture on Tagore in the City Hall in Cape Town, and sermons in Durban and Pretoria Cathedrals, and in places like the Indian Association Hall, Phagli, a repeated theme being, in connection with a reminder of Tagore's Nobel Prize for Literature, that India 'was and is a civilised country, that even her coolies are heirs to a traditional culture and spirituality'. (26) There was also a full involvement in the negotiations with Smuts, and the closest of encounters with the leaders of the Indian struggle and in particular with Gandhi.

Andrews wrote for Gokhale a very full account of his part in the offical negotiations. It is clear from this that by establishing an immediate understanding of Gandhi's inner motivation, he was able to make a helpful contribution. He put this in a letter to Tagore.

> I had no difficulty in seeing from the first Mr
> Gandhi's position and accepting it; for in principle
> it is essentially yours and Mahatamaji's (Munshi Ram)
> – a true independence, a reliance upon spiritual
> force, a fearless courage in the face of temporal
> power, and withall a deep and burning charity for all
> men. His watchword is 'We Indians must cease being
> mendicants. We must be ready to suffer anything
> rather than take that position of degradation and be
> ready to win back our moral position in the world by
> suffering'.

Although involved in the detailed presentation of the Indian case, his main achievement, as he saw it, was the establishing of this principle, of what he called Indian 'honour', with Smuts, and securing the latter's public acknowledgement of it 'for the Back-Veldters and Natal planters to see'. (27) This, too, is how Polak and Gandhi saw it, Polak later writing that 'Andrews rendered great service in interpreting the Indian viewpoint to Smuts and the Commission'. (28) The final settlement of this phase of the South African Indian struggle had to wait upon a bill in the South African parliament six months later. During the debate in parliament, despite vehement opposition to allowing freer access for 'the refuse of the backparts of India' to 'overrun' the country, Gandhi commented in his journal that Andrews' spirit 'seemed to watch and guide the deliberations of the House'. When the settlement came, Gandhi and his associates modestly attributed its achievement principally to the 'suffering of thousands of resisters' over the previous eight years, but they were also deeply grateful for Andrews' 'great assistance' in the form both of 'wise counsel' and of spreading 'a spirit of sympathy and love all round'.

Later, and with exaggerated modesty, Gandhi was to pay Andrews a remarkable
tribute.

> If I were to compete with him as to which of us
> had the greatest influence with these people in
> South Africa, I am not sure that he would not floor
> me. (29)

In India itself, the Tribune vindicated both Andrews' original argument
about the missionary significance of the South African situation, and his
intervention, admitting that his work and example had 'helped to remove a
certain prejudice which mere proselytism caused in the minds of people',
and also compared his work to Christian missionary involvement in such
issues as the emancipation of slaves. (30) Andrews himself, despite being
invited by the Viceroy to dine with him in Simla on his return, saw his
achievement in terms of a much closer identification with the Indian
people. He wrote to Munshi Ram on his return journey to India that he was
'now a child of Aryavarta not merely in name and thought, but in deed and
act', though he emphasised to him that his motivation in what he had done
had been his Christian faith. (31)

Despite the quite exceptional immediate significance of his visit to South
Africa, there was an even more important long-term effect, and that was the
establishment during these days of a deep friendship with Gandhi. Because
'no life lived' at that time 'could be more moving' than Gandhi's, Andrews
had envisaged his visit as 'a pilgrimage to touch his feet'. We can,
nevertheless, trace through his frequent letters, particularly those to
Munshi Ram and Tagore, the steady development of a deeply affectionate
relationship, so that they were soon 'close as brothers and closer'. He
found in Gandhi 'a new Indian element the Gujerati character', and missed a
sense of what he called 'unity of spirit', which he associated with Tagore.
Nevertheless, he was soon able to tell Gandhi that he was a part of his
life 'as Mahatmaji and Gurudev (Tagore) and Sushil (Rudra) are'. (32)
Andrews' affection was immediately reciprocated, as Gandhi later recalled,
at the time of Andrews' death in 1940.

> When we met in South Africa we simply met as brothers
> and remained as such to the end.

At the time, he spoke of 'the loneliness there would be' for him when
Andrews left. (33)

One important consequence of this new friendship is reflected in a painting
by Abanindranath Tagore, now at Santiniketan, depicting Gandhi and Tagore
talking together, with Andrews slightly in the background, the message
being that he brought them together. This was, indeed, the case, but only
as part of a wider process whereby Andrews was instrumental in creating
important links for the national movement. Even while he was in South
Africa, Tagore acknowledged this in a letter to Munshi Ram.

> We have come close to each other through the common
> love of our dear friend Charlie Andrews and the
> common aim we both have set before us.

Similarly, soon after Gandhi's own return to India in 1915, Pearson
reported that he had spoken 'of the great debt of gratitude he owed to
Andrews for having brought him into such close and intimate touch with
three of India's greatest sons, the poet Rabindranath Tagore, Mahatmaji and
Mr Rudra'. From then to the date of Rudra's retirement in 1923, whenever
he happened to be in Delhi, Gandhi stayed in the Principal's house, and 'it
was here that he first met Tagore, and where he used to receive leaders
like Tilak, Motil Lal Nehru, Maulana Mohammed Ali, Hakim Ajmal Khan,
Maulana Azad, Jawaharlal Nehru ...'. Gandhi himself later acknowledged the
point in Young India.

> My open letter to the Viceroy giving concrete shape
> to the Khilafat claim was conceived and drafted under
> Principal Rudra's roof. He and Charlie Andrews were
> my revisionists. Non-co-operation was conceived and
> hatched under his hospitable roof. (34)

There can be no doubt that Andrews was fully aware of what he was doing in his frequent references, in conversation with Gandhi in South Africa, to his other close friends, and that he saw himself as forging these links for the national movement.

Another important aspect of the friendship was Andrews' interest in the religious dimension of Gandhi's political work. For Gandhi himself, of course, the initially pragmatic political technique of passive-resistance had already become satyagraha or 'truth-force', with its concomitant ahimsa, or non-violence, an important expression of his emerging philosophy of life as a search for truth. Andrews' first few days in South Africa confirmed for him that Gandhi was essentially a religious man, 'a saint', though 'of the heroic type, a saint of action rather than of contemplation', while the form this took seemed to have universal significance, representing 'that which we have all been groping after - a moral equivalent for war'. (35)

Andrews' handling of the question of the sources of Gandhi's ideas is important. Gandhi had himself many years previously discovered Tolstoy and his interpretation of the Sermon on the Mount, and had subsequently corresponded with Tolstoy - a correspondence part of which Andrews saw at this time. Not surprisingly, then, Andrews saw satyagraha as 'the Hindus, under Mr. Gandhi ... presenting to the world almost literally the ideal of the Sermon on the Mount'. He went so far, indeed, as to claim that he had 'found Christ and worshipped him, amid the little groups of Indian passive resisters fresh from prison - Hindus almost all of them'. (36) He nevertheless acknowledged the importance of Gandhi's Hindu sources, and gives us an interesting account of how the latter developed his theory.

> The principle of 'passive resistance' ... has been
> taken ... originally from Tolstoy's writings. But
> this has been ... drastically remodelled and
> re-interpreted in the light of Hindu religion. The
> parallel to Hinduism was found by Mr. Gandhi in his
> recollection of the methods by which caste discipline
> was silently and effectively observed in Kathiawar,
> without the aid of external law, or the use of

weapons of force. But later on the principle was
carried by him much deeper still, back to the very
heart of Hindu religion. Its parallel was found, on
the one hand, in the doctrine of ahimsa, on the other
hand, in the doctrine of the supreme reality of the
atman.

In the matter of the former 'doctrine', of ahimsa, Andrews found in Gandhi
a new illustration of the phenomenon discovered in his encounters with
Tagore and Munshi Ram, namely a correlation between his understanding of
'the Christ of the Gospels' and 'Hindu India and its ideals', but a more
significant one in this case because it was at the important level of
'ideas ... (applied) to the test of action'. He developed this further in
a letter to Tagore shortly after leaving South Africa.

> The Hindu ideal is often termed 'passive' .... This
> is of course outrageous. The real touchstone is
> ahimsa. Is physical force, domination, aggression,
> the true attitude in life, or is ahimsa? There is
> the dividing line. The Jew, the Roman, the modern
> Englishman would instinctively say the former:
> Christ says the latter: - 'My kingdom is not of this
> world, else would my servants fight, but now is my
> kingdom not from hence .... He that is of the Truth
> heareth my voice'. (37)

The implication here is clear enough, that a Hindu like Gandhi, in his
practice of ahimsa, had his part in that kingdom, and was 'of the Truth.'

His response to Gandhi's 'doctrine of the supreme reality of the atman', as
he understood it, was, if anything, even more enthusiastic. Though later
he was to differ radically over the latter's understanding of this, over
his 'equation of the essential self of man with the atman and the
consequent rejection of the body and all matter as the source of all
selfishness', it is evident that at this stage he was looking at the
concept from another angle. (38) 'The message of the Upanishads, that

man's deliverance comes through realisation of the <u>Atman</u>', had assumed for
Andrews 'a new and living meaning'.

> The pure human spirit is in essence one with the
> divine. This alone gives the clue to mortal
> existence. Without this all human life becomes chaos
> and despair.

If there seems to be here a tendency towards an anthropology more Hindu
than Christian, the main point that he is trying to make would seem to be
that in this doctrine there was an affirmation of the dignity of the human
person over against the denials implicit in South African oppression: the
chief lesson that he had learnt from Gandhi in South Africa, he explained,
was of 'the supremacy of "spiritual independence" over all other human
forces'. He saw this supremacy embodied in Gandhi, and it had been
attained in and through 'the struggle'.

> His spiritual realisation in action has been so
> complete, during all these years of conflict and
> imprisonment, that I long merely to bow my head in
> silence and thus express my reverence.

If some of Andrews' commentary on Gandhi's 'doctrine' is somewhat
ambiguous, the point he is trying to make is clear enough. Nor was there
much room for misunderstanding in his concluding observation. He had seen
in Gandhi, he wrote, 'the fulfilment in action of those ideals which as a
Christian I longed to realise'. (39)

His own Christian allegiance, in other words, he did not regard as in
question, though it is clear from what we can gather from his first
surviving letter to Gandhi, written a week after setting sail from Cape
Town, that he now clung to the primacy and '<u>distinctiveness</u>' of Christ amid
almost overwhelming confusions. His desire to 'meet ... (Gandhi's) own
mind, and that of others', would, he could see, mean 'a lonely pilgrimage',
in which he would be regarded by everyone in the West whom he knew and
loved as 'a heretic of the most dangerous kind', led away by his

'pro-Indian bias and infatuation', and yet, in the same letter he affirmed, tenaciously, though never less offensively, his faith in the universal significance of 'the meek and lowly Christ', the 'child of the East and West in one', in whose coming 'something far greater' than all that Indian tradition had yet produced, even in the Buddha, took place, because Christ '<u>lived</u>' what had previously been only 'beautiful thoughts'. (40)

Testing out some of his related new ideas on 'the organic development of religion' in this letter, Andrews asked Gandhi for his criticisms. He recognised that there were bound to be points of disagreement in the dialogue now opening up, but he was confident that Gandhi's love for him would grow, provided only that he could remain certain that Andrews was 'struggling towards the truth and not shirking the task'. Regrettably, we have no indication of Gandhi's response to Andrews at this time, other than his gratitude for his help in the negotiations with Smuts and his deepening affection and respect for him. For the dialogue which they were to develop over the next quarter century, only the foundations had been laid. These, nevertheless, clearly were laid, in the deeply affectionate relationship which had been established, in Andrews' unfeigned admiration for Gandhi's achievement, his willingness to acknowledge that this had its roots close to 'the very heart of Hindu religion', and his continuing sense of freedom to affirm both the primacy in his own faith of the person of Jesus Christ, and Christ's universal significance.

Thus began a further relationship with someone of another faith. Andrews arrrived back in India, by way of London and a deepened friendship with Gokhale, on 17 April 1914. (41) The <u>Tribune</u> summed up his visit to South Africa as a 'mission of love'. (42)

6. 'The sympathetic school of Mr Andrews'

Andrews' missionary years, the years of these friendships, or of the beginning of them, coincided with the emergence in India of what came to be known as the 'fufilment school', a group of Indian Christians and missionaries who saw Christ or Christianity as, in one way or another, fulfilling the other religions, and who, in consequence, looked upon these

religions with a new sympathy. 'The great sages of India were
schoolmasters to bring the Indians to Christ', said the Bishop of Bombay at
the Pan-Anglican Congress. (1) His claim, however, that this notion was
'behind the whole conception of modern missions', was somewhat exaggerated,
and there were many opponents of this approach, 'the sympathetic school of
Mr. Andrews', as one critic called it. One Anglican missionary wrote that
before coming to India, he had believed many good things of Hinduism.

> My ideas ... were moulded very much on the lines C.F.
> Andrews always follows. Most of my opinions have
> changed .... Some of us get severe shocks if we read
> too much 'Andrewsism' at home.

Another critic said of Andrews' expectation of finding good in Hinduism,
that 'it would be just as reasonable to expect to draw sweet water from a
bitter spring', while an S.P.G. missionary, whose views Bishop Montgomery
had solicited to check against those of Andrews and Rudra, wrote that
'where Christianity offers the perfect solution of all the problems raised
by religious consciousness, Hinduism merely offers contradictory, absurd
and usually immoral and blasphemous hypotheses'. (2) There is,
nevertheless, some justification in describing the 'sympathetic school' -
not least after the popularisation of these ideas at the World Missionary
Conference in Edinburgh in 1910 - as 'the new orthodoxy'. (3) Andrews, his
name several times coupled with that of Rudra, was regarded by many as a
representative exponent of this important development in the Christian
attitude to other faiths and their adherents. (4)

In spite of this, Andrews' appreciation of other religions, and in
particular of Hinduism, was not without qualification. In particular, he
had little sympathy with popular Hinduism as he saw it at this time. When,
for example, he saw cows receiving acts of devotion at Benares, he
exclaimed, 'How repulsive it was, and yet how full of pathos!' (5) From
his first report, written for S.P.G. in February 1905, through to the
Renaissance in India, published in 1912, he markedly failed to appreciate
what he called 'idolatry', and he frequently criticised it as a source of
spiritual and moral degradation within the Hindu community. Similarly, he

attacked astrology, and the ideas which lay behind it. He was highly
critical, as we have seen, of certain social expressions of Hinduism, in
particular of aspects of caste, the more serious because he recognised
caste as 'still the real church of Hinduism', and 'at the very centre of
Hinduism'. (6) With much of which he was critical, then, he was clear that
'a Reformation ... (was) needed in India as well as a Renaissance'. (7)

Not surprisingly, therefore, it was in what he called Hinduism's 'higher
religious history', and in the reforming movements that he found most to
admire, and in the latter that he made his close friendships beyond the
Christian community. Although he often drew attention to passages of
'spiritual beauty and moral insight' in the classical texts of the Indian
religions, and went on to claim that 'the Eternal Word was the Light of the
Buddha and Tulsi Das in their measure, even as he was, in so much greater a
degree, the Light of the Hebrew Prophets', it was largely in relation to
the modern movements and the 'intellectual, strong and independent men' who
supported them, that he developed his more sympathetic reflections, his
'Andrewsism'. (8)

He justified his sympathy from the New Testament. His most distinctive
contribution here was to go behind such, by then, relatively commonplace
concepts as that of the Johannine 'Eternal Word' as employed, for example,
by Farquhar in his Crown of Hinduism, and to cite Christ's own attitude in
the Synoptics. (9) Thus, for example, 'when Christ chooses His example of
truly noble conduct, He selects not a Jewish Priest, but a Samaritan for
His word of commendation', because 'moral and spiritual character is the
only criterion of Christ, ... (and) race, birth, religion, even, are as
nothing compared with character'. 'Christ', he says in another place,
'recognised kinship in the things of the Spirit far beyond the limits of
any one religion, according to His own great saying - "He that doeth the
will of my Father which is in heaven, the same is my brother ...."'. (10)
'I lay stress', he reported to Commission 4 of the Edinburgh Conference,
'on the picture of Christ in the Synoptic Gospels as he accredits and
approves this person and that, not as belonging to God's chosen people, but
as being humble, devout sincere, unselfish'.

It was not only on the basis of such criteria, however, that Andrews
justified his welcome for the reforming movements in Hinduism and Indian
Islam. He also said that, because the predominant new religious factor
which had given rise to the reforming movements in British India was
Christianity, some of them were 'on the very borderland of the Christian
faith', and, because they had assimilated certain central Christian ideas,
'especially the great commanding and correlative thoughts of the Fatherhood
of God and the Brotherhood of Man', were functioning as 'Christian leaven
... penetrating the great mass of Indian life'. (11) In consequence, new
attitudes were called for.

> There must be no longer the desire to capture
> converts from Hinduism, by any and every means, and
> take advantage of her hour of weakness and
> desolation; but rather the desire to come to her help
> in the needful time of trouble, and to aid her in the
> fufilment of duties which she has long neglected ....
> If we sincerely believe the great words of our Lord,
> 'I came not to destroy but to fulfil', we shall
> hesitate before we undertake destructive work in a
> country which has aimed so high as India. (12)

The Christian attitude must, nevertheless, be discriminating. India's
religious development could not be merely a 'smooth, graduated evolution',
for there was 'much in Hinduism that must perish, ... much that must die
and be reborn'. (13) At the same time, Christianity itself might hope to
benefit from this new encounter: there were, for example, 'crude' features
of Western Christianity, 'transcendent ideas of God, ... individualistic
ideas of human personality, ... creationist theories of the universe', to
which 'the Vedanta Philosophy' might offer a corrective, leading to 'a
more balanced and complete Christian philosophy'. (14)

It is not difficult to see why the term 'Andrewsism' was coined. Andrews
had not set out, like Farquhar in the Crown of Hinduism, to work out a
comprehensive argument about the relationship between Christianity and
Hinduism, but, writing briefly and in a wide variety of places, he clearly

sought to encourage a new attitude of openness and sympathy as an appropriate Christian and missiological response to people of other faiths, and especially to the reformers among them. The invitation in early 1911 to write a book on Christianity and the 'educated Hindu classes', nevertheless, gave him an opportunity to draw together much that he had written over the previous years, and to write, <u>inter alia</u>, a sympathetic survey and evaluation from a Christian standpoint of the reforming movements. <u>The Renaissance in India</u>, completed by mid-1912, sums up the sort of approach for which Andrews had become known over the previous six or seven years.

Almost simultaneously with its publication, however, Andrews met Rabindranath Tagore, and entered into the first of that series of profound friendships with some of the most important figures in neo-Hinduism, which was to fill the last two years of his missionary decade. At the end of a chapter on 'The New Reformation' in <u>The Renaissance in India</u>, he had written that 'a wide sympathy and tolerance for the work of others, such as Christ inculcated, should only deepen and enlarge our own faith'. (15) Certainly, the impact of these three drove him to a serious reconsideration of his own position, in contrast with which, the approach he had previously sought to popularise looks relatively conventional.

We can trace the course of his thinking in his letters to Tagore, Munshi Ram and Gandhi at this time. (16) There are two central and related points with which he was exercised. First, a view of religious history which gave a very high valuation to Indian religious experience. He first tried out his ideas on this with Munshi Ram, and later with Gandhi. To the latter, he wrote that there were 'two great races which possessed religious <u>genius</u>, - the Semitic and the Indo-Aryan'; nevertheless, he continues, 'the <u>mother</u> source of inspiration' was India, demonstrably influencing both the East and (in thinkers such as Plato) the West. (17) It was in this context of a reconsideration of what has come to be known as salvation history, that he made his second point, about Christ. He wrote to Tagore of his growing conviction 'that both the Semitic and the Hindu-Buddhist element are to be found in the Christ of the Gospels: that the two great fountain heads of higher religion - from Palestine and from India - actually met and gave

birth to Christianity in its essential primitive form'. (18) His fullest
exposition of this 'new discovery', as he called it, is to be found in a
letter to Tagore, written on 2 March 1914, the 'main issue' being that, in
contradistinction from the 'old, hard, aggressive Jewish ... view of life,
Christ, the Jewish peasant, lived instinctively, as part of his own
fundamental nature, ... (a) non-Jewish ideal, which ... (was) so akin to
Hinduism'.

> He lived it, not artificially, not as a superimposed
> creed, but as naturally and freely as the birds of
> the air and the lilies of the field lived out their
> nature. ... He has the Universal Compassion for all
> nature and all mankind .... He has also the Universal
> Charity, like that of God ... and this nature wells
> up at all times. It is as marked in the agony of
> crucifixion as on the sunny Galilean hills .... If
> this is really so, then surely the life of Christ
> cannot be unrelated to the only soil which, up to
> then, had produced ... this type of nature, ... the
> Hindu-Buddhist stream, which ... had for long ages
> been the greatest moral and spiritual force in all
> the world.

The relationship, he suggested, was not dependent on any direct historical
links, for which he conceded that there was no evidence, but was
'spiritual', its identification dependent on 'a fine spiritual instinct ...
like a good ear in music'. The main issues in this long and interesting
letter were later very sympathetically but severely criticised by Farquhar,
and it is clear that Andrews himself was not entirely confident about them,
for he asked Tagore whether he did not think him 'extravagant and
speculative'. Certainly, he had moved far beyond the 'new orthodoxy' of
the 'fulfilment school', but the context of the letter at least helps us to
understand how it came to be written. He wrote it while at sea, just
eleven days out of Cape Town, and it is, in Farquhar's perceptive words, 'a
blazing sign of the depths to which ... (his) Christian soul was moved by
the grossness and cruelty of Christian people in South Africa in their

dealing with people of other races'. (19) That is part of the context, and
the other is his encounter with Gandhi, this following closely upon the
deep impressions made already by Tagore himself, and by Munshi Ram, which
gave substance to the notion of 'the Hindu-Buddhist ideal'. In his new
friends he saw much that he regarded as Christ-like, and yet how to say
this without giving an impression of religious arrogance? He dismisses the
theory of Christ as the Logos as 'a piece of theological jugglery', but
finds it possible to speak of Jesus as 'the true Son of Man' whom he 'can
worship' precisely because he is 'the true lineal descendant of India as
well as Palestine'. He is led from this to some final reflections on how
Christians who share his main position might 'sit at the feet of India the
Mother', in order to fully understand their own religion and correct the
faults in their own civilization, while Hindus might also learn and study,
without any sense of humiliation, the further truths which have been added
by Christianity to their own original deposit of faith.

Andrews did not pursue these matters further at this time. His return to
India pitched him into the very busy and deeply distressing closing months
of his missionary decade, in which, hardly surprisingly, his 'Christian
position' was, as he wrote to Tagore, in question. (20) His theorizing in
this corespondence, nevertheless, is extremely interesting as an indication
of the strength of the challenge which was presented to his understanding
of Christ by what he saw in South Africa of white racism, and also, more
positively, by what he discerned in the depths of his friendship with these
people of other faiths.

As important, in the long run, as these speculations into which he was led,
were the friendships which preceded and helped to shape them. (21) In this
respect, the first friendship, with Zaka Ullah, was important in disclosing
to Andrews the possibility of deep friendship beyond the Christian fold,
and is important in illustrating the possibilities of deep and creative
fellowship and dialogue between Christian and Muslim. That with Munshi
Ram, so amply illustrated in the surviving correspondence, has a singular
value as an example of 'fruitful dialogue ... in practice' in a region left
otherwise almost exclusively to fierce polemics, and also because it
includes such a clear indication of Munshi Ram's amazing response to

Andrews' initiatives. (22)

The friendship with Tagore had its less satisfactory side, in that Andrews was so clearly overwhelmed by Tagore's powerful personality. And yet this friendship, along with that with Gandhi, was very important, because these two represented in their different ways, 'as no one else could hope to, the spirit of the new Hinduism', the former distilling and disseminating in unique ways 'the sweet essence of Hinduism', the 'unique ways' including the art of poetry, a valuable point of access for Andrews. (23) An important element which distinguishes the friendship and dialogue with Gandhi, quite apart from the unusually close relationship with one who was to fulfil such a central role in the history of modern India, was the frequency with which they exchanged moral and religious views in considering Gandhi's specific actions in the national struggle. So dialogue was carried into new and important areas of human concern, into what Hinduism calls the way of action, and others politics, as had indeed been the case from the beginning, through Andrews' involvement with Gandhi in the South African struggle.

In these friendships and their accompanying dialogue, there is no question but that Andrews' own ultimate loyalty to Christ was never in question and always apparent and affirmed. This is very clear from Hoyland's observation of Andrews in discussion with Munshi Ram, but even in the 1914 correspondence with Tagore and Gandhi, his new speculations are an occasion to underline the universal significance and appeal of Christ as 'of the East and of the West'. If Andrews' orthodoxy was in question among his Christian contemporaries, the centrality of Jesus Christ for his own life and faith was always made clear to his friends, and was one of the enduring impressions that he left with them. (24) Even as he was reaching the point of finally detaching himself from a formal missionary role, then, he was developing, in his 'participation ... in the life' of these men of other faiths, his own distinctive mode of Christian witness. (25)

In his dream, forty years earlier, of a new Alexandria, Westcott had envisaged the formation of a community in India made up of people 'as thoroughly Hindu as they ... (were) Christian'. Andrews shared this ideal

for the Church, and worked for its realization. At the same time, he
discovered among his friends of other faiths those who were, by his
criteria, as he might have put it, though not necessarily to them, as
thoroughly Christian as they were Hindu or Muslim, and, as such, members of
what he called 'that larger Church of Christ, the Church of aspiring
Humanity, the Church of Him who is the Son of Man'. There were a number of
factors which helped to propel Andrews out of formal missionary work, but,
along with them as we shall see, was this very positive one, this
discovery, and its determination of his own new and distinctive vocation.

NOTES: Chapter Six

1. Introductory

1 NI p. 236. His knowledge of Indian texts was, of course,
   limited almost exclusively to those available in English
   translation.

2 The MS life of the prophet Muhammad is in NAI.

3 Andrews' Introduction runs to 17 pages. The first four volumes
   appeared between 1910 and 1913, the fourth including an
   'Appreciation' by Puran Singh which quotes extensively Andrews'
   remarks on the Swami in RI. After Amir Chand's execution in
   1914, there was a pause until a further four volumes were
   published in 1931-2, the first of these repeating the passage
   from RI.

4 Tribune 7 Apr 1911; IR Jul 1910 and MR Jul 1913

5 Rudra CC 1909; SSC Mag Apr 1910; Andrews CC 1910

6 DMN Jan 1912; DMN Jul 1911

7 DMN Jan 1908; Jan 1909; Jan 1912; DMN Jul 1908; NI p. 144. Among
   the CT series, in particular 18, 25 Nov 1910, 'The Christian
   Borderland' and 'The Hindu Challenge to the Church'

8 Guardian 28 Feb 1913; SM Apr 1913 (Andrews responded in SM Jun
   1913). Two reviews in Britain were appreciative, TEW Oct 1912,
   CMI Dec 1912.

9 Macnicol Ind Int Jan 1913, cf. Farquhar YMOI Jan 1914; another
   enthusiastic missionary reviewer was Andrews' new colleague,
   P.N.F. Young DMN Jan 1913. For an Indian Christian review, NMI
   Mar 1913. Nationalist reviews included HR Feb-Mar 1913, cf.
   Tribune 9 Oct 1912 (it was also quoted in an editorial of 13 Feb
   1913), IR Mar 1914.

10 CMI Dec 1912

11 SM Apr 1913. In one missionary household where Micklem's
    strictures were read out, 'there were emphatic expressions of
    approval that he had so faithfully and boldly stated the truth
    about Hinduism as it really is' M.M. Underhill to T. Tatlow, 24
    Aug 1912 (SCM).

12 Gulam Masih NMI May–Jun 1912

2. 'The New Islam'

1 Gairdner 1910, p. 248; Sharp 1921, p. 101
2 Smith 1943, p. 44; NI p. 132
3 Spear 1951, p. 144. Smith 1943 identifies nine principal figures
   in the Aligarh Movement, among them Andrews' three friends.
4 Andrews later wrote a booklet, Hakim Ajmal Khan, in a series,
   'Biographies of Eminent Indians'.
5 RI p. 126
6 NI p. 134; SM May 1910; ZU p. 1. Except where otherwise stated,
   all further quotations in this section are from ZU.
7 MR Apr 1910
8 SM May 1910
9 TEW Oct 1905; SM May 1910; NI p. 135. In one of his best known
   papers, Lefroy, an acknowledged authority on Islam, chose to
   quote at length a passage from a letter of Andrews' on this last,
   'the ritual aspect of the Mohammedan creed and life' – Montgomery
   1907, p. 287.
10 Lefroy 1894; RI pp. 213, 248
11 ZU, also MR Apr 1911, Tribune 14 Dec 1910
12 Harcourt Butler 'Note on the Political Outlook in India' 20 Apr
    1910 (Minto – NLS)
13 ZU, also MR Apr 1911, Andrews True India p. 198
14 NI p. 130
15 Spear 1949, p. 186
16 ZU, also MR Apr 1911
17 SM May 1910; Tribune 14 Dec 1910; MR Apr 1911
18 MR Nov 1924 – Aug 1925
19 Andrews' account occurs in Andrews 1930, pp. 109–110.
    Contemporary reports include Tribune 26 Feb, 16 Mar 1907.
20 Hardinge to Meston, 13 Dec 1914 (Hardinge – CUL)
21 Andrews stayed with Ali Imam in his house at Simla in May 1913,
    and clearly knew him well – Andrews to Munshi Ram, n.d. (mid–May
    1913) (Chaturvedi – NAI).

22 On hearing of the success of the Viceroy's visit to Cawnpore,
'Later in the day I sent for a young Mussalman extremist of the
Mahomed Ali school ... and he said, "We shall all be with the
Viceroy now"' Andrews to Lady Hardinge, 19 Oct 1913 (Hardinge -
CUL).

23 Meston to Hardinge, 26 Aug 1913 (Hailey - IOL& R)

24 Andrews to Tagore, 1 Sep 1913 (Santiniketan)

25 Meston to Hardinge, 26 Aug 1913 (Hailey - IOL& R). Meston
went on to refer to Andrews' 'almost pathetic anxiety to be a
successful peacemaker', and added, 'he is the most fascinating of
idealists; and I wish I had one tenth of his single-mindedness'.
Several years later, Meston spoke of his friendship with Andrews
having 'survived many vicissitudes' Challenge 13 May 1921.

26 Andrews attended some of the old-style disputations in the
Bickersteth Hall in Delhi NI pp. 133-4, cf. Allnutt DMN Jul
1909; Paisa Akhbar 19 Mar 1906 (PNNR); Preparatory Paper
for Commission 4 (WMC); Lefroy in Montgomery 1907, pp. 282, 304

27 Andrews included an English translation of Nazir Ahmad's Memoir
in ZU.

28 MR Mar 1924

29 MR Apr 1911

30 SM May 1910

3. 'The Divine Preceptor'

1 Farquhar 1915, p. 29

2 NI p. 211. Andrews' statistical appendix in RI indicates the
decline of the Brahmo Samaj. He noted in 1913 that Satyendranath
Tagore was 'troubled because the whole Theistic movement in
Bengal seems to be on the point of collapse' Andrews to Munshi
Ram, 3 Aug 1913 (Chaturvedi - NAI)

3 IR Mar 1909; CT 18 Nov 1910

4 Farquhar 1915, p. 384

5 RI p. 184; he first drew attention to Tagore's impact in MR Nov
1908; MR Mar 1912, cf. Ezra Pound's later observation that Tagore

had 'sung Bengal into a nation'.

6 N.C. Chaudhuri 1974

7 MR Aug 1912, also in Tribune 10 Aug 1912; MR Jan 1913

8 MR Aug 1912; Tagore to Mrs Andrews (mother of C.F. Andrews) 31
   Dec 1913 (Santiniketan)

9 Andrews' influence, if any, on the English text of Gitanjali is
   not easy to determine. His assistance in the editing of Tagore's
   prose writings was a much happier affair. Tagore eventually
   entrusted him with the preparation of an edition of his complete
   prose writings – Tagore to Macmillan, 10 Apr 1938 (Macmillan –
   B.L.).

10 Andrews to Tagore, 8 May and 15 May 1913 (Santiniketan) (All
   subsequent quotations from Andrews' correspondence with Tagore
   are from the collection at Santiniketan; Tribune 28 May 1913;
   Pioneer 28 May 1913. The Tribune reproduced the text in full, the
   Pioneer summarized it at length. The full text also appeared in
   MR Jun, Jul 1913.

11 HR Aug 1913

12 Andrews to Munshi Ram, 31 May 1913 (Chaturvedi – NAI)

13 Biog p. 125; Tribune 20 Feb 1914

14 MR Jul 1913

15 Andrews to Hardinge, 24 Jan 1915 (Hardinge – CUL)

16 Andrews to Tagore, 7 Dec 1913

17 MR Jul 1913; the reference to Underhill is in Andrews to Tagore,
   14 Jan 1914. For an explanation of Tagore's leading idea of the
   Jivan-Devata, see Thompson 1921, pp. 26–30, 74–76.

18 MR Jul 1913; Tribune 4 Dec 1912, also his poem 'On Reading
   Gitanjali' MR Apr 1913

19 Andrews to Tagore, 21 Aug 1913

20 MR Jun 1913; Andrews to Tagore, 21 Aug 1913

21 Andrews to Tagore, 12 Dec 1912, 8 May 1913; 13 Dec 1913; 1 Jan
   1914; 14 Jan 1914

22 Quoted in Pearson 1917, pp. 15–16

23 Andrews to Tagore, Feb 1913; Andrews to Munshi Ram, 12 Jul 1913
   (Chaturvedi – NAI); Andrews to Tagore 1 Sep 1913; 26 Apr
   1914; 14 Jan 1914

24 Andrews to Tagore, 2 Mar 1914; 14 Jan 1914; 11 Feb 1914

25 Andrews to Tagore, 21 Feb, 2 Mar 1914; MR Jul 1913

26 In 1922, he published several of these letters to Tagore of 1913-14, introducing them as having been written during a period when he was 'passing through a religious crisis' and a period of suffering had come to his inner life MR Jul 1922. In a slightly later review of his developing thought, he said 'There have to be taken into account the influences of strong and remarkable personalities... It is never quite easy to tell how far these may have disturbed the balance of judgement' YMOI 1928 Vol. XL p. 443. His arguments were carefully examined and refuted by Farquhar when the letters were published in 1922 - YMOI 1922 Vol. XXXIII pp. 490-4. Such ideas had had some currency in the nineteenth century, and were to be taken up again later, by Radhakrishnan and more recently by an American scholar, Amore - Chadwick 1970, Part 2 p. 39; Radhakrishnan 1939, p. 186; Amore 1978.

27 Andrews to Tagore, 11 Feb 1914

28 Andrews to Tagore, 2 Mar 1914, cf. RI p. 163

29 Tagore 1912, p. 9

30 Young India Oct 1921

31 Spear 1949, pp. 23, 26

32 Zaehner 1966, p. 192

33 Thomas 1967, p. 84

4. 'In the Heart of the Universal Mother'

1 Census 1911: Arya Samaj 243,514; Brahmo Samaj 5,304

2 For Hindu sensitivity to the information made available in the Census, see Jones 1976, p. 144.

3 Jones 1976, p. 30

4 Bickersteth CC 1879 reported that an enquirer who had recently left the Mission School had been drawn into the Arya Samaj. Allnutt 1886 records that a branch of the Samaj was formed in Delhi shortly before 1885, and that students of the College were showing an interest.

5 Williams worked with his wife at the out-station at Rewari from
1884 to his death in 1900. There he wrote a number of tracts
with words like 'Exposure' and 'Farce' in their titles. He also
encountered the Arya Samaj during bazaar preaching, as at Hissar,
where 'the Aryas turned out in all their force and beset me like
hornets', an encounter that led on to a private correspondence
with the Arya Pandit - Williams CC 1892. Allnutt and Williams
had been contemporaries at Cambridge, where the latter had
studied Sanskrit and Arabic; Allnutt said that Williams was 'the
only one of our staff who had any real claim to be considered an
Oriental Scholar', though he often used to regret that he was 'so
trenchant in his attack' CC 1900.

6 Bickersteth CC 1878; Allnutt 1897, but DMN Apr 1895; Lefroy -
Preparatory Paper for Commission 3 (WMC); Rudra CT 17 May
1912; for Sharp's visit to Hardwar, SSC Mag 4 May 1910, also
Tribune 4 May 1910

7 In a review of Lillingston 1901, DMN Oct 1901

8 DMN Jul 1909. Both staff and students of St Stephen's had links
with the Samaj during these years: students were involved in
fund-raising Tribune 16 Sep 1908; Andrews' colleague and friend,
Raghubar Dayal was a little later appointed an examiner of a
thesis for the Gurukula at Hardwar Tribune 17 Mar 1914.

9 RI pp. 119-20, cf. CT 25 Nov 1910, CC 1910

10 NI pp. 196-7, cf. MR Jul 1908, Preparatory Paper for Commission 4
(WMC)

11 Ram 1902, p. 11

12 Tribune 24 Mar 1908; 16 Mar 1909; 30 Apr 1913

13 Preparatory Paper for Commission 4 (WMC), cf. NI p. 196

14 On the basis of his early visit, Andrews wrote 2 articles MR Mar
1913, Tribune 29 Apr 1913. Of the former, he wrote 'All Calcutta
was full of it when I was there' Andrews to Munshi Ram 7 Mar 1913
(Chaturvedi - NAI) (All subsequent correspondence quoted
between Andrews and Munshi Ram is from this collection).

15 See my account of this correspondence in Gispert-Sauch 1973,
pp. 73-83.

16 Tribune 4 Apr 1911. Elsewhere, he put it in more Anglicised

terminology 'It is as though we could get hold of the Balliol scholars and the lights of Trinity and bring them under one roof at Cuddesdon – no beef, no tobacco, and no racy stories' Ram 1914, p. iv.

17 Tribune 29 Apr 1913

18 MR Mar 1913

19 CMI Sep 1907. Holland repeated his views in his Preparatory Paper for Commission 1 (WMC) 'Though remorseless in its anti-Christian antagonism, it is yet so true a reform and advance upon popular Hinduism that it is undoubtedly preparing the way of the Lord'. Not surprisingly, another friend of Andrews, K.C. Chatterjee, whose missionary endeavours in the Hoshiarpur district of Punjab had been so long sustained and effective, in his Preparatory Paper, noted of the Samaj that there continued to be 'special antagonistic influences in this district'.

20 MacDonald 1910, p. 53. Was it with Andrews' encouragement that MacDonald and other members of the Public Service Commission visited the Gurukula, as reported in Tribune 26 Nov 1913? Certainly, Andrews discussed MacDonald's visit with him, in advance – Andrews to Munshi Ram, 15 Nov 1913. MacDonald also visited Santiniketan a few days later Tribune 14 Jan 1914.

21 Pioneer 9 May; 11 Jul 1913. The novel was written by Edmund Candler, principal of a private school in the princely state of Patiala, whose ruler was very hostile to the Arya Samaj – Tribune 11 Aug 1906, 27 Nov 1909, 30 Jan 1914. The Arya Samaj, the Gurukula and its 'Pundit' figure largely in the novel, and we get, interestingly, a glimpse of a 'young Cambridge missionary, Moon', who is portrayed as disingenuously sympathetic towards the movement. The book reflects a great deal of the current situation as seen by the majority of the Anglo-Indian community. Andrews noted that 'all Simla was reading it', conceded that it was 'clever', and surmised that, published anonymously, it was 'probably the work of a C.I.D. man' Andrews to Munshi Ram, 26 May 1913.

22 Pioneer 27 Oct 1913; HR Feb 1914, cf. Tribune 29 Oct 1913; Tribune 3, 8 Aug, 20 Sep 1913

23 Munshi Ram 'gave me the best advice of all as to the way to make
    it a success, and helped me more than anyone practically. It was
    due to him also that the Arya Samaj entered so whole-heartedly
    into the Celebration' Andrews to Hardinge, 5 Jul 1913 (Hardinge –
    CUL).

24 Andrews to Munshi Ram, 31 May 1913. The meeting took place in
    early September. Andrews was present. He also arranged for
    Munshi Ram to meet Sir Michael O'Dwyer, the new Lt Governor of
    the Punjab, on whom the visit left 'a very happy impression', the
    latter told the Viceroy. Andrews also took Munshi Ram's chief
    assistant, Ram Deva, to meet Lady Hardinge, at the latter's
    request. Andrews told Lady Hardinge that Ram Deva's daughter was
    ill, at which she sent her personal physician to attend to the
    child. This was reported as 'A Gracious Act of Lady Har3dinge' in
    the Vedic Magazine, and revealed 'a genuine Aryan heart' Tribune,
    6 Jul 1913.

25 Printed Memo 21 Jul 1913, in response to a query as to whether he
    thought the 1912 bomb outrage presaged a revival of anarchy
    (IOL& R). Meston cited the case of Munshi Ram, among others, as
    evidence that the Arya Samaj was not dangerous.

26 Andrews to Munshi Ram, 26 May, 7 Jun 1913; Andrews to Tagore, 15
    May 1913; Andrews to Munshi Ram, 8 Jun, 21 May 1913.

27 Hoyland 1940, p. 15

28 Rudra to Munshi Ram, 30 Mar 1913 (Chaturvedi – NAI); Munshi
    Ram to Andrews, 25 Apr 1913; Andrews to Munshi Ram, 26 Apr 1913.
    Tagore was 'far away, up in the clouds'.

29 Passing on his letters to and from Stanton, Lefroy, Montgomery
    and Allnutt, he wrote 'I want you to share with me everything and
    I can only do this by sending you such letters as these' Andrews
    to Munshi Ram, 27 Jul 1913, cf. 28 Jul 1913.

30 Andrews to Munshi Ram, 21; 26; 30 Apr; 13 Jul; 28 Oct 1913

31 Andrews to Munshi Ram, 26 Apr 1913, N.b. his position some three
    years previously, when he wrote that, although he regarded the
    currently banned national song, 'Bande Mataram' as 'wonderful',
    he thought that 'a religion of Mother India', in which 'the very
    soil of India itself has been made sacred' (probably deriving

from 'a prolonged retention of primitive forms of nature
worship') was bound to become 'among the educated ... more and
more untenable' <u>IR</u> Jan 1910.

32 Andrews to Munshi Ram, 28 Oct, 28 Jul 1913

33 Munshi Ram to Andrews, 25 Apr 1913

5. 'A saint of action'

1 <u>Biog</u> p. 126

2 During these years, the <u>Tribune</u> carried reports on indenture in
Fiji (18 Dec 1910) and Mauritius (28 Jan, 21 Feb 1911), as well
as South Africa; lack of progress in controlling the system in
South Africa caused increasing concern (19 Jan 1910, 14 Jan 1911,
18 Mar 1912). The Anglo-Indian <u>Pioneer</u> was unsympathetic,
complaining that 'the Indian coolies' in British Guiana were
'rather given to desertion', without considering possible causes
(5 May 1904), and describing the use of the term 'slavery' of the
conditions of (Chinese) indentured labourers in South Africa as
'absolutely irrational' (14 Jun 1904).

3 The <u>Tribune</u> followed the 1906 legislation closely, and concluded
that the entire Indian community in South Africa were 'Helots at
last' (3 Aug 1907). From mid-1913 to mid-1914, the <u>Tribune</u>
carried at least 63 items on the subject.

4 Curzon and Ampthill both spoke out against the treatment of South
African Indians <u>TEW</u> Jan 1909, and Ampthill, on returning to
Britain, became an energetic President of the South African
Indian Committee, as the <u>Tribune</u> of 17 Jan 1908 noted with
satisfaction. Subsequently, the nationalists welcomed Minto's
order discontinuing indenture in the Straits Settlements <u>Tribune</u>
18 Oct 1910.

5 Huttenback 1976, p. 323

6 E.g. <u>Tribune</u> 3 Aug 1907, 21 Mar 1908

7 <u>Tribune</u> 2 Jan 1910

8 A link existed in the person of A. French, who in 1906 went from
the Delhi Mission to the Indian Mission in Durban, from where he
reported on the hostility of the white colonists to the 'free

Indians' <u>DMN</u> Oct 1906

9   <u>TEW</u> Jan 1909; <u>Tribune</u> 9 Jan 1909, 4 Feb 1910

10 Rudra quoted <u>Tribune</u> 5 Sep 1912; Allnutt to Stanton, Dec 1913
    (CMD)

11 <u>RI</u> p. 171; <u>TEW</u> Jul 1910, <u>SM</u> Apr 1908

12 Printed <u>Tribune</u> 25 Jan 1908; Andrews to Dunlop Smith, 28 Jan 1908
    (Minto - NLS). A few days earlier, Andrews had spent a day with
    W.H. Nevinson, 'foremost among journalist friends of the Indian
    people' (<u>MR</u> May 1909) who was on his way to speak in Lahore
    on 'Indian Oppression in the Transvaal' <u>Tribune</u> 22 Jan 1908.

13 <u>SSC Mag</u> Jan 1914

14 <u>Tribune</u> 24 Jul 1910. Minto took Andrews' letter as 'another
    proof of the very deep and widespread feeling of resentment at
    the treatment of Indians in South Africa' Minto to Godley, 30 Jan
    1908 (Minto to NAI)

15 <u>Tribune</u> 25 Jan 1908

16 Andrews to Hardinge, 5 Jul 1913; Hardinge to Andrews, 12 Jul 1913
    (Hardinge - CUL)

17 Andrews to Lefroy, 29 Oct 1913; 13 Nov 1913 (BC Cal)

18 It is not clear when exactly Andrews met Polak. He later said
    that Polak was the only person whom he knew among the welcoming
    party when he reached Durban (typescript 'Lecture in the Indian
    Association Hall, Phagli', Chaturvedi - NAI). Polak visited
    the Punjab during his tour.

19 <u>MR</u> May 1910, <u>Ind Int</u> Oct 1909; <u>MR</u> Jan 1914

20 The appeal appeared in <u>Tribune</u> 9 Nov 1913; Andrews to Gokhale,
    16 Nov 1913 (Gokhale - NAI). Andrews offered his life-
    savings, of which Gokhale accepted Rs. 1,000. Other donors at
    the time included Lefroy (Circular Letter to bishops, 21 Jan 1914
    - BC Cal), Ramsay MacDonald and the Gurukula students <u>Tribune</u>
    20 Nov 1913. Gokhale visited St Stephen's to collect the
    students' contribution. Rudra welcomed him as 'an emblem of
    absolute loyalty to the King and magnificent service to the
    Motherland', and at the end of the meeting, with 'cheers to
    Messrs. Gandhi and Polak, and the singing of the National Anthem,
    the gathering dispersed' <u>Tribune</u>, 21, 19 Nov 1913.

21 Typescript (press release?), 26 Nov 1913 (Gokhale – NAI)

22 Critical comments were made in the Pioneer, by the Calcutta
    correspondent of the Guardian, and by a correspondent to CT,
    although an article in this last saw the mission as important;
    the Archbishop of Cape Town hoped that Andrews would see that
    there were two sides to the question – Archbishop of Cape Town to
    Montgomery, 9 Jan 1914 (SPG). Nationalist comments in MR
    Dec 1913, Tribune 31 Dec 1913

23 Tribune 21 Dec 1913, MR Jan 1914

24 Tinker 1979, p. 143

25 In addition to at least 11 substantial articles, he published an
    important collection of data, Documents Relating to the Indian
    Question.

26 MR Mar 1914

27 Andrews to Tagore, 6 Jan 1914, Andrews to Gokhale, 23 Jan 1914
    (Gokhale – NAI); the letter of 30 Jan is also essential for
    Andrews' contribution to the negotiations.

28 Polak 1949, p. 91

29 Andrews Documents p. 27; Indian Opinion 17 Jun 1914; Tribune
    6 Jul 1914; 22 Jan 1914; Gandhi Collected Works Vol. XLVIII,
    p. 123

30 Tribune 8 Jan 1914, 18 Feb 1914

31 Andrews to Munshi Ram, 5 Apr 1914

32 Andrews to Munshi Ram, 12 Dec 1913 (Andrews did, of course,
    literally touch Gandhi's feet on meeting him, to the
    consternation both of Gandhi himself and also of the white
    onlookers); Andrews to Gokhale, 30 Jan 1914 (Gokhale – NAI);
    Andrews to Tagore, 14 Jan 1914; Andrews to Gandhi, 26 Feb 1914
    (Gandhi S.S.S.) (All subsequent letters from Andrews to Gandhi
    are from this collection).

33 Harijan, 19 Apr 1940; Andrews to Gandhi, 26 Feb 1914. That
    Gandhi should entrust his sons to Andrews' care on their return
    to India, indicates that there were elements of respect and
    trust, as well as affection, here. Andrews arranged that they
    should stay in turn with Rudra, Munshi Ram and Tagore Tribune
    10 Nov 1914; SSC Mag Easter 1923; Andrews to Munshi Ram, 24 Nov

1914.

34 Tagore to Munshi Ram, 15 Jan 1914 (Santiniketan); Pearson to
    Rudra, 27 Sep 1915 (Berkeley); _Stephanian_ Oct 1969; _Young India_
    9 Jul 1924.

35 Andrews to Tagore, 14 Jan 1914; _MR_ Jun 1914, cf. Tolstoy to
    Gandhi, 7 Sep 1910, included in Andrews _Documents_ 'Your activity
    in the Transvaal ... is the most ... important of all the work
    being done in the world'.

36 Andrews to Tagore, 2 Mar, 11 Feb 1914

37 _MR_ May 1914; Andrews to Munshi Ram, 28 Oct 1913; Andrews to
    Tagore, 11 Feb 1914; 2 Mar 1914

38 Thomas 1970, p. 226

39 _MR_ Jul 1914

40 Andrews to Gandhi, 26 Feb 1914

41 'The ten days I had with him (Gokhale) were precious to me in a
    peculiar degree' Andrews to Gandhi, 5 Apr 1914. They had long
    discussions on Andrews' new religious ideas, and on Gokhale's
    understanding of the relation between politics and religion.

42 _Tribune_ 18 Jul 1914

6.   'The sympathetic school of Mr Andrews'

1 _Pan-Anglican Congress_ Vol. 3, p. 15

2 _SM_ Apr 1913; Underhill to Tatlow, 24 Aug 1913 (SCM); a writer
   in the _Cowley Evangelist_, quoted in _DMN_ Jan 1912; Gardiner to
   Montgomery, 26 Dec 1912 (CMD).

3 Sharpe 1977, p. 36

4 _SM_ Mar 1912, _CT_ 19 Dec 1913

5 _NI_ p. 79, cf. the 'evil-looking _sadhus_' at Cawnpore, p. 110, and
   the 'gross heathenism' at Kotgur, p. 154

6 'Idolatry' _CC_ 1905, _TEW_ Oct 1905, _Ep_ 6 Oct 1906, _HR_ Jan 1907,
   _NI_ pp. 80-1, _RI_ pp. 81, 160. Hindu reviewers took exception to
   his attitude to this as to little else in his views, _MR_ Jul 1909.
   _IR_ Mar 1914. Astrology _SSC Mag_ Dec 1911. Caste - Preparatory
   Paper for Commission 4 (WMC), _RI_ p. 247.

7 _NI_ p. 210

8   <u>RI</u> p. 163; <u>Ind Int</u> Oct 1909; <u>RI</u> p. 163; <u>MR</u> Mar 1908

9   Farquhar 1913, p. 27

10 <u>Ind Int</u> Oct 1909, cf. <u>SM</u> Nov 1909, <u>Ep</u> 25 Nov 1911, <u>RI</u> p. 179

11 <u>RI</u> pp. 274, 280; <u>IR</u> Jun 1912

12 'India in Transition' 1910

13 <u>RI</u> p. 144, cf. <u>TEW</u> Jan 1911

14 Andrews developed some of these ideas in <u>MR</u> Apr 1909. R.G.
Milburn, on the staff of Bishop's College, Calcutta, caused a
good deal of controversy with a similar view, in 'Christian
Vedantism' <u>Ind Int</u> Jan 1913. A young Christian woman in the
Punjab saw nothing but danger in such an accommodation: 'The
"Siren notes" of Vedantism, its subtle and deep philosophies, will
bring that stupor and sleep upon the West out of which the East
is just arising' M. Ahmad Shah <u>HR</u> Sep 1913.

15 <u>RI</u> p. 144

16 Only one aspect of his new ideas found its way into print at this
time, a lecture which he delivered at the Brahmo Mandir in
Calcutta in Jul 1913, and revised and expanded into 'The Body of
Humanity' <u>MR</u> Sept and Oct 1913. In this, he begins by explaining
that he is responding to Tagore's call 'to carry forward the work
of the "Making of Man"', by examining the social implications of
the various world religions and their potential contribution to
the well-being of 'the body of humanity'. The connection with
his subsequent reflections lies in the claim that 'Christianity
is no longer divorced from other world religions'. He confessed
that he found the subject beyond his powers - Andrews to Tagore,
1 Sep 1913.

17 Andrews to Gandhi, 26 Feb 1914, cf. Andrews to Munshi Ram, 13 Sep
1913. He wrote a few days later of 'the world's higher
religions' as 'a branching family tree' Andrews to Tagore, 2 Mar
1914, a metaphor also used by Gandhi.

18 Andrews to Tagore, 21 Feb 1914

19 <u>YMOI</u> Sep 1922

20 Andrews to Tagore, 13 Apr 1914

21 It is the friendships that are held up as a model for dialogue,
e.g. Samartha 1971, p. 21, and Cracknell 1980, pp. 23-4.

22 R.H. Lesser _Indian Journal of Theology_ Jul–Dec 1978

23 Zaehner 1966, pp. 187–8

24 On Andrews' death, Tagore wrote that nowhere had he seen 'such a triumph of Christianity', and Gandhi called him 'love incarnate' – both in an appendix to Andrews _Sandhya Meditations_ 1940, pp. 172, 5.

25 Andrews' 'participation ... in the life of Gandhi' as a model for a new mode of mission, Smith 1969

CHAPTER SEVEN
MOVING ON

1. Introductory

On 15 June 1914, Andrews left Rudra and St Stephen's College, the Cambridge
Brotherhood and Delhi, and went to his new home at Tagore's Santiniketan in
Bengal, thus bringing his missionary decade to an end. The last two or so
years of that decade, from mid-1912, were a time of intense and varied
activity, so that he spoke of 'this crowded, urgent existence, ...
overburdened ... with activities and impetuosities'. (1) It was also a
time of great personal confusion and distress, as he approached the point
of decision about leaving the Delhi Mission.

It is not to be thought, however, that the explanation for his decision lay
solely in the particular experiences of 1912-14. In some respects, the
seed was sown in his attending the 1906 meeting of the Congress, and he
himself later said that a growing sense of an incongruity between his
nationalist sympathies and his place in the Delhi Mission stemmed from that
time. (2) In another respect, what he saw as the 'religious imperialism'
of the Christian missions had been a source of disquiet from his earliest
days in India, so that, almost throughout the decade, and particularly from
the time of his meeting S.E. Stokes, he 'felt more and more like a fish out
of water' in his formal missionary role. Only, as he himself was later to
acknowledge, the sympathetic understanding of Rudra and Allnutt, and the
relatively 'liberal' attitude of the Cambridge Mission, enabled him to stay
as long as he did. (3) It has also to be said that there were factors in
his personality which had made him from the beginning a somewhat uncertain
member of the Delhi Mission. (4)

The last two years of Andrews' missionary decade, nevertheless, provide a
number of indications of factors which helped to shape his decision.

2.   'Education on indigenous lines'

The move from St Stephen's College to Santiniketan was a move from one type
of educational institution to another of a somewhat different type. Was
Andrews' decision to move in any way determined by this difference? In
order to answer this question, we need to look at his views on education in
India. Not surprisingly for one with a considerable reputation as an
educationalist, he gave a good deal of attention to educational questions
throughout his missionary decade and wrote several notable articles on the
subject. (1)

Significant changes in education were, in fact, afoot at this time. From
the official side, there was Curzon's reform of the universities, with its
bold emphasis on Indian studies, a reform consolidated with Harcourt
Butlers's appointment in 1910 as the first member for education in the
Viceroy's Council. The University of the Punjab was a particular focus of
this type of reform. A movement for change from within the emerging
political nation was reflected in the resolution of the 1906 Congress
stressing the importance of what was called 'National Education'.

Andrews himself sought to describe and evaluate these changes, most
typically by surveying the history of Western education in India. His own
attitudes were considerably modified during the decade. Thus, at the
beginning, he called Macaulay, whose minute had led to the introduction of
Western education, ' one of the greatest friends which India ever had'. At
the end of the decade, he was referring to 'that vandal and iconoclast
Macaulay'. (2) In the years between, we find a series of attempts to
evaluate and re-evaluate the impact of Western education. Throughout, he
continued to acknowledge that the thrust of Macaulay's minute was 'a true
one, ... probably right for the time ... The hour of the indigenous
revival had not yet come. A shock from without was needed.' Macaulay's
approach had, nevertheless, been 'extremely short-sighted', and its defects
were now being understood in the national movement, the 'lack of
appreciation of the greatness of India's past, and his blindness to the
claims of the vernaculars'. What was most characteristic of Macaulay's
'vandalism' was 'the neglect of Indian tradition', his forgetting that

India was not a _tabula rasa_, but, rather, 'an illuminated manuscript ...
rich with the spoils of time and inscribed with the wisdom of the ages'.
Over against this attractive image, he drew a parable of the Western
educational enterprise from the architecture of Delhi - 'a sham Gothic
clock-tower, and a terra-cotta Town Hall built like a Greek Temple', placed
side by side in 'the noble' Chandhi Chowk, 'the most famous street in all
India', a perpetual record of British taste at its worst. And this 'vandal
spirit' still characterised the education system.

> Since Macaulay's time, we have remained crudely,
> almost brutally English ... We ourselves are in
> danger of becoming vandals in our turn.

The effect of this was a system widely felt to be failing, a mere
'make-shift for education'. (3) These were views strongly corroborated by
Rudra. In a paper on 'Indian Students', he quoted approvingly a British
educationist in India to the effect that 'Dead Sea fruit we have been
giving to the students instead of the bread of culture. With Dead Sea
fruit and ashes we have fed them until they have come, many of them, to
believe that these things are the bread of life', himself adding that 'for
the majority of students, ... the wonder is that their mental balance is
not upset. The spring of their youthful nature survives only because they
do not really attend to all the lectures'. (4)

Andrews went on to describe more accurately the 'inadequacy of Macaulay's
legacy'. (5) He did so in an original and interesting excursus on the
commonplace analogy between the Roman and British empires. Macaulay's
educational policy, which aimed 'to make the Hindu more English than
Indian', and so, Andrews added, 'to attach him to England by the strongest
of all ties, - the tie of sentiment', had found its justification in Roman
imperial practice. Indeed, it was this that 'turned the scale in favour of
the adoption of English as the medium of Indian Higher Education and thus
set once for all the type of teaching to be adopted'. The adequacy of the
analogy was still taken for granted: Seeley had 'gloried in it', and
Andrews took to task, in the _Hindustan Review_, a retired civil servant who
used it uncritically in an article in the _Indian Review_. (6) It rested,

however, on a fallacy, as the latest research on education in the Roman empire made clear.

> Rome's method of education in her dependencies
> contains one of the most startling warnings in
> history as to the danger of Imperialism ... a) The
> educated classes in the Provinces become more and
> more separated from their own countrymen ... b) Owing
> to the exotic nature of the education given and its
> lack of appeal to indigenous instincts, the highest
> talents of the conquered Provincials become
> sterilised and unfruitful. (7)

In addition to this negative argument, drawn from this analogy, he several times drew attention to 'the best modern theory of education', namely, 'utilising to the full every innate instinct and tradition of the pupil in building up the structure of intelligence and character'.

> It is now seen, as it was not understood in
> Macaulay's time, that true education must proceed
> from within and lay hold of every innate faculty and
> indigenous instinct ... The wholesale
> transplantation of a foreign culture into an
> unsuitable soil, the cutting adrift of the tender
> human plant from its own natural environment – such
> things are as antiquated and unscientific in the eyes
> of the modern educationalist as astrology and alchemy
> are in other spheres. The whole trend of modern
> thought is in the direction of education on
> indigenous lines. (8)

Andrews' principal reflections on this theme, in the <u>Hindustan Review</u>, were very widely and enthusiastically welcomed, and it is not surprising to find the <u>Tribune</u>, a little later, echoing in its editorial columns the same ideas. (9) The presuppositions, then, on which the British educational enterprise in India had been founded, were, for a number of reasons, false.

We went wrong at the very outset, and we have
perpetuated a wrong and vicious system. (10)

Having said this, it has to be said that Andrews nowhere criticises the
education provided at St Stephen's College, and, indeed, he specifically
quoted a student, Thandi Ram, who had claimed that the College was a
'National College' because no differences of caste, colour or creed existed
within it, and it provided 'lessons of wholesome patriotism'. (11) These
reasons did not, of course, touch the important cultural question, but it
is noteworthy that the College was by no means unrelievedly anglicized
during Andrews' years. Quite apart from able and distinguished teachers in
the Indian tradition, the College produced exceptionally fine orientalists
among the students at that time, and Andrews was always quick to draw
attention to this in the College magazine. (12) We have also seen how he
drew attention, addressing a Christian readership, to the special
significance of colleges like St Stephen's as an essential link between the
Church and the national movement. He did admit, shortly after leaving,
that what he called 'all the paraphernalia of a Government-aided College'
meant that 'the sense of compromise' was always with him. (13) The very
fact, though, that, on leaving the College, he agreed to return annually to
teach for a couple of months - a scheme that proved impracticable in the
event - is indicative of his very positive view of the education provided.
St Stephen's remained for him, throughout his life, 'one of the most sacred
spots on earth'. (14)

Even so, he was very enthusiastic about what he regarded as a more
indigenous type of education, and on several occasions he drew attention to
various institutions that seemed to him to be of increasing significance as
representing the principle of 'assimilation', promoting a 'harmony between
Western knowledge and Eastern culture'. (15) Into this category, of
course, fell Munshi Ram's Gurukula and Tagore's Santiniketan, both first
discovered by Andrews in the last two years of his missionary decade.
Immediately after his first visit to the former, he wrote an article for
the Modern Review almost euphoric in its enthusiasm: the Gurukula had
given him 'a new vision ... (of) the New India', receiving 'the impulse

from the West' through the medium of Sanskrit and Hindi, forming character
'in harmony with the genius of the country'. Despite his objections to the
Aryan claims for the Vedas as containing all knowledge (a problem he would
not have at Santiniketan), he acknowledged that the teaching of what he
called 'the higher modern subjects', economics, history, science, etc.,
through the vernacular was singularly effective. (16) He was emphatic, as
he was to be at Santiniketan also, about the need to remain free of
Government and Government aid. (17) It was all 'full of hope for the
future'. (18) Santiniketan, he discovered a few months later, was 'closely
akin, in many respects, in spirit', and, like the Gurukula, seemed to him
to be 'at the very heart of young aspiring India in its organic
development'. (19)

The move from St Stephen's College to Santiniketan does seem to have
involved for Andrews, then, some weighing of the different approaches of
the two institutions, though this could by no means be described as a
decisive determining factor.

3. 'Church of England religion'

While in England in 1912, Andrews and Rudra came into conflict with the
India Sub-committee of SPG, and this experience was much more clearly
determinative of Andrews' decision to move. Rudra and Andrews met the
Sub-committee to seek approval for a proposed revised Constitution for the
College, the revision having already been approved by the Mission Council
in Delhi, and by the Cambridge Committee of the Delhi Mission. The Sub-
committee was concerned over two questions in connection with the College,
co-operation with the Baptists (in particular, the employment of C.B. Young
as a teacher), and the participation of Hindu and Muslim members of the
staff in the programme of religious and moral instruction and in the
administration of the College. The request for approval of the new
Constitution afforded the Sub-committee an opportunity to question these
developments, and the arrival of Rudra and Andrews in London enabled them
to confront the chief architects, as they were held to be, of both of them.
The details of this long and convoluted controversy need not concern us
here. It stretched from 1910 to December 1914, when a Constitution that

has passed the test of time, and which bore unmistakably the stamp of
Rudra's and Andrews' ideals, though firmly limiting the role of
non-Anglicans and non-Christians, was finally approved. C.B. Young,
writing many years later, and recalling Andrews' 'consuming passion for
unity', described this Constitution as 'one of the greatest of his specific
services' to St Stephen's College.

> In its essential features, the constitution embodied
> the ideal of inter-racial and inter-credal unity. It
> gave to the Staff powerful representation on the
> Governing Body, and while providing for the inclusion
> of non-Anglicans and non-Christians, it positively
> required the inclusion of Indian members of the
> Staff. Thus it not only anticipated by nearly 20
> years, in its opposition to racial exclusiveness, the
> recommendations of the Lindsay Commission, ... but it
> went beyond the latter's subsequent recommendations
> in its repudiation of credal tests. In both respects
> it illustrated the basal principles of Andrews' life
> and work in and for India. (1)

In achievement of this, however, we need to note the inflexibility of
the 'irreconcilables', or 'old fogies', as Bishop Montgomery called them,
of the Sub-committee with whom Rudra and Andrews were confronted in
London. (2)

The Sub-committee insisted that the College teach only 'Church of England
religion', and that 'members of the Oriental Religions' were to be
preferred as teachers to 'Nonconformists ... who could not teach on Church
lines'. (3) Rudra saw things very differently. In the face of 'the
stupendous fact', which the Sub-committee seemed not to understand, of
living 'in the midst of an overwhelming non-Christian world', the co-
operation of the Baptists was 'no hindrance to the progress of the Gospel',
but rather, as a demonstration to his students that Anglicans and Baptists
were 'members of one another in Christ', a solemn duty. (4) Andrews added
a very interesting argument in support of Anglican-Baptist collaboration.

> Perhaps the consideration of the 'reserve' in
> Christian teaching during the early centuries may
> help to a realization of our position in India. In a
> very real sense, that 'reserve' in respect of the
> deeper mysteries of our faith must be observed today
> in our Christian Colleges. The doctrine of the
> Church's ministry and sacraments comes under that
> head. It is this very necessity of 'reserve' on such
> subjects that makes co- operation in religious
> teaching possible and practical, without compromise
> or sacrifice of principle. (5)

The question of the place and standing of Hindu and Muslim teachers in the
College aroused much less opposition among the Sub-committee, although one
member, the Reverend Lord William Gascoyne-Cecil, was 'aghast' at the idea
of giving them any place in the management of the College because of their
inevitable tendency to intrigue, while an ex-missionary from South India,
A.F. Gardiner, advised Bishop Montgomery that co-operation with
'Mohammedanism and Heathenism' was impossible, and that 'the control must
be exclusively and aggressively Christian'. (6) Again, Rudra and Andrews
took a very different line. With regard to participation in religious and
moral instruction, Rudra argued that in getting Hindu and Muslim colleagues
to teach on 'such questions as belief in God - Sin - Duty', they were all
'moving in the same direction', while Andrews pointed out that the
College's practice was in line with 'the general findings of the Edinburgh
Commission'. (7)

On both questions, it should be added, Rudra and Andrews were supported by
most of their Delhi Mission colleagues, not least by Allnutt, who had
himself done so much to encourage ecumenical co-operation in Delhi, as also
by Lefroy, the Cambridge Committee, and even, in some measure, by
Montgomery of SPG. The attitudes disclosed in the Sub-committee, however,
made a deep impression on Rudra and Andrews.

This bad impression was darkened by a further factor, the treatment of

Rudra, 'the saddest side of all which you cannot possibly understand',
Andrews wrote to Stanton, 'viz:- the <u>racial</u> feeling'. (8)   There were
several ways in which Rudra was made to feel this.   First, Montgomery
published proposals regarding the College without consulting him, an
action, Andrews protested, that would require an apology.   Secondly,
Bishop Lefroy, receiving enquiries from SPG about the College, by-passed
Rudra and referred them to his European Vice-Principal, F.J. Western.
Thirdly, the Sub-committee refused to invite Rudra to some of their
meetings when the College was being discussed. (9)   These and similar snubs
led Rudra to observe that he would not have been so treated had he been an
Englishman. (10)

The 'moral revulsion' which Andrews experienced as a result of this 'racial
feeling', and also more generally as a result of his and Rudra's encounters
with the 'ecclesiastical spirit and domination of the West with all its
Pharisaism and narrowness, ... the sectarian spirit in religion, ... the
pettiness and the meanness of that spirit', was 'in a great measure' the
immediate cause of Andrews' decision to leave formal missionary work. (11)

4.   'The Divinity of our Blessed Lord'

To what extent were Andrews' beliefs changing, as he moved towards a break
with his formal missionary role, and had this anything to do with the
break?

There is no doubt that Andrews' understanding of Christian faith had
changed during his time in India, though in his Preparatory Paper for
Commission 4 of the World Missionary Conference, he said that he preferred
to see this as a 'widening ... of the dogmatic side of the faith' rather
than a weakening of it.   He was, by that time, he said, 'not so anxious,
for instance, as in the past, to <u>define</u> the Divinity of our Blessed Lord'.

> Greek Theology appears to me, in its later stages
> especially, to have gone too far in definition, and
> Latin Theology still more narrowly to have defined
> and confined the Faith, which should have been left

more wholly a matter of heart and moral apprehension
than a matter of intellect and logical reasoning. I
should not condemn anyone who said he did not <u>wish</u> to
define his belief in the Divinity of Christ, but who
could from his heart say with the Apostle Thomas 'My
Lord and my God', or with Simon Peter 'Lord, to whom
else should we go? Thou hast the words of eternal
life'. I should not condemn anyone who could not
hold as an article of faith the Virgin Birth, but who
could make the above confession of Simon Peter and
Thomas. I would not condemn a doubt as to the
'objectivity' of the Resurrection of Christ, if the
fact of the Living Christ were granted and his Living
Presence were a daily experience.

Less anxious, then, than hitherto, to define Christian doctrine, the
Divinity of Christ was to him 'more than before the centre of thought'.

Despite such affirmations, Andrews' association with his neo-Hindu friends
from 1912 onwards, and in particular from the time of his visit to South
Africa, aroused much uncertainty about his position. His surmise, after
meeting Gandhi, that he would be regarded as 'a heretic of the most
dangerous kind' proved only too true. Even while he was in South Africa,
his Christian position was in question in a number of ways. First, his
'missionary purpose' in going to South Africa at all was questioned by a
correspondent in the Church Times, though Andrews was stoutly defended in
replies from Allnutt and Rudra and others, including B.K. Cunningham. (1)
Secondly, it is evident that Rudra had heard about and been worried by his
new ideas about the relation of Christianity to 'the Hindu-Buddhist ideal',
for Andrews wrote to Gandhi to say that he felt sure Rudra would understand
when he had seen him and been able to 'put things clearly to him'.
Thirdly, while he was still out of India, Allnutt had found cause for
concern, presumably on the same grounds, for he had written to demand that
he define his 'Christian position' in writing. Fourthly, the vernacular
newspapers of the Punjab were triumphantly retailing the rumour that he was
to become a Hindu. On his return to India, the new Bishop of Lahore joined

in with a demand that he should declare himself a Christian. (2)

A visit to Lahore a fortnight later, at the beginning of May, was a painful occasion, with the Indian Christians up in arms and charging him with 'betraying the cause', and he wrote to Munshi Ram about the 'almost universal outcry from the so-called Christian world' at his decision to go to make his home at Santiniketan. (3) An invitation to preach in the Cathedral on this visit to Lahore gave him an opportunity to make a thoroughly public confession of his faith. His sermon is a powerful testimony to the continuing 'widening' of his understanding of the Christian faith that he had referred to in 1909.

> This, then, is what it means to be a Christian, to
> follow Christ; not the expression of an outward
> creed, but the learning of an inner life. Men in
> every age have tried to bind the Christian spirit
> within the walls of external formulae, but it has
> been futile. The living spirit has escaped them all.
> For its very essence is a life, a character, a
> personal devotion; and these can never be confined
> within such narrow bounds. I say this today with a
> new emphasis, because I myself had formerly a narrow
> outlook; and I have been learning at last, painfully,
> eagerly, wistfully learning, to look first at the
> life rather than the creed. And as my outlook has
> widened, I have found Christ in strange, unlooked-for
> places, far beyond the boundary of sect or dogma, of
> church or chapel, far beyond the formal definition of
> man's devising, or of man's exclusive pride ... In
> South Africa, I found Christ's presence ... far more
> intimately ... in the Indian and Kaffir locations
> placed outside the cities of the Rand, than in those
> cities themselves built up of gold with all its fatal
> curse upon it.

While the _Tribune_ welcomed this as an important statement from 'this great

Christian thinker', and published the sermon in full, Andrews had to report
that it did nothing to satisfy the Christian community, and in fact only
made matters worse. 'I am sure there is nothing to do but remain silent',
he wrote to Munshi Ram. 'It is deeds not words that are the test: And if
my deeds are not Christian my words shall never make me one'. (4) However,
he went on to say that Rudra was 'wholly' with him, and the fact is that
those who knew him well, whatever concern they may have expressed about his
public position, seem not to have been greatly concerned about his faith as
such. His close friend, the thoroughly orthodox Baptist, C.B. Young,
responded to an anxious enquiry from J.N. Farquhar, reassuring him that
Andrews' faith had not changed. (5) His colleagues in the Brotherhood seem
also to have been satisfied, referring to his move to Bengal in mid-June as
'transference to another diocese', and saying that he would be nevertheless
'still one of' them, while Allnutt noted that he went 'with the full
approval' of Bishop Lefroy, now Metropolitan. (6)

When he went to Santiniketan on 15 June, he was particularly glad that it
had been possible to find him a small church in which to minister in nearby
Burdwar, since this showed to 'the outside world' that he had gone 'as a
Christian'. At the same time, his public declaration at Lahore had
disclosed his uneasiness with 'outward creed' and 'external formulae'.
Living with Tagore, 'in the daily presence of a man ... to whom deception
in any form is hateful and impossible', brought him quickly to a crisis
about this, in particular about some specifically Anglican questions, 'the
semi-Calvinist strain that runs through much of the Prayer Book and the
Articles', and he decided, both for his own integrity and lest he bind
these as burdens on Indian Christians, to give up his 'ministerial
obligations'. (7) He wrote to Montgomery of SPG to this effect on 16
August, and more or less simultaneously published a public statement in
India to the effect that he had 'resigned ministerial duties as a clergyman
of the Church of England owing to difficulties with regard to the articles
of belief proposed by that body'. (8) He added that he intended to 'remain
a Christian layman', Tagore insisting on the inclusion of the word
'Christian'. (9)

Beside this, in attempting to understand the various factors involved in

Andrews' moving from the Delhi Mission to Santiniketan, we have to recall
the growing authority for him of his own experience as a Christian <u>bhakta</u>,
expressed most fully in his letter explaining his move to Bishop Talbot.

> But in the Gospels I found more and more delight.
> There it was all different. There I found all that I
> had been learning to love so deeply in Indian
> religious life and thought ... And so I found myself
> more and more going right back to Christ Himself, and
> living day by day more consciously in His life;
> accepting His standards and making these the main
> objectives of my own life, rather than laying
> emphasis on any special doctrines or religious
> observances. And a wonderful illumination came. The
> life itself had a new meaning and a new fulness to
> me, which was continually growing deeper.

There was, then around the time of Andrews' move, besides a growing
disinterest in Christian doctrines, a very positive development in Andrews'
self-understanding as a Christian, in terms of 'personal devotion' and
'deeds not words'.

5. 'The dwelling place of ... Christ'

About the association of Christianity in India with the imperial project,
Andrews had always been ambivalent, and, while he had never been an
enthusiast for what he called 'a Church and Empire creed', he continued
throughout most of his missionary decade to take a somewhat 'Westcottian'
view, preaching at Cambridge, for example, in 1912, on 'Imperial
Responsibilities', and proving a willing collaborator with such liberal
administrators as Lord Hardinge and Sir John Meston. (1)

As late as the beginning of 1912, indeed, he initiated a major plan for St
Stephen's College which envisaged and required for its fulfilment the
closest association with the Imperial Government. This was in connection
with the transfer of the capital to Delhi, and his instant vision of a new

residential college in the new city. It would be, he argued, 'an object lesson at the centre of Indian Government'. (2) Rudra saw the new college very much in terms of mission, whereby the Delhi Mission would be able to hold its own in the new city. The aim would be, 'where the cream of the intellect of the Empire will be congregated, to establish the moral supremacy of Christian work and worth, and thus to win the homage of all to Christ and his power'. (3) Nevertheless, the links with the imperial system were to be very strong, and about this Andrews must have been perfectly clear. Rudra had had to confer with the Education Secretary, Sir Harcourt Butler, over the plans, the Government made a gift of a site for the college and put aside funds for the new building, and Andrews himself had accompanied Rudra for discussion with Butler's staff and with W.M. Hailey, Chief Commissioner for Delhi, who was 'anxious that the Government should foster the growth' of the College, and publicly expressed his pleasure at the association, 'the College authorities, hand-in-hand with the Imperial Government'. (4)

By the time that Andrews had left Delhi, just over a year later, his attitude had changed dramatically. Recalling the situation at the time of the 'Indian Unrest' a few years earlier, he wrote with evident satisfaction that St Stephen's had been at that time 'like no other Mission College in India. It was the bugbear of Government'. What had pushed the pendulum of Andrews' thought to this other extreme in the matter of a year, so that he no longer found it tolerable, because half his college stipend came from Government funds, to be 'a half-paid member of a foreign ruling race'? (5) He had been uneasy about these things for some time. He wrote to Tagore in 1913 that 'the longing ... to become freed from all these chains ... of Government and Mission and Anglo-India' had been growing from before 1912, though meeting with Tagore had intensified it. (6)

The determinative influence seems to have been his experience in South Africa. He had gone with a warning from Gokhale that what he saw there would be a great shock to his Christianity. (7) This was indeed so, to the extent that his long-held views about the contradiction between 'European racial arrogance' and 'the vision of Christ, the meek and lowly Son of Man', or, as he put it to Tagore at the time, between 'the creed ... held

for centuries' and 'the conventional life ... being lived', were confirmed
decisively. He concluded that 'the West' was in a state of virtual
apostasy, worshipping only 'Money and Race', while 'the meek and lowly
Christ' was to be 'found and worshipped ... amid the little groups of
Indian passive resisters fresh from prison - Hindus almost all of them'.
(8)

He brought his reflections on this experience into something of a
definitive form in the sermon which he preached in Lahore Cathedral on his
return to India. He seems to have regarded this sermon as something of a
formal statement of his position on leaving the Delhi Mission, drawing his
general conclusions from his particular South African experiences.
Developing in a very original way the much-used analogy between
contemporary British imperial rule and the Roman empire, he depicts Jesus
as rejecting the rich and cultured world of Chorazin, Bethsaida and
Capernaum, 'the direct social outgrowth of the great Roman system of
government', for 'the simple, child-like peasant poor, ... the poor, tired
labourers, ... half-famished', and then turns to the contemporary world,
characterized in bold, prophetic terms.

> The question came upon me with a sad, a terrible
> insistence, as I travelled across many seas, past
> many shores, whether the modern, aggressive, wealthy
> nations of the world, armed to the teeth against each
> other, trafficking in the souls of men for gain, can
> be for long the dwelling place of the meek and lowly
> Christ; whether the hour may not be near when He will
> say unto them ... 'Woe unto you', and will turn
> instead to the poor and down-trodden peoples of the
> earth and say unto them, 'Come unto me'. For in His
> Kingdom, 'there are many that are last that shall be
> first, and first that shall be last'. (9)

It is clear that it was in the context of this insistent question, and the
implied answer, that Andrews was inviting his hearers to interpret and
understand his own decision to leave the Delhi Mission for Santiniketan.

'Asato ma sat gamayo', he wrote to Munshi Ram after a last painful visit to the 'official world' of Simla, where he found himself, to all except the Viceroy himself and a small circle of very senior civilians, 'an outcaste and a pariah', 'I am being led from the unreal to the real'. (10) That leading, though, and that reality, as the Lahore sermon had made clear, had a profound Christological dimension.

6. 'The divine call'

In spite of the rumours of his abandonment of Christian faith, and in spite of the fact that he did, indeed, for a number of years from 1914, experience a deep spiritual and emotional crisis, only recovering the fulness of his faith in the 1920's, Andrews left Delhi and went to Santiniketan a professing Christian, not seeking to hide his convictions from his Hindu friends. His hope was, as he told Tagore, 'from a completely independent standpoint, ... to try to express Christian thought here in the East'. More than this, he saw his decision as a vocation, so that to remain longer in a missionary society he would have been 'untrue to the divine call'. (1)

This is not to say that he abandoned his work in Delhi lightly or easily. To leave Rudra in particular was clearly very painful, and the decision was talked over 'a hundred times', with Rudra his 'counsellor and adviser in each step', until Andrews at last convinced himself that Rudra was giving him up for 'a greater work and a greater need'. (2) Allnutt, too, was 'very kind and good', and Andrews acknowledged that he had always given him 'the most wonderful liberty'. (3)

That liberty, however, was not enough, and Andrews repeated to Gandhi his sense of a divine vocation in his decision to go to Santiniketan.

> One thing is perfectly clear, the call has come to me
> to follow Christ, simply and truly, in this summons
> to ... (Santiniketan) which has come to me'. (4)

There was in this an ascetic impulse, 'inward and spiritual and personal',

which was at the same time evangelical, to strip himself 'bare of anything
that could stand in the way as a barrier against complete oneness with
Indians'. To Munshi Ram, he wrote of this as 'the call of the sanyasi',
which he had been feeling more and more.

> - to cut myself free from ... (the) worldly ties of
> an assured income and place in a fixed society and a
> work which is in a great measure prescribed, and to
> give myself wholly into the hands of God to go where
> he leads. (5)

He referred also, on several occasions, to hoping 'to help ... and to share
in the true new life of India', believing that 'in serving India most
wholly', he would be 'acting most in the spirit of Christ'. (6) Two
important substantiations of Andrews' continuing missionary vocation come
from two of his closest Delhi colleagues. Thus, Allnutt, in the Delhi
Mission News.

> He feels out of touch with so much of our current
> Mission policy, that it will be a relief to him to be
> independent and free to work out the problem of how
> best to adapt the Christian message to meet the needs
> and aspirations of educated Hindus, on the lines
> which his nine years' intimate experience of this
> class of our fellow-subjects, deepening as the years
> have gone on, has led him to conceive as those best
> fitted to commend the Gospel of Christ to them.

C.B. Young, in writing to Farquhar to explain the situation, told him that
Andrews felt that 'these modern movements, the Brahmo Samaj and the Arya
Samaj, were doing a good deal to bring in the Kingdom of Christ, and that
they might, in the future, even bear some relationship to the Church'.

> In his sympathy for them, then, he was ready to go
> and work under Rabindra. (7)

Andrews' integrity, if not his wisdom, was not in the end questioned by
those who knew him well. (8)

There was, then, in addition to the strong negative factors in Andrews'
decision to leave Delhi for Santiniketan, and in addition to the very
personal element, the friendship with Tagore, a very unambiguous positive
factor, a sense of missionary vocation. That this found the joyful
response that it did beyond the Christian circle, is some measure of its
significance. Rudra had seen Andrews' original coming to St Stephen's
College as 'a gift from above'. (9) It was in just precisely the same
terms that Rabindranath Tagore welcomed him to Santiniketan, 'as a gift of
the Lord'. (10)

NOTES: Chapter Seven

1. Introductory

1 Andrews to Tagore, 25, 23 May 1914

2 Biog p. 87

3 Andrews to Talbot n.d. (late 1914) (Berkeley). This letter to
   E.S. Talbot, Bishop of Winchester, a lengthy explanation of his
   action in leaving the Delhi Mission, provides much of the
   background for this chapter. Talbot had been his bishop in his
   Pembroke College Mission days, had ordained him, and conducted a
   service of commendation for him in Southwark Cathedral on the eve
   of his original departure for India, so that Andrews must have
   felt a special obligation to explain his move to Santiniketan to
   him.

4 Allnutt wrote, on Andrews' leaving, that he had felt 'that our
   late colleague's diversity from our general standpoint (diverse
   as that is in many ways) had exceeded the limits our sense of
   unity demands to make fellowship real' DMN Jul 1914. Allnutt
   clearly was often exasperated with Andrews, as were some of the
   other members.

2. 'Education on indigenous lines'

1 His main ideas are to be found in two articles for an Indian
   readership, MR Jul 1908, and HR Jan, Feb 1909, and, for a
   readership in Britain, in Guardian, 16, 30 Dec 1908, and Ch. 2
   of RI. He also contributed a number of items to the Tribune,
   chiefly in the correspondence columns regarding the University of
   Lahore – 18 Jun 1907, 12 Jan 1909, 21 Apr 1910, 22 Apr 1910, 17
   Nov 1910. He also contributed in a small way to a Calcutta
   journal which supported the movement for National Education,
   Dawn.

2 Tribune 13 Nov 1906; Andrews to Hardinge, 24 Jan 1915 (Hardinge –
   CUL)

3 MR Jul 1908, RI p. 36, MR Jun 1913; RI p. 36, NI p. 23; IR

Dec 1910, <u>MR</u> Jul 1908; 'India in Transition' 1910; <u>Guardian</u>
30 Dec 1908, <u>MR</u> May 1913; <u>HR</u> Jan 1909

4 'Indian Students' 1910

5 The phrase is R.A. Butler's, commenting on Andrews views in
   Gilbert 1966, p. 254.

6 <u>HR</u> Jan 1909

7 <u>MR</u> Jul 1908. Andrews quotes here, and in his other articles on
   Indian education, from Bigg 1905.

8 <u>MR</u> Jul 1908; <u>HR</u> Jan 1909

9 They were welcomed in <u>Indian Daily Telegraph</u>, <u>Hindu</u>, <u>Indian
   Patriot</u> (all quoted in <u>HR</u> Feb 1909), <u>IR</u> Feb 1909, <u>Tribune</u> 31 Jan,
   22 Apr 1909, and echoed in <u>Tribune</u> 9 Nov 1909.

10 <u>MR</u> Jul 1908

11 <u>SSC Mag</u> Nov 1908

12 Among Hindu students, Har Dayal, who went on to be Boden Sanskrit
   Scholar at Oxford <u>SSC Mag</u> Dec 1907; among Muslims, Gulam Yazdani,
   who became a distinguished archaeologist, member of the Royal
   Asiatic Society, and contributor to the 'Bibliotheca Indica' <u>SSC
   Mag</u> May 1911; among Christians, Joel Waiz Lal, later to become a
   principal translator of the Urdu New Testament, was tutored in
   College by Nazir Ahmad, won 6 university gold medals, and stood
   first in his year in the Lahore degree of Master of Oriental
   Learning <u>SSC Mag</u> Apr 1909.

13 Andrews to Talbot, n.d. (Berkeley)

14 <u>Stephanian</u> Jun 1939

15 <u>HR</u> Jan 1909, cf. <u>Tribune</u> 23 Aug 1910

16 <u>MR</u> Mar 1913; <u>Tribune</u> 28 Apr 1913

17 Andrews to Munshi Ram, 7 Jun 1913, Andrews to Tagore, 19 Oct 1913

18 Andrews to Tagore, 31 Mar 1913

19 Andrews to Munshi Ram, 12 Jul 1913; Andrews to Talbot, n.d.
   (Berkeley)

3. 'Church of England religion'

1 <u>Stephanian</u> Jun 1940

2 Lefroy to Stanton, 17 Apr 1912; Montgomery to Stanton, 25 Sep

1912 (CMD)

3 C.E. Phipps to Stanton, 10 Oct 1912; the opinion of Sir Theodore Hope, in Montgomery to Stanton, 31 Oct 1912 (CMD)

4 Rudra's Memorandum of July 1912 (CMD); Rudra to Allnutt, 1 Sep 1911 (CMD)

5 Andrews' Memorandum, n.d. (CMD)

6 Gascoyne-Cecil to Stanton, 5 Nov 1912; Gardiner to Montgomery, 26 Dec 1912 (CMD)

7 Rudra to Allnutt, 1 Sep 1911; Andrews to Lefroy, Nov 1912 (CMD)

8 Andrews to Stanton, 15 Sep 1912 (CMD)

9 Andrews to Montgomery, 10 Sep 1912 (SPG); Andrews to Stanton, 15 Sep 1912 (CMD); Rudra to Montgomery, 2 Sep 1912 (SPG). Montgomery's credentials in the matter of racism have been questioned - Huttenback 1976, p. 49.

10 Andrews to Stanton, 15 Sep 1912 (CMD)

11 Andrews to Stanton, n.d. (1913) (Chaturvedi - NAI); Andrews to Talbot, n.d. (Berkeley)

4. 'The Divinity of our Blessed Lord'

1 The critic was C.R.N. Blakiston CT 12 Dec 1913. His champions were J. Lee and B.K. Cunningham CT 19 Dec 1913, and Allnutt and Rudra CT 23 Jan 1914. The Tribune 8 Jan 1914, also came to Andrews' defence, claiming that 'the gravamen of the charge against Mr Andrews is that he lacks the bigotry of the latter-day missionary'.

2 Andrews to Gandhi, 13 Apr 1914; Andrews to Munshi Ram, 22 May 1914

3 Andrews to Munshi Ram, 22 May 1914

4 Tribune 6 May 1914; Andrews to Munshi Ram, 22 May 1914

5 Farquhar to J.R. Mott, 4 Jun 1914 (New York)

6 DMN Jul 1914

7 Andrews to Talbot, n.d. (Berkeley)

8 Indian Social Reformer 23 Aug 1914

9 Andrews to Talbot, n.d. (Berkeley)

5. 'The dwelling place of ... Christ'

1 The sermon was printed in MR May 1913, Tribune 7 May 1913. An editorial note in the latter on 4 May 1913, found it 'ennobling'.
2 Andrews to SPG India Sub-committee, 21 May 1912 (CMD)
3 CC 1912
4 The Chief Commissioner was speaking at the College speech day - SSC Mag Jun 1913.
5 Andrews to Talbot, n.d. (Berkeley)
6 Andrews to Tagore, 8 May 1913
7 Andrews to Tagore, 11 Feb 1914
8 MR May 1913; Andrews to Tagore, 2 Mar 1914; Andrews to Gandhi, 26 Feb 1914; Andrews to Tagore, 11 Feb 1914
9 Tribune 6 May 1914
10 Andrews to Munshi Ram, 22 May 1914

6. 'The divine call'

1 Andrews to Tagore, 28 Jul 1913; Andrews to Munshi Ram, 20 Jan 1914
2 Andrews to Tagore, 21 Aug, 7 Dec 1913, 26 Apr, 27 May 1914, Andrews to Munshi Ram, 20 Jan, 22 May 1914; Andrews to Talbot, n.d. (Berkeley); Andrews to Rudra, 1915 (Berkeley). Whether Rudra really felt this, we cannot be sure. He acknowledged that it was 'more and more difficult for the Western Church to preach Christianity in India', but he clearly saw St Stephen's College as a place where, because of Andrews' presence, it had become possible 'with great confidence to preach the Christian faith' CC 1914.
3 Andrews to Talbot, n.d. (Berkeley). Something of Allnutt's capacity to appreciate Andrews' position comes over in his comments on his resignation from the Delhi Mission: 'If men like Andrews seem precipitate and inclined to break too easily with the older traditions, I am inclined to say that ... we have come to the time when we need bold ventures ... It may be that some day we shall have reason to be thankful for what such men

have been able to achieve as pioneers in a new era of missionary enterprise' DMN Jul 1914.

4   Andrews to Gandhi, 13 Apr 1914

5   Andrews to Munshi Ram, 5 May 1913; Andrews to Talbot, n.d. (Berkeley)

6   Andrews to Tagore, 8 May 1913; Andrews to Stanton, n.d. (1913) (Chaturvedi - NAI). Did Andrews read into his view of Margaret Noble, Vivekananda's disciple, something of his understanding of his own actions, in his poem, 'Sister Nivedita' 1916?

> She loved, and though she left the outer fold
> Of Christ, to love's commandment she was true,
> Leaving her home, to make a stranger's woes
> Her own in Christ-like act ...

7   DMN Jul 1914; quoted in Farquhar to Mott, 4 Jun 1914 (New York)

8   Farquhar, in his letter to Mott, accepted Young's explanation, but thought Andrews was 'grievously mistaken ... I hope that within a few months he will see the impossibility of doing any serious service where he is, and revert ... The beaten track of progressive conservatism seems safest, does it not? We can be scholarly and accurate and sympathetic, without running so far to meet the enemy that we lose our bearings - and our distinctive message'. Farquhar continued to be supportive of Andrews throughout his most troubled years, continuing to publish articles by him in YMOI.

9   CC 1915

10 From a poem written for the occasion, quoted in Chaturvedi and Sykes 1949, p. 104

CONCLUSION

The decade which Andrews spent as a member of the Cambridge Mission to
Delhi was in some respects only a prelude to his most important work in
India, even, it might be said, to his most important missionary work, and
yet it was a phase of his life profoundly interesting in itself, full of
remarkable achievements and insights, and the essential seedbed of all that
was to follow, establishing the approach and adumbrating many of the themes
which he was to develop during the subsequent twenty-six years of his life
and work, the years for which he has hitherto been best known.

It would not be inappropriate, in the light of the preceding chapters, to
characterise this striking decade within the parameters suggested by the
theology of mission which Westcott and French had sketched out for the
Cambridge Mission. Certainly, such a way of looking at Andrews' work is
inclusive, and provides a means of seeing it as all of a piece. In 1914,
Rudra had felt obliged to disclaim the fulfilment of Westcott's dream in
and through St Stephen's College, saying that, although they were
establishing the College in the new capital as one 'of real significance
for the true intellectual and spiritual welfare of India', it was 'perhaps
not as an Alexandria on the Jumna'. (1) Andrews' own work, nevertheless,
during the years that he was a member of the College, was in many
essentials just such a fulfilment.

This, in retrospect, Andrews himself might even have been willing to
concede. In the closing year or so of his life, he looked back on the
friends with whom he had been especially closely associated at that time,
or beginning to be closely associated, as embodying in themselves much of
what Westcott had hoped for. Thus, at the laying of the foundation stone
of the new St Stephen's College, in March 1939 (the ceremony in the area at
the front of the College, to be known as Andrews Court), he reminisced
about Westcott and their talks together many years before, when Westcott
had spoken of the role that he believed that India would play in Asia as
comparable with that of Greece in Europe. In those talks, we must also
recall here, Westcott had gone one to say that India would thus in time
become 'the missionary of Christ to Asia'.

> If Bishop Westcott had lived long enough to see the
> place that the names of Tagore and Gandhi have
> taken in contemporary history, he would have realised
> how marvellously his prophetic words had been
> fulfilled. (2)

When we consider how, within Hinduism, as Andrews was already discovering
towards the end of his missionary decade, these two 'wonderfully expressed
the spirit of Christ', and when we consider his own subsequent influence
upon them, so that the former called Andrews' friendship 'the highest
blessing' of his life, and the latter's foremost Indian biographer could
say, 'Gandhi ... needed ... Andrews', it begins to be possible to speak of
Andrews' part in this fulfilment. (3)

In the same year, 1939, he recalled how Westcott, in his old age, 'like an
ancient seer, with a vision of the future before his eyes', had prophesied
that 'the intellectual and spiritual appreciation of ... (St John's Gospel)
would come most fully and richly at last from great Indian Christian
thinkers when they had gone far beyond the period of tutelage from the
West, and had learnt to think for themselves on these profound subjects'.
He then went on to recall his own Indian Christian friends associated
essentially with his missionary decade.

> Both Susil Rudra and the Sadhu showed me clearly how
> true that prophecy was, and how quickly it was coming
> to pass. (4)

Andrews' encouragement and support of the former, in the context of perhaps
the deepest of all his friendships, and his early and enthusiastic
association with the latter, are, along with so much more of his work in
promoting the development of an Indian Church, further aspects of his
realization of Westcott's dream.

Even at the time, in 1909, as he reflected upon his experience of much that
he believed derived from 'the eternal Word', both in India's 'wonderful

religious history' and also in the noble acts of modern educated Hindus of
the new political nation, Andrews had turned to the Alexandrian analogy.

> I find myself here in India in something of the same
> position as the first Christian thinkers, when they
> passed from the confines of Palestine and came face
> to face with the writings of Plato and the nobler
> Greek classics. (5)

It was, of course, as we have seen, particularly in the living issues that
confronted people in their struggle towards nationhood, rather than in a
more speculative sphere, that he developed his own theological formulations
and made a beginning at a theology of national renaissance. The analogy
with the Alexandrian approach was, nevertheless, a valid one, as he sought
to find a way of speaking of Christ in the context of the all-important
centre of the thought of educated Hindus, the desire to be a nation.
Indeed, he argued with some justification that it was more valid than the
more speculative essays of some of his contemporaries. This, too, would
have chimed in with one of Westcott's own deepest convictions, that
'speculative and historical criticism', for all its attraction, was 'wholly
subsidiary to action', which was for him 'the characteristic of man', and
that, in consequence, the Gospel, 'which claims to have the power to deal
with every practical question of human conduct', should be vindicated 'on
the broad fields of life'. (6)

Beneath all the rich variety, then, of Andrews' involvements and
commitments during his missionary decade, in the matter of nationalism, in
the building up of an Indian Church, and in relationships with people of
other faiths, a profound and profoundly consistent missiology is to be
discerned. Its soundness as a classical missiology was the guarantee of
its appropriateness and usefulness in a completely new context. So
conscious was he of the novelty of the context, and the critical nature of
the times, that he spoke of arriving 'in the New World of the East' at 'the
very epoch of its renaissance'. That he should identify, there and then,
in so much that was going on both within and beyond the Christian fold,
disclosures that were, he believed, 'a part of the Revelation' of Christ,

is a striking reminder of Westcott's expectation for India of a great new
'epoch of revelation'. That continues to unfold, in what has been called
'the coming of the Third Church', but in his missionary decade he
participated in and contributed to it in a distinctive and creative and
distinguished way. (7)

The next step in Andrews' pilgrimage in mission, which involved leaving the
Delhi Mission, and even, for a time, the sacramental life and ministry of
the Church, raises deep and difficult questions that would be another
'mission study' in themselves. His valedictory Lahore sermon had hinted,
in its allusion to Christ's rejection of 'the rich and cultured world' of
Chorazin, etc., at a new phase of mission marked by an identification with
the poor in their struggles. This, too, would have made good sense to the
founder of the Cambridge Mission to Delhi, for whom the proclamation of a
Gospel to the poor was 'the crowning sign of Christ'. (8) It also made
sense in Andrews' own perspective, as that which would be required of
Christianity in the emerging Indian situation, once the identification with
national aspirations had been secured. It could, then, be argued, that
Andrews' moving on from Delhi, seen in this perspective, was a prophetic
sign wholly congruous with a missionary approach that required a
penetration of the culture of the mission field in question, and the
formulation from within it of what Westcott had called 'new illustrations
of the one infinite and eternal Gospel'. (9) Those new illustrations were
certainly to follow, as, over the subsequent years, be earned from the
Indian people the title, Deenabandhu, 'friend of the poor'. Less
specifically, but clearly as a logical development of his missionary
vocation, that was how his nationalist friends saw his move in 1914. The
Tribune - and the last word might reasonably be with that voice in the
Punjab of Indian nationalism, which had borne such remarkable testimony to
his endeavours - claimed that the 'respect and esteem' which this
'Christlike man' had won from the people of India, were likely to be
increased by this step, which was 'characteristic'. (10)

Notes: CONCLUSION

1 SSC Mag Apr 1914

2 Statesman 28 Mar 1939

3 The Inner Life 1939, p. 13; from a tribute dated Jan 1941, included as
   a Foreword to Andrews 1942; B.R. Nanda 1971

4 The Inner Life 1939, p. 32

5 Ind Int Oct 1909

6 From Westcott's first address as Bishop of Durham to the Diocesan
   Conference, quoted in Edwards 1971, p. 217

7 Ind Int Oct 1909; 'Third Church' Bühlmann 1976

8 Westcott 1892, p. 230

9 Quoted in Monk 1935, p. ii

10 Tribune 7 Apr 1914

GLOSSARY OF INDIAN WORDS

Most of the words from Indian languages used in the text are in the
Anglicised forms adopted in the eighteenth and nineteenth centuries. They
are given here in that form.

ADVAITA   (lit. 'non-duality') This is the principle upon which one
                 of the leading Hindu philosophical systems, developed by
                 Sankara, the VEDANTA, often referred to as the ADVAITA
                 VEDANTA (which proposes the identity of BRAHMAN, the
                 supreme being, and the ATMAN, the human soul), is based.

AHIMSA   (lit. 'harmlessness') The name under which reverence for
                 all forms of organic life has been taught in the Jain and
                 Hindu traditions. Developed by Gandhi as a political
                 methodology of non-violent resistance.

ARYA   (lit. 'noble') The term denotes the Nordic people who
                 entered the sub-continent, ARYAVARTA, the land of the
                 Aryans, during the second millenium B.C.E. (though it is,
                 in fact, a linguistic term indicating a speech-group of
                 Indo-European origin). The word acquired a fresh currency
                 as national consciousness developed in the nineteenth
                 century, not least through the association known as the ARYA
                 SAMAJ.

ASHRAM   (lit. 'a place of self-mortification') The tradition of
                 Hindu ascetics, or hermits, living in a group of huts known
                 as an ASHRAM, seems to originate about 700 B.C.E. Rudra's
                 proposal for a Christian ashram, in 1910, appears to be the
                 first such idea in the Christian community. The first was
                 founded about a decade later. The word can also mean one of
                 the four stages of life, as understood in Hindu tradition.

ATMAN   (lit. 'breath') The later, most widely received meaning is
                 'soul', the inmost being of the individual person. Gandhi

and Munshi Ram were both known as MAHATMA, 'great-souled'.

BASTI   (lit. 'abode') Used of the small houses or huts, or a cluster of these, in a town or city.

BHAGAT   (lit. 'devotee') A North Indian type of wandering preacher and theologian, fit to associate with scholars but ready to preach to the people in their own language. The devotion is to the BHAGAVAN, the Lord; much of this is focussed in the BHAGAVAD GITA, the Song of the Lord, part of the epic, the MAHABHARATA.

BHAKTI   (lit. 'sharing or participating in') A devotional tradition within Hinduism, deriving from an experience of participation in the life of God, and of God's participation in the life of people. A person devoted either meditatively or emotionally to the Lord is a BHAKTA.

BRAHMAN   (lit. 'sacred utterance') The developed meaning is the immutable and eternal ground of the universe. A member of the highest caste, that performed the priestly role in relation to BRAHMAN, had either the same name or was known as a BRAHMIN. In the first stage of life, a young Hindu is known as a BRAHMACHARI ('faring according to BRAHMAN'), and lives an austere and celibate life at the home of the teacher.

DHARMA   (lit. 'decree, custom') The duty special to each individual, its fulfilment being in Hinduism a condition of salvation. Munshi Ram's use of the adjective DHARMIC of his educational system is probably best translated 'orthodox'.

DHOTI   A cloth worn round the waist, passing between the legs and fastening behind.

DURBAR   A royal audience, an assembly in the presence of the ruler.

FAQIR (lit. 'poor', 'poor man') Originally a Muslim religious mendicant, applied more widely to Hindu ascetics.

GURU (lit. 'teacher') A religious teacher, whose students would often live as a household or family with the GURU in the GURUKULA. Tagore was popularly known as GURUDEV, the divine teacher.

KAYASTH The writer caste.

KSHATRIYA The second or military caste.

MAHARAJ Sovereign, emperor.

MANDIR Temple, house of God.

MULLAH A Muslim learned in theology.

PANDIT (lit. 'learned, skilled') A learned Brahmin, versed in Sanskrit.

PARAMHAMSA One who has reached the fourth, most advanced stage of asceticism among the orders of SANNYASIS.

PARDAH (lit. 'curtain, screen') The social practice of separating women from all men except immediate family.

PURANAS (lit. 'old, ancient') In the corpus of Hindu sacred literature, long mythological works in verse, extolling one or other of the great gods.

RAJ (lit. 'reign') Used of British rule in India.

SADHU (lit. 'perfect') A holy or pious person, usually belonging to an ascetic order.

SAHIB　　　　　(lit. 'lord, master') Used widely of Europeans during the British imperial period.

SALAAM　　　　(lit. 'peace') A greeting, or a gesture of obeisance.

SAMAJ　　　　　(lit. 'meeting, assembly') Used of various associations or organisations, such as the ARYA SAMAJ, BRAHMO SAMAJ, PRARTHANA SAMAJ.

SANYASIN　　　(lit. 'laying aside') A wandering ascetic who had embraced some form of SANNYASA or monastic renunciation.

SATYAGRAHA　　(lit. 'truth-force') A new word coined by Gandhi in preference to 'passive resistance', based on his conviction that in the search for truth, the goal of life, the methods employed in human action and conflict should never injure another's integrity or prevent another's search for truth.

SHASTRA　　　　(lit. 'order, command') Hindu religious books, particularly law books.

SHIVAM　　　　Goodness.

SUDRA　　　　　A member of the lowest of the four Hindu castes, generally associated with such occupations as labourer, servant.

SWADESHI　　　(lit. 'belonging to one's own country') The name of a movement started early in the twentieth century to encourage Indian industries.

SWAMI　　　　　(lit. 'master') A Hindu religious teacher.

SWARAJ　　　　Self-rule, self-government.

UPANISHADS　　(lit. 'to sit down beside') Denoting the posture of the disciple, so the word came to indicate one of the main

categories of Hindu sacred literature, a collection of some
one hundred spiritual treatises.

VEDA   (lit. 'knowledge') A collection of hymns that represent the
earliest and most sacred Hindu scriptures. There are four
VEDAS. Munshi Ram uses the word VEDIC rather as some
Christians use the word 'biblical' to legitimate their own
views.

ZENANA   The secluded women's apartments in a Persian or Indian
Muslim house.

ABBREVIATIONS

BC Cal	Bishop's College, Calcutta
Biog	'Register containing biographical notes' (Chaturvedi – N.A.I.)
BL	British Library
C&MG	Civil and Military Gazette
CC	Mission Reports: The SPG and Cambridge Mission in Delhi and the South Punjab
CMD	Cambridge Mission to Delhi
CMI	Church Missionary Intelligencer
CMR	Church Missionary Review
CMS	Church Missionary Society
CQR	Church Quarterly Review
CSS Review	Christa Seva Sangha Review
CT	Church Times
CUL	Cambridge University Library
DCI	Reports of the Director of Criminal Intelligence (NAI)
DMN	Delhi Mission News
Ep	Epiphany

Gandhi SSS   Gandhi Smarak Sangrahalaya Samiti

HR   Hindustan Review

Ind Int   Indian Interpreter

IOL&R   India Office Library and Records

IR   Indian Review

IRM   International Review of Missions

IW   Indian Witness

JRAS   Journal of the Royal Asiatic Society

MCCM   Madras Christian College Magazine

MR   Modern Review

NAI   National Archives of India

NI   North India

NL   Nehru Memorial Museum and Library

NLS   National Library of Scotland

NMI   National Missionary Intelligencer

PNNR   Punjab Native Newspaper Reports (IOL&R)

RI   The Renaissance in India

SCM   Student Christian Movement

<u>SM</u>	<u>Student Movement</u>
SPG	Society for the Propagation of the Gospel
<u>SSC Mag</u>	<u>St Stephen's College Magazine</u>
<u>TEW</u>	<u>The East and the West</u>
<u>TLS</u>	<u>Times Literary Supplement</u>
<u>WIOC</u>	<u>What I Owe to Christ</u>
WMC	World Missionary Conference (Edinburgh 1910)
WSCF	World Student Christian Federation
<u>WSCF</u>	Andrews' paper for the 1911 WSCF Conference
<u>YMOI</u>	<u>Young Men of India</u>
<u>ZU</u>	<u>Zaka Ullah of Delhi</u>

314

BIBLIOGRAPHY

A. UNPUBLISHED SOURCES

1. St Stephen's College, Delhi

Monk's File: papers collected by F.F. Monk in preparing his history of the College, including correspondence re Rudra's appointment as Principal, student's recollections

Staff Meeting Minutes Book

2. Brotherhood of the Ascended Christ, Delhi

Brotherhood Minutes Book

3. National Archives of India, New Delhi

Home Department. Political (including DCI)
Gokhale Papers
Ampthill Papers (microfilm)
Minto Papers (microfilm)
Morley Papers (microfilm)
Chaturvedi Collection, including:

Andrews' correspondence with Munshi Ram (includes drafts of letters to V.H. Stanton, etc)

Articles and Speeches of C.F. Andrews in ms

Register containing biographical notes on Andrews, made by Chaturvedi, much of it dictated (1921?)

Collection of Press Clippings

'A Short Life of Muhammad. Translated from the Urdu' –

Andrews' handwriting.   Deposited by M.R. Bansal

4. Gandhi Smarak Sangrahalaya Samiti, Delhi

  Correspondence between Andrews and Gandhi, beginning Feb 1914

5. Nehru Memorial Museum and Library, New Delhi

  Har Dayal Papers

6. Rabindra Bhavana, Santiniketan

  Correspondence between Andrews and Tagore, beginning Aug 1912

7. Bishop's College, Calcutta

  Box 'Africa'

8. Vidyajyoti Library, Delhi

  Hosten Papers (Vols 33-9 contain material on Sundar Singh)

9. United Society for the Propagation of the Gospel Archives, Oxford

  Lahore Letters Received (Copied), Vols III-V, 1904-14
  SPG Missionary Reports (Originals) 1907
  SPG Letters Received (Originals) Africa 1, 1914
  SPG Standing Committee Minutes

10. Cambridge Mission to Delhi (Archives with USPG)

  Papers on 'College History'
  'College Constitution' 1911-13
  'Papers on Early Mission History' 1891-1918
  Appointment of Rudra as Principal, 1907
  'College Building Fund'

College Correspondence 1902-38
General Correspondence 1914-30
'Past Members of Mission. Men'
Candidature Papers
Box of Press Clippings

11. Church Missionary Society Archives, Birmingham

T.V. French. Letters and Reports 1850-74
Punjab and Sindh Précis 1904-10, 1910-19

12. Conference for World Mission, London

United Council for Missionary Study, Minutes 1911-12

13. India Office Library and Records

Ampthill Papers
Fleetwood-Wilson Papers
Hailey Papers
Morley Papers
Judicial and Public Department. File on Delhi Conspiracy Trial
Selections from Native Newspapers published in the Punjab 1905-14

14. British Library, London

Macmillan Archives 1913-39

15. University Library, Cambridge

Hardinge Papers

16. Pembroke College, Cambridge

Pembroke College Mission Reports 1889-1900
Letters and papers relating to the College Mission 1890-99

Correspondence of Andrews with Prior family 1899–1900

17. SCM Archives, Selly Oak, Birmingham

Papers, correspondence on Student Volunteer Missionary Union, etc
(unsorted at time of inspection) including, by Andrews,
'Conishead and India' (1908) and 'Missionary Service'
(1911)

18. National Library of Scotland, Edinburgh

Minto Papers

19. Christ's College, Aberdeen

Preparatory Papers for WMC, Edinburgh 1910

20. World Council of Churches, Geneva

Preparatory Papers for WMC, Edinburgh 1910

21. Missionary Research Library, New York

Preparatory Papers for WMC, Edinburgh 1910

22. Y.M.C.A. Historical Library, New York

Correspondence of J.N. Farquhar

23. Houghton Library, Harvard

Rothenstein Papers

24. South and South East Asia Library, Berkeley, California

Correspondence of Andrews (with Rudra, Talbot, etc.)

----

25. Unpublished theses

Barrier, N.G. <u>Punjab Politics and the Disturbances of 1907</u> PhD,
Duke 1966

Jones, K.W. <u>The Arya Samaj in the Punjab: A Study of Social Reform
and Revivalism 1877-1902</u> PhD, Berkeley 1966

A. PUBLISHED SOURCES

1. Mission Reports

<u>Report of the Delhi and Kurnaul Missions of the SPG 1868</u> ff.
(Delhi 1869) The title varies slightly over the subsequent
years. From 1880, it appears annually as: <u>The SPG and
Cambridge Mission in Delhi and the South Punjab, Report of
the Cambridge Committee, with which is incorporated the
General Report of the Branches of the Mission</u> (1880 Report
published Allahabad 1881). By 1904, it was published from
Cambridge.

2. Contemporary Newspapers and Periodicals

Amrita Bazar Patrika
Bengalee
Civil and Military Gazette
Church Missionary Intelligencer
Church Missionary Review
Church Quarterly Review
Church Times
Contemporary Review

Delhi Mission News

East and West

The East and the West

Epiphany

Guardian

Hindustan Review

Indian Interpreter

Indian Review

Indian Social Reformer

Indian Witness

Indian World

Leader

Madras Christian College Magazine

Modern Review

National Missionary Intelligencer

Nineteenth Century and After

Pioneer

St Stephen's College Magazine

Spectator

Stephanian

Student Movement

Tribune

Young India

Young Men of India

3. Printed Sources: Andrews

(The list is more or less complete to 1914; thereafter, only items
cited in the text and notes are given)

The Relation of Christianity to the Conflict between Capital and
Labour London 1896

    (ed. C.F. Andrews) C.H. Prior The Presence of God, and Other
    Sermons Cambridge 1904

'Indian Character: An Appreciation. I' DMN Jul 1905

'Indian Character: An Appreciation. II' DMN Oct 1905

'The Religious Unrest of Northern India' <u>CMI</u> Oct 1905

'The Effect of the Japanese Victories upon India' <u>TEW</u> Oct 1905

'Indian Character: An Appreciation. III' <u>DMN</u> Jan 1906

'Change of Times' (letter) <u>C&MG</u> 8 Sep 1906

'The Education of our Children' (letter) <u>Tribune</u> 17 Sep 1906

'Change of Times' (letter) <u>C&MG</u> 30 Sep 1906

'The National Sin of Idolatry' (letter) <u>Ep</u> 6 Oct 1906

'The National Congress of 1906' (letter) <u>Tribune</u> 17 Oct 1906

'A Letter' <u>SM</u> Oct 1906

'Indian Nationality' <u>Tribune</u> 13 Nov 1906

'An Indian School in the Hills' (letter) <u>Tribune</u> 13 Dec 1906

'Indian Nationalism' <u>Tribune</u> 16 Dec 1906

'Hopes and Difficulties of Indian Nationalism' <u>Tribune</u> 25 Dec 1906

'The Ideal of Indian Nationality' <u>Bengalee</u> 28 Dec 1906, etc.

'An Englishman's Impression of the National Congress' <u>Bengalee</u>
   28 Dec 1906

'The New Indian Nation' (poem) <u>HR</u> Dec 1906

'Indian Students in British Colleges' <u>SM</u> Dec 1906

'Indian Students in England' <u>CMR</u> Jan 1907

'Further Thoughts on Prayer' <u>SM</u> Apr 1907

'The Junior Clergy Missionary Association' <u>TEW</u> Apr 1907

'The Spiritual Force of Christianity' <u>Ep</u> 20 Apr 1907, also as
   'Great Religious Movements in the West' <u>SSC Mag</u> May 1907

'Indian Nationality: Last Words' <u>HR</u> May 1907

'M.A. English Courses in the University' (letter) <u>Tribune</u>
   18 Jun 1907

'Shakespeare and Nationality' <u>MR</u> Jul 1907

'Swadeshi I' <u>Tribune</u> 16 Aug 1907

'The Religious Basis of a National Movement' <u>Ep</u> 17 Aug 1907

'The Government and Swadeshi' (letter) <u>Tribune</u> 8 Sep 1907

'Swadeshi II' <u>Tribune</u> 27 Sep 1907

'The Situation in the East' <u>TEW</u> Oct 1907

'A Needed Reform in Indian Education' (letter) <u>Spectator</u> 26 Oct 1907

'A Door Open in India ' <u>SM</u> Nov 1907

'Christianity and Nationalism' (letter) <u>Ep</u> 9 Nov 1907

'Christianity in Japan' <u>SSC Mag</u> Dec 1907

'The Outlook' MR Dec 1907

North India London 1908

'A New Year's Message' NMI Jan 1908

'A Hindu Apologetic' DMN Jan 1908, also as 'The Creation Theory of
the Universe' MR Apr 1909

'The Transvaal Problem' (letter) Tribune 25 Jan 1908

'Religion and Patriotism' Ep 25 Jan 1908, etc.

'One in Christ' YMOI Feb 1908

'Reply to the criticism of the Gwalior Mission Journal' (letter) NMI
Feb 1908

(Syrian Christian students - letter) Guardian 25 Mar 1908

'Racial Unity' SM Apr 1908

'Educational Missions in India' DMN Apr 1908

'First Principles of a National Movement' SSC Mag May 1908

'The Motherland' (poem) MR May 1908

'India and England: Some Aspects of the Economic Relation' IR Jun
1908

'The Future of Indian Education' MR Jul 1908, etc

'A Punjab Religious Movement' DMN Jul 1908

'Indian Christians and the National Movement' YMOI Sep 1908

'Indian History: Its Lessons for Today' MR Sep 1908, etc

(Relations with Nestorian Christians - letter) Guardian 7 Oct 1908

'Malaria and its causes' SSC Mag Nov 1908

'Possibilities of Social Service' SSC Mag Nov 1908

'National Literature and Art' MR Nov 1908

'The Awakening' (poem) MR Dec 1908

'The Church and Education in India I' Guardian 16 Dec 1908

'The Church and Education in India II' Guardian 30 Dec 1908

'A Modern Hindu Apologetic' DMN Jan 1909

'The Minto-Morley Reforms' IR Jan 1909

'Hope the Conqueror' IR Jan 1909, etc

'The Punjab University' Tribune 12 Jan 1909

'Indian Higher Education: A Criticism' HR Jan and Feb 1909, etc

'The Awakening of the East: Its Meaning and Significance' Tribune
20 Feb 1909, etc

'The Practice of the Sermon on the Mount' SM Mar 1909

'Science and Forgiveness' _Ep_ 13 Mar 1909

'A Retreat near Delhi' _SM_ May 1909

'Educational Needs' _DMN_ Jul 1909

'A Great Educational Experiment' _SSC Mag_ Jul 1909

'The Dawn' (poem) _MR_ Jul 1909, etc

'The Teaching of Politics in Colleges' (letter) _Tribune_ 24 Sep 1909

'A Missionary's Experience' _Ind Int_ Oct 1909, etc

'A Review of the Modern World. I Asia' _MR_ Nov 1909, etc

'A Review of the Modern World. II Europe' _MR_ Dec 1909

Intro. to Ram Tirtha _In Woods of God-Realization_ Delhi 1910

'Ordination Study in India' CMD Occasional Paper 1910

'India in Transition' CMD Occasional Paper 1910, also as 'India in
the Victorian Age' _IR_ Dec 1910

'Christ and Educated India' _YMOI_ Jan 1910

'Nationalism and Religion' _IR_ Jan 1910

'A Review of the Modern World. III Africa' _MR_ Jan 1910

'Christianity and Patriotism' _NMI_ Feb 1910, etc

'A Review of the Modern World. IV Australia' _MR_ Feb 1910

'Arya Varta' (poem) _HR_ Feb 1910, etc

'A Review of the Modern World. V America' _MR_ Mar 1910

'A Review of the Modern World. VI India' _MR_ Apr 1910

'The University Year. I' _Tribune_ 21 Apr 1910

'The University Year. II' _Tribune_ 22 Apr 1910

'How to Serve my Country. I' _Tribune_ 27 Apr 1910

'The Inner Spirit of Islam' _SM_ May 1910

'Social Service: Nursing the Sick' _MR_ May 1910

'The Endowment of Indian Education' _Tribune_ 4 May 1910

'How to Serve my Country. II' _Tribune_ 13 May 1910

'Social Service: Temperance Work' _MR_ Jun 1910

Review of P.T. Forsyth _SM_ Jun 1910

'Malaria' _SSC Mag_ Jul 1910

'In Memoriam: Lala Rang Lal' _SSC Mag_ Jul 1910

'Race within the Christian Church' _TEW_ Jul 1910

'India's Death Rate' _Tribune_ 18, 20, 23 Aug 1910, etc

'A Holiday in the Hills' _Tribune_ 2 Sep 1910

'Colour and Caste' _IW_ 6 Sep 1910

'A Grave Moral Danger' MR Oct 1910, etc

'Christian Life in the Primitive Church' Ep 15 Oct 1910

'Indian Church Problems. I Introductory' CT 21 Oct 1910

'Missions and "The Drain"' IW 25 Oct 1910, etc

'The Day of Opportunity in India' NMI Nov 1910

'Indian Church Problems. II Interpretation of Christian Doctrine'
   CT 4 Nov 1910

'Honours Students' Tribune 17 Nov 1910

'Indian Church Problems. III The Christian Borderland' CT
   18 Nov 1910

'Indian Church Problems. IV The Hindu Challenge to the Church' CT
   25 Nov 1910

'Indian Church Problems. V Caste and the Church' CT 2 Dec 1910

'Zaka Ullah' (letter) Tribune 13 Dec 1910

'Munshi Zaka Ullah' Tribune 14 Dec 1910

'Indian Church Problems. VI Indigenous Development' CT 16 Dec 1910

Oremus. An Office Book for the Use of Missionary Communities in
   India Cawnpore 1911

'The Indian Missionary Ideal' TEW Jan 1911

'The Evolution of Liberty in Europe' HR Jan 1911

'Lord Acton on Nationality' HR Feb 1911

'Toru Dutt: A Memoir' MR Feb 1911

'From the East and from the West' SSC Mag Feb 1911

'The Indigenous Expression of Christian Truth. I' YMOI Mar 1911

'The Decennial Conference' IW 7 Mar 1911

'The Indigenous Expression of Christian Truth. II' YMOI Apr 1911

'Munshi Zaka Ulla: A Great Educationist' MR Apr 1911

'Students and the Application of Christ's Teachings to Modern Life:
   To International and Racial Relations' WSCF Conference Report
   1911

'The Malarial Parasite' SSC Mag May 1911

'A Visit to Dharmpur' MR Jun 1911, etc

'The Secret of Jesus' Ind Int Jul 1911, etc

'The Increase of Intemperance in the Panjab' (letter) Tribune
   24 Sept 1911

'A Notable Government Report' Tribune 14 Oct 1911

'Christianity and the Test of Vitality' Ep 28 Oct 1911

'A March in the Simla Hills' MR Nov 1911

'The Christian Moral Standard I' Ep 25 Nov 1911

'Astrology and Religion' SSC Mag Dec 1911

'Malaria in Delhi' SSC Mag Dec 1911

'Shelley's Personality' SSC Mag Dec 1911

'The Christian Moral Standard II' Ep 2 Dec 1911

The Renaissance in India. Its Missionary Aspect London 1912

'Uplifting the Depressed Classes' in The Depressed Classes Madras
    1912

'The King's Visit' YMOI Jan 1912

'What is Hinduism?' DMN Jan 1912

'The Problem of Reunion' (letter) TEW Jan 1912

'To Rabindranath Tagore' (poem) MR Mar 1912

'Sister Nivedita' (poem) MR Apr 1912

'The Doctrine of Atonement' IR Jun 1912

'The Day of Opportunity. India' in The Day of Opportunity London
    1912

'The King's Announcement at Delhi' TEW Jul 1912

'An Evening with Rabindra' MR Aug 1912

'Race Within the Christian Church. II' TEW Oct 1912

'An Advent Hymn' (poem) SM Dec 1912, etc

Review of Gitanjali Tribune 4 Dec 1912

Preface to S.E. Stokes The Historical Character of the Gospel
    Madras 1913

'To Sarojini Naidu' (poem) HR Jan 1913

'With Rabindra in England' MR Jan 1913

'Student Life and the Character of Hamlet' SSC Mag Jan 1913

'Christ and Social Reconstruction I' Ep 18 Jan 1913

'A Young Bengali Writer' MR Feb 1913

'Christ and Social Reconstruction II' Ep 15 Feb 1913

'Hardwar and its Gurukula' MR Mar 1913

'Christ and Social Reconstruction III' Ep 8 Mar 1913

'On Reading the Translation of Gitanjali' (poem) MR Apr 1913

'Lady Hardinge's Children's Day' (letter) Tribune 11 Apr 1913

'The Gurukula and its Ideals' Tribune 29 Apr 1913

'A Cambridge University Sermon' MR May 1913, etc

'Death the Revealer' (poem) MR Jun 1913

'Tagore and the Renaissance in Bengal' Contemporary Review Jun 1913

'The Renaissance in India' (letter) SM Jun 1913

'Rabindranath Tagore I' MR Jun 1913

'Rabindranath Tagore II' MR Jul 1913

'Siri Ram, Revolutionist' (letter) Pioneer 11 Jul 1913

'The Ideal of the Christian Church' Ep 12 Jul 1913

'The Body of Humanity I' MR Sep 1913

'The Body of Humanity II' MR Oct 1913

Review of Sarkar's Chaitanya MR Oct 1913

'The Patriot' (poem) MR Nov 1913

Review of Tagore's The Gardner MR Dec 1913

'Indians Outside India' IR Dec 1913

'The Struggle in South Africa' Tribune 21 Dec 1913

'The Abolition of Indenture' MR Jan 1914

'Bharat Mata' (poem) MR Jan 1914

'Indians in South Africa' (letter) Cape Times in Tribune 25 Feb 1914

'Letter from Natal' MR Mar 1914

'Intercommunion of Races' (letter) CT 6 Mar 1914

'The Spirit of India' Tribune 20 Mar 1914

'New Behar' (poem) MR Apr 1914

'Mr Gandhi at Phoenix' MR May 1914

'A Sermon Preached in Lahore Cathedral' Tribune 5 May 1914, etc

'Mr Gandhi Vindicated' (letter) Pioneer 20 May 1914, etc

'Mr Gandhi and the Commission' MR Jul 1914

'A Tirtha in South Africa' MR Aug 1914

'Helpers in the Struggle I' MR Sep 1914

'Helpers in the Struggle II' MR Oct 1914

'Race Within the Church III' TEW Oct 1914

'Mr Gandhi's Children' (letter) Tribune 10 Nov 1914

Documents Relating to the Indian Question Cape Town n.d. (1914?)

The Motherland, and other poems Allahabad 1916

'How India Can be Free' Madras 1921

'India and the Empire' Madras 1921

'National Education' Madras 1921

Hakim Ajmal Khan: A Sketch of his Life and Career Madras 1922

'The Oppression of the Poor' Madras 1922

'Buddhism and Christianity' MR Jul, Aug, Sep 1922

'Tribute to Principal Rudra' SSC Mag Easter 1923

'Christ and India' MR Mar 1924

'Old Delhi' MR Nov 1924 - Aug 1925

'A Quest for Truth' YMOI Aug - Dec 1928

Mahatma Gandhi's Ideas London 1929

Zaka Ullah of Delhi Cambridge 1929

India and the Simon Report London 1930

What I Owe to Christ London 1932

Christ in the Silence London 1933

Sadhu Sundar Singh: A Personal Memoir London 1934

India and Britain: A Moral Challenge London 1935

The Challenge of the North-West Frontier London 1937

(with G. Mookherjee) The Rise and Growth of the Congress London 1938

The Inner Life London 1939

The True India London 1939

'On the Rock of Faith' Stephanian Jun 1939

The Good Shepherd London 1940

Sandhya Meditations Madras 1940

The Sermon on the Mount London 1942

4. Books, reports and articles

Abhishiktananda Towards the Renewal of the Indian Church Cochin 1970

Abraham, C.E. The Founders of the National Missionary Society
    Madras 1947

Allnutt, S.S. 'Educational Work in 1885' CMD Occ. Paper No. 10,
    Cambridge 1886

----- 'Education as a Missionary Agency' Short Papers of the
    SPG and CMD, No. 6, St Albans 1897

----- 'What has happened in India?' DNM Jul 1911

----- 'The Racial Problem' DMN Jul 1911

----- 'Christian Indebtedness' DMN Oct 1914

Ambalavanar, D.J. The Gospel in the World: Essays in honour of

Bishop Kulandran Madras 1985

Amore, R.C. Two Masters, One Message. The lives and teachings of Gautama and Jesus Nashville 1978

Animananda, B. Swami Upadhyay Brahmabandhav Calcutta 1908

Argov, D. Moderates and Extremists in the Indian Nationalist Movement 1883-1920 London 1967

Armstrong, C.J.R. Evelyn Underhill (1875-1941) London 1975

Ashby, E. Universities: British, Indian, African. A Study in the Ecology of Education London 1966

Aziz, K.K. The Making of Pakistan: A Study in Nationalism London 1967

Baago, K. Pioneers of Indigenous Christianity Bangalore 1969

Barrier, N.G. 'The Punjab Disturbances of 1907; the response of the British Government in India to Agrarian Unrest' Modern Asian Studies I.iv 1967

Barrier, N.G. Banned: Controversial Literature and Political Control in British India 1907-47 Columbia 1974

Barrier, N.G. and Wallace, P. The Punjab Press 1880-1905 Michigan 1970

Basham, A.L. A Cultural History of India Oxford 1975

Behari, A. Liberty 1913

Bevan, E. Indian Nationalism: An Independent Estimate London 1913

Bickersteth, E. 'A Letter to Rev. Canon Westcott, D.D.' CMD Occ. Paper No. 2, Cambridge 1881

Bigg, C. The Church's Task Under the Roman Empire Oxford 1905

Birks, H. The Life and Correspondence of Thomas Valpy French, First Bishop of Lahore London 1895

Bolt, C. Victorian Attitudes to Race London 1971

Bondurant, J.V. The Conquest of Violence. The Gandhian Philosophy of Conflict Princeton (revised ed.) 1965

Borker, S. 'At the altar of National Freedom' Stephanian 1972-3

Boyd, R.H.S. An Introduction to Indian Christian Theology Madras 1969

Brown, E.C. Har Dayal, Hindu Revolutionary and Rationalist Arizona 1975

Brown, J.M. Gandhi's Rise to Power: Indian Politics 1915-1922

Cambridge 1972

Bruce, J.F. <u>A History of the University of the Panjab</u> Lahore 1933

Buck, E.J. <u>Simla Past and Present</u> Calcutta 1904

Bühlmann, W. <u>The Coming of the Third Church. An analysis of the present and future of the Church</u> (Eng. Tr.) Slough 1976

----- <u>The Church of the Future: A model for the year 2001</u> (Eng. tr.) New York 1986

<u>Bunch of Letters: To Rabindranath Tagore and M.K. Gandhi</u> Andrews' Papers No. 4, Calcutta 1971

Butler, H. <u>India Insistent</u> London 1931

Butler, H.M. 'Sermon by the Master of Trinity on the 50th Anniversary of the outbreak of the Mutiny at Delhi, 11 May 1907' <u>DMN</u> Jul 1907

<u>Cambridge Companion to the Bible</u> London 1893

Candler, E. <u>The Unveiling of Lhasa</u> London 1905

----- ('anon') <u>Siri Ram, Revolutionist. A Transcript from Life 1901-11</u> London 1912

Carter, J. 'Glimpses of Delhi' <u>DMN</u> Apr 1907

Chadwick, H. 'The Vindication of Christianity in Westcott's Thought' Cambridge 1960

Chadwick, O. 'Westcott and the University' Cambridge 1962

----- <u>The Victorian Church</u> London 1970

Chand, H. 'Our Trip to Hardwar' <u>SSC Mag</u> Jul 1910

Chandra, B. <u>The Rise and Growth of Economic Nationalism in India</u> New Delhi 1966

Chatterji, S.C. 'Indian Christians and National Ideals' <u>TEW</u> Apr 1914

Chaturvedi, B. and Sykes, M. <u>Charles Freer Andrews. A Narrative</u> London 1949

Chaudhuri, N.C. 'The True and the False' <u>TLS</u> 27 Sep 1974

Chirol, V. <u>Indian Unrest</u> London 1910

Clark, I.D.L. <u>C.F. Andrews - Deenabandhu</u> Delhi 1970

Cracknell, K. 'Why Dialogue? A First British Comment on the W.C.C. Guidelines' London 1980

Crosthwaite, A. <u>II Corinthians</u> Madras 1916

Daniélou, J. Couratin, A.H. and Kent J. <u>Historical Theology</u> Harmondsworth 1969

Darling, M. Apprentice to Power, India 1904-1908 London 1966

Datta, S.K. The Desire of India London 1908

Davies, A.W. 'The "New Thought" and the Missionary Message' SM
    Mar 1912

Dayal, H. 'Karl Marx: A Modern Rishi' MR Mar 1912

-----   'Yugantar Circular: The Delhi Bomb' San Francisco 1913

-----   Hints for Self-Culture ed. Bombay 1960

Dayananda, S. Satyarth Prakash (English trans.) Lahore 1908

The Day of Opportunity: A Report of the Proceedings of the S.P.G
    Summer School held at York 1912 London 1912

Deva, R. The Arya Samaj and Its Detractors Kangri 1911

Directory of Graduates of the University of the Panjab Up to and
    including the year 1914 Lahore 1919

Doke, J.J. M.K. Gandhi; An Indian Patriot in South Africa
    London 1909

Donaldson, St C. 'Varieties of Method of Missionary Work in India'
    TEW Jan 1904

Ebright, D.F. The National Missionary Society of India 1905-1942
    Chicago 1944

Eddy, G.S. A Pilgrimage of Ideas London 1935

Edwardes, M. The High Noon of Empire: India under Curzon
    London 1965

Edwards, D.L. Leaders of the Church of England 1828-1944 London 1971

Ellison, J. and Walpole, G.H.S. Church and Empire: A Series of
    Essays on the Responsibilities of Empire London 1908

Estborn, S. The Religion of Tagore in the Light of the Gospel
    Madras 1949

Farquhar, J.N. Gita and Gospel Madras 1903

-----   The College St Matthew Madras 1909

-----   The Crown of Hinduism Oxford 1913

-----   Modern Religious Movements in India New York 1915

-----   'Mr C.F. Andrews on Buddhism and Christianity' YMOI
                Sep 1922

Forman, H. The Arya Samaj. Its teachings and an estimate of it
    Allahabad 1887

Forrester, D.B. Caste and Christianity: Attitudes and Policies on

Caste of Anglo-Saxon Protestant Missions in India London 1980

Fraser, L. At Delhi Bombay 1903

French, T.V. 'The Proposed Cambridge University Mission in North India' Cambridge 1876

Gairdner, W.H.T. The Reproach of Islam London 1910

Gallagher, J., Johnston, G. and Seal, A. (eds.) Locality, Province and Nation. Essays on Indian Politics 1870-1940 Cambridge 1973

Gandhi, M.K. Satyagraha in South Africa Madras 1928

----- The Collected Works Delhi and Allahabad 1958 ff.

Gardner, C.E. The Life of Father Goreh London 1900

Ghose, S.A.C. 'The Indian Nation and Christianity' SM May 1907

Gilbert, M. Servant of India. A Study of Imperial Rule from 1905 to 1910 as told through the correspondence and diaries of Sir James Dunlop Smith London 1966

Gispert-Sauch, G., S.J. 'The Sanskrit Hymns of Brahmabandhav Upadhyay' Religion and Society Dec 1972

----- (ed.) God's Word Among Men Delhi 1973

Graham, G.F.I. The Life and Work of Sir Syed Ahmad Khan London 1909

Grimes, C.J. Towards an Indian Church London 1946

Guha, A.C. First Spark of Revolution: The Early Phase of India's Struggle for Independence 1900-1920 Bombay 1971

Hardie, J.K. India. Impressions and Suggestions London 1909

Hardinge, Lord My Indian Years 1910-1916 London 1948

Hartford, R.R. Godfrey Day: Missionary, Pastor and Primate Dublin 1940

Hayes, M.E. At Work. Letters of Marie Elizabeth Hayes, M.B., Missionary Doctor, Delhi 1905-8 London n.d.

Heiler, F. The Gospel of Sadhu Sundar Singh ed. Lucknow 1970

Heimsath, C.H. Indian Nationalism and Hindu Social Reform Princeton 1964

Henderson, L.F. (ed.) The Cambridge Mission to Delhi: A Brief History London 1931

Hibbert-Ware, G. 'The Place of Education in Missionary Work' CMD Occ. Paper No. 31, Cambridge 1904

-----   'Christ and the Oppressed Classes of India' Ep 17 Aug 1907

Hobson, J.A. Imperialism London 1902

Hocking, W.J. (ed.) The Church and New Century Problems London 1900

Holland, W.E.S. 'Young India' CMI May 1910

Hollis, M. Paternalism and the Church London 1962

Holroyd, M. Lytton Strachey: A Critical Biography London 1967

Hooper, W. Christian Doctrine in Contrast with Hinduism and Islam Madras 1896

Hooker, R.H. Journey into Varanasi London 1978

Hoyland, J.S. C.F. Andrews. Minister of Reconciliation London 1940

Huttenback, R.A. Gandhi in South Africa: British Imperialism and the Indian Question 1860-1914 Ithaca and London 1971

-----   Racism and Empire: White Settlers and Colored Immigrants in the British Self-Governing Colonies 1830-1910 Cornell 1976

Hyam, R. Britain's Imperial Century 1815-1914. A Study of Empire and Expansion London 1976

Jacob, E. Professor Yesudas Ramchandra of Delhi. A Memoir Cawnpore 1902

Jambunathan, R.R. (ed.) Swami Shraddhanand New Delhi 1961

Jones, K.W. Arya Dharm: Hindu Consciousness in 19th Century Punjab California 1976

Jones, P.d'A. The Christian Socialist Revival 1877-1914 Princeton 1968

Joshi, D.L. 'A Call to Indian Christians' CMI Mar 1906

Karve, D.G. and Ambedkar, D.V. (eds.) Speeches and Writings of Gopal Krishna Gokhale Poona 1967

Kaur, Rajkumari A. 'C.F. Andrews the Man' Stephanian 1964

Kiernan, V.G. The Lords of Humankind: European Attitudes to the outside world in the imperial age Harmondsworth 1972

Kingsley, C. Alexandria and Her Schools Cambridge 1854

Kipling, R. Plain Tales from the Hills ed. London 1890

Koss, J. John Morley at the India Office 1905-1910 Yale 1969

Kripalani, K. Rabindranath Tagore. A Biography London 1962

----- 'Andrews, Gandhi and Tagore' National Seminar, New Delhi 21 Nov 1971 (cyclostyled)

Krüger, H. 'Indian National Revolutionaries in Paris before World War I' Archiv Orientalni 4.45 Prague 1977

Latourette, K.S. 'Indigenous Christianity in the Light of History' IRM Oct 1940

----- Christianity in a Revolutionary Age New York 1958

Lefroy, G.A. 'The Leather Workers of Daryaganj' CMD Occ. Paper No. 7 Cambridge 1884

----- 'Missionary Work in India' CMD Occ. Paper No. 12, Cambridge 1887

----- 'Christ the Goal of India' CMD Occ. Paper No. 15, Cambridge 1889

----- 'Mohammedanism, Its Strengths and Weaknesses' CMD Occ. Paper No. 21, Cambridge 1894

----- 'The Moral Tone of India' TEW Apr 1903

----- 'British Indians in the Transvaal: An Empire Problem' TEW Jan 1909

Leitner, G.W. History of Indigenous Education in the Panjab since Annexation and in 1882 Calcutta 1882

Lillingston, F. The Brahmo Somaj and Arya Somaj in their bearing upon Christianity London 1901

Low, D.A. Lion Rampant: Essays in the Study of British Imperialism London 1973

-----(ed.) Soundings in Modern South Asian History London 1968

M.S. 'Glimpses of a Forgotten Stephanian' Stephanian 1972-3

McClymont, A.W. The Travelling Bookman: John Murdoch of Madras London 1947

MacDonald, J.R. The Awakening of India London 1910

----- 'India and South Africa' SSC Mag Jan 1914

McDonough, S. The Authority of the Past: A Study of Three Muslim Modernists 1970

Macnicol, N. 'Spiritual Forces in India' Contemporary Review Sep 1909

----- C.F. Andrews, Friend of India London 1944

Majumdar, R.C., Raychaudhuri, H.C. and Datta, K. An Advanced History
of India London
1964

Mason, P. Patterns of Dominance London 1970

Maurice, F.D. The Religions of the World and their Relation to
Christianity London 1846

----- Lincoln's Inn Sermons ed. London 1892

Meer, F. Apprenticeship of a Mahatma Phoenix 1970

'A Member of the Brotherhood of the Imitation' Divine Incarnation
Madras 1913

Milburn, R.G. 'Christian Vedantism' Ind Int Jan 1913

Minto, Mary, Countess of India: Minto and Morley 1905-1910
London 1935

Minz, N. Mahatma Gandhi and Hindu-Christian Dialogue Madras 1970

Monk, F.F. St Stephen's College, Delhi. A History Calcutta 1935

Montgomery, H.H. Foreign Missions London 1902

----- Life and Letters of George Alfred Lefroy London
1920

----- (ed.) Mankind and the Church, Being an Attempt to
Estimate the Responsibilities of the Great Races
to the Fulness of the Church of God. By Seven
Bishops London 1907

Mudford, P. Birds of a Different Plumage: A Study of British-
Indian Relations from Akbar to Curzon London 1974

Mukarji, S.N. 'Address by the Principal at the Memorial Service held
in College, May 4 1940' Stephanian Jun 1940

Mukerji, S.C. 'The Presentation of Christianity to Hindus' Ind Int
Apr 1909

Mukherjee, H. and U.M. The Origins of the National Education
Movement (1905-1910) Calcutta 1957

Müller, M. India: What can it teach us? London 1883

Murdoch, J. Vedic Hinduism and the Arya Samaj: An Appeal to
Educated Hindus Madras 1902

Myrdal, G. Asian Drama: An Inquiry into the Poverty of Nations
London 1968

Nanda, B.R. 'C.F. Andrews: The Bridge-Builder' National Seminar,

New Delhi 21 Nov 1971 (cyclostyled)

Nehru, J. An Autobiography: With Musings on Recent Events in India
Delhi 1936

Neill, S. A History of Christian Missions Harmondsworth 1964

Newsome, D. Two Classes of Men: Platonism and English Romantic
Thought London 1974

O'Connor, D. The Testimony of C.F. Andrews Madras 1974

O'Dwyer, G. India as I knew it 1885–1925 London 1925

Oldham, J.H. Christianity and the Race Problem London 1924

O'Malley, L.S.S. (ed.) Modern India and the West London 1941

Owen, R. and Sutcliffe, B. Studies in the Theory of Imperialism
London 1972

Pakenham–Walsh, H. I–III John Madras 1910

Palmer, M. History of the Indians in Natal Cape Town 1957

The Pan–Anglican Congress 1908 London 1908

Pannikar, K.M. Common Sense About India London 1960

Paradkar, B.A. Theology of Goreh Bangalore 1969

Parliamentary Debates 4th Series Vol. 170 London 1907

Paul, R.D. They Kept the Faith Lucknow 1968

Pearson, W.W. Shantiniketan: The Bolpur School of Rabindranath
Tagore London 1917

Pelly, A.C. 'The First Summer School of Study in India' SM Oct 1911

Pfander, C.G. The Mizanu'l Haqq English ed. London 1910

Phillips, G.E. The Outcaste's Hope: Or Work Among the Depressed
Classes in India London 1912

Polak, H.S.L. M.K. Gandhi Madras 1909?

-----   The Indians of South Africa: helots within the empire
and how they are treated Madras 1909

-----   'Indians in the Transvaal' Tribune 29 Aug 1909

-----   'The Spirit of the Transvaal Indian Struggle' Ind Int
Oct 1909

-----   'The Transvaal Indians' MR May 1910

Polak H.S.L., Brailsford, H.N. and Pethick–Lawrence, Lord, Mahatma
Gandhi London 1949

Potts, E.D. British Baptist Missionaries in India 1793–1837
Cambridge 1967

Radhakrishnan, S. Eastern Religions and Western Thought second ed.
                 London, 1940
Rai, L.L. The Story of My Deportation Lahore 1908
Raleigh, T. (ed.) Lord Curzon in India. Being a Selection from His
                 Speeches as Viceroy and Governor-General of
                 India 1898-1905 London 1906
Ram, L.R. The Rules and the Scheme of Studies of the Gurukula,
                 Sanctioned by the Arya Pratindhi Sabha, Punjab
                 Lahore 1902
Ram, M. The Gurukula Through European Eyes Kangri 1914
Ramachandran, G. Presidential Address, National Seminar, New Delhi
                 20 Nov 1971 (cyclostyled)
Report of the 22nd Indian National Congress held at Calcutta on the
     26th to 29th December 1906 Calcutta 1907
Report of the Conference of the World Student Christian Federation
     Robert College, Constantinople April 24-28 1911 London 1911
Robertson, E.H. Lund 1952: An Account of the Third World Conference
     on Faith and Order London 1952
Robinson, F. Letters to His Friends London 1904
Roy, M.C. 'Indian Christians and the National Movement' MR May 1910
Roy, R.M. English Works Allahabad 1906
Royal Commission on Public Services in India London 1915
Roychaudhury, P.C. C.F. Andrews: his life and times Bombay 1971
Rudra, Sudhir K. 'The Student Movement: The Call of India' YMOI
     Jan 1914
Rudra, S.K. 'Some Stray Musings of an Indian Visitor' DMN Oct 1905
-----   'Is India Thirsting for Religious Truth' TEW Jan 1906
-----   'Missionary Education in India' Pan-Anglican Papers 1908
-----   'Indian Students: Their Training and Guidance in
                 Missionary Colleges' CMD Unnumbered Papers. London
                 1910
-----   'Christ and Modern India' SM Jan 1910
-----   'Indian National Missionary Work' YMOI Dec 1910
-----   'The Christian Idea of the Incarnation' Madras 1911
-----   'Religious Changes in India during the British Period'
                 TEW Jul 1913

----- 'An Indian Christian's Confession of Faith' SM Jun 1912

Said, E.W. Orientalism London 1978

Samartha, S.J. The Hindu Response to the Unbound Christ Madras 1974

----- (ed.) Living Faiths and the Ecumenical Movement Geneva 1971

Schweitzer, E. The Quest of the Historical Jesus tr. London 1910

Seeley, J.R. The Expansion of England London 1883

Seshagiri Rao, K.L. Mahatma Gandhi and C.F. Andrews: A Study in
Hindu-Christian Dialogue Patiala 1969

Sharp, H. Delhi: Its Story and Buildings London 1921

Sharpe, E.J. Not to Destroy But to Fulfil: The Contribution of J.N.
Farquhar to Protestant Missionary Thought in India
before 1914 Uppsala 1965

----- Faith Meets Faith. Some Christian Attitudes to
Hinduism in the 19th and 20th Centuries London 1977

Shaw, P.E. The Catholic Apostolic Church, sometimes called
Irvingite. A Historical Study New York 1964

Singh, H. (ed.) Approaches to the Study of Religion Patiala n.d.

Singh, S. Freedom Movement in Delhi (1858-1919) New Delhi 1972

Singha, S.S. 'A Retreat near Delhi' SM May 1909

----- More Yarns About India London n.d.

Sitaramayya, B.P. The History of the Indian National Congress 1885-
1935 Allahabad 1935

Smith, W.C. Modern Islam in India: A Social Analysis Lahore 1943

----- 'Participation: The Changing Christian Role in Other
Cultures' Occasional Bulletin New York, Apr 1969

Smith, W. and Wace, H. A Dictionary of Christian Biography London
1877 ff.

Spear, T.G.P. 'C.F. Andrews' Stephanian Jun 1940

----- India, Pakistan and the West London 1949

----- The Twilight of the Mughuls: Studies in Late Mughul
Delhi Cambridge 1951

----- India: A Modern History Ann Arbor 1961

----- A History of India Vol. 2. Harmondsworth 1965

Stanton, V.H. (ed.) The Story of the Delhi Mission London 1908

Stokes, S.E. 'Interpreting Christ to India' TEW Apr 1908

----- ('anon') 'A Scheme for a Christian Gurukula' n.d.

-----   The Love of God: A Book of Prose and Verse
      Croydon 1908

-----   The Historical Character of the Gospel Madras 1913

Sudarisanam, A.N. (ed.) Rethinking Christianity in India Madras 1938

Summary of the Administration of Lord Hardinge of Penshurst, Viceroy
 and Governor-General of India, November 1910-March 1916
 Delhi 1916

Sundkler, B. The Church of South India: The Movement towards Union
      1900-1947 London 1954

Sykes, M. 'The Rebel Devotee' (pamphlet) Calcutta 1971

-----   C.F. Andrews: Representative Writings New Delhi 1973

Tagore, Gitanjali (Song Offerings) London 1912

Tandon, P. Panjabi Century 1857-1947 London 1963

Tatlow, T. The Story of the Student Christian Movement in Great
      Britain and Ireland London 1933

Taylor, R.F.L. In the Land of the Five Rivers Edinburgh 1906

Taylor, R.W. (ed.) Society and Religion: Essays in Honour of M.M.
      Thomas Madras 1976

Thomas, M.M. The Christian Response to the Asian Revolution
      Lucknow 1967

-----   The Acknowledged Christ of the Indian Renaissance
      Madras 1970

-----   The Secular Ideologies of India and the Secular Meaning
      of Christ Madras 1976

Thompson, E.J. Rabindranath Tagore: His Life and Work Calcutta 1921

Tinker, H. A New System of Slavery: The Export of Indian Labour
      Overseas 1830-1920 London 1974

-----   Separate and Unequal: India and the Indians in the
      British Commonwealth 1920-1950 London 1976

-----   The Ordeal of Love: C.F. Andrews and India Delhi 1979

Tirath, R. In Woods of God-Realization Delhi 1910

Tirath, S.D. 'The Work of a Christian Preacher' Ind Int Oct 1911

Tripathi, A. The Extremist Challenge: India between 1890 and 1910
      Delhi 1967

Walker, T. Philippians Madras 1909

-----   Acts of the Apostles Madras 1912

Waller, E.H.M. The Revelation of St John the Divine Madras 1909

Weber, H.R. Asia and the Ecumenical Movement 1895-1961 London 1966

Webster, J.C.B. The Christian Community and Change in 19th Century
           North India Delhi 1976

-----   'Arya Evidences - A Study of Christian influence'
           Indian Church History Review Jul 1978

Weitbrecht, H.U. St Matthew Madras 1912

Westcott, A. (ed.) Life and Letters of B.F. Westcott London 1903

Westcott, B.F. On Some Points in the Religious Office of the
           Universities London 1873

-----   'Origen and the Beginnings of Christian Philosophy'
           Contemporary Review May, Jun 1879

-----   'The Cambridge Mission and Higher Education at Delhi'
           CMD Occ. Paper No. 3. Cambridge 1882

-----   Social Aspects of Christianity London 1887

-----   Essays in the History of Religious Thought in the
           West London 1891

-----   The Gospel of Life: Thoughts Introductory to the
           The Study of Christian Doctrine London 1892

-----   'The Obligations of Empire' (pamphlet) London 1900

Western, F.J. 'The Lahore Diocesan Conference' DMN Jan 1907

-----   The Early History of the Cambridge Mission to Delhi
           (cyclostyled) 1950

Whaling, F. 'Indian Christian Theology - The Humanity of Christ and
           the New Humanity' Scottish Journal of Theology 31.4
           1978

Whitehead, H. 'Our Mission Policy in India' Guardian 4 Sep 1907

Williams, R.T. Exposure of Dayananda Saraswate Delhi 1889

-----   A Farce - A Religion professedly based on a book,
           which, as translated for that religion, has no
           existence (3 vols.) Rewari 1892, 4, 5

Winslow, J.C. The Eyelids of the Dawn London 1954

Wolpert, S.A. Tilak and Gokhale: Revolution and Reform in the
           Making of Modern India Berkeley and Los
           Angeles 1962

Wood, H.G. Frederick Denison Maurice Cambridge 1950

Woodcock, G. Anarchism: A History of Libertarian Ideas and
                 Movements Harmondsworth 1975

World Missionary Conference 1910 Report Edinburgh and London 1910

Yanuck, M. 'The Kanpur Mosque Affair of 1913' Muslim World Oct 1974

Yazdani, G. 'C.F. Andrews' Stephanian Jun 1940

Young, C.B. 'C.F. Andrews' Stephanian Jun 1940

Young, R.F. Resistant Hinduism: Sanskrit Sources of Anti-Christian
                 Apologetics in Early 19th Century India Vienna 1981

Zaehner, R.C. Hinduism Oxford 1966

INDEX

Abyssinia 223

Acton, Lord 16, 122f, 135, 150

Ahmad, Nazir 216ff, 297

Akhbar, emperor 135

Alexandria, Alexandrian Fathers 7ff, 18, 21, 22, 24, 39, 54, 164, 195,
     200, 204, 235, 262, 301, 303

Ali, Maulana Mohammed 251, 266

Aligarh Movement, Aligarh School 216, 218, 219, 222, 265

Allahabad 83

All-Indian Theistic Conference 137

Allnutt, Samuel Scott 14, 19, 22, 27, 39, 64, 66, 79, 85, 87, 93, 99, 104,
     127, 131, 145, 153, 157, 167, 169ff, 184, 202, 235, 245, 269, 271,
     278, 285, 287, 289, 293f, 296, 298, 299

Ambala 238

Ampthill, Lord 30, 65, 272

Andrews Court (St Stephen's College) 301

Andrews, John Edward (father) 14

Andrews, Mary Charlotte (mother) 231

Arya Samaj   54, 167, 214, 234ff, 268, 269, 270, 271, 294

Arya Samaj Gurukula, Hardwar   22, 179, 207, 235ff, 269, 270, 273, 282f

Arya Samaj Mandir, Simla   228

Asoka, emperor   135

Azad, Maulana   251

Azariah, V.S.   61, 157, 167, 202, 204

Bahksh, Canon Ali   160, 195, 202

Bakunin, M.A.   130

Balfour, Lord   145

Ball, Canon   70

Ballantyne, J.R.   13

Balliol College, Oxford   270

'Bande Mataram'   271

Banerjea, Krishna Mohan   13, 193

Bannerjee, Surendranath   85, 86, 88, 98, 149

Banerji, Kali Charan   86

Baptists   184f, 283f

Bateman, R.   209

Behari, Awadh 128f, 152

Benares (Varanasi) 80, 215, 256

Bengal 43, 80, 121, 225ff, 278

Bengalee 90 et passim

Besant, Annie 86

Bhagavad Gita 242

'Bibilotheca Indica' 297

Bickersteth, E.H. 7, 235

Bickersteth Hall, Delhi 266

Birdwood, Sir George 182

Birmingham 14, 99

Bishop's College, Calcutta 202

Blakiston, C.R.N. 101, 298

Boden Sanskrit Scholar, Oxford 297

Bombay (Bombay) 80

Bombay, Bishop of (E.J. Palmer) 256

Bose, Rash Behari 128

Brahmo Samaj 60, 137, 225ff, 266, 294

Brahmo Samaj Mandir, Calcutta   276

Brahmo Samaj Mandir, Lahore   124, 225

Brahmo Samaj Mandir, Simla   228

Branch, Mr   270

Bright, John   219

British Guiana   272

Brotherhood of the Imitation of Jesus   156, 178ff, 230

Brown, Canon E.F.   85, 99

Browne, E.G.   16

Buddha, Buddhist ideal   229, 233, 255, 257

Burdwar   289

Burrows, R.M.   147

Butler, Sir Harcourt   279, 291

Butler (R.A.), Lord   297

Butler, H.M. (Trinity College, Cambridge)   15, 65

Calcutta   43, 80, 161

Calcutta, Bishop of (R.S. Copleston)   204

Callaway, R.F.   189f

Cambridge 8, 15ff, 28, 37, 61, 105, 169ff, 290

Cambridge Committee 27f, 168, 283, 285

Cambridge Mission to Delhi, Delhi Mission, Cambridge Brotherhood 6, 7ff,
18ff, 25f, 48, 87, 119, 121, 127, 145, 161, 167ff, 216, 223, 235,
245, 272, 278, 283, 285, 289, 291, 292, 301, 304

Campbell, R.J. 155

Candler, E. 270

Canning, Lord 105

Cape Town 228, 248, 254, 260, 274

Cape Town, Archbishop of 247

Carey, W. 13

Carlyon, H.C. 170f

Catholic Apostolic Church 14f, 17

Cawnpore (Kanpur) 161, 221f

Cecil, Lord Hugh 146

Celsus 7

Chaitanya 174

Chakkarai, V. 200, 204, 211

Chand, Amir 88, 127ff, 153, 213f, 264

Chatterjee, K.C. 270

Chatterji, Justice P.C. 60

Chatterji, Ramananda 90

Chenchiah, P. 157, 200, 211

Chirol, V. 132

Christa Seva Sangh, Poona 183, 209

Christian Endeavour 156

Christian Social Union 17, 116

Christianity and the Conflict Between Capital and Labour (Burney Prize
        Essay) 17, 141

Church Missionary Intelligencer 50 et passim

Church Missionary Society 7, 43, 50, 157, 174, 184, 207, 209

Church of England in India 103, 166

Church Times 92, 157, 214 et passim

Civil and Military Gazette 68ff, 75, 76, 92, 95

Clement of Alexandria 11, 13

Clerk Maxwell, J. 12

Columbia, Bishop of 147

Convention of Religions (1911) 210

Coomaraswamy, A.K. 123

Corrie, D. 209

Cotton, Sir Henry 72

Cuddesdon 270

Cunningham, B.K. 93, 101, 287, 298

Curzon, Lord, Viceroy 30, 31, 34, 35, 41, 51, 56, 65, 70, 74, 272, 279

Dar, Bishan Narayan 104

Das, Ishwar 126

Das, Tulsi 257

Datta, S.K. 61

Davitt, Michael 130

Day, J.G.F. 39, 42, 59, 202

Dayal, Har 28, 106, 127ff, 152

Dayal, Raghubar 40, 59, 85, 88, 106, 126, 152

Dayanand Anglo-Vedic College, Lahore 235

Dayananda, Swami 234, 235, 237, 243, 244

Delhi College 216

Delhi Conspiracy 128, 228

Delhi Durbar   106, 115

Delhi Mission News   50, 92, et passim

Derozio, H.L.   131

Deussen, P.   213

Deva, Ram   243, 271

Devanandan, P.D.   200

Dev Samaj   214

Director of Criminal Intelligence   127

Duff, Alexander   43

Dunlop-Smith, Sir James   60, 108

Durban   273

Durban Cathedral   248

Durham   15f

Durrant, H.B. (4th Bishop of Lahore)   287f

Dutt, R.   107

East and West   100

The East and the West   50, 92 et passim

Eddy, G.S.   167

Edessa 7

Edward VI, King 33

Edwardes, H. 105

Epiphany 91, 123, 157 et passim

Episcopal Synod (1900, 1908) 76f, 166

Fairbairn, A.M. 210

Farquhar, J.N. 94, 114, 120, 125, 132, 134, 136, 154, 157, 208, 214, 257,
    258, 260, 289, 294, 300

Fiji 272

Fleetwood-Wilson, Sir Guy 145

Forman College, Lahore 39,40, 83

Fraser, A.G. 204

French, A. 272

French, B.P.W. 169

French, T.V. (1st Bishop of Lahore) 7ff, 19, 24, 173, 195, 200, 209, 301

Gandhi, M.K. 1, 2, 23, 44, 61, 102f, 104, 149, 233, 244ff, 251, 295ff,
    273, 274, 275, 276, 277, 287, 293, 302

Garde, Dr. (Gadre?) 133

Gardiner, A.F. 285

Garibaldi, G.   130

Gascoyne-Cecil, The Revd Lord William   285

Ghose, B.N.   209

Ghose, J.J.   160

Ghose, S.A.C.   40, 42, 53, 59, 78, 99, 117f, 127, 158, 173, 195, 202, 206

Gitanjali   226, 227, 229, 232, 233, 267

Gladstone, W.   219

Gladstone, Lord   228

Gokhale, G.K.   35, 39, 86, 98, 99, 107, 109, 117, 247, 248, 255, 273, 275,
     291

Gore, C.   43, 164, 191

Goreh, N.N.   13, 193, 195

Government College, Lahore   39, 127

Greaves, E.   197

Gupta, Ishwar Chandra   36

Guardian   92, 157

Gurdaspur   238

Hailey, W.M.   291

Hardinge, Lord, Viceroy   35, 100, 108, 128, 145, 222f, 228, 238f, 246, 250,

290, 293

Hardinge, Lady 238f, 271

Harnack, A. 194, 196

Hasan, Faizal 27

Hibbert-Ware, G. 39, 41, 58, 59, 168, 202, 203

Hilary of Poitiers 155

Hindu-Buddhist ideal 232f, 242, 253, 259ff, 268, 287

Hinduism 47, 54, 214, 219, 225ff, 234ff, 244ff, 255ff

Hindustan Review 90 et passim

Hissar 268

Hobson, J.A. 104, 146

Holland, W.E.S. 238, 270

Hooper, W. 195

Hope, Sir Theodore 298

Hort, F.J.A. 172

Hoshiarpur 270

Hoyland, J.S. 100, 239f, 262

Hume, R.A. 97

Ibbetson, Sir Denzil 66

Imad-ud Din 26, 195, 209

Imam, Sir Ali 222, 265

Indenture 244ff

Indian Association Hall, Phagli 248

Indian Church Commentaries 157, 194

Indian Councils (Minto-Morley) Act (1909) 87, 102, 121, 127, 152

Indian Interpreter 91, 123 et passim

Indian Mission, Durban 272

Indian Missionary School of Study 156, 214

Indian National Congress 80ff, 89, 98, 117, 121, 122, 140, 245, 246,
  278, 279

Indian Review 90, 142 et passim

Indian Witness 91 et passim

Indian World 100

Isananda, Swami 178

Islam 22, 26, 38, 54, 214, 215ff, 258, 261, 265

Jacob, Mr. 207

Japan 37, 159, 202

Julian 7

Justin 12

Kabir 229

Kathiawar 252

Keir Hardic, J. 59, 146

Kelley, W.S. 170

Khan, Hakim Ajmal 122, 216, 251

Khan, Sir Syed Ahmad 216, 218f

Khilafat 251

Kikuyu Controversy 210

Kingsley, C. 13, 22

Kipling, R. 56, 68

Kitchener, Lord 78, 110

Kotgarh 174

Kumarappa 61

Labour Movement 159

Lahore 43, 54, 65, 68, 76, 83, 234, 273, 288

Lahore Cathedral 83, 288, 289, 292f, 304

Lahore Diocesan Conference (1906, 1909) 62, 82, 160, 166, 172

Lahore Diocese 82, 184

Lahore Divinity School 7ff, 195

Lahore Indian Association 72

Lahore University - see Punjab University, Lahore

Lal, Gobind Bihari 43, 126, 127

Lal, Harkishen 83, 85, 97

Lal, Joel Waiz 297

Lal, Parmeshwar 84

Lambeth Conference (1908) 77

Latourette, K.S. 165

Lawrence, Sir Henry 105

Lawrence Military Asylum/School, Sanawar 67, 71, 95

Lee, J. 298

Lefroy, G.A. (3rd Bishop of Lahore) 14, 19, 22, 23, 31, 51, 67, 74ff, 89,
         96, 103, 104, 105, 117, 161, 166, 167, 170f, 174, 177, 180, 194,
         195ff, 204, 218, 223f, 235, 245, 247, 265, 271, 273, 285f, 289

Libanius 7

Lightfoot, J.B. 14

Lindsay Commission   284

London   255

Lucknow Diocese   82

Lund   185

Macaulay, T.B.   229, 279f

MacDonald, J. Ramsay   38, 132, 139, 154, 237, 246, 270, 273

Machhli Bazar Mosque, Cawnpore   222f, 266

McLeod Campbell, J.   194

Macmillan, Mr.   207

Macmillan and Co.   227, 267

Macnicol, N.   91, 94, 123, 132, 214f

Madras   246

Majeetia, Sirdar Dayal Singh   88

Majumdar, A.C.   60

Malaviya, Madan Mohan   83, 84

Marsh, N.C.   169

Marx, K.   130, 139

Masih, Abdul   209

Maurice, F.D. 13, 18, 134, 139, 140, 141, 155

Mauritius 272

Mazzini, G. 130, 137

Mecca 220

Medina 220

Meston, Sir John 145, 222, 239, 266, 271, 290

Metcalfe, Sir Charles 76

Micklem, N. 215, 264

Milburn, R.G. 276

Mill, J.S. 150

Mill, W.A. 13, 210

Miller, W. 97

Minto, Lord, Viceroy 31, 65, 72, 76, 78, 79, 108, 132, 246, 272, 273

Modern Review 90 et passim

Mohammedan Anglo-Oriental College, Aligarh 216, 222

Monier-Williams, M. 13

Monkwearmouth 17

Montgomery, H.H. 62, 93, 164, 191, 271, 284ff, 289, 298

Morley, John, Viscount   72, 75, 79, 96

Mott, J.R.   300

Muir, J.   13

Mukerji, N.C.   116

Müller, M.   13, 19, 62

Murdoch, J.   94

Muslim League   122

Naoroji, Dadabhai   81, 85f, 107

Natesan, G.A.   142, 245

Nath, Lala Baij   213

National Education   85, 228, 237, 279ff, 296

National Missionary Intelligencer   91, 157, 167ff et passim

National Missionary Society   156, 183, 186

Nehru, Jawaharlal   101, 251

Nehru, Motilal   251

Nestorian Church   230

Nevinson, W.C.   226, 273

Newcastle   14

Nicholls, G.E. 32

Nicholson, Sir John 65

Nisibis 7

Nivedita, Sister (Margaret Noble) 300

Nobel Prize for Literature 226, 248

Non-Cooperation 251

North India 92, 111, 156f, 214 et passim

Nundy, Alfred 89, 100

O'Dwyer, Sir Michael 34, 271

Oldham, J.H. 148

Origen 11ff

Outram, Sir James 105

Oxford 121, 127, 297

Oxford Brotherhood, Oxford Mission, Calcutta 43, 48, 85, 123

Pal, B.C. 85

Palestine, Holy Land 241, 261

Pan-Anglican Congress (1908) 77, 103, 104, 107, 147, 156, 161, 164,
    204, 256

Panjabee 88 et passim

Papworth, J.W.   71

Pariala   27, 270

Paul, K.T.   61, 157, 160, 168, 204

Pearson, W.W.   229, 248, 251

Pembroke College, Cambridge   15f

Pembroke College Mission   15ff, 296

Pennell, J.L.   96

Petrovskie, S.   130

Pfander, C.G.   195

Pioneer   92 et passim

Plato, Neo-Platonism   10, 11, 54, 63, 228, 259, 303

Polak, H.   247, 249, 273

Porphyry   7

Pound, E.   267

Prarthana Samaj   137

Prem Sangat   214

Presbyterians   184

Pretoria Cathedral   248

Prior, C.H.   16

Provincial Synod (1912)   166f

Punjab   31, 35f, 39, 54, 66, 85, 87, 88, 102, 158, 177, 202, 215, 234ff,
    273, 304

Punjab University, Lahore   22, 25, 236, 279, 297

Purton, G.A.   169, 202

Qur'an   216, 218

Rai, Lajpat   36, 59, 71, 88, 127, 151

Ram, Munshi (Swami Shraddhanand)   22, 44, 207, 237ff, 248, 249, 250, 251,
253, 259ff, 271, 274, 288, 289, 293, 294

Ram, Thandi   282

Ranade, M.G.   107, 117, 123

Rawalpindi   27

Raza, Syed Haidar   88, 126, 127

Redman, J.C.   174

Renaissance in India   92, 157, 214f, 259 et passim

Rewari   269

Ripon, Lord, Viceroy   64

Risley, H.   213

Rivaz, Sir Charles   72

Robertson, A.   91, 94, 123

Robinson, F.   16, 82

Roman Catholic Church 205, 211

Roman Empire   31ff, 97, 280f, 292

Rosebery, Lord   150

Rothenstein, W.   226, 227

Rousseau, J.J.   130

Roy, Ram Mohun   36, 225, 234

Royal Asiatic Society   297

Royal Commission on the Public Services in India (1912)   270

Royal Visit (1911-12)   102, 106f, 146, 239

Rudra, P.M.   43

Rudra, Suddhir   44, 67, 139, 243

Rudra, Susil Kumar   18, 23, 38, 39, 43ff, 53, 61, 62, 67, 75, 93, 95, 106,
    110, 117, 127, 131, 136, 141, 158, 160f, 163, 165, 166, 167ff, 173,
    175f, 192f, 202, 203, 205, 206, 209, 211, 214, 235, 240, 245, 250,
    256, 273, 278, 280, 283ff, 287, 289, 291, 293, 295, 298, 299, 301,
    302

Sabathu   175

St John's College, Agra 7

St Stephen's College, Delhi 14, 18, 25, 26, 38ff, 44, 49f, 58, 59, 60, 82,
        95, 106, 126ff, 175, 206, 214, 217, 235, 247, 269, 273, 278, 279,
        282ff, 290f, 295, 299

St Stephen's College Magazine 92, 246 et passim

Santiniketan 1, 227, 228, 229, 231f, 237, 278, 282f, 288, 289, 292, 293ff

Sapru, Tej Bahadur 83

Sargodha 238

Schweitzer, A. 204

Seeley, J.R. 109, 280

Sen, K.C. 203

Serampore 167

Sermon on the Mount 41, 54f, 252

Shah, M. Ahmad 276

Shams-ud Din 26, 32, 56, 88

Sharp, C. 236

Simla 26, 30, 32f, 43, 56, 153, 174f, 228, 232, 293

Singh, Kirthi 65

Singh, Puran 264

Singh, Sundar   174ff, 206, 207, 209, 302

Singha, Shoran   206

Sinha, Saccidananda   90

Siri Ram, Revolutionist   238

Smith, V.   154

Smuts, J.C.   248, 255

Society for the Propagation of the Gospel   146, 161, 184, 186, 191, 256, 283ff

Socrates   195

South Africa   2, 77, 103, 190, 228, 244ff, 260, 261, 272, 273, 287, 288

South African Indian Committee   272

Southwark Cathedral   269

Spectator   92

Staffordshire   227

Stanton, V.H.   19, 27f, 271, 286

Stead, W.T.   80

Stock, E.   194

Stokes, S.E.   174ff, 206, 207, 208, 209, 278

Straits Settlements   272

Student Christian Movement   156

Student Movement   92, 157 et passim

Student Volunteer Missionary Movement   156

Sundkler, B.   187

Surat   87, 127

Syrian Church   230

Tagore, Abanindranath   123, 251

Tagore, Maharshi Devendranath   226, 228, 231f

Tagore, Rabindranath   44, 61, 109, 119, 203, 226ff, 237, 240, 248, 249,
      250, 251, 253, 259ff, 267, 271, 274, 276, 277, 278, 289, 291,
      293ff, 302

Tagore, Satyendranath   266

Talbot, E.S.   15, 290, 296

Tatlow, T.   82

Tavernier   130

Tennyson, A.   41

Thomas, M.M.   200, 211

Tibet   30, 34f

Tilak, B.G.   85, 88, 133, 251

Timur, House of   217, 218

Tirath, Swami Dhar   178, 207

Tirath, Swami Ram   213f, 264

Tolstoy, L.N.   252, 275

Tranquebar   187

Tribute   73, 75f, 88f, 98, 100, 118, 153, 304 et passim

Trinity College, Cambridge   270

Ullah, Zaka   216ff, 261

Underhill, E.   230, 232

Upadhyaya, Brahmabandhab   13, 193, 210

Upanishads   229, 242, 253

Vaishnava Hymns   229

Vassulitch, V.   130

Vaswani, T.L.   155

Vedas, Vedanta, Vedic   54, 213, 235, 236, 237, 242, 258, 276, 283

Victoria, Queen   70, 71, 105, 218

Vivekanand   174, 300

Voltaire, F.M.A.   130

Walworth   17

Weitbrecht, H.U.   208

Westcott, Basil   16, 18

Westcott, Brook Foss   7ff, 14ff, 21, 77, 103, 139, 141, 154, 155, 158,
      171f, 195, 200, 204, 210, 214, 262, 290, 301, 302, 304

Westcott, Foss   17, 166, 204

Westcott, George   17, 210

Westcott House, Cambridge   15

Western, F.J.   168ff, 178ff, 202, 286

Whitehead, H.A., Bishop of Madras   115, 161ff

Williams, R.T.   235, 269

Winslow, J.C.   209

Winter, R.R.   13

World Missionary Conference (Edinburgh 1910)   77, 145, 156, 161, 163, 164,
      173, 177, 186, 198f, 204, 256, 257, 285

World Student Christian Federation (1907, 1911)   147, 156, 184, 202

Wright, J.W.T.   18, 39, 44

Yazdani, Gulam   297

Yeats, W.B.   226

Young, C.B.   283f, 289, 294, 300

Young, P.N.F.   98, 264

Young Liberals League   100

Young Men of India   92,   157 et passim

Y.M.C.A. Triennial Convention (1907)   112

Zaka Ullah of Delhi   221 et passim

STUDIEN ZUR INTERKULTURELLEN GESCHICHTE DES CHRISTENTUMS
ETUDES D'HISTOIRE INTERCULTURELLE DU CHRISTIANISME
STUDIES IN THE INTERCULTURAL HISTORY OF CHRISTIANITY

Begründet von/fondé par/founded by
Hans Jochen Margull †, Hamburg

Herausgegeben von/edité par/edited by

Richard Friedli   Walter J. Hollenweger   Theo Sundermeier
Université de Fribourg   University of Birmingham   Universität Heidelberg

Jan A.B. Jongeneel
Rijksuniversiteit Utrecht

Band   1   Wolfram Weiße: Südafrika und das Antirassismusprogramm. Kirchen im Spannungsfeld einer Rassengesellschaft.

Band   2   Ingo Lembke: Christentum unter den Bedingungen Lateinamerikas. Die katholische Kirche vor den Problemen der Abhängigkeit und Unterentwicklung.

Band   3   Gerd Uwe Kliewer: Das neue Volk der Pfingstler. Religion, Unterentwicklung und sozialer Wandel in Lateinamerika.

Band   4   Joachim Wietzke: Theologie im modernen Indien - Paul David Devanandan.

Band   5   Werner Ustorf: Afrikanische Initiative. Das aktive Leiden des Propheten Simon Kimbangu.

Band   6   Erhard Kamphausen: Anfänge der kirchlichen Unabhängigkeitsbewegung in Südafrika. Geschichte und Theologie der äthiopischen Bewegung. 1880-1910.

Band   7   Lothar Engel: Kolonialismus und Nationalismus im deutschen Protestantismus in Namibia 1907-1945. Beiträge zur Geschichte der deutschen evangelischen Mission und Kirche im ehemaligen Kolonial- und Mandatsgebiet Südwestafrika.

Band   8   Pamela M. Binyon: The Concepts of "Spirit" and "Demon". A Study in the use of different languages describing the same phenomena.

Band   9   Neville Richardson: The World Council of Churches and Race Relations. 1960 to 1969.

Band   10   Jörg Müller: Uppsala II. Erneuerung in der Mission. Eine redaktionsgeschichtliche Studie und Dokumentation zu Sektion II der 4. Vollversammlung des Ökumenischen Rates der Kirchen, Uppsala 1968.

Band   11   Hans Schöpfer: Theologie und Gesellschaft. Interdisziplinäre Grundlagenbibliographie zur Einführung in die befreiungs- und polittheologische Problematik: 1960-1975.

Band   12   Werner Hoerschelmann: Christliche Gurus. Darstellung von Selbstverständnis und Funktion indigenen Christseins durch unabhängige charismatisch geführte Gruppen in Südindien.

Band   13   Claude Schaller: L'Eglise en quête de dialogue. Vergriffen.

Band   14   Theo Tschuy: Hundert Jahre kubanischer Protestantismus (1868-1961). Versuch einer kirchengeschichtlichen Darstellung.

Band   15   Werner Korte: Wir sind die Kirchen der unteren Klassen. Entstehung, Organisation und gesellschaftliche Funktionen unabhängiger Kirchen in Afrika.

Band   16   Arnold Bittlinger: Pabst und Pfingstler. Der römisch katholisch-pfingstliche Dialog und seine ökumenische Relevanz.

Band   17   Ingemar Lindén: The Last Trump. An historico-genetical study of some important chapters in the making and development of the Seventh-day Adventist Church.

Band   18   Zwinglio Dias: Krisen und Aufgaben im brasilianischen Protestantismus. Eine Studie zu den sozialgeschichtlichen Bedingungen und volkspädagogischen Möglichkeiten der Evangelisation.

Band   19   Mary Hall: A quest for the liberated Christian, Examined on the basis of a mission, a man and a movement as agents of liberation.

Band 20 Arturo Blatezky: Sprache des Glaubens in Lateinamerika. Eine Studie zu Selbstverständnis und Methode der "Theologie der Befreiung".

Band 21 Anthony Mookenthottam: Indian Theological Tendencies. Approaches and problems for further research as seen in the works of some leading Indian theologicans.

Band 22 George Thomas: Christian Indians and Indian Nationalism 1885-1950. An Interpretation in Historical and Theological Perspectives.

Band 23 Essiben Madiba: Evangélisation et Colonisation en Afrique: L'Héritage scolaire du Cameroun (1885-1965).

Band 24 Katsumi Takizawa: Reflexionen über die universale Grundlage von Buddhismus und Christentum.

Band 25 S.W. Sykes (editor): England and Germany. Studies in theological diplomacy.

Band 26 James Haire: The Character and Theological Struggle of the Church in Halmahera, Indonesia, 1941-1979.

Band 27 David Ford: Barth and God's Story. Biblical Narrative and the Theological Method of Karl Barth in the Church Dogmatics.

Band 28 Kortright Davis: Mission for Carribean Change. Carribean Development As Theological Enterprice.

Band 29 Origen V. Jathanna: The Decisiveness of the Christ-Event and the Universality of Christianity in a world of Religious Plurality. With Special Reference to Hendrik Kraemer and Alfred George Hogg as well as to William Ernest Hocking and Pandipeddi Chenchiah.

Band 30 Joyce V. Thurman: New Wineskins. A Study of the House Church Movement.

Band 31 John May: Meaning, Consensus and Dialogue in Buddhist-Christian-Communication. A study in the Construction of Meaning.

Band 32 Friedhelm Voges: Das Denken von Thomas Chalmers im kirchen- und sozialgeschichtlichen Kontext.

Band 33 George MacDonald Mulrain: Theology in Folk Culture. The Theological Significance of Haitian Folk Religion.

Band 34 Alan Ford: The Protestant Reformation in Ireland, 1590-1641. 2. unveränderte Auflage.

Band 35 Harold Tonks: Faith, Hope and Decision-Making. The Kingdom of God and Social Policy-Making. The Work of Arthur Rich of Zürich.

Band 36 Bingham Tembe: Integrationismus und Afrikanismus. Zur Rolle der kirchlichen Unabhängigkeitsbewegung in der Auseinandersetzung um die Landfrage und die Bildung der Afrikaner in Südafrika, 1880-1960.

Band 37 Kingsley Lewis: The Moravian Mission in Barbados 1816-1886. A Study of the Historical Context and Theological Signifcance of a Minority Church Among an Oppressed People.

Band 38 Ulrich M. Dehn: Indische Christen in der gesellschaftlichen Verantwortung. Eine theologische und religionssoziologische Untersuchung politischer Theologie im gegenwärtigen Indien.

Band 39 Walter J. Hollenweger (Ed.): Pentecostal Research in Europe: Problems, Promises and People. Proceedings from the Pentecostal Research Conference at the University of Birmingham (England) April 26th to 29th 1984.

Band 40 P. Solomon Raj: A Christian Folk-Religion in India. A Study of the Small Church Movement in Andhra Pradesh, with a Special Reference to the Bible Mission of Devadas.

Band 41 Karl-Wilhelm Westmeier: Reconciling Heaven and earth: The Transcendental Enthusiasm and Growth of an Urban Protestant Community, Bogota, Colombia.

Band 42 George A. Hood: Mission Accomplished? The English Presbyterian Mission in Lingtung, South China. A Study of the Interplay between Mission Methods and their Historical Context.

Band 43 Emmanuel Yartekwei Lartey: Pastoral Counselling in Inter-Cultural Perspective: A Study of some African (Ghanaian) and Anglo-American viwes on human existence and councelling.

Band 44 Jerry L. Sandidge: Roman Catholic/Pentecostal Dialogue (1977-1982): A Study in Developing Ecumenism.

Band 45 Friedeborg L. Müller: The History of German Lutheran Congregations in England, 1900-1950.

Band 46 Roger B. Edrington: Everyday Men: Living in a Climate of Unbelief.

Band 47 Bongani Mazibuko: Education in Mission/Mission in Education. A Critical Comparative Study of Selected Approaches.

Band 48 Jochanan Hesse (Ed.): Mitten im Tod - vom Leben umfangen. Gedenkschrift für Werner Kohler.

Band 49 Elisabeth A. Kasper: Afrobrasilianische Religion. Der Mensch in der Beziehung zu Natur, Kosmos und Gemeinschaft im Candomblé - eine tiefenpsychologische Studie.

Band 50 Charles Chikezie Agu: Secularization in Igboland. Socio-religious Change and its Challenges to the Church Among the Igbo.

Band 51 Abraham Adu Berinyuu: Pastoral Care to the Sick in Africa. An Approach to Transcultural Pastoral Theology.

Band 52 Boo-Woong Yoo: Korean Pentecostalism. Its History and Theology.

Band 53 Roger H. Hooker: Themes in Hinduism and Christianity. A Comparative Study.

Band 54 Jean-Daniel Plüss: Therapeutic and Prophetic Narratives in Worship. A Hermeneutic Study of Testimonies and Visions. Their Potential Significance for Christian Worship and Secular Society.

Band 55 John Mansford Prior: Church and Marriage in an Indonesian Village. A Study of Customary and Church Marriage among the Ata Lio of Central Flores, Indonesia, as a Paradigm of the Ecclesial Interrelationship between village and Institutional Catholicism.

Band 56 Werner Kohler: Umkehr und Umdenken. Grundzüge einer Theologie der Mission (herausgegeben von Jörg Salaquarda).

Band 57 Martin Maw: Visions of India. Fulfilment Theology, the Aryan Race Theory, & the Work of British Protestant Missionaries in Victorian India.

Band 58 Aasulv Lande: Meiji Protestantism in History and Historiography. A Comparative Study of Japanese and Western Interpretation of Early Protestantism in Japan.

Band 59 Enyi Ben Udoh: Guest Christology. An interpretative view of the christological problem in Africa.

Band 60 Peter Schüttke-Scherle: From Contextual to Ecumenical Theology? A Dialogue between Minjung Theology and 'Theology after Auschwitz'.

Band 61 Michael S. Northcott: The Church and Secularisation. Urban Industrial Mission in North East England.

Band 62 Daniel O'Connor: Gospel, Raj and Swaraj. The Missionary Years of C. F. Andrews 1904-14.

Band 63 Paul D. Matheny: Dogmatics and Ethics. The Theological Realism and Ethics of Karl Barth's Church Dogmatics.

Band 64 Warren Kinne: A People's Church? The Mindanao-Sulu Church Debacle.

Band 65 Jane Collier: The culture of economism. An exploration of barriers to faith-as-praxis.

Band 66 Michael Biehl: Der Fall Sadhu Sundar Singh. Theologie zwischen den Kulturen.

Martin Maw

Visions of India
Fulfilment Theology, the Aryan Race Theory, and the
Work of British Protestant Missionaries in Victorian
India

Frankfurt/M., Bern, New York, Paris, 1988. abt. 400 pp.
Studies in the intercultural history of christianity. Vol 57
Editor: Prof. Dr. Walter J. Hollenweger
ISBN 3-631-40544-8   hardback DM 99.--/sFr. 90.--

The Oxford academic F.M. Müller, and B.F. Westcott, Bishop of Durham, were both Victorians who posited an idealist relationship between India and the West. Müller believed them part of the same Aryan culture; Westcott, that they were essentially members of the same
Church. Missionaries absorbed these ideas. Many read Müller. The
Cambridge University Mission to Delhi embodied Westcott's notions.
He also influenced a mission from Trinity College, Dublin, and had
several children who were themselves missionaries. Such links permit
a close analysis of idea becoming practice. Evidence from the World
Missionary Conference, 1910, shows that missionaries accepted such
liberal thinking. Ultimately, though, Müller and Westcott's ideals proved inadequate. They were grounded in Romanticism and semantics,
and could not bear the weight of experience in India itself.

Contents: F. M. Müller and the Aryan Race Theory - Obstacles to
Aryan Solidarity - B.F. Westcott and the Cambridge University Missi-
on to Delhi - Other Missionary Brotherhoods - The World Missionary
Conference, Edinburgh 1910.

Verlag Peter Lang Frankfurt a.M. · Bern · New York · Paris
Auslieferung: Verlag Peter Lang AG, Jupiterstr. 15, CH-3000 Bern 15
Telefon (004131) 321122, Telex pela ch 912 651, Telefax (004131) 321131
- Preisänderungen vorbehalten -